The Rivers of Money

Adi Imsirovic · Colin Bryce

The Rivers of Money

Social and Economic History of Modern Oil Trading

palgrave
macmillan

Adi Imsirovic
Surrey Clean Energy
Ascot, UK

Colin Bryce
Energex Partners
London, UK

ISBN 978-3-031-91805-6 ISBN 978-3-031-91806-3 (eBook)
https://doi.org/10.1007/978-3-031-91806-3

Cover Credit: Yuichiro Chino via Getty Images

This Palgrave Macmillan imprint is published by the registered company Springer Nature Switzerland AG
The registered company address is: Gewerbestrasse 11, 6330 Cham, Switzerland

Acknowledgements When two people write a book, pride of authorship does not work. Fortunately, neither one of us suffers from an inflated view of the beauty of our respective prose and we have both happily given way to each other without a crossword between us.

The task of reminiscing has been an enjoyable one, recalling as it does, good times past albeit with the occasional recollection of extreme embarrassment and with the ever-present sense of how quickly the years have slipped by.

Reconnecting with old colleagues, friends, and the occasional adversary has been cathartic, reminding us how fortunate we were to have landed on our feet in the world of oil trading all these years ago.

Some may view our business as a branch of high finance—popularly conceived as a turbo-charged, fast-moving, and ruthless business. Traders are supposed to: 'Eat what they kill'.

Yet, almost without exception, the folks who we knew in the business and who so kindly helped memorialise, are down-to-earth, regular folks.

It is to them (listed in alphabetical order) and their recollective gaze that we offer our thanks. Any errors, omissions, poetic licence, and accidental falsehoods are solely our responsibility.

With thanks to: Adrian Binks, Andy Whitrow, Ann Summers, Brendan Connellan, Charles Tuke, Chris Evans, Chris Heilpern, Colm Kelleher, Dave Ernsberger, David Hufton, David Peniket, Dennis Kongsiri, Fereidun Fesharaki, Gary King, Gene Grabinski, Goran Trapp, Greg Newman, Hiromichi Kaburaki, Ingeborg Srenger, Javier Blas, John Chapman, John Driscoll, John Hunt, John Rodger, Jonathan Martland, Junichi Kasahara, Justus Van Der Spuy, Ken Leask, Kevin O'Reilly, Kurt Chapman, Lawrence Ho, Liz Bossley, Lourdes Rodriguez, Marc Crandall, Marc Moure, Mark Quartermain, Mick Conway, Milan Kratka, Nancy Kropp Galdy, Neal Shear, Neil Atkinson, Neil Fleming, Nigel Whiteley, Owain Johnson, Paul Chapman, Paul Clausen, Paul Horsnell, Paul Newman, Pavel Pojdl, Peter Bosworth, Peter Smith, Phil Pollock, Richard Johnstone, Robin Burley, Rod Gavshon, Ron Davidson, Rowan Bainbridge, Russell Newton, Scott Brown, Seana Lanigan, Stephen Chow, Stephen Lim, Steve Gutteridge, Steve Jones, Steve Mawer, Stuart Saint, Taraneh Azad, Tim Bullock, Tom Galdy, Tom Leaver, Tony Dillon, Trish Collins, Tula Weis, and Weimin Yuan.

Competing Interests The authors have no competing interests to declare that are relevant to the content of this manuscript.

Contents

About the Authors

Adi Imsirovic is a Lecturer at the Master's course in Energy Systems, Department of Engineering, University of Oxford. He is also a Senior Associate (Non-resident), in the Energy Security and Climate Change Programme at the Centre for Strategic and International Studies (CSIS) in Washington.

Adi Imsirovic has 35 years of experience in oil trading. He has held a number of senior trading positions, including global head of oil at Gazprom Marketing & Trading and regional manager of Texaco oil trading for Asia. Dr. Imsirovic was a Fulbright scholar and studied at Harvard University's Graduate School of Arts and Sciences. For a number of years, he was a Senior Research Fellow at the Oxford Institute for Energy Studies.

Adi has a Ph.D. in economics and a Master's Degree in Energy Economics. He has written a number of papers and articles on the topic of oil and gas prices, benchmarks, and energy security. Adi is the Author of two books: '*Trading and Price Discovery for Crude Oils: Growth and Development of International Oil Markets*', published by Palgrave in August 2021, and '*International Oil Markets in the Age of Climate Change*', published by Palgrave in July 2024. Adi also edited the book '*Brent Crude Oil: Genesis and Development of the World's Most Important Oil Benchmark*', published by Palgrave in June 2023.

Colin Bryce began his career in 1978 in the Oil Pricing Unit of the British National Oil Corporation (BNOC) after earning a Degree in Geography and Political Economy from the University of Glasgow. In 1982, he joined

Britoil's Supply and Trading division before moving to Morgan Stanley in 1987 to help establish its oil trading business outside the United States.

During his tenure at Morgan Stanley, Colin held several senior leadership roles, including Co-Head of Global Commodities, Head of EMEA Institutional Sales and Trading (covering Equities, Fixed Income, and Commodities), and Chairman of Morgan Stanley Bank International Ltd. He also served for 19 years on the board of Morgan Stanley & Co. Ltd. and was a member of the firm's Global Management Committee.

A founding partner of the energy consultancy Energex Partners, Colin is also co-owner, alongside his wife, of Laundry Cottage Stud Farm. In his free time, he enjoys watching rugby, playing the piano, and flying light aircraft.

List of Figures

1

The Introduction: The 'Rivers of Money'

Why Did We Write This Book?

This book explores the development and growth of modern trading in the world's largest international commodity market since the 1970s. It builds naturally on the foundation of our 2023 book, '*Brent Crude Oil—Genesis and Development of the World's Most Important Oil Benchmark*'.[1]

Paul Horsnell, a veteran industry analyst, observer, and author, perfectly captured the essence of our intent when he endorsed that book: '*... even the most important markets in the world are created by and sustained by the interplay between people, many larger-than-life... bringing this story together before it is covered up by the sands of time*'. His observation underscores a core theme of this book: markets are far more than abstract, number-driven systems. They are deeply social constructs that emerge from human interaction, shaped by individuals and places, and created for the benefit of society.

In writing the social and economic history of Brent, the world's most important oil benchmark, we sought to emphasise this human dimension. However, we soon realised the need to broaden our scope to include the wider narrative of modern oil trading, capturing its complexities and the remarkable individuals who shaped it. The result is this book.

The decline of the oil Majors' oligopoly in the late 1970s, combined with the wave of liberalisation in the United Kingdom and the United States during the 1980s, set the stage for the re-emergence of markets and the evolution of modern oil trading. From these turbulent beginnings, a handful of visionary individuals took on the challenge of linking buyers and sellers in what was then a nascent and highly fragmented market. Over the course of

A. Imsirovic and C. Bryce, *The Rivers of Money*,
https://doi.org/10.1007/978-3-031-91806-3_1

a few decades, they transformed the industry from one of the most tightly controlled global oligopolies into one of the most efficient and resilient commodity markets in the world. This book focusses on the evolution of the crude oil market since the 1970s, with an emphasis on its key hubs in the United States, Europe, and Asia.

The significance of oil trading cannot be overstated. Every day, billions of dollars change hands for crude oil and petroleum products.[2] Yet, this is merely the visible crest of a wave of a vast financial river and a glimpse of an underlying ecosystem encompassing futures, forwards, swaps, options, and other derivatives. Around this market, an intricate network of traders, brokers, analysts, price-reporters, journalists, shippers, inspectors, financiers, and logisticians has emerged, creating a web of interactions that drives the industry forward.

It is this very complexity that makes the oil market so resilient. Despite geopolitical upheavals, financial crises, and global disruptions—including the Iran–Iraq War, two Gulf Wars, the 1998 Asian Financial Crisis, the Great Recession of 2008, the COVID-19 pandemic, and the 2022 Russian invasion of Ukraine—oil has continued to flow. Prices have been volatile, but the adaptability of this intricate system has ensured that shortages of energy have been avoided.

Given the sheer importance of this market, an in-depth examination is essential. While experts, analysts, and journalists scrutinise the economics of oil daily, relatively little has been written about the individuals and companies involved in the marketplace. Rather than focussing solely on economic abstractions, this book aims to tell the story of modern oil trading through the eyes of those who built and navigated it—the traders, brokers, and all the characters who transformed the way oil is bought and sold.

There is an additional reason for writing this book—a deeper, fundamental interest of the authors in examining oil markets, their benefits and flaws.

Markets and Politics

We are living in a time defined by political polarisation, deglobalisation, and rising government intervention in markets. Many young people, who have no memory of the economic landscape before the 1990s, are growing sceptical of market forces as a reliable way to allocate scarce resources.[3] At the same time, governments are increasingly adopting protectionism and enacting industrial policies that, if adopted globally, could stifle economic growth and reduce global prosperity.[4]

In certain circles, markets are seen as obstacles, rather than the essential tools for navigating the complexities of the modern economy. There are some good reasons for this. The last few decades have seen a large increase in inequality across the globe.[5] The main reasons for this rise have been domestic economic policies, technological progress, globalisation, and commodity price cycles. A further reason for mistrusting markets has been: '*... an epidemic of tax evasion and avoidance that has reached an unprecedented scale*'.[6]

In 2025, the U.S. President Donald Trump ordered the Department of Justice to halt the enforcement of a U.S. anti-corruption law, which bars American companies and individuals from bribing foreign government officials in order to win business.[7] As a result, 'Crony Capitalism' in which business success depends on close relationships between business people and government officials,[8] and '*Winners Take All*' economy have resulted in many individuals being '*left behind*'.[9]

What is often forgotten is that markets play a crucial function in a modern, complex economy. But this view should not be equated with 'market fundamentalism', the idea that markets are best left to their own devices, without state interference.[10] Both market scepticism and market fundamentalism are extreme positions. On one hand, it is impossible for governments to coordinate the economic activities of all the economic agents with different preferences. On the other hand, those very agents consume public goods such as clean air and water, stable climate, common defence as well as some socially desirable level of health and education.[11] These are some of the most important goods for which we have little or no natural markets.[12]

It follows that we desperately need markets to send the correct signals and incentives in the economy, with an understanding of their limitations and the need to support, protect, and augment their function in society. Therefore, it is essential to study markets in a social context where people and places play a central role.

Oil Markets: A River of Money

The global oil market resembles a powerful river of capital, constantly flowing towards the most profitable and cost-efficient opportunities, much like water seeking the path of least resistance. While this flow cannot be halted, it can be strategically guided to maximise social benefits.

Oil traders navigate these swirling waters, leveraging arbitrage opportunities to channel that commodity across borders to the places of most efficient usage. The sheer scale of the financial currents propelled by the immense volume and value of oil become relentless, powerful streams of both oil and money carving their way through the global economy.

Markets, much like rivers, are essential to human progress and the functioning of modern economies. However, they are not always inherently ethical. They flow according to the 'gravity' of human desire, following the natural contours of opportunity. At the same time, markets must be embedded within a broader social framework of norms, values, and ethical boundaries.

Just as human structures regulate a riverbed to guide its flow and harness its power, trading activity is shaped by societal norms and values. These boundaries and rules ensure markets serve the collective good, redirecting their course to align with shared objectives and foster progress. Social contexts play a crucial role in shaping how markets operate, defining what is deemed acceptable. For example, while creating a marketplace for human organs might efficiently match donors with recipients, such transactions are considered morally and ethically unacceptable in most societies.[13] Such societal boundaries are vital to all markets, but they are particularly pronounced in the oil markets, where the scale and impact of trading activities often bring ethical considerations into sharp focus.

Trading is not merely a tool for efficiency but it is a business in itself, enhancing price visibility, engendering liquidity, enabling the transfer of risk, and promoting the movement of goods and commodities across regions, systems, and even time. Trading emerges spontaneously, connecting societies in the most efficient ways. The rewards are shared—traders grow wealthier, and consumers gain access to new products and better prices.

It is hardly surprising that early human societies engaged in extensive trade networks. An essential mark of humanity, trading has naturally emerged even in the most unlikely places such as prisons, refugee camps, and continued between peoples even during conflict.[14]

The flow of trade does much more than foster prosperity and economic growth. Like a river carrying resources from one place to another, trade serves as a conduit for the exchange of knowledge, technology, and culture in general.[15] It connects societies peacefully, enriching them and fostering unity. Without trade, economies would be isolated and limited to local resources, stifling not only growth and development, but also knowledge, art, and culture. From the ancient Silk Road to modern global supply chains, trade has been instrumental in shaping civilisations and connecting humanity.

Trading is not just an economic activity but a reflection of what makes us uniquely human—our ability to create networks of cooperation that transcend borders, cultures, and generations we connect and collaborate for mutual benefit.[16] Humans have elevated trade into a complex system governed by trust, negotiation, and mutual benefit. The ability to recognise the value of cooperation, to specialise, and to create systems of exchange reflects higher cognitive and social capabilities. It is a fundamental aspect of society and a defining characteristic of what it means to be human. We are hard-wired for trade.

Attempts to arrest the progress of the river of money eventually always fail. As a society, we should preserve the message it carries and focus on shaping its direction and flow. In other words, governments should abstain from tinkering with prices and focus on making markets function better and fairer. The latter can be hard, but we have fiscal means and welfare policies to redistribute some windfall profits.

The modern oil market began as a small, untamed stream, with governments and companies struggling to regulate its unruly flow. Over time, it grew into a mighty river of money, shaped by the confluence of new players, evolving markets, and external interventions. Like a river fed by tributaries, oil trading gained momentum from innovation, infrastructure, and seminal events that altered its direction and velocity. Barriers—whether technical, regulatory, or geopolitical—tested its adaptability, while external forces sought to harness its energy for broader benefit. At its peak, the flow steadied into a mature, vast, and predictable system, though not without occasional floods and breaches.

We examine the people, the places, and the events constituting the rivers of money from the rising of the first spring, through its youthful stage as it received tributaries, was altered in course by external events, became a torrent, and eventually deepened and matured into the biggest but least known and arguably most personally rewarding industry that bears enormous influence on economies and the lives of peoples across the globe.

You will hear of the upstream and the downstream, waves of selling, floods of orders, streams of income, flows of business, turbulent waters, and safe harbours in describing the rivers of money. This is a story of how money flowed—sometimes cleanly, sometimes less so—through the mainstream and the eddies of one of the most consequential industries of our time.

The Layout of the Book

Our story begins in Chapter Two when the trading money primarily flowed up and down the Hudson and Rhine rivers—a small flow derived from the surplus volumes of petroleum products around hubs such as Rotterdam and New York harbour. Sovereign states who produced crude oil were still neutered by the hegemony of the Seven Sisters, and within these Major oil companies, crude oil trading didn't exist.

Swapping of different grades of oil, volumes, and locations was common within this international oil oligopoly, and there was hardly any meaningful price other than the price 'posted' by them. The cost of shipping was far greater than the price of a barrel of oil and getting the logistics right saved the companies a lot of money. Freight was king.

The period leading up to the emergence of the first spring of oil trading was a transformative time marked by significant events such as the Suez Crisis, the decline of European colonialism, the Soviet launch of Sputnik, and the triumph of the Cuban Revolution. These developments sparked a shift in the aspirations of oil-producing nations, leading them to take collective action through the establishment of the Organisation of Petroleum Exporting Countries (OPEC). However, the first decade of OPEC's existence remained relatively uneventful, with oil continuing to flow through the established systems controlled by the Seven Sisters.[17]

Markets spontaneously appear when there is a gaping arbitrage opportunity for making easy money.[18] Governments have a history of poor interventions in the markets, and the U.S. government of Richard Nixon was a good example. The 1973 'Emergency Petroleum Allocation Act', which created a two-tiered pricing system for domestically produced crude oil, distinguishing between 'old oil' and 'new oil'.[19] The regulation was effectively a tax on the domestic producers of 'old' oil and a subsidy for the consumption of 'new', 'stripper', and imported oil. But oil is a fungible commodity, and there was no difference in the molecules of these different types, except in their price. Controlling the flow of oil that was subjectively labelled and priced differently was virtually impossible, opening a massive arbitrage opportunity for trading cheap oil for the expensive one, resulting in a boom in trading activity.

This legislative or 'Nixon arbitrage' might have been a simple and inglorious beginning of a large-scale, modern crude oil trading, but some traders such as the infamous Marc Rich learned from it, including how to channel the flows of the 'rivers of money' via fictitious foreign oil deals, fake invoices, and channel them into offshore havens, away from the U.S. tax authorities.

But new springs emerged, and the independent traders of Rotterdam were able to score financially and to seize new opportunities presented on the margin by producers and the weakening majors. In the absence of regulatory arbitrage, European traders grew their businesses around the Amsterdam-Rotterdam-Antwerp area, moving smaller volumes of excess products, too small for the oil Majors to bother about. Such traders were Mabanaft, Vanoil, Mebro, Naftamondial, and others, who learned the ropes in the trading business. One notable individual at the time was John Deuss, the infamous Dutchman who founded Joc Oil in 1967 to trade jet fuel. Many of these small traders disappeared in the volatile 1970s, and early 1980s, but the flexible and resilient ones such as Vitol and Mabanaft would remain to this day.

One large pool of trading talent came from the oil Majors. Early bulk sales and supply teams could not match the remuneration opportunities of the trading companies, and BP in particular saw an exodus of talent in the 1970s to various traders including Philipp Brothers. That company was the master of the trading strategy of 'doing difficult things with difficult people in difficult places—quietly'. These events are discussed in Chapter Three.

A seminal moment for oil trading was the departure of Marc Rich and Pinky Green from the Philipp Brothers to set up their own trading entity Marc Rich + Co. in Switzerland. The location, individuals involved, and the approach to trading of the duo would be replicated for decades to come and would spawn dozens of key traders and companies, including Glencore and Trafigura, discussed in subsequent chapters.

The 1970s shook up the world of oil. It was like a river falling over a waterfall. The Majors lost control and the OPEC cartel, while massively influential, could not exert the same level of control over the market. They were unable to 'fix' prices, and price volatility increased significantly. In markets where power was shifting, pricing structures were evolving, and volatility was on the rise, conditions became ideal for traders to step in and step up.

The chaotic nature of this 'messy business' presented lucrative opportunities. At the same time, high oil prices of the late 70 s incentivised production outside OPEC control, and Alaskan and North Sea oil started to flow and was a game changer in establishing the oil trading business. In particular, the structure of the Petroleum Revenue Tax (PRT) in the United Kingdom incentivised buying and selling of equity oil by the Majors, playing a pivotal role in the development of the forward Brent market and leading to the demise of the British National Oil Corporation and their 'Pin Striped Sheiks'.[20] Growing 'spot' trading also gave rise to a whole ecosystem of players and institutions such as brokers, price assessment (PRA) agencies, and exchanges.

There was money to be made, not just by corporations, but by individuals who could brand themselves as 'oil traders' and parlay their way to a comfortable remuneration. Self-interest was a powerful motive in promulgating the efficacy of the nascent oil markets.

At the heart of this revolution was: '*The London market [which] spread all over the world*'. The London location mattered: Vendome or the Guinea Grill for lunch, Morton's in Berkeley Square for after-work cocktails followed by Marks Club or Les Ambassadeurs (clubs for those who didn't qualify on breeding grounds for the proper men's clubs of St James) for supper. Members of even lower echelons might then end up in Tokyo Joe's nightclub or, horror upon horrors, the Dover Street wine bar or the Stork Club on Aire Street. This story is the subject of chapters four and five.

The traders and buccaneers of the early days had emotional intelligence to burn-gregarious, sociable, and clubbable (at least night-clubbable) and they could just as easily negotiate their way around the salons and restaurants of Paris and London as around a typical business problem of the day. Ambition, a will to win, intensity (also the key differentiator in sporting brilliance), self-belief, and a capacity for hard work took a trader a long way then as now and some of those individual stories that shaped the market are the subject of Chapter Six.

Despite all the lunching, carousing, golfing, and gossiping in 'high life' places, the turbulent waters of the trading industry were developing with a rapidly increasing seriousness of purpose and direction. It was an industry that would in future years become one of the most influential yet one of the least understood by the outsiders. Oil trading would impact the global economy by setting the price of oil. And it would make some people very rich indeed, mostly by honest toil but also, at times, by operating on the dark side. Self-regulation of the Brent forward market, with the help of brokers was a feature, preventing some trading houses from 'behaving badly'. There was more bad behaviour in playing another 'legislative arbitrage', busting sanctions against South Africa, Rhodesia, and Israel.

Less dark side was the Wall Street banks that joined the feeding frenzy in the river of new oil trading opportunities. Different cultures and approaches taken by the two key players, J. Aron a commodity trading arm of Goldman Sachs and Morgan Stanley, and the impact the two banks made are the subject of chapter seven. Wall Street was to be the catalyst for a series of new forward, as opposed to futures, products that came to be core and central to oil trading and to oil price risk management. From the mid-1980s onwards, products such as Brent and Dubai partials, Dated-to-Paper or CFD swaps,

OTC Options, and other instruments became available for anyone interested in oil.

It took the advent of Wall Street refiners to make the concept of the 'bonus' common in the oil trading industry. It was perhaps inevitable, in order to retain the talent (Chapter Two talks about the early exodus of traders from BP). This would be the tool of enrichment which would eventually be taken up by oil companies Shell and BP and the growing number of independent traders. Hundreds of thousands were paid, not only the rainmakers who added their contributions to the river of money, but also a lucky cadre of coat-tailers, folks who were, in the basketball language so loved by the trading fraternity, 'hanging around the hoop'. As the rivers of money deepened and the flow accelerated, 'money men' such as hedge funds became attracted to oil trading. Hundreds of thousands paid to the traders turned into millions.

Growing volatility in the oil markets had some negative consequences, causing further problems in the Brent market, mainly due to 'traders behaving badly'. With a great deal of money at stake, the chains of forward Brent trades would break down as false dates were passed from one company to another, resulting in several nominations for cargo loading in the period allotted for one or two shipments only. Pin-Striped Sheiks would come to the rescue, recommending that Shell should act as the informal regulator of the Brent market. This they had a financial interest in doing and the river continued to flow within the banks of self-regulation.

Of course, the policing was done on behalf of the 'spinners', the Major oil companies who were minting money out of the forward Brent market by optimising their tax exposure. Their traders were being amply rewarded for the effort, playing the legal tax arbitrage. Self-interest, corporate and personal, was a strong motivator to keep the show going and the 'rivers of money' flowing. Some of the early alleged squeezes in Brent and bad practices by the futures exchange 'local' traders are the subject of Chapter Eight.

Chapter Nine switches attention to the growing importance of Asia. While Tokyo was initially the place to do oil business, the attitude of the government and the local oil community where the trading houses (Sogo Shosha) had a close relationship with the end users, was not favourable to development of international trading. Singapore already had a number of refineries and some petroleum products trading around that hub. But from 1989, Singapore had something that always attracted the profit-seeking community: low tax. From January of that year, Singapore introduced the Approved Oil Trader (AOT) scheme—and it charged the approved oil trading companies only 10 per cent tax, a significant improvement from the usual (and not unreasonable) 27 per cent. Later, under the 'Global Trader Programme', the tax could be as low as 5 per cent. The money river just found a new path.

The same chapter traces the development of Singapore as an international trading hub, following several characters that contributed to its growth. From Weimin Yuan to OK Lim and his Hin Leong trading company, the trading hub grew along with its port and the refining business, both very much supported by government policy. Singapore bars, restaurants, and schools mirrored those of any major Western city and significantly contributed to making it an attractive place to live and work. Singapore was, and still is a great place to trade oil. Dubai and Tapis were the mainstays of the early crude oil trading there, but it quickly expanded to 'paper' oil as well. A handful of London traders who moved there quickly imported the Brent trading techniques, taking the Singapore hub to another level.

Paper trading in general is the subject of the next chapter. It traces the development and the growth of the Dubai swap market and how the growth of China changed the Brent-Dubai arbitrage through the eyes of the people who shaped it. Chinese 'Majors' simply had too much exposure to hedge it and instead, became the key price-makers in the Asian market. Culture was changing too. London traders brought with them long lunches and wine drinking. Chinese restaurants quickly learned that big margins were to be made on selling wine. To encourage wine drinking, it was common for them not to remove empty wine bottles from the table. For Western traders, this could be rather embarrassing as a long lunch could leave many empty bottles on the table!

Chapter Eleven expands on the Derivatives Revolution and swaps in particular. Financial markets, particularly fixed income (bonds) and foreign exchange traders, had been long-time users of swaps. The technology was familiar to the Wall Street as well as other commercial banks already present in the oil markets. There was an avalanche of new entrants—Societe General, Paribas, Barclays Capital, CRT, Chase Manhattan, JP Morgan, Chemical Bank, and a host of other names.

It was airlines that were the obvious first customers. Aviation fuel (jet) can make as much as half of the total operating cost of an airline. Holiday makers often book their favourite destinations many months in advance. Fixing the cost of fuel as soon as tickets are sold is a sensible strategy for any air carrier.

Similar logic can easily be extended to bus companies, cement makers, glass manufacturers, and almost any other industry where fuel constitutes a significant proportion of operating costs. Oil refineries are a special case. Buying or building a refinery is simply a massive trade of being long petroleum products and short crude oil. Refining can be a cyclical business and it makes sense to cash in some of the profit in good times, when petroleum products trade well above the price of crude oil. We follow the narratives of the people involved in derivatives trading and broking these deals from the earliest days.

Chapter Twelve follows the end of Marc Rich + Co. and two beginnings—of Glencore and Trafigura. The mantle of qualitative trading—'Not *judging deals, but judging the people who brought them*' would successfully pass on to these two trading houses. They knew the flows well and how to take advantage of rough waters in the river of money.

The oil markets experienced something of great moderation between the end of the Gulf War in early 1991 and mid-1996. The River of Money began to meander. Traders who had feasted on volatility and the growing interest of consumers in oil markets and associated derivative products and an array of banks providing liquidity, began to start twiddling their thumbs. But a new great opportunity came out of the blue—the collapse of the Soviet Union.

The chapter follows personal experiences in dealing in the region, from Soyuzneftexport to privatised entities such as Lukoil and Rosneft. We discuss how traders entered the unchartered territory from bartering tights for oil to buying from oil producers through Russian proxies. This is where some of the greatest 'rivers of money' were channelled for the private benefit of the few. Despite Russia's vast oil reserves, a sizable refining industry, robust domestic and export markets, and encouragement from Western business interests over time, no traded oil markets have emerged inside the country. Having opaque structures served some private individuals well, allowing them to 'milk the system' for decades.

Some western companies did poorly out of their investments in the country. But the companies used to dealing in 'difficult places and with difficult people' did well. Vitol and Glencore owe their current size and status to a considerable extent thanks to their early entry and selective deal-making in Russia.

Success in trading is about having superior information and assets are one way of having that information. Many an oil trader have graduated by working for one of the Majors and benefited from having first-hand knowledge of refinery margins, fundamentals of, production, inventory levels, individual grade differentials, freight costs, and so on. This topic is covered in chapter thirteen.

Sticking to the superiority of information, the chapter also covers the early days of Enron Online. Moving trading to an electronic platform was a great idea. However, the true value in trading is in the provision of liquidity and this was not provided by Enron, but by the most active oil traders of the time: J Aron, Morgan Stanley, BP, and Shell. The value of liquidity and the information it generated resided with them, and allowing Enron to profit from it would have been a critical mistake. This insight led the major players in oil trading to look for ways to wrest control of that competitive advantage from Enron, the interloper. These companies (later, a few others as well) worked together to acquire their own electronic platform and each company would pledge a certain volume of trades on it. The chapter is a first-hand account of the Intercontinental Exchange (ICE) becoming a major oil trading platform and the home of the Brent benchmark. At least for a while, it would monopolise the futures Brent trade and become a major arbiter of the flow of that river.

The last quarter of a century has seen an incredible growth of trading companies and the river of money cascaded like a torrent entering the flood plain. The lucky owners of independent trading companies have been multi-millionaires and even billionaire profiters. Fired up by COVID-19 and the Russian invasion of Ukraine, the cascade has plentifully endowed those who have been positioned to intermediate between producers and consumers and to direct and redirect, as required, the flows and course of the much-deepened river of money.

Operating in regions where standards of conduct can vary widely from those in developed nations, many trading companies find themselves navigating a delicate boundary between legality and illegality. Commercially, they often push this line, testing limits to stay competitive. Often, they pay the price. We go back to them in chapter fourteen and focus on Vitol, 'Rich renegades'—Trafigura, Glencore, and Mansfield as well as Mercuria and Hetco. Wherever possible, we stick to the first-hand accounts not published before.

And then, there were also the flows of money, less ethical, from Lagos to London, Moscow to Geneva and Dubai, and Baghdad to Houston—that were to enrich a certain class of company and individual who fished in the same river. Chapter Fifteen examines the rise of Arcadia, a trader in both physical and paper (especially, Brent and WTI) markets and the United Nations-controlled 'Oil-for-Food' programme in which a handful of traders ended up controlling a majority of the Iraqi oil exports. The '*UN management of the oil-for-food 'operated in an ineffective, wasteful, and unsatisfactory manner', leading to some $5 million in documented contractor overpayments, and 'undoubtedly much higher'* losses not discovered by the limited UN audits, reminding us how a misguided political intervention in well-functioning international markets can have major, negative consequences.

Financialisaton of the oil market was in full swing at the turn of the century. Exchange Traded Funds (EFTs) and other financial instruments enabled retail investors to invest in high-risk assets such as oil. This development amplified the impact of the Financial Crisis (the Great Recession) of 2007–8 on the oil market where oil prices fell by some $100 a barrel in one year. The event was followed by a torrent of government regulations, gradually squeezing banks out of the physical oil market and some market-making roles.

The independent traders and liquidity providers, poised like wolverines to capitalise on the opportunity to scale up and compete with BP, Shell, and Total, were unlikely to prioritise liquidity provision for 'clients' in the future. As a result, oil trading was set to increasingly bifurcate into two distinct areas: asset-backed trading benefiting the firm itself, and proprietary trading driven by quantitative modelling, algorithms, and data science. Although the latter did generate a lot of liquidity, it did not typically focus on market-making. This topic as well as an inside story of disposing some of the banks-owned commodity trading assets is the topic of chapter sixteen.

Our narrative moves on to companies that stepped into the empty space left by major banks and focus on financial players and 'liquidity providers'. We refer to them as 'Paper Boys' and they are the subject of Chapter Seventeen. Heavy on technology and data mining to support their decision-making processes and hedging, they have come to dominate high-risk paper market liquidity. They are '*momentum creators*'.

Citadel and Millenium, the two most active companies, operate at opposite ends of the risk scale. Citadel is a maximum-risk organisation, confident in its deep data-led views. They are willing to sit with losing positions until they hopefully come right and they trade large-sized positions. Their willingness to hold onto positions harks back to the methods employed by Phibro in the Andy Hall days. This approach is experiencing a revival in some traditional trading firms such as Vitol as deep data spawns confidence that markets will eventually do what the data says they will do. Millenium on the other hand is tightly risk controlled. Set up in a structure of individual risk 'pods', their traders are kept on a much shorter leash. Consequently, they have not experienced the large losses and profits of a Citadel.

Generally, though, hedge funds and CTA's (Commodity Trading Advisors) are market followers. Often referred to as 'momentum' traders, they follow signals and trends, going with and exaggerating the flow with their rules-based trading. And they hunt as a pack. Their growth has been explosive. Strategies of these funds differ greatly, but all of them often move in the same direction and exacerbate directional price moves and volatility in the short run.

Whether technology can take over the role of the trader in totality is a moot point. Some see traders as '*artisans, restless, humans with heightened sensory perception. They can pick up the signals from the things not said*'.[21] On the other hand, there are those who believe that the human touch of the trader creating value is of lesser consequence.

Finally....

The history of trading, much like the river's course, is marked by inflection points, challenges, and transformations. Technology and innovations have changed trade and trade has induced more innovation and technology. The provision of a huge volume of information in the modern oil market has certainly made the use of Artificial Intelligence and algorithms indispensable, especially following the declining cost of computation and its widespread adoption in other markets such as electricity trading. We are now firmly in the era of data and the impact of the data scientist on the business of oil trading.

Not all present-day market operators have abandoned the past. Certainly not the large independent traders like Vitol and Trafigura, BP, and Shell. This is just as well as if they had done so and had abandoned their asset-backed optionality-mining physical trading business, they would have missed out on three of the most remunerative years ever experienced in oil markets in 2021, 2022 and 2023. Partly due to the effects of COVID-19, partly due to the disruption of the normal flows of commerce consequent on Russia's invasion of Ukraine, and partly due to the growth of U.S. shale oil as an internationally traded stream and partly due to the Brent benchmark, these companies were able to adapt and profit.

Despite episodes of bad behaviour, whether in futures, forwards, or physical markets, it is well worth remembering that the great majority of market participants act in good faith. It is those who have made money trading oil but have resisted the temptation to engage in market manipulation or bribery who can take great credit for trading profitably, transparently, and honestly. They are the ones who have added true value in the process of directing the river of money from source to the most efficient and effective place of disposal and who have, by application of trading instruments available in futures and forward markets, made things cheaper and better for all of us.

This book does not aim to provide a sensationalised account of daring exploits, nor is it designed to be populist or judgemental. Instead, its purpose is to preserve and present, in an accessible fashion and before it is too late, the genesis and evolution of the modern oil trading business.

Notes

1. Imsirovic A. ed (2023). These two authors wrote chapters 1,2,4 and 9 in the book.
2. At $70 a barrel oil price and overall demand of about 105 million barrels a day, $7.35 billion worth of oil changes hands each day. Add to that a greater amount of petroleum products to get the value of just physical oil changing hands.
3. Personal experience of one of the authors while teaching a module within a course on Energy Systems at University of Oxford.
4. See: https://www.ecb.europa.eu/press/blog/date/2023/html/ecb.blog230712~085871737a.en.html#:~:text=The%20deglobalising%20effects%20of%20reshoring,and%20increase%20domestic%20production%20costs.
5. 'From 1990 to 2015, the share of income going to the top 1 per cent of the global population increased in 46 out of 57 countries…' https://www.un.org/en/un75/inequality-bridging-divide#:~:text=From%201990%20to%202015%2C%20the,per%20cent%20of%20overall%20income. Para. 5.
6. 'Since 2015, the richest 1% have more wealth than the rest of the world combined.' Ibid, paragraph 3.
7. https://www.ft.com/content/f880bfc3-6069-427b-9873-51255d4e0b8c
8. See: https://www.journals.uchicago.edu/doi/10.1086/686474#:~:text=Definition%201%3A,business%20people%20and%20government%20officials
9. https://knowledge.wharton.upenn.edu/podcast/knowledge-at-wharton-podcast/anand-giridharadas-winners-take-all/
10. https://u.osu.edu/introhumanitiesonline/tag/market-fundamentalism/
11. Public goods are goods where one person's use of them cannot diminish or exclude others using it.
12. There is some basic level of health and education that societies want to have for all citizens.

13. Most societies have rejected this idea because of the potential for exploitation, coercion, and the violation of human dignity. For example, see: https://pmc.ncbi.nlm.nih.gov/articles/PMC10155689/
14. See Radford (1945) describing exchange in prisoners of war camp. Another good source of wonderful examples is Davies (2019)—a highly recommended read for anyone interested in markets.
15. https://insights.som.yale.edu/insights/how-has-trade-shaped-the-world?utm_source=chatgpt.com
16. For example, bartering among animals for food or grooming.
17. Oil Majors were (their more modern names are used here):Exxon, Mobil, Chevron, Texaco, Gulf, BP and Shell.
18. This was pointed out back by Adam Smith (1776) in the Wealth of Nations: '…certain propensity in human nature, which has in view no such extensive utility; the propensity to truck, barter, and exchange one thing for another.' Book1, Chapter 2, first paragraph.
19. https://www.congress.gov/bill/93rd-congress/house-bill/8863#:~:text=Shown%20Here%3A&text=Emergency%20Petroleum%20Allocation%20Act%20%2D%20States,in%20their%20national%20distribution%20system.
20. Sunday Times Business Section 06/02/1983.
21. Communication with Brendan Connellan an ex-trader and playwright on 24/08/2024.

Bibliography

Casson, Mark and John S. Lee (2011): 'The Origin and Development of Markets: A Business History Perspective', Business History Review 85 (Spring 2011): 9–37. https://doi.org/10.1017/S0007680511000018

Davies R. (2019): 'Extreme Economies: Survival, Failure, Future—Lessons from the World's Limits', Bantam Press.

Imsirovic A. ed (2023): 'Brent Crude Oil—Genesis and Development of the World's Most Important Oil Benchmark,' Palgrave.

Radford, R.A. (1945): 'The Economic Organisation of a P.O.W. Camp', Economica, New Series, Vol. 12, No. 48 (Nov., 1945), pp. 189–201.

Smith, Adam (1776): 'An Inquiry into the Nature and Causes of the Wealth of Nations'.

2

Freight is the King

Freight is the King

Robin Burley was staring intently at a sheet of paper—still the cutting-edge office technology of the day. British Petroleum (BP) was 'long' crude oil,[1] but the timing of cargoes and the quality of oil was not always what his refineries wanted. The trader had a cargo of heavy, high sulphur oil from Kuwait, scheduled to sail to Northwest Europe, but right now, he needed a cargo of Arab Light for his Mediterranean refinery.

In 1967, a barrel of Arab Light crude oil was valued at just $1.30, yet the shipping cost to Rotterdam far exceeded the price of the oil itself. Efficient logistics were paramount. There was no trading, markets, or market prices to speak of. Oil prices were made up and 'posted' by an oligopoly of oil Majors who controlled the world supply.[2] Posted prices were used to pay Royalties to the producing nations and were kept low and stable. As a result, profits soared, royalties remained minimal, and vast rivers of money flowed, steadily controlled and carefully managed by a select few international oil companies.

There was just endless swapping of cargoes and destinations, usually with one of the 'Sisters'[3] such as Exxon, Shell, Mobil, Chevron, Texaco, or Gulf. Sourcing the right crude oil for his refinery and taking the shortest possible shipping route there would save BP millions. And it was not exactly that hard for a Natural Sciences major from Cambridge. '*Who needs trading when you can make all this money without taking any risk? Freight is king*', Robin thought.[4] However, this oil swap had to wait. Markets were static, and prices were fixed. In those days, the oil market moved at a slow pace—nothing happened in a hurry. There was always tomorrow.

A. Imsirovic and C. Bryce, *The Rivers of Money*,
https://doi.org/10.1007/978-3-031-91806-3_2

As was customary in those days, it was time for lunch, and he wasn't about to let the lads head off without him. The Shell boys were already into their first pint at the Cricketers Club of London on Blandford Street. They hardly ever ventured there, but it was a BP invite and they were happy to come in early for a few aperitifs. The lunch was sure to be another boozy affair, but as long as one returned to the office in a reasonably sober state, both BP and Shell were happy to turn a blind eye. It wouldn't have been the first time a swap deal was hashed out right there, over a pint, at the Cricketers. This was simply how business was done in those easy-going times.

But the lazy oil industry orchestrated by the oil Majors was slowly changing. And it all started a few years earlier, in the 1950s with the discovery of oil in new places.

Dr Hammer

In 1956, the French discovered oil in Algeria, and by the end of the War of Independence in 1962, the country was supplying 40 per cent of all the French oil imports. Having signed a favourable joint venture agreement with Getty Oil, the Algerian government was to become one of the leading hawks in pressing the oil companies for better concession terms.[5] In 1956, BP and Shell found oil in Nigeria, opening West Africa as a new oil frontier. Some majors, such as crude-short Shell and Jersey Standard (now ExxonMobil) welcomed the new finds which provided more diversified supplies, away from the Persian Gulf.

A 1957 round of concessions in Venezuela attracted 'independent' U.S. oil companies such as Sun, Phillips, and Sinclair, and soon they produced about 10% of the country's output. In the same year, the National Iranian Oil Company (NIOC) granted a number of offshore concessions. NIOC agreed to their development through '50/50' joint ventures with Agip, a subsidiary of the Italian state-owned ENI[6] and an U.S. 'independent', Amoco.[7]

In the same year, Saudi Arabia signed a similar agreement with the Japanese Petroleum Trading Company (JPTC) for exploration and production in the offshore part of the Neutral Zone. The onshore section of the Zone had been awarded to another U.S. independent, Getty Oil, a few years earlier. Similar deals were signed in Kuwait. These 'independents' such as J.P. Getty paid more for concessions and offered higher royalties. Getty still made a fortune, which did not go unnoticed among the producers.[8]

Russian production also started to take-off, with volumes growing annually at 14 per cent in the 1950–1963 period, eventually reaching over 4 million barrels per day. By the end of the 1950s, the USSR became the second-largest producer in the world, after the United States, and produced a volume of oil that could compete with the Middle East.[9] Italian ENI was one of the first companies to start importing cheap Russian oil from the Urals region into Italy, undercutting prices set by the oil majors.[10]

The Iranian crisis of the early 1950s and the closure of the Suez Canal during the 1956–1957 Suez crisis made Libya, an oil producer with direct access to the Mediterranean, a strategically important country. The Libyan 1955 Petroleum Law offered a large number of small concessions and stricter terms for exploration than the existing Middle East contracts. Still, the proximity to the European market and the light, low sulphur crude oil in the country attracted a large number of international bidders, most of them without refinery systems.

Dr Armand Hammer established the once small and 'independent'[11] Occidental Petroleum in 1957. About a decade later, the company struck oil in its Libyan concession, catapulting it into the ranks of major players in the oil industry.

Some sixty concessions awarded by 1957 included those to U.S. 'independents' such as Occidental, Conoco, Bunker Hunt, Continental, Marathon, and Amerada (the latter three forming the 'Oasis group') and later a major, Jersey Standard (Exxon). More than half of the Libyan production ended up in the hands of companies that had no European refining systems. Between 1962 and 1970, the oil production in the country went from 182,000 to 3,318,000 barrels![12]

When a messy coup in Libya brought the notorious Colonel Muammar al-Qaddafi to power in 1969, his determined anti-western agenda was to turbocharge a process that had been settling into place over the preceding ten years. And it would be Dr Hammer and Oxy (as Occidental were known to all) who would be the straws that broke a most important camel's back.

Forever and a day, the oil business has been run by a small group of seven major oil companies. Better known as the 'Seven Sisters',[13] a term credited to the charismatic outsider, Enrico Mattei (the founder of the Italian company ENI).[14] The 'Sisters' consisted of Esso, Texaco, BP, Shell, Chevron, Gulf, and Mobil.[15] The group controlled the exploration, production, transportation, refining, distribution, and marketing of oil across the globe with only minor competition coming from a group of smaller 'independents' such as Oxy, Philips, and Conoco. The 'Sisters' acted as '*one big organisation who took care of the world*'.[16]

Except, they had been remiss in taking too much care of themselves as '… *during the 1950's and 1960's the price of oil fell and it became very cheap*'.[17] Two other factors were driving the oil price lower. The 1958 recession (the Eisenhower Recession)[18] was sharp and also spread to Europe and Canada, driving oil demand lower. Just a year later, protectionist measures in the United States resulted in an oil import quota being imposed, effectively shutting the largest oil market to foreign competition.

Stranded overseas, the U.S. 'independent' producers had to sell their oil to national refineries in Europe, Japan, and Latin America at the best price they could get, driving prices down. The price of oil that traded outside the vertically integrated systems of the Majors fell from $1.93 in 1956 to $1.60 in 1959, and then to $1.30 in 1967.[19]

Qaddafi changed all this, and, with his policy of Libyan expansionism, was able to prise open a crack that was to begin the process of retreat by the Sisters. He did this by attacking the weakest link, Dr Hammers' Oxy. Ordered to cut production,[20] under the threat of expropriation and having been denied help by Esso, Hammer capitulated and conceded an increase in Libya's profit share and an increase in the prices that they agreed to pay for Libyan oil (the so-called Posted Price).[21]

All this put the Majors in a difficult position with the existing producers who were all hoping for higher prices and more revenues. From this point on, the hegemony of the Sisters was undermined, a cascade of renegotiations ensued across the Gulf, Africa, and Latin America and oil began to leak in gradually increasing amounts outside the aegis of the majors. The royalty terms changed and the concept of 'participation' for the producer states first appeared as concession agreements came under renegotiation.[22]

Revolutionary Times

This was also a revolutionary period, a decade marked by the Suez crisis of 1956, the end of European colonialism, the 1957 Sputnik launch, and the 1959 victory of the Cuban revolution. In Iraq, a group of officers overthrew the British-installed monarchy and established a republic. A year later, a revolution in Venezuela removed a military dictator and elected a democratic government; the country increased taxes on the oil industry to almost 70 per cent.[23] A new wave of populist leaders emerged in oil-producing nations, including Gamal Abdel Nasser in Egypt, Muammar al-Qaddafi in Libya, Houari Boumediene in Algeria, Abdullah Tariki in Saudi Arabia, and Pérez Alfonso in Venezuela. These leaders, primarily hailing from countries recently freed from colonial rule, grappled with declining prices for the vital resources that fuelled their economies. The Major oil companies were seen as vestiges of the old, colonial system.

Oil was a key commodity for their national aspirations and this time they were planning collectively. The roots of the Organisation of the Petroleum Exporting Countries (OPEC) were in an unofficial 'understanding' on the sidelines of the First Arab Petroleum Congress in Cairo in 1958. Representatives from S. Arabia, Kuwait, Egypt, Syria, Iran, and Venezuela came up with a wish list: increase their share of oil revenues, support prices (on which tax revenues were based), be consulted before any changes are made in posted prices, increase the refining throughput inside the producing countries, establish national oil companies and coordinate production policies through a commission that was to meet annually. While the meeting had no legal consequences,[24] this, so-called 'Maadi Agreement' (the meeting took place at the Maadi Yachting Club in Cairo) was a blueprint for everything the producing nations would strive to achieve in the future.[25]

The agreement was followed by the formal establishment of OPEC in Baghdad in September 1960, with Venezuela, Saudi Arabia, Iran, Iraq, and Kuwait as the founding members. Within months, they were joined by Libya.

In its first decade, OPEC had little effect, but the oil market underwent significant changes. At the heart of these changes was a collapse in the traditional pricing system. The Majors could no longer control the market by limiting supply, and with tax payments tied to posted prices, their revenues became unpredictable. Unable to maintain stable posted prices, the Majors shifted the financial burden onto oil-producing nations by lowering posted prices, reducing producer revenues at a time when these countries were eager for higher income. The once orderly flow of 'rivers of money' fragmented into numerous chaotic streams, each redirected by new players—companies or governments—into the market.

One of the most ambitious leaders of this era was Shah Reza Pahlavi of Iran. Following the Six-Day War in June 1967, the Shah covertly partnered with Israel to establish a company that, within a few years, constructed a pipeline between the Israeli ports of Eilat on the Red Sea and Ashkelon on the Mediterranean.[26] In its first year of operation, over 70 million barrels of Iranian oil were exported through this pipeline, nearly half of which remained in Israel. This arrangement was mutually beneficial: Israel secured a steady oil supply, and the Shah gained a secret channel for bypassing the Majors' system, enriching himself in the process.

This marked the start of a slow but decisive shift in control. The tipping point came when Libya successfully confronted weaker concessionaires, specifically Hammer's Occidental Petroleum. Libya's victory inspired other producing nations, sparking a wave of negotiations that progressively wrested control from Big Oil. Producing countries introduced improved royalty terms, price hikes, 'participation' agreements, and buyback discounts—where the Majors purchased oil under the producers' aegis at reduced rates. These efforts led to significant gains for OPEC nations, as they increasingly reasserted control over supply and pricing at the expense of the oil Majors.

Even the Saudis got involved. They were unhappy with high inflation in the United States eroding the dollar and the effective purchasing power of each barrel of their oil. They started selling some barrels at a price which included a gold-price 'escalator'. The logic was that, as the dollar value fell, gold trading in a relatively liquid market would increase in price and the 'escalator' would increase the price accordingly.

'Free' Oil

It was oil from Libya, supplied by the independent companies into Europe, that made a major contribution to the development of trading at the time, especially in the large, deep ports such as Rotterdam.[27] A significant portion of this 'free' oil was processed into petroleum products at independent refineries in the Mediterranean, particularly in Italy and Greece. From there, cargoes of heating oil and fuel oil were transported to Rotterdam, where they were divided into smaller lots in a process known as bulk-breaking. These smaller shipments were then barged down the Rhine to supply industrial Europe.

Tunisian barrels were among the first to reach the open market, followed closely by Syrian crude. Meanwhile, under the Shah, Iran pursued its own independent path, engaging in various barter arrangements. Enrico Mattei orchestrated a deal exchanging steel pipes for Russian oil, which was either refined in Italy or sold to India. Syria swapped oil for buses with FIAT, while Voest Alpine bartered steel for Iranian crude.

While Saudi Arabia tended to be more scrupulous when it came to offering barrels outside the traditional channels, there was no shortage of oil on the market from other OPEC countries. In the early 1970s, Abu Dhabi, Kuwait, and Qatar were especially active in tendering their Royalty oil and even some Participation oil which, in periods of low prices, the concessionaires would decline to buyback. Bids came from companies as widely spread as Petrobras, United Refining of Warren Pennsylvania, Cirillo Brothers of New York, Charter Oil, Philips Petroleum, John Sheehan (a Canadian refiner), and Swiss trader Nafta Mundial among others.

The Nixon Arbitrage

Trading opportunities are particularly based on optionality and arbitrage, or price differences in different markets.[28] But, in the 1960s, there were few such opportunities. The crude oil market was tightly controlled by a powerful oligopoly of the oil Majors, leaving little oil or petroleum products available outside their integrated systems. Trading was minimal, as there was little oil to trade; most production was retained within the Majors' integrated systems.

Instead of market transactions, joint ventures and swaps between companies were common. Oil prices remained stable, primarily because they were strategically set to minimise royalties and taxes paid to producing countries.[29]

Any trading in petroleum focussed on smaller volumes of petroleum products, usually around hubs such as Rotterdam and New York harbour. Both are deep-water ports at the mouth of rivers, linked to global markets as well as with access to large, inland markets. Some excess volumes of petroleum products could be traded on barges and were sufficiently small for the oil Majors not to bother with.[30]

But, in August 1971, a significant arbitrage opportunity emerged due to a decision by the U.S. government. This opportunity was created when President Richard Nixon's administration implemented wage-and-price controls in a misguided attempt to curb inflation. However, inflation had little to do with wages or energy prices; it was primarily driven by excessive money printing to finance the Vietnam War, which led to the U.S. abandoning the gold standard that very same month. This economic shift, well before the October 1973 Arab Oil Embargo,[31] was the true underlying cause of fuel shortages in the country, not the oil crisis itself.[32]

The legislation in question implemented in the United States in the decade after 1971 is best summarised as complex: '*The controls were amended several hundred times, either by rule making, legislation or through issuance of 'interpretative guidelines*'.[33] Complexity has long been a strategic advantage for professional traders, providing opportunities to exploit regulatory loopholes for profit.

One of the most significant moments for such arbitrage came with the Emergency Petroleum Allocation Act of 1973. This legislation created a two-tiered pricing system for domestically produced crude oil, distinguishing between 'old oil' and 'new oil'. 'Old oil' referred to crude from wells drilled before 1972, while 'new oil' was extracted from wells drilled after that year. Additionally, there was a category for 'stripper oil', which came from small, ageing wells nearing the end of their production life.[34] In 1974, the wellhead price for new oil was set at $10.13 per barrel, while old oil had a price cap of

$5.03 per barrel. Notably, the price of stripper oil and imported oil were not subject to these price controls, offering further opportunities for arbitrage.[35]

What is immediately obvious is that the regulation was effectively a tax on the domestic producers of 'old' oil and a subsidy for the consumption of 'new', 'stripper' and imported oil. But oil is a fungible commodity and there was no difference in the molecules of these different types, except in their price.

Unsurprisingly, the refiners would ask producers for as much 'old' oil as possible and to 'sweeten' the deal, they would pay a premium over the market for 'new' oil. To prevent this, the government made several changes to the legislation, eventually giving each refinery an old oil entitlement equal to the national average ratio of controlled to uncontrolled crude.[36] However, controlling the flow of oil that was arbitrarily labelled and priced differently was very hard.

Due to weak regulation, parties involved in the oil market began exploiting price discrepancies through a chain of trades designed to arbitrage between the different oil price tiers. For example, an oil gatherer could purchase 'old' oil at $5.25 per barrel, then sell it to a friendly trader (Trader A) at $5.40, making a $0.15 profit—this markup was the maximum allowed by government regulations. The oil would then pass through several other traders (B, C, D…), each marking up the price by $0.15. By the time the oil reached the original gatherer again, it could be sold at $9.40 per barrel. The gatherer would then sell it to a refiner at $9.55, effectively passing off the oil as 'new' oil and profiting from the price difference, circumventing the price controls meant to prevent such manipulation.[37]

What in reality happened was that the oil gatherer bought the 'old' oil at the government-mandated price of $5.25 and sold it to the refiner, at $9.55 a barrel, below the market price of say $10 (to sweeten the deal given that the oil was not 'new' but 'old'). The regulatory arbitrage of $4.75 ($10–$5.25) was a massive profit that could be shared between the 'daisy chain' of the producer, gatherer, refiner, and traders and would never benefit the end consumer—as the government hoped. All that the 'traders' in the middle needed was a telephone line and a telex machine.

The result was a boom in oil trading: '*Over 100 new firms, the great majority of which did not have storage facilities or transportation equipment, would enter in the 1973–77 period*'.[38] Regulatory arbitrage was all the rage and there were many other examples of dubious or simply obviously illegal trading. One Robert Sutton was accused by the Department of Energy (DOE) of fraudulently certifying hundreds of millions of barrels of old oil as 'stripper oil' (which was not restricted in price by the government). In 1973, Mr. Sutton started with a borrowed telephone and soon registered over fifty trading companies.[39]

Eventually, the infamous Marc Rich and Pincus Green[40] joined the frenzy, only they put a twist to it—they compensated companies via fictitious foreign oil deals, issued fake invoices, and moved profits overseas, away from the U.S. tax authorities.[41] Within a few years, the trading game of 'Nixon arbitrage' was over. The newly elected President Ronald Reagan ended the Byzantine price controls in January 1981.[42]

Modern oil trading might have had an inglorious start, but it had only just started.

Rotterdam Market: Bulk Breakers, Small Traders, and the Big Boys

The Port of Rotterdam is a fine example of locational geography perfection. Sited on an ample alluvial plain where the River Rhine meets the North Sea, with deep water and a large harbour area, its wider situation offers preferential access to a heavily populated hinterland stretching Southeast into industrial Germany and on to Switzerland and Central Europe. In close proximity to the North and Northwest, the United Kingdom, Low Countries, and Scandinavia are also very large markets for petroleum products. All in all, the port is a perfect location for entrepot activities.

The Rotterdam spot market, although an ethereal concept geographically, took its name for the reason that the oil industry became busy at that location in the early days of trading. One of the leading oil consultants of the day, Joe Roeber contends that '*If there is such a thing as a Rotterdam market, it is not a market and it is not at Rotterdam*'.[43] It was, and is, an '*everywhere and nowhere market*'.[44]

However, in the early days, the majority of the bulk-breaking companies importing cargoes of gas oil and fuel oil to Rotterdam and distributing the products by barge up the River Rhine were indeed mostly based in the Rotterdam area or at least in the contiguous location known as ARA (Amsterdam, Rotterdam, Antwerp).

While it was the movement of heavy fuel oil upon which the Amsterdam-Rotterdam-Antwerp (ARA) area was founded, Rotterdam began to become a storage and refining centre in the 1960s. Crude oil from the Independent's Concessions (especially in North Africa, Russia, and Syria) made its way to the mouth of the Rhine, and new storage companies Paktank and Matex were set up. For many of the smaller traders, it was the less than sophisticated strategy of buying heating oil in the summer and storing it until (they hoped) prices rose in the winter that was their trading mainstay.

Amsterdam had been the site of the Mobil oil refinery, set up to supply gas oil to the U.S. East Coast, although when they eventually closed the refinery in 1982, Amsterdam became more of a blending and storage hub.

Without deep water in the age of the supertanker, Antwerp suffered a relative disadvantage. A pipeline was constructed from Rotterdam to ship crude oil to its refineries and while this further interconnected the different areas of ARA, Antwerp tended to specialise increasingly in petrochemicals.

One of the earliest and most significant of these bulk breakers was Mabanaft, a company whose agile reinventions over almost 80 years of existence make it probably the 'father of the house'. Established in 1947[45] as 'Marquard and Bahls' by Theodore Weisser, they pre-date their erstwhile competitors such as Vitol and Bulk Oil and they remain active and relevant to this day having reaped the benefit of their home country, Germany, lacking a national oil company. Although they started life in the business of distribution of lubricating oil, as long ago as the late 1950s, they were processing Russian and Kuwaiti crude oil (via purchases from Gulf Oil) at Kalundborg in Denmark.[46]

Mabanaft was not afraid to expand beyond the home area and by 1972 they were buying 15,000 barrels a day of Khafji crude from a Japanese trader, Kanematsu-Gosho, which they refined at the Come-By-Chance refinery in Newfoundland (then owned by Canadian entrepreneur, John Sheheen) in return for a delivery of oil products. Khafji was a crude produced by the Japanese-owned Arabian Oil Company in the Neutral Zone in the Arabian Gulf to which the Japanese Sogo Shosha Kanematsu, had obtained access, and then sold it for profit.

Through cooperation with other players in the oil market and integration along the value chain, both at home and internationally, Mabanaft was able to be entrepreneurial and protective of capital. They understood, and still do, their changing competitive advantage and have been able to use this insight to reinvent their strategic agenda and make adjustments to their business model as necessary over time.

In addition to their Rotterdam and Italian processing, in 1979 Mabanaft purchased the 100,000 barrel-a-day Albatross Refinery in Antwerp from a German petroleum company, Wintershall.[47] The trader was planning to add a cracker (a specialised piece of equipment that serves to produce better and more valuable products in an oil refinery) to what was a simple refinery that mainly produced low-quality products such as fuel oil. But with an operating environment of poor profitability for refiners at the time and with a utilisation rate at less than 60 per cent of capacity, Mabanaft instead sold the plant in 1982.

The financial woes of European refining can trace their origin to the 1973 imposition of price controls in the United States.[48] With U.S. refiners able to bid up the price of crude oil and resist the attraction of product imports to their own domestic market, European refiners were beset by high input costs and low output revenues. As pointed out by Europ-Oil Prices in 1975, '*US refiners set a level of product selling prices and a level of buying prices for imported crude oil which between them make life impossible for Europe*'.[49]

After the construction of the Saras refinery in Italy in 1965, Europe experienced a rash of refinery construction in the Mediterranean and Northwest Europe with plants by Texaco at Ghent, Amoco at Milford Haven, Fina at Immingham, Mobil at Amsterdam, and Chevron at Feluy in Belgium and others. There were some less than sensible ideas for refinery locations such as BP's plans to build a refinery in the English Midlands and one by U.S. refiner, Murphy to begin construction at Bishopton on the River Clyde in Scotland, upstream of a basalt dyke that almost wholly closed the river to shipping![50]

As refinery margins went into free fall from 1973 onwards, the rush into the refining sector proved to be a strategic mistake of some significance for the industry. By 1976, the Italian refineries were only operating at 46 per cent of capacity. Compare that to the 100 per cent utilisation in the U.S. at that time.[51] Indeed, Dr H.L. Pellas, a representative of German oil company Wintershall, revealed at a Cologne energy conference[52] that in mid-1976, a simple refinery in Europe was only able to cover 95 per cent of its cash costs at the low level of product prices of that time.

Much later, post the 2008 Financial Crisis, when international trading became difficult due to credit availability, Mabanaft withdrew from its foreign operations. By 2018 however, they felt comfortable enough to return to the fray by establishing Mabanaft Energy Trading in Houston, Texas to trade middle distillate products.

There are few firms that have thrived and survived in the changing world of oil trading over the last half a century, but Mabanaft and the Weisser family who are still running the business are a shining example of success.

In the early days of the Rotterdam spot market, their most serious competitor was perhaps Bulk Oil. Based in Amsterdam and founded by the 'dour' Jacob Schreiber, Bulk Oil was one of the early cargo/barge traders in the Rotterdam milieu as well as being an early trader and 'a pioneer in trader processing'.[53] Schreiber also had strong contacts in Israel at the time of the 1973 oil embargo, and during the 1970s and 80 s, they had expanded aggressively overseas. From their London office in upmarket Berkeley Square, they were neck and neck with Mabanaft on traded volumes. Ultimately, they were to prove less agile and resilient. Regardless, the Bulk Oil annual International Petroleum (IP) week party at Park Lane's Grosvenor House Hotel regularly outdid that of their main competitors!

Prior to the price rises of 1970s, the financial commitment required to trade small-volume barges was not excessive. Such businesses attracted a large number of entities. Vanol, founded by Andre Von Gils, was one who grew into a reasonably active crude oil trader in the 1980s from their starting point in the Rotterdam markets.

A number of other small traders operated in and around the Rotterdam market at the time. Mabanaft was already very strong in Germany but some of their people left to form other trading companies such as Mebro and Naftamondial, the latter focussing on sourcing and selling Russian products. There was Joc Oil, founded in 1967 by the infamous Dutchman, John Deuss, trading jet fuel, and later Russian crude oil.

Patrician brokers Lambert and Bendall were very focussed on the heavy fuel oil business. Their man in Milan, Marco Bevilacqua, would source product from the Italian refineries Saras and Montedison for shipment up the Rotterdam. In many ways, the relationship between the Mediterranean third-party processing refinery source of product with the distribution and consumption hub of Rotterdam mimicked the relationship between the U.S. Gulf and the Caribbean with the U.S. East Coast.

Vitol was founded in 1966 by Henk Vietor (the name came from combining 'Vietor' and 'oil') and Jacques Detiger. Their first business was trading around barges on the Rhine and excess refinery production in ARA. Vitol was in direct competition with Van Gils' Vanol, who became one of the more active players in the naphtha[54] market. That market was originally organised by Phil Pollock, the owner of the brokerage company Aspen Oil, and by Theo Walti of Dow Chemicals, who wrote the original naphtha contract.[55]

In Milan, Branko Srenger set up Petraco to take advantage of what began to look as the beginning of the end of the total control of the seven sisters with Libyan, Russian, and Nigerian oil spilling into the spot markets (for growth of the spot market, see Fig. 2.1).

Another significant trader at the time was Tampimex, which had strong contacts in Iran and Israel. The company was linked to the secretive construction of and supply from the pipeline from Eilat in Israel to Askelon on the Mediterranean Sea. Headed up by Clive Oatley, they ploughed a not dissimilar furrow to Bulk Oil.

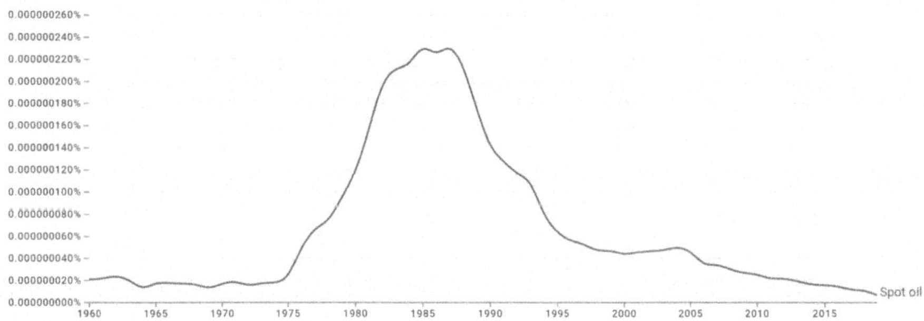

Fig. 2.1 'Spot oil' mentioned in english literature since 1960. Author, using Google Ngram viewer

Atlas Continental was based in London's swanky Park Lane and was subsequently bought by Koch, while Peter de Savary's Wilco, another small trading company, was also active. Not all staffers came from the traditional oil company backgrounds, and none were more exotic than Texas legend Oscar Wyatt's Coastal, run in Paris by interior designer Don Munsen and Armagnac producer Olivier de Montel.

The combative Wyatt has been an ever-present figure in the oil trading, refining, and production world for over fifty years. Coastal traded aggressively by leveraging its assets, especially its refineries in Eagle Point in Philadelphia, Corpus Christi, and Aruba, all of which were eager for heavier types of crude oil from the Middle East and West Africa.[56]

Referred to in one article as '*meaner than a junkyard dog*',[57] he was renowned for giving nothing away in a negotiation. While Wyatt was rumbustious and sought conflict, his long-time consigliere, Sam Wilson, took a different tack, one of pleading for consideration when trying to close a deal on his terms. He would use the very Texas expression '*ma' ass is hangin' out*' to evoke sympathy from his counterparty in what was an unusual example of the use of emotional intelligence in the rough and tumble oil patch!

The 1980s saw Oscar Wyatt run a lean team of oil traders in Houston and London. The London crew consisted of the experienced hands Carl Winberg, Mike Church, and Nigel Whiteley.[58] Most of their money came from getting involved in the Iranian prefinancing deals with Western, mainly German banks where Coastal would simply secure letters of credit and guarantee purchases of oil. Their other niches were Iraqi and Egyptian barrels. They managed to load very large crude carriers (VLCCS) and bring them to the U.S. Gulf Coast (USGC) with some oil for their own system and some for trading.

Wyatt conducted business, most controversially in Iraq, that eventually saw him fall foul of the U.S. authorities and spend a short time behind bars for his troubles.[59] By then, he had cashed in by selling the company to El Paso for $17 billion, which probably went a long way to soothe the pain.[60] Despite this interregnum, Wyatt and his well connected wife, Lynn, remained scions of Houston high society.[61]

Scan Trading, which subsequently became Scanoil and was a temporary home for a succession of traders 'in between jobs' over the years, was active from the very earliest days of the spot market. Their trading volume was significant at 5 million tonnes a year by 1974, almost half of which consisted of business into the U.S. East Coast.[62] They had begun by trading a good deal of fuel oil, much of it through Norwegian brokers, Fearnoil—a firm that had a ship-owning and broking background and who was owned by the wealthy Astrup family from Norway.

Kuwait National Petroleum Company, KNPC, was active in London at the time from their offices in St James's. They marketed refined products from their Mina al Ahmadi refinery and from Kuwaiti crude which they had third-party processed in the Med, Europe, East Africa, Pakistan, and Japan among other places and it was a very 'multi-cultural place to work'.[63] One of the early trainees who worked there in 1972 was Nader Sultan, a Pakistani-born son of a Kuwaiti diplomat who would later lead that company in its heyday.

A number of entities trading in the Levant were also active although their reputation for performance at the time was not always first class. Khalil Ghattas will appear at a later stage when his company, Gatoil, almost brought the Brent market to its knees. BBNaft were Lebanese and did much of their business in the Eastern Mediterranean while Petrogulf, which had links to Pakistan got caught up in the scandal that engulfed the notorious bank, BCCI.

The Americans, who were larger and better capitalised than many other traders, were able to benefit from the price rises of 1973 and survive the slacker time from 1975 to 1978 better than many of the smaller Rotterdam spot market players. These American traders were well represented by the likes of PetroSun, Anchutz, Northeast, and Houston Oil among others.

Not all the Americans were based in Europe. In New York, companies like Melanol, a name no longer active, thrived. Set up by two German-Jewish émigré's Rolf Noether and Eric Sondheimer, they had contracts with Iberian refiners Cepsa and Petrogal, while also bringing products from Europe into U.S. clients such as Hess and NEPCO. Northville, a highly successful and long-lasting products importer and distributor in the Northeast of the United

States, had begun their involvement in oil in 1956 and was to become, under successive generations of the Bernstein family, the biggest importer of gasoline to their market area. Northville was also a prime participant in the construction of the pipeline across the Isthmus of Panama which facilitated the movement of Alaskan North Slope oil to the U.S. Gulf Coast. More recently they became a predominantly futures market player however.[64]

In response to the interesting amount of business being done outside their systems, the majors BP, Shell, and Esso set up Anro, Petra, and Impco respectively to attempt to capture bulk-breaking profits. Anro, with superior relationships with the BP affiliates, was the most successful of these three. Headed up in the early days by a well-loved BP veteran, the late Chris Houseman, they were eventually pushed aside when Deutsche BP flexed their trading muscles at the end of the 1970s.

Going Bust

Trader participation in the market became particularly intense after the oil shock of 1973–74, since the costs of entry into the industry were low (basically a telex and telephone) and the potential rewards were high. As a result, the number of traders proliferated to more than 300 in the Rotterdam area alone, though the trade was dominated by those with access to crude and products at the same time, such as the Majors' offspring.

During the slack period of 1975–78 a large number of these traders went bankrupt. One company that was robust enough to survive the shakeout was Magna. In the equal ownership of ex-Shell supply man, Trevor Simmons and the Houston, Texas firm BAC (who were voracious buyers of European gas oil pre-embargo), Magna remained close to Simmons' old employer, Shell. This was a smart move and it was an arrangement, not unusual at the time, which suited both the Shell exile's firm and also the alma mater. If Magna found themselves in a bit of bother, they had a line back into Shell to help them out. And the favours worked both ways as Shell was most likely able to rely on Magna to prosecute business quietly for them outside the usual channels.

Simmonds was assisted by Bob Leonard, Bridie Tobin, and Andy Whitrow in the early days. Leonard, who had joined from Gulf, was a big guy and he proved to be especially adept when the sanctity of a contract needed to be observed with the application of a little additional persuasion. Bridie Tobin had been a colleague of Simmons at Shell and was one of the first women to be involved in the front-line supply and trading business at an oil major. A

Trinity College Dublin geologist, Bridie was blessed with the Irish facility for outgoing friendliness, and she was a popular trader of the time. At a later stage in her career, she was tapped to head up the Supply and Trading Department of Britoil, the privatised oil production firm that had been part of the British National Oil Corporation (BNOC). She was rarely without client guests who had flew up from London or further afield to meet at her Glasgow offices.

Bridie and her colleagues enjoyed taking the visitors to lunch, usually at the well renowned Rogano Oyster Bar, an epicurean oasis in the city of the mutton pie. On one occasion, well remembered, Bridie sensed that she had ingested a bad oyster. Immediately, she called for a tumbler full of neat vodka and in a scene reminiscent of a Fresher's Week drinking boat race, she downed what was the best part of a half bottle of the neat spirit in one long gulp. Then, Bridie declared with certainty that any bacteria would have been well and truly drowned. In the true form of a member of a nationality known for their pot-stilling and extreme carousing, she walked back to the office completely unaided and proceeded to complete a full day's work, according to a member of her trading staff who was present at the lunch.[65]

Alcohol has played a central role in the oil business over the years. The offshore rig men of the upstream business were required to remain abstemious during their two-week shift but no such restraint burdened the men of Mayfair, Midtown, and Marunouchi (and as we will see, they were largely at that time, men).

The three-pint or three-martini liquid lunch was not unusual and would be followed by a snooze in one's private office under the angle-poise light, with the door closed. Yet, a few instances of alcohol abuse did occur. Most who were engaged in the industry at the time will recall the eviction, still discussed among the trading community today, from a second-floor window of the Norwegian Embassy in London, of a valuable oil painting of the then King of that country. A well-refreshed trader had removed it from the wall in the Embassy banqueting hall and had decided to heave it out onto the street below. It was one of the very few public instances of serious misbehaviour from these days.

In later years when trading took its electronic turn, there would be more than one instance of an unfortunate trader returning from an extended lunch only to slump over a live trading terminal keyboard and accidentally trade up an expensive storm.[66]

Generally, while alcohol was consumed in large quantities, standards of behaviour were largely maintained. This was despite the effects of excessive drinking on speech and carriage, especially in a business world that relied heavily on face-to-face interactions and verbal negotiations.

Back in the sober reality of the world, the established elites were facing a shake-up, as plenty of new players arrived to challenge their dominance.

Notes

1. In the early 1960's BP produced more oil than it refined.
2. For details, see Imsirovic (2021), page 74: 'Towards the International Cartel'.
3. 'The seven sisters were the Standard Oil Company of New Jersey (later Exxon), the Standard Oil Company of New York (Socony, later Mobil, which eventually merged with Exxon), the Standard Oil Company of California (Socal, later renamed Chevron), the Texas Oil Company (later renamed Texaco), Gulf Oil (which later merged with Chevron), Anglo-Persian (later British Petroleum), and Royal Dutch/Shell.' https://history.state.gov/milestones/1921-1936/red-line#:~:text=The%20seven%20sisters%20were%20the,Gulf%20Oil%20(which%20later%20merged
4. Little did he know that later in his career, he would get pretty close to a real king and serve as a personal advisor and a mentor to then 'young prince', Abdulaziz bin Salman Al Saud. Robin's success of running the 'Oxford-Princeton' oil trading programme for over two decades made him well known across the oil industry and finally landed him the lucrative job of mentoring the 'young prince' in all things trading.
5. CIA (1970), page. 7.
6. ENI stands for 'Ente Nazionale Idrocarburi'.
7. Amoco was much later bought by BP. This section of the chapter draws a lot on Imsirovic (2021), chapter 7, 'New Kids on the Block', page 90.
8. A. Sampson page 157.
9. Data from the National Petroleum Council Report (1964, pp. 18, 29, 74, 101).
10. https://www.govinfo.gov/content/pkg/CHRG-87shrg86868/pdf/CHRG-87shrg86868.pdf see page 13.
11. For a definition, see: https://guides.loc.gov/oil-and-gas-industry/companies#:~:text=Researching%20oil%20and%20gas%20companies&text=An%20independent%20company%20focuses%20on,oil%20during%20a%20given%20year.
12. Blair (1976), page 221.

13. https://www.americanforeignrelations.com/O-W/Oil-The-seven-sisters.html
14. https://archiviostorico.eni.com/aseni/en/news/IT-ENI-CMS0001-000064
15. Now, all 'Seven Sisters' are consolidated into ExxonMobil (Merged with Mobil), Chevron (merged with Texaco and took over Gulf), BP and Shell.
16. From the interview with John Hunt formerly of Gulf Oil and Citizens Energy 09/02/2024.
17. Yergin D., 1991, p. 524.
18. https://academic.oup.com/oep/article-abstract/10/1/34/2360066
19. Blair (1976), page 213.
20. https://www.nytimes.com/1975/09/03/archives/occidental-petroleum-to-protest-libyan-plan-to-cut-output-of-oil.html
21. Since there was no oil market to speak of before that, the oligopoly of Majors would simply 'post' the price for oil and it would serve the basis for their tax payments (or royalties) to the producing governments. Needless to say, they kept them pretty low.
22. Parra, 2004, p. 154.
23. Parra (2004), page 89.
24. Most participants had no authority to sign such agreement on behalf of their countries, so they signed it in their personal capacity.
25. Rubino (2008), page 174.
26. Amman (2009), page 65.
27. Razavi (1986), page 16.
28. In general, traders move commodities in space, time andquality across regulatory regimes. For more details, see Imsirovic (2024), chapter 3.
29. For details, see Imsirovic (2021), 'Discriminatory pricing, page 77.
30. Razavi (1986), 'Rotterdam market', page 16.
31. Embargo followed President Nixon's request to Congress for $2.2 billion in emergency aid to Israel during the Yom Kippur War.
32. To this day, history books claim that the shortages were caused by the Arab embargo. See: https://www.history.com/news/energy-crisis-1970s-innovation
33. Murphy (2018), page 64.
34. https://nswa.us/stripper-wells/
35. Kalt 1981, page 18.
36. Murphy (2018), page 66.
37. The example is from Bradley (1996), page 690.
38. Ibid, page 690.

39. Ibid, page 710.
40. A lot more on them in the subsequent chapters.
41. Marc Rich Indictment (1984) pages 14–18. Pincus Green, Clyde Meltzer, Mark Rich + Co. International Limited Indictment, US District Court Southern District of New York. FBI Records (The Vault): https://vault.fbi.gov/marc-rich/Marc%20Rich%20Part%2005%20of%2024
42. https://www.washingtonpost.com/archive/politics/1981/01/29/reagan-decontrols-gasoline-crude-in-deregulation-debut/fa3134b7-f70a-4bdd-92be-3c92f43e6112/
43. Roeber, 1979, p. 2.
44. Vinocur, July 8, 1979, Section F,p. 1.
45. According to the Mabanaft website. That would almost certainly make it the oldest trading company in Europe. https://www.mabanaft.com/en/about-us/overview/
46. Kalundborg Refinery has been part of the Klesch Group since January 1, 2022. https://www.heiderefinery.com/en/about-us/raffinerie-kalundborg
47. Europ-Oil (Prices) London 07/09/1979. Wintershall was founded at the beginning of 1894 as a potash drilling company. https://wintershalldea.com/en/who-we-are/history/history-general#:~:text=Wintershall%20is%20founded%20at%20the,the%20extraction%20of%20potash%20salts.
48. https://www.archives.gov/research/guide-fed-records/groups/432.html
49. Europ-Oil (Prices) London 07/03/1975, p. 2.
50. Bryce, C:The Growth of Bishopton—unpublished dissertation, University of Glasgow 1978.
51. Europ-Oil (Prices) London 27/08/1976, p. 2.
52. Europ-Oil (Prices) London 27/08/1976.
53. Roeber, p. 4.
54. A light petroleum product from distillation of crude oil, used for production of petrol (gasoline) and petrochemical products.
55. Discussion with Phil Pollock on 26/06/2024. We shall revert to the naphtha contract later in Chapter 5.
56. From interviews with Nigel Whiteley on 5 September 2024 and 23 January 2025.
57. Russell, Jan Jarboe: Texas Monthly April 1991.
58. Carl and Nigel worked together at Metallgesellschaft (MG) office in London. From interview with N. Whitley, Ibid.

59. https://www.cnbc.com/2007/10/01/texas-oilman-pleads-guilty-in-oil forfood-scandal.html
60. https://www.ftc.gov/news-events/news/press-releases/2001/01/ftc-cle ars-merger-el-paso-energy-coastal-corp
61. '[Lynn's] annual birthday parties, at villas in the South of France, were considered high points of the summer season—drawing her friends, who ranged from Prince Rainier and Princess Grace of Monaco to Elton John, Estée Lauder, David Niven, Joan Collins, and West German chancellor Helmut Schmidt.'.
    https://www.vanityfair.com/culture/2016/01/lynn-wyatt-texas-soc ialite?srsltid=AfmBOooDrlQuLjTaFt1l0Fvy8BHxp-ZN6V65TTAaOl Eu9rW1ywCM-Nnz
62. Europ-Oil (Prices) London 24/09/1976, p. 3.
63. Discussion with Richard Johnstone 24/04/2024.
64. 'They also tried power trading until one of their traders lost tens of million on a NY-Philly power spread back in the mid 90's,' According to a source who wished to stay anonymous.
65. Your author was there.
66. For example, see: https://www.reuters.com/article/world/china/oil-bro kerage-pvm-names-rogue-trader-behind-oil-spike-idUSTRE5621U5/

Bibliography

Blair J.M. (1976): 'The Control of Oil', Pantheon books, New York.

Casson, Mark and John S. Lee (2011): 'The Origin and Development of Markets: A Business History Perspective', Business History Review 85 (Spring 2011): 9–37. https://doi.org/10.1017/S0007680511000018

CIA Intelligence Assessment (1986): The Libyan Oil Industry: Dependence on Foreign Companies, Directorate of Intelligence, January 1986.

CIA Intelligence Memorandum (1970): Algeria: The Importance of the Oil Industry, Directorate of Intelligence, October 1970.

Davies, Richard (2019): 'Extreme Economies', Bantam Press.

Hearing Before the Committee on Energy and Natural Resources (1983): 'World Petroleum Outlook—1983', US Government Printing Office, Washington, DC.

Imsirovic, Adi (2021): 'Trading and Price Discovery for Crude Oils', Palgrave.

Kalt, Joseph. 1981. The Economics and Politics of Oil Price Regulation. Cambridge, MA. MIT Press.

Mark Rich Indictment (1984): 'Mark Rich, Pincus Green, Clyde Meltzer, Mark Rich + Co. International Limited Indictment', US District Court Southern

District of New York. FBI Records (The Vault): https://vault.fbi.gov/marc-rich/Marc%20Rich%20Part%2005%20of%2024
Murphy, Robert P. (2018): 'Removing the 1970s Crude Oil Price Controls: Lessons for Free-Market Reform', The Journal of Private Enterprise 33(1), 2018, 63–78.
National Petroleum Council Report (1964): Impact of Oil Exports from the Soviet Block, Supplement to the 1962 Report, MPC, March 19, Washington.
Parra F. (2004): Oil Politics, A Modern History of Petroleum, I.B. Taurus Co. Ltd.
Roeber, J: The Rotterdam Oil Market Petroleum Economist 1979
Roeber, J: The Evolution of Oil Markets: 'Trading Instruments and Their Role in Price Formation.' Royal Institute of International Affairs, 1993.
Razavi Hossein, (1986): 'The New Era of Petroleum Trading', World Bank Technical paper number 96.
Rubino A. (2008): Queen of the Oil Club, Beacon Press, Boston.
Sampson, A.: 'The Seven Sisters, The Great Oil Companies and The World They Shaped', Cornet Books, 1975 and 1988 editions.
Vinocur, J: The Great Noses of Rotterdam New York Times 08/07/1979
Yergin, Daniel: The Prize—The Epic Quest for Oil, Money and Power Simon and Schuster 1993

3

Difficult Deals in Difficult Places

Trading at the 'Sisters'

While the new entrepreneurs of oil trading were buccaneering their way around the oil-producing world, the majors, especially the Seven Sisters, were in different ways contemplating their futures.

The commercial departments of these companies looked after supply and distribution. There was no trading. Henry Longhurst's 1959 book on the history of BP runs to 286 pages without once mentioning the word 'trading'.[1] Rather, the Sisters' market [2]representatives were known as 'supply men'.

BP and Shell were the European Sisters but they were, at least in the early days, very different types of entities and their response to the events unleashed in the early 1970s was to differ from the response of the American Sisters—Texaco, Chevron, Gulf, Mobil, and Esso.

All the Sisters had 'Bulk Sales' teams who moved their excess production from their Concessions to customers in the consuming countries short of crude oil, often the Far East. Texaco, as the most supply-balanced of the group, would be the least active in this respect while BP supposedly had 300 or so employees in Bulk Sales. With excess crude from Kuwait, Iran, and Nigeria, BP was the most active Sister, with Gulf Oil probably a close second.[3]

The other side of the commercial departments dealt with refinery crude supply, external processing, affiliate supply, crude and petroleum product exchanges, and distribution. But 'nothing was being done that resembled trading'.[4]

A. Imsirovic and C. Bryce, *The Rivers of Money*,
https://doi.org/10.1007/978-3-031-91806-3_3

Shell, always short of crude oil, was known for their marketing prowess and, at times, their ruthless edge and was noted as having the 'commerciality of the Dutch and the duplicity of the English'.[5] Much later in September 1985, when Margaret Thatcher agreed to the Al-Yamamah arms deal[6]in exchange for oil, BP was offered the full quantity of exchanged oil. This was a very generous deal in which Her Majesty's Government allowed BP to receive the oil at a discounted price of $1 a barrel below the official prices.[7] However, BP felt uncomfortable taking on the full quantity of oil and asked Shell if they would join the venture on an equal basis. Shell rewarded BP by attempting to persuade the British government to award them the whole deal. In fact, the Shell Central Supply Department was already very active in the early 1970s. They were lifting some 30 VLCC per month from the Persian Gulf, destined for various Shell Affiliates.

BP was considered to be very Civil Service, Oxbridge-like, and very much less commercial than Shell. They were 'an archaic culture with a spread of assets in the wrong places'.[8] David Hufton, who subsequently played an especially important role in the development of spot markets in the North Sea as a founder of the London arm of the brokerage firm PVM, recalls that, as a graduate of a lesser-known University and with the regional accent of a 'Northerner', he found: '*class discrimination in BP to be rife*'.[9]

Yet it was BP, led by senior figures like Russell Seal and Bryan Sanderson, who were to emerge in the early days as the most successful traders among the Majors and the earliest of adaptors of 'proprietary' trading.[10] Seal was close to the industry price reporter, geopolitical sage, and proprietor of Europ-Oil (Prices) London, Jan Nasmyth. Europ-Oil was the publication most consulted by traders and oil company senior management. In a manner that has become common among politicians, he would leak information to Nasmyth mainly to test the industry's reaction, but also to promulgate interest in trading. Seal 'made sure that Jan was well informed about what was going on in the Rotterdam market'.[11]

Of the U.S. Sisters, Texaco, considered to be very right wing in their outlook (they had been the major supplier to Franco's Spain),[12] was the least in need of buying and selling to cover shortfalls or to remove surpluses and were unpopular among their peers. 'We all hate Texaco' said an Esso man.[13] With their international department based in White Plains, New York, Texaco would attend lunches with their U.S. 'Sisters: Gulf, Mobil, Exxon, and Chevron. Each week there was a rota of lunch appointments—if it's Wednesday, it would be Exxon and so on. There they would divide up business 'in a tranquil fashion'.[14]

For example, if Esso had supplied, say, Cepsa last month, then it would be the turn of Mobil this month and then Chevron next month in a sort of a rotation. Only when there were special needs would brokers be involved. For example, when Esso needed to source heavy fuel oil to cover their utility commitments[15] without the wider market knowing what was going on they would use Bruggeman brokers in New York. Otherwise, surpluses and deficits were normally settled by the Majors through exchanges, and these occurred regularly.

For example, Gulf Oil liked to run Bu Attifel crude oil from Libya but were not themselves producers of this particular grade. Italian Agip (now part of the ENI Group), who produced it, preferred Arab Light crude oil. Gulf Oil would then acquire Arab Light from Texaco in return for Nigerian and then exchanged Arab Light for Bu Attifel with Agip. Valuations would take place through internal discussion of the relative worth of the products from each grade being exchanged and a quantity premium or discount would be applied to equalise value.

Exxon was known for being engineering-centric and rarely promoted those lacking refining experience to the most senior positions. Mobil, under the 17-year-long Chairmanship of the formidable Rawleigh Warner, were mavericks and would plough the loneliest of furrows among their peers who were often frustrated that Mobil would do their own thing without thought for the overall interests of the Sisters 'club'. Gulf, like BP, were suppliers of the marginal barrel from their long crude oil position. In fact, Gulf supplied Shell with 600,000 barrels a day of Kuwaiti oil for many years while BP tended to sell their allocation to Esso and Mobil, all the while keeping business nicely within the club.

'Lot of contracts were quality exchange contracts among the Majors' says Nigel Whiteley, who was at the Bulk Trading department of BP in the 1970s, 'There was no spot business. It was a comfortable market, just based on oil exchanges'.[16] Thus together, the sisters ruled the biggest commodity market in the world.

If joining the European Sisters mostly required an Oxbridge academic pedigree and if Exxon required one to be an engineer, no such encumbrances were necessary at Gulf Oil. John Hunt was, in his own words, a 'ski bum' but, answering a Wall St Journal advertisement where individuals with international experience were sought, he found that his few years living with his family overseas as a teenager, qualified him for the role and he was hired by Gulf Oil for their International Commercial desk in New York. The company would, though, be the first of the Sisters to begin to retreat from the International arena as early as 1974 and they were eventually to be taken over by Chevron some ten years later.

This was a time of rapid change and the old vertically integrated ways where the majors controlled the value chain from production to consumption were being fractured. To compete with the newly minted trading companies, the big guys had to change.

The change was led by BP and Shell who began to de-integrate their businesses and enable their affiliates to operate with some independence in the new commercial world. This process was known as 'arms lengthing'[17] and, in the case of Shell, it led to the establishment of Shell International Trading Company or SITCO in 1975. The company's mission was to compete in supplying affiliates such as Deutsche Shell and Shell Nederland and to benefit from central purchasing rather than having individual affiliates competing with each other in the market.

It took SITCO a full ten years to accomplish what they had set out to achieve from when their first CEO, Geoffrey Harbe, commenced the 'arms-lengthing' process.

BP got the joke early and trading quickly became a valued competency. So, like Shell, they created a trading department in July 1975, known thereafter as the trading 'bench', implying not individual offices with closed doors, but a communal trading area. BP was to become the dominant source of trading talent for the wider world as markets expanded over the next ten years. It was the early departure in 1970 of Len Dickinson to Koch which, internally, set off a lot of talks and then action about better-paid opportunities outside the majors.[18] Early on, BP was to lose Steve Paice to Phillip Brothers, Meg Annesley to a small trading company, Tricentrol, David Hufton went to brokers PVM, Urs Reider to Scan Trading, Marcus Green to Phillip Brothers, Andy Hall to BP trading in the United States and so on.

While having to continually retrain staff when their top commercial dealers were tempted away, there were also some advantages in having, and indeed at times encouraging, the establishment of an external alumni group. Being able to operate quietly outside company strictures was a useful facility.

If the Sisters ran a tight ship, at least up until the early 1970s, there was a group of large Independents snapping at their heels. They were tolerated and even proved useful when selected for oil exchanges from time to time. These were companies like Koch, Philips Petroleum, Arco, Ashland, Conoco, Coastal, and Sun in the United States, state-owned entities like CFP in France, Fina in Belgium, and ENI in Italy, along with various other scattered firms like Petrobras in Brazil, Idemitsu, and Kanematsu in Japan and Soyuzneftexport in Russia.

During the 1960s and 1970s, the independents were able to buy supplies from the producer states directly at official prices, with some discounts or premiums, depending on the market conditions. However, their cost of crude was always above the prices the Majors paid and they had to work very hard on the distribution and retail aspect of the business to compete. They would be forced to reduce their profit margins by engaging in price cutting both at the retail level and ex-tank bulk sales and later would attract consumers to their forecourts through hosting convenience store products.

In the Middle of the Deal

Much of the business being developed at this time was conducted through the intermediation of brokers. Erwin Spuller (with his thick horned-rimmed spectacles and neatly coloured hair) had been first on the block with his company Fretoil, when they opened an office on Rue MarBoeuf in Paris in 1938. Their involvement over time was focussed on the trade of Russian oil coming into Europe, the cargo and barge markets of Rotterdam, the inputs and outputs from the Mediterranean third-party processing refineries and in serving both the independent and, quietly, major oil companies.

In an age without the technological support of today, the oil brokers held a very privileged position. Information access, as ever, was key, and it was they who knew who wanted to buy or sell and at what price. Brokers were the ones who could choose to whom they would show deal possibilities. A powerful position and one not worn lightly by Erwin Spuller, whose frequent interviews with the oil trading press and regular conference speeches, usually bemoaning the entry of speculators to the marketplace, were widely reported.

Indeed, the advent of speculator interest was to grate with the old ways for many. Europ-Oil Prices reported in 1974 that: '*In the last 18 months, fresh persons have appeared in the products markets and now in crude oil for whom speculation rather than expertise is the breath of lif*e!'.[19]

At the same time, the brokerage business was thriving in New York, where another notable figure, Thomas Galdy, was making a name for himself at Commerce Oil. Galdy, who would later transition into the world of Fine Art—particularly Old Masters Drawings—was already an accomplished art connoisseur. From his townhouse just steps away from Florence's iconic Ponte Vecchio, he remains today a knowledgeable guide to the lesser-known frescoes and significant works tucked away in various buildings across that cultured city.

However, it was not his expertise in art that led him to work at Commerce Oil in New York after graduating in 1969. Instead, Galdy's talent as a polyglot, fluent in five European languages, made him an invaluable asset. At a time when global markets were rapidly expanding, his linguistic skills were highly sought after, earning him a key role at the company.

Unlike Fretoil in Paris whose origins were in shipbroking, Commerce Oil, based in Rockefeller Plaza and chaired by Harry R. Louis, had aspirations to be an international oil trader rather than just a broker. However, these aspirations came to a crashing halt when, having arranged to import heavy fuel oil from Romania by means of a contract with Petrolexport, a state oil export monopoly in that country, the Wall Street Journal ran a front-page story alleging that Commerce Oil was trading with the enemy and consorting with Communists![20]

Still, brokerage was not a bad way to earn a living, and having been relocated to Zurich in 1971, Galdy became involved in the sale of surplus Royalty oil from producer states. This was a category of oil unlike a Concession holder's Equity oil or Participation barrels. It was effectively an additional tax in kind and the oil, available directly from producer states, was outside the major oil companies' ambit and often found its way into the hands of traders. Working extensively with traders to place these barrels with the Rotterdam, Italian, and the U.S. markets, the standard broker remuneration was a fee of 1% on products and 1 cent per barrel on crude oil.[21]

And of course, there was also business to be done quietly behind the so-called 'Swiss Curtain'[22] from where 'outlaw'[23] crude from the North Rumaila field in Iraq and the Sarir oil field in Libya, along with Russian material, found its way into markets in Europe as well as India and Brazil.[24]

If a number of 'fresh persons' had entered the market in 1974, it was also a time when the undercapitalised and underfunded smaller firms were exiting the space. Prices were rising dramatically as were the consequent risks and oil trading became a business only for the bigger fish.

Difficult Deals in Difficult Places

Before the Arab Oil Embargo of October 1973, the oil markets—such as they were—were dominated by four distinct groups. First, there were the 'traders': specialists in sourcing crude oil that had 'leaked' from places like Russia, Syria, and North Africa, adept at navigating difficult deals in even more difficult locations. Second, the bulk-breaking merchants and distributors, primarily based in Rotterdam, played a pivotal role in creating the so-called Rotterdam Spot Market. Third, the market featured the 'Supply Men' of the Sisters, alongside a fragmented network of independent oil companies and third-party refiners, especially in the Mediterranean and the Caribbean. Lastly, there were the producer states, most notably the members of OPEC.

Among the 'Traders' was a company that would go on to pioneer the model that, refined over fifty years, came to define the independent oil trader of the 2020s: Philipp Brothers.

By the late 1960s, Phillip Brothers had earned a reputation as the world's leading independent commodities merchant, though oil was not yet a core part of its portfolio. Over the next two decades, however, the company would rise to become the largest and most successful oil trader in the world.

Like so many other embryonic oil trading firms who saw an opportunity opening as barrels appeared outside the ambit of the Seven Sisters, Philipp Brothers was a firm of German and Central European Jewish émigrés. Ludwig Jesselson, a kindly but 'conservative and cautious'[25] individual, was a back-to-back man who liked both sides of a deal, purchase and sale, to be contemporaneously 'tightly secured'.[26]

The company's first oil deal was indeed tightly secured. The cultured, opera-loving, sophisticated Brit, Alan Flacks,[27] who then ran the Milan office had come across a small parcel of Tunisian crude that was available for immediate lifting. Having found an Italian refiner willing to take the cargo, Flacks secured both sides of the deal at an attractive margin.[28]

This business model of knowing people in sometimes exotic locations in an age of opacity served Philipp Brothers well for many years. They and traders like them could straddle the globe buying, selling, and earning a risk-free margin before technology predicated an alternative model based on the availability of perfect information and the mining of data the likes of which prevails today and which we will encounter later.

The Philipp Brothers model was one of accomplishing difficult things in difficult places, and this involved dealing with rogue producers, acquiring newly freed up 'royalty barrels',[29] and sourcing oil from Independents who owned concession rights. On the demand side, they would cosy up to states where supply restrictions were in place, countries without a major national oil company. and where the Sisters' footprint was light on the ground.

All the traders were soon overshadowed by a pair of young hands at Philipp Brothers. Their early entry into the oil market proper had been led by Marc Rich working out of the Madrid office, along with his long-time colleague, Pincus Green who was working from Zug in Switzerland. Rich handled the trading, while Green was the 'traffic' man.[30] If Rich made the money, Green's job was to protect it.

Marc Rich was a colleague of Alan Flacks at the time and had been running the Madrid office. And it was to be Rich and not Flacks who built on the Tunisian deal and who with a fierce work ethic, ambition, nerve and arguably, unburdened by scruples, would introduce the firm to the easy margins to be made by mining the oil trading opportunity.

So, when Richard Johnstone, then a young supply executive at BP sold a cargo of Iranian Light to Cepsa[31] back in 1971, the deal was brokered for 1 cent per barrel by Marc Rich, then at Philipp Brothers.[32] BP, long crude oil at that time from Kuwait, Iran, and Nigeria, always had difficulty placing the Iranian grades, and the newcomer, Rich, was a helpful trading facilitator.

Pinky Green, who spoke Farsi, had close contacts in Iran, while Marc Rich had a friend in the government of General Franco of Spain.[33] Working as a team, Pinky would send Iranian oil via the Israeli pipeline to Ashkelon and Marc would make sure that the oil was a part of the sizeable, thirty per cent quota of the Spanish government, which he managed to obtain through his government contacts. Franco did not recognise Israel, but the business was too good for all the parties concerned for this detail to be a deal-breaker.

Marc Rich also brought oil from Egypt to Spain, based on a debt-repayment deal, and some oil was sold to Italy as well.[34] Later, in their own company, the infamous duo would make the most profitable oil trades by supplying the apartheid regime of South Africa, Castro's Cuba, Marxist Angola, the Nicaraguan Sandinistas, Gaddafi's Libya, Ceauşescu's Romania, and Pinochet's Chile.[35]

Global outlook and reliance on 'special relationships' was a skill mastered at Philipp Brothers, back in New York. And if the seminal developments of 1973 and 1974—the embargo, rapidly rising demand, the imposition of price controls in the United States, and the lifting of import quotas in the same country were easy to identify, there was a further event that took place which was to prove to be of seminal importance in the development of oil trading.

That event was the resignation from the Philipp Brothers of Marc Rich and the founding of his own firm, Marc Rich + Co. Not only would this provide the market with a second big international trade player but it would also galvanise a response from Philipp Brothers that was to be especially important over the succeeding years.[36]

Whether Rich the risk taker became too much of a handful for his boss, the conservative Ludwig Jesselson, whether they argued about compensation or whether Rich just wanted his own show, he and colleague Pincus Green left the firm in early 1974 armed with contacts in Iran, West Africa and further afield.

Their departure left a gaping hole in Philipp Brothers' growing oil business. Ludwig Jesselson called not on an oil man, but on metals trader Tom O'Malley to take over the oil side of the business. O'Malley, who we shall hear about more later, wasted no time in recruiting a bench of traders from the majors. But one of the foremost among the 'younger' crop of traders that he relied on was Patrick De Barros.[37]

French-educated and of a Portuguese background, De Barros had already been persuaded by O'Malley to leave his existing role at Sonarep, a Portuguese entity operating extensively in Africa, to come to New York to run the oil trading relationship with Brazil, a major consumer at the time and a destination for much of the West African crude that the firm handled. When Rich and Green exited, O'Malley put De Barros in charge of most of the oil business except the (mainly North African) business handled by Peter Arbenz in Zug.

De Barros[38] recalls that the Philipp Brothers team then consisted of Al Kaplan, David Tobey, and Vin Boemio (latterly of the failed Houston Oil Refining and Bomar) in New York, Juan Luiz Gonzalez in Madrid, Steve Paice (and later Ron Gray) in London, Peter Arbenz in Zug, and George Tanaka (along with, later, Marcus Green) in Tokyo.[39] This was as powerful a set of guns as could be imagined, and they were to make serious waves in the succeeding ten or so years as oil markets grew dramatically.

This was the beginning of the trading strategy of 'doing difficult things with difficult people in difficult places-quietly!' The Philipp Brothers' guns moved in what was, at least on the face of it, exalted company. Jorge Almeida in his book on De Barros (Uma Vida a Bolina), relates encounters with King Juan Carlos, Cyrus Vance, Bridget Bardot, and a variety of African and other assorted 'Potentates'.

Introduced to Madame Claude, the infamous Parisian 'Madame', by a French aristocratic school friend, De Barros leveraged this connection to arrange a meeting with Reza Pahlavi, the Shah of Iran—who was allegedly one of Madame Claude's clients. This audience with the Shah secured De Barros a contract to purchase Iranian crude oil under the name 'Interoil'. These barrels reportedly often found their way to Southern Africa and other sanctioned regions.

De Barros also found success in Africa, particularly in Nigeria, where the locals showed a clear preference for the Portuguese over the French, who were also active in the region. This advantage enabled him to secure a contract for Bonny Light crude, with profit margins so substantial that O'Malley reportedly described them as 'absolutely shocking'.[40]

Phillip Brothers faced a significant obstacle in accessing the coveted Arab Light crude, having been blacklisted by the Saudis due to the company's Jewish leadership. However, a direct intervention by Jesselson, coupled with the negotiation of an additional 'shipping services fee' discreetly paid to an appropriate offshore account, secured a contract. To circumvent the blacklist, the deal was conducted under the name of a Luxembourg company rather than Philipp Brothers itself.

This was an era defined by 'introduction fees', face-to-face negotiations, and the art of understanding people in high places and their unique quirks. A glass of fine red wine, a tailored suit, and a stylish pocket square often closed deals—and very lucrative ones at that. Social finesse and charm frequently outweighed raw intellect, though street smarts remained indispensable.

Marc Rich and his team also excelled at handling 'difficult things', and their efforts spurred Philipp Brothers into action. By the mid-1970s, the two firms were fierce competitors, vying for marginal barrels of oil destined for hard-to-reach locations, as the trading landscape rapidly expanded. Of course, Rich knew all about this style of trading when he set out his own stall, and it would not be long before he became embroiled in controversial trading activities within the U.S. domestic oil complex.

Rich was the one more willing to take risks and explore new opportunities. When Angola needed a company to handle a distressed cargo of crude oil from the Soyo stream, it was Rich who stepped in when Philipp Brothers had declined. His new company successfully lifted the cargo and was rewarded by the Angolans with an exclusive agency to operate there.[41]

Marc Rich + Co's confidence knew no bounds but on one occasion their swagger was put down in classic fashion. Having had the temerity to ask the Finance Director of Shell International Trading Company (SITCO) if he could give them a bank guarantee, the response to Rich was: '*And which bank would you like us to guarantee sir?*'.[42]

Marc Rich + Co. and Phillip Brothers were not alone in their pursuit of marginal oil opportunities. Among their contemporaries was John Deuss,[43] a figure once described by an industry insider as '*Bond villain-like*' in his demeanour and methods.[44] Rotterdam-born Deuss had been operating on the fringes of the market for years, donning various guises—including car salesman, fashion house owner, and oil trader.[45] Persistent rumours of his connections to the CIA had swirled since the 1970s, adding an air of intrigue to his already colourful reputation.[46]

At the time, the most notable Deuss business which was conducted through his company JOC Oil (John's Oil Company apparently) was the supply of Russian crude which had been destined for Cuba but which Deuss persuaded Soyuzneftexport, the Soviet oil export monopoly at the time, to sell to him while he fulfilled the Russian commitment to Cuba with oil sourced from Mexican. Deuss was later to fall out with Russia over allegations of an unpaid bill for a cargo of oil and then, further down the road, he was, through his new entity, Transworld Oil, to fall out with the North Sea trading 'club' in a big way, as we will later discover.

In the absence of regulatory arbitrage, European traders grew around the Amsterdam-Rotterdam-Antwerp area moving smaller volumes of excess products, too small for the oil Majors to bother about. Initially, the bulk sales department of the oil Majors was the main source of talent for the growing business of oil trading. But the seminal moment for oil trading was the departure of Marc Rich and Pinky Green from Phillips Brothers and the setting up of their own trading entity Marc Rich + Co. in Switzerland.

The individuals involved and the approach to trading of the infamous duo would be replicated for decades to come and would spawn dozens of traders and companies including Glencore and Trafigura, discussed in subsequent chapters. Marc Rich and Pinky Green may not invented spot oil trading as it is sometimes alleged, but they certainly made it international!

Notes

1. Longhurst 1959.
2. Often referred to as such by Jan Nasmyth in his weekly leader article in Europ-Oil Prices (London).
3. Discussion with David Hufton 24/04/2024.
4. Discussion with Richard Johnstone 24/04/2024.
5. Discussion with Ron Davidson and John Rodger 26/04/2024.
6. https://www.bbc.co.uk/news/uk-politics-37167251
7. Discussion with Ron Davidson and John Rodger 26/04/2024.
8. Discussion with S Saint 20/03/2024.
9. Discussion with David Hufton 24/04/2024.
10. Pure trading for profit.
11. Heren, Patrick–Jan Nasmyth's Small Platoon: The Early Years, in Nasmyth's Memorial Dinner booklet 12/10 2009, p. 10.
12. Sampson A., 1988, p. 97.
13. Sampson A., 1975, p. 209.

14. Interview with John Hunt 09/02/2024.
15. At the time fuel oil was used by utilities for electricity generation. They would buy this fuel oil on long-term contracts. Subject to the type of crude oil refineries were running, they would produce more or less than these commitments to the long-term contracts.
16. Interviews with N. Whitley on 5/9/24 and 23/1/25.
17. Europ-Oil (Prices) London 27/08/1974.
18. From an interview with Nigel Whitley on 5/9/2024.
19. Europ-Oil Prices (London) 19/08/1974.
20. Discussion with Thomas Galdy 07/02/2024. He recalls the incident from when he worked at Commerce oil, commenting that it blew over quickly but ended the company's thoughts of 'doing business with the enemy'.
21. Discussion with Thomas Galdy 07/02/2024.
22. A euphemistic description of possibly illegal business.
23. This was oil which producer states who had fallen out with the concession holders on contract terms were appropriating and selling "illegally" on the spot market.
24. Europ-Oil (Prices) London 29/10/1972.
25. Waszkis, 1987, p. 210.
26. Ibid, p. 210.
27. Tom Galdy described Alan Flacks as: '*A low key, sophisticated gentleman who was a key senior fellow in the Phibro organisation.*' Interview with Thomas Galdy on 07/02/2024.
28. Waszkis, 1987, p. 208.
29. 'Royalty oil' refers to a share of oil production that is paid to the country (the owner of mineral rights) from which the oil is extracted.
30. Green was mainly concerned with contracts and operational matters.
31. A Spanish integrated oil company: https://www.cepsa.com/en/the-company/cepsa-history
32. Conversation with RSB Johnstone on 20/07/2024.
33. The friend was Alfredo Santos Blanco, who later became Spain's minister of industry. Amman (2009), pages 69, 93.
34. Amman (2009), pages 68–70.
35. Ibid.
36. Waszkis, 1987, p. 218.
37. Almeida, 2017 p. 148.
38. Ibid, p. 149.
39. Ibid, p. 149.
40. Ibid, p. 144.

41. Discussion with Thomas Galdy 07/02/2024.
42. Discussion with Steve Gutteridge 24/01/2024.
43. Johannes Christiaan Martinus Augustinus Maria "John" Deuss!
44. See: https://www.theguardian.com/business/2006/oct/16/crime.uknews
45. See: https://www.youtube.com/watch?v=e81RkAH9f4A
46. Norman, 2008.

Bibliography

Almeida, Jorge: Patrick Monteiro de Barros Uma Vida a Bolima Publicacoes Dom Quixote 2017

Amman D. (2009): 'The King of Oil—The Secret Lives of Marc Rich', St. Martin's Griffin, N. York.

CIA Intelligence Assessment (1986): The Libyan Oil Industry: Dependence on Foreign Companies, Directorate of Intelligence, January 1986.

CIA Intelligence Memorandum (1970): Algeria: The Importance of the Oil Industry, Directorate of Intelligence, October 1970.

Copetas, Craig A. (1985): 'Metal Men', Futura publications, 1987 ed.

Davies, Richard (2019): 'Extreme Economies', Bantam Press.

Imsirovic, Adi (2021): 'Trading and Price Discovery for Crude Oils', Palgrave.

Longhurst, Henry: 'Adventure in Oil. The Story of British Petroleum', Sidgwick and Jackson, 1959

Norman, James R: 'The Oil Card', Trine Day, 2008

Parra F. (2004): Oil Politics, A Modern History of Petroleum, I.B. Taurus Co. Ltd.

Razavi Hossein, (1986): 'The New Era of Petroleum Trading', World Bank Technical paper number 96.

Sampson, A.: 'The Seven Sisters, The Great Oil Companies and The World They Shaped', Cornet Books, 1975 and 1988 editions.

Waszkis, Helmut: Phillip Brothers—The Rise and Fall of a Trading Giant Metal, Bulletin Books 1987

4

Messy Business

Messy Business

In markets where power is shifting, pricing structures are evolving, and volatility is on the rise, conditions become ideal for traders to step in. The chaotic nature of these 'messy' times in the oil markets presented no shortage of lucrative opportunities for those with optionality in existing portfolios[1] and adept at navigating uncertainty.

In 1973, Andy Whitrow left BP's oil supply team in pursuit of greater opportunities and higher earnings. He joined Magna, a small trading operation founded by Trevor Simmonds, a former Shell trader based in London about whom we have already heard. Magna actually operated as a front for Caiman Oil, a Bermuda-based trading company, and collaborated with BAC Houston, a U.S. trading firm established by John Draughon, an ex-Esso (Exxon) Chemicals employee. Magna's initial strategy focussed on sourcing inexpensive European gas oil and shipping it to the United States.[2]

One notable deal of the time involved Andy securing 100,000 metric tonnes (Mt) of Saudi Arab Light crude oil from Petro Rico, a small trading outfit likely owned by Bert Bock, another ex-Exxon employee. The cargo was contracted at a fixed price with a gold-price escalation clause. Magna resold half the cargo to another trader, Wilco, who then sold it to Shell.

However, Petro Rico defaulted on the sale, lacking any Saudi Arab Light crude. Instead, they offered Magna a large shipment of Iranian Light crude. Trevor Simmonds leveraged his contacts at Shell to buy oil from them and fulfil the deal with Wilco, which in turn completed its sale to Shell, creating

A. Imsirovic and C. Bryce, *The Rivers of Money*,
https://doi.org/10.1007/978-3-031-91806-3_4

a chain that saved the transaction. Remarkably, Simmonds also managed to sell the Iranian Light crude at a profit.

But the complications didn't end there. Petro Rico defaulted again, this time on the Iranian Light crude, offering instead Iranian Heavy crude. When this, too, fell short, they delivered only half a cargo of Iranian Heavy, supplemented with half a cargo of Kuwaiti oil, which was similar in quality to Iranian Heavy. Despite the cascading defaults, the deal was salvaged through a mix of resourcefulness and connections.

To honour its commitments, Magna enlisted the help of a French oil broker, Fretoil, who connected them with Petrofina, a Belgian refiner willing to exchange Iranian Heavy crude for Iranian Light. This arrangement allowed Magna to fulfil its sale obligations for Iranian Light. The Kuwaiti cargo, meanwhile, was successfully sold to a Greek refiner.

'*It was very messy*', recalled Andy Whitrow, 'But prices were going up and up, and we managed to make money in the end!'

Turning back to the broader global landscape, Big Oil suffered a significant blow. In 1973, following the Yom Kippur War, an Arab-led oil embargo targeted nations perceived as overly supportive of Israel, including the United States, the United Kingdom, Canada, Portugal, the Netherlands, and South Africa. This embargo, often referred to as the oil market's 'Big Bang', upended the Majors' control over oil supply. In the months that followed, demand kept growing, prices skyrocketed, quadrupling, and marking a pivotal moment in the evolution of oil trading and competitive markets. Unsurprisingly, the upheaval attracted a swarm of new players eager to capitalise on the emerging opportunities in the oil trading business.

It was a favourable moment to establish a foothold. The oil embargo had upended the status quo. Between 1970 and 1973, oil demand in the developed world surged by over 20 per cent, rendering outdated policies like the U.S. import quota system—established by Eisenhower in 1959 to limit imports to 13 per cent of domestic needs—ineffective. As domestic demand outpaced supply,[3] spot prices for increasingly accessible crude oil rose above-posted prices in a scramble for supply. In response, price controls were imposed on U.S.-produced oil, further amplifying market turbulence.[4]

The price controls acted as a subsidy to imports of foreign crude oil,[5] as U.S.-based refiners were able to bid up the price of their favoured foreign light sweet crude oils. Since refiners had access to a baseload of lower priced controlled domestic crude, they were able to pay more for foreign oil and average up their acquisition cost, but within the regulated parameters.[6] With U.S. domestic oil production barely able to service the demand needs of the country, companies needed to look overseas.

Not only did the Independent oil refiners in the United States need to set up their own international divisions—usually in New York (Pittsburgh and Philadelphia the case of Gulf and Arco, respectively) rather than in the oil production-orientated Houston—but they suddenly needed international trading expertise given their increased interest in foreign crude oils. This was to result in the growing presence of U.S. entities in the developing centres of oil commerce in Western Europe and the Mediterranean-London, Paris, Milan, and, especially, Rotterdam.

The rolling wave of change was well underway. Seminal change tends to occur in an evolutionary manner over time, triggered by discrete events. The first half of the 1970s was not short of discrete events of some considerable relevance in the development of the business of oil trading. Abolition of import quotas,[7] the imposition of price controls, the embargo, growing demand, and the arrival of crude oil traders, were all events of consequence.

Prices of 'freely available' oil were changing frequently and markets began to emerge. Prior concern with cost alone was being usurped by a concern with price and value.

Out of Control

The oligopoly power of the Majors was finally broken in the 1970s, starting with nationalisations of the oil resources and culminating with the 1979 Iranian Revolution.

On 16th October 1973, at a meeting in Kuwait, OPEC agreed on a higher posted price for the main Saudi grade Arab Light, essentially proclaiming that the organisation and not the oil Majors would be the sole arbiter and administrator of oil prices, and Arab Light would be their key price benchmark.[8] OPEC was as naïve as the Majors were arrogant—the organisation had no way of balancing the market in order to maintain the price they agreed on. They had no quotas and no vertically integrated system like the oil majors had, which would ensure control of all the barrels they produced. Ultimately, the price of oil is derived from the demand for oil products. Without ships, pipelines, refineries, and pumps that sell the product, OPEC's information and control of the market was poor.

Both the 'would be' cartel and newly formed traders were very lucky in one respect: Growing demand ensured that prices kept rising, and the traders looked as if they were in control. Derivative markets were non-existent, and the usual trading strategy was to buy the oil ('go long') and sell it later at a profit. Throughout the 1970s, growing demand pushed prices higher (see

Fig. 4.1) and traders going long and selling later generally made money. They were lucky. The producers were in a similar situation. As prices kept increasing, various OPEC conferences would agree to 'increase' prices. In reality, they were just riding an upward-trending market price, giving them an illusion they were 'in control'. If they were, oil trading would never have thrived. But it did.

A decade later, they would realise their error and introduce production quotas. But it was too late. In the meantime, volatile prices and fluctuating refinery margins caused frequent product optimisation by refiners, especially in busy hubs such as Rotterdam. This supported trading activity to the extent that: '*... the market was also recognised by the government of many countries as a "free" market for petroleum, on which many domestic prices control policies could be based*'.[9]

The change in the oil pricing structure did not happen overnight. Throughout the 1970s, oil traded at premiums or discounts to the official and posted prices. The Majors were also 'lifting' oil at the official selling prices (OSPs) and selling them at a premium or discount, depending on the market conditions. These could also take the form of longer or shorter credit terms and various 'fees'. In 1979, following the Iranian revolution,[10] such premiums jumped to over \$8 a barrel: '*The trend began with Nigeria and Iraq. In mid-1979 Nigeria asked its long-term contract agents to pay for half of their liftings at spot prices (giving an effective premium of \$6/b); and Iraq required*

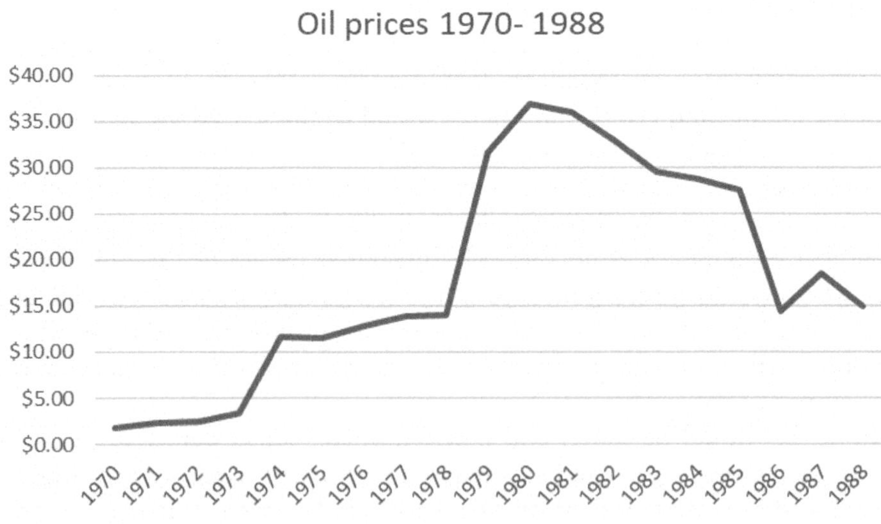

Fig. 4.1 Oil prices (year average), Arabian light at Ras Tanura (1969–1983). From 1984, Brent dated. BP statistical review

new contract customers to pay a $10/b premium payable in advance as a lump sum non-refundable signature bonus'.[11]

Oil producers also bartered crude oil or used it to repay debts. For example, former Yugoslavia carried out a number of civil engineering projects in Libya, Iran, Kuwait, and Iraq, and those projects and debts were generally paid in crude oil.[12] Iran did similar deals with Austria, Brazil, Greece, Pakistan, Spain, Syria, Taiwan, Turkey, and others. Saudi Arabia purchased Boeing airliners and the UAE bought Mirage jet fighters in return for oil.[13]

Particularly popular were oil 'processing' deals, where a company or a trader would supply crude oil to a refinery with excess capacity or credit problems and would take back oil products after having paid a processing 'fee' in oil. Such deals were being struck from Indonesia to the Mediterranean.[14] They were popular with trading companies since their complexity and lack of transparency led to potentially large profits.

Producing countries were particularly keen on barter deals in the 1980s when oil prices came under pressure from falling demand. In such deals, OPEC countries could sell oil in exchange for goods without breaking OPEC agreements and 'official' prices. In a barter deal, the price of oil can be kept at the OSP, but the price of imported goods can be inflated, effectively meaning the oil is sold at a discount. Such discounting, when coupled with different credit terms, subsidised shipping, free storage, and other trading tricks, is almost impossible to detect.

Following the Iranian revolution, a two-tier official price system developed, with little regard for market prices or their relative refining values. Greed came before any agreements. In May 1980, the Government Selling Price (GSP) for Arab Light was $28 a barrel. At the same time, the GSP for Iranian Light crude of similar quality was $35.37. High-quality Nigerian oil had a GSP of $35.29 a barrel.[15]

Selling oil 'spot' was a way to achieve higher prices, and even though OPEC members agreed in June 1979 to limit spot sales, high spot prices often proved to be too tempting. While Saudi Arabia, Venezuela, and Algeria refused to participate in the spot market, Iraq, Libya, and Nigeria used it frequently and Iran even used it exclusively for a while.

While officially hostile to the spot markets, some OPEC members effectively facilitated its creation. Another reason the cartel helped the creation of the 'free market' for oil was the nationalisation of oil resources in producing countries. Faced with uncertainty, oil companies were already shifting their investment to less politically volatile oil regions in the 1960s. This resulted in large, but expensive to produce finds in Prudhoe Bay on Alaska's North Slope in 1967 and the Ekofisk field in the Norwegian sector of the North Sea in

1969. In a remarkably short time, the share of spot trades rocketed, from less than five per cent prior to January 1979, to about a quarter by November of the very same year.

As oil prices climbed in the early 1970s, the financial demands on trading companies grew increasingly burdensome, causing opportunities in the sector to stagnate during the quieter years of 1975–78. This led to a decline in the number of companies participating in the barge and cargo markets at Rotterdam. By 1979, it was estimated that seven companies controlled two-thirds of the activity, with an additional 12 entities handling a further 25 per cent of the market.[16] By this stage, gas oil movements accounted for over 60 per cent of the barge trade and almost 60 per cent of these movements were by companies identified as 'traders' as opposed to refiners or distributors.[17]

At the same time, majors such as BP were sharpening their trading skills. Traditionally 'long' crude oil, BP lost its supply from Iran and Nigeria in quick succession. This forced the Major into the market to look for alternative supplies. '*It was quickly realised that the Bulk Trading Department had to change into a more nimble Supply and Trading team with a very flat structure, enabling quick decision-making*', says Nigel Whiteley.[18] He worked in a small team headed by Chris Wright, together with traders Bob Sexton and Tom Mackey.

By design or by chance, BP's timing was perfect. '*In the three years, between 1981 and 1983, probably a half of the small trading companies got wiped out by the price volatility. The forward Brent market picked up and in 1983, WTI futures contract started. BP hired Urs Reider from Marc Rich + Co. in Switzerland. We had Ceri Evans who was a wizard in stitching up forward Brent chains to maximise our operational tolerance and therefore profitability. This disaster of 1979 was probably one of the reasons why BP became such a dominant force in oil trading, and remained so to this day*', concludes Whiteley.

Alaskan North Slope (ANS) and the North Sea oil

The impact of the discovery of the Alaskan North Slope crude oil (ANS) in 1968 would have a global supply significance. It would only be dwarfed in importance as a new source by North Sea oil a couple of years later. Interesting domestic markets were to develop around ANS as a benchmark and a tradeable crude and these would have something of an impact on the way oil was traded, both locally and internationally.

Bringing a major oil discovery to the market is a laborious process, and it took fully ten years from the discovery of oil in Prudhoe Bay[19] until the first cargo was exported from Port Valdez in the fjord of Prince William Sound in Alaska in the late summer of 1977.[20] In the end, it didn't go very far, as under the U.S. Export Administration Act of 1979 'no domestically produced crude oil transported through the Alaskan pipeline system may be exported from the United States'.[21]

So, the market for ANS was constrained to the U.S. West Coast and Gulf Coast, frustrated from finding a home further afield by the Merchant Marine Act of 1920 (popularly known as the Jones Act).[22] The act made transportation of crude subject to the availability of U.S. flagship vessels, and with difficult access across the Isthmus of Panama, most of the production of ANS remained on the U.S. West Coast, replacing Ecuadorian, Indonesian, and some Arab Gulf grades of oil.

Both Morgan Stanley (in 1988) and Trafigura (in 1989) attempted to sponsor the development of a viable forward market but with limited success. Consequently, the foreign grades of crude arriving in the United States, which were priced by reference to ANS operated off a small set of visible transactions. Although the export ban was lifted in 1995, by that time the international oil trading attention was focussed elsewhere in more liquid venues.

In fact, the immediate effect that ANS supply had on the global markets balance was minimal, at least until the early 1980s and in no way could it compare with the impact that the North Sea would have on the price of oil and, more especially, the impact that it was to have on the extent to which oil became a traded commodity and eventually an asset class in its own right.

If the discovery of oil in the North Sea, within short-haul distance from major markets, was both fortuitous and seminal in the development of trading, the strategic actions of a succession of the U.K. governments were to unwittingly accelerate these developments.

Not only was oil discovered in the U.K. sector of the North Sea, but it was also discovered in size in the Norwegian sector as well. Discoveries in Danish and Dutch waters were of less significance volumetrically, and neither of these Governments, nor the Government of Norway, employed the taxation and supply security strategies that were to influence markets in anything like the way that the United Kingdom's action did (we will later see that Norway came to play its part in different ways).

The first oil well to be drilled in the North Sea was in 1964, and within a year gas had been discovered in the West Sole area by BP. Sold to the U.K. gas supply monopoly, the Gas Council, at a low price, the strategic policy of the U.K. government was clear—to achieve the lowest possible price of gas for the benefit of U.K. consumers.[23]

In 1968, the first oil was found in what became known as the Cod Field. The limited volumes, produceable only at a high price relative to the single dollar level of Posted Prices at that time, did not engender great excitement. It was not until the major finds of Ekofisk in the Norwegian sector in 1969 followed by Brent the same year and Forties in 1970 that it became clear that a major oil province had been uncovered.

This came as something of a surprise to many and not least to the Chairman of BP, Sir Eric Drake. As late as 1970, Sir Eric had commented that: 'There would be no major discovery in the North Sea'.[24] Yet by the autumn of 1971, BP was announcing that: 'The Forties field was a giant one'.[25] Indeed, not many months prior to the Forties discovery, Sir Eric had agreed to sell the block to Gulf Oil only for the Gulf board of directors to turn down the opportunity at the last moment.

The first oil to be landed from the North Sea was from the Norwegian sector and it arrived at Fina's Lindsay refinery in the East of England on the 2nd of November 1971. The 34,000-tonne parcel was carried by the vessel Theogennitor and was the first of many shipments that would be made on the 'Inter U.K.-Cont' route in the succeeding 50-plus years.[26]

Oil from the U.K. sector took a while more time to arrive and it was not until 1975 that the first cargo of oil from the Argyll field arrived at BP's Isle of Grain refinery on the Thames, having been sold by equity holder Rio Tinto. The field operator, Hamilton Brothers, was subjected to some unfair criticism from Scottish Nationalists who viewed North Sea oil as Scotland's oil and who felt insulted that the first cargo should be landed in England. Any blame should have lain with BP as the buyer though, as was pointed out in a private communication between the American Consul in Edinburgh and their Embassy in London.[27]

BNOC Surplus

The Petroleum and Submarine Pipe-lines Act (1975),[28] which regulated the petroleum industry in the United Kingdom during the exploration boom in the United Kingdom might not be one's bedtime reading of choice. More Her Majesty's Stationary Office than John Grisham, it nevertheless occupies an important place in the enabling of the business of oil trading, because this was the Act of Parliament that passed into the U.K. law, the creation of The British National Oil Corporation (BNOC), an organisation that was to perform an especially influential if unintended role in the early development of oil markets.

While the Act deals with the North Sea Oil in bland legalese, there was nothing bland about the exploration, discovery, and production of this new and important source of non-OPEC oil. The mere words conceal a business of environmental and engineering enormity, one where a brave and skilled workforce operated at the edge of technological possibility in the often-deadly weather conditions of John Bacchus Dykes[29] 'foaming deep'. Those who worked in 'peril on the sea' contrast with the traders—the folks 'who get rid of the stuff'.[30]

Although a steamy negotiating session in Lagos or a sweaty session in the NYMEX[31] crude pit in New York might be somewhat inconvenient, the habitat of the trader was more usually the padded office chair somewhere in Mayfair or Midtown, not too terrible places to spend the working day.

And the conditions were equally as harsh on the Alaskan North Slope at Deadhorse on Prudhoe Bay. Up there though it was ice, snow and, to put it mildly, a fresh breeze that the pioneers of harsh environment oil production would have to suffer. No wonder then that the tool pushers and roustabouts would refer to the traders as flaneurs and boulevardiers, having an easy time deciding which cocktail party to attend or who to take to lunch today.

The bigger picture, though, will not record the relative daily toils of the operatives. Rather, it will record that the discovery of oil in the North Sea, in Alaska and, contemporaneously in Mexico, would dramatically change the power dynamics in geopolitics, oil markets, and oil trading.

After some years of haggling in Parliament and with the owners and operators of the North Sea oil fields, the U.K. Government decided to create a new entity, the British National Oil Corporation (BNOC). What was it for? Therein lies a matter of great consequence in the way in which oil markets were to develop over the following 10 years.

From the very start, there was an incoherent evolution of the strategic objectives of Glasgow-based BNOC (Secretary of State for Scotland, Willie Ross's constituency of Kilmarnock was just down the road, and so Glasgow it was, rather than Aberdeen or Edinburgh). Across the North Sea, the Norwegian government was clear on the role of the company that they created to deal with oil matters, Statoil. Set up in 1972, it was '*to acquire and hold participation rights and direct licences in the industry*'[32] and it did this by assuming a carried interest in fields being developed and then investing in successful projects. More widely, the Norwegians had a strategic plan of greater vision than in the United Kingdom and 'the explicit goal was a fully integrated oil company'.[33] While the Norwegians lacked a company like BP which, already in existence, presented a trickier situation for the United Kingdom to negotiate, there is little doubt in hindsight that they set themselves onto a more remunerative long-term path than did the United Kingdom.

A major difficulty in the United Kingdom had been the complete lack of a bi-partisan approach to the issues presented by the potential windfall.[34] Ideologically, the Labour Party demands progressed from appropriation by the state to 'Participation' supposedly to guarantee the security of supply to the United Kingdom. However, rather like the process that had taken place between OPEC members and Concession holders some few years earlier, the real desire was control of the resources seen to be 'of the state'. Not price maximisation for the exchequer or even security of supply, it was a control that the Labour government of the time sought. The Tory Party in the United Kingdom was much less concerned with the creation of a new company or with the need for state control. After all, the United Kingdom already had BP. Did they really need another state oil company?

The outcome in the United Kingdom was a two-tier system of Taxation and Participation, a combination that was to prove to be a godsend for the trading community but a nightmare for politicians and the U.K. public purse. It was a combination that was to operate against price stability, despite frequent government and company claims to the contrary, and to bring the U.K. government into international oil geopolitics in a manner that was to aggrieve both the major oil companies and OPEC. BNOC was a political and ideological creation with little cogent thought seemingly given to commerciality.

Broadly, agreements were negotiated (at times aggressively by BNOC Managing Director Alistair Morton's attack dog lieutenants)[35] granting a majority Participation right to the state which would leave the equity holders no better or no worse off. Given the actions of the OPEC states in the early 1970s,[36] Participation was a word, which would rile the oil companies as the word implied, at least to them, appropriation. In addition, a Royalty provision, either in cash or in kind, covered twelve and a half per cent of each owner's interest and added to the quantity of oil to be handled by BNOC. Although sale backs were negotiated with the major players such as Shell, Esso, and BP, the rights established by Participation (along with Royalty and their own Equity oil) gave BNOC the opportunity to buy and then resell a very significant volume of crude oil (well over 1 million barrels per day by the early 1980s).

With this as the background, the first serious operational mistake was made when BNOC Chairman, Frank (Lord) Kearton, exercised the participation options in full. This came as a complete surprise all around. '*He's going to exercise 100 percent. I thought he'd go for 5 percent*', commented a shocked BNOC MD of Trading, Ian Goskirk.[37] The dapper Cumbrian and ex-Shell executive Goskirk was not the only one to be wrongfooted. Jan Nasmyth commented that: '*There were few in the industry who ever believed the right would be exercised*'.[38]

Perhaps, if there had been a greater awareness of Kearton's ambitions, there would have been an enhanced interest in assessing the pros and cons of BNOC investing in the downstream refining sector and/or in acquiring storage. As it was, the company was destined to become a weak seller, forced to buy and price every quarter before attempting to subsequently on—sell at, hopefully, at least the same price. Yet, as financial market participants were so devastatingly reminded in the Financial Crisis of 2008, such an asset and liability mismatch are inviting the possibility of ruin. Well-regarded Oil Economist Peter Odell commented in hindsight that: '*Perhaps the main problem with BNOC was that the terms of reference were made much too narrow*'.[39]

Considering the difficult environment that refiners were confronting at that time—crude oil prices had risen due to the 1973 embargo, there were domestic price controls in the United States, and there was a serious degree of overcapacity in refining internationally—it is perhaps understandable that downstream looked like a bad place to be. The later suggestion by Odell that BNOC might consider purchasing the then for-sale Gulf Oil refinery in Rotterdam fell on deaf ears.[40]

BNOC and its civil servant controllers may not have felt inclined to broaden the mandate but there were other politicians who clearly saw the need for a safety net. Both Dr J Dickson Mabon and Ted Rowlands, Labour members for Greenock and Merthyr Tydfil respectively, raised the matter of a lack of refining or storage in order to offset the risk of BNOC being exposed middlemen, in Parliament and at the Select Committee level on numerous occasions.[41] Even booking refining or storage space as a precautionary action could have had a disproportionally positive effect on the situation and could have tempered the all-pervasive view of BNOC as a totally exposed weak hand at the mercy of the markets.

And the inevitable happened. When oil demand took a downward turn in the very early 1980s BNOC quickly found themselves to be exposed as a transparent, weak seller of significant volumes with the result that their short-haul oil was offered in the spot market in some volume. The '*BNOC Surplus*' became the basic problem.

But there was another factor layered on top which was to cause further pain for BNOC and the U.K. Government in weak markets and which was to prove to be manna for the embryonic trading community. This was the matter of tax and, in particular, the Petroleum Revenue Tax (PRT), levied on the producers of North Sea Oil.

The largest producers were companies such as Shell, Esso, BP, Conoco, and others, many of whom also had downstream interests in the United Kingdom, which attracted Corporation Tax. As Corporation Tax was set at a significantly lower level than PRT, if the integrated companies could transfer profits from upstream to downstream, they could reap enhanced rewards from the differential tax rates. They did this by means of 'spinning'. Basically, this allowed them to trade their equity cargoes in the spot market but not to declare until the last minute, which cargoes would be defined as their equity cargoes and thus liable to PRT. They would, of course, declare the lowest-priced cargo, and in a falling market they would always have an incentive to continue spinning.

This activity served to undermine the BNOC price (determined quarterly) as there was a continual incentive for the integrated companies to continue to sell, buyback if the price went lower, sell again, and keep at it until prices reached a nadir. As we will see, matters became even worse for BNOC and the U.K. exchequer when, in July 1983, Shell and Esso were given permission by the Oil Taxation Office to 'spin' Participation as well as equity crude (BP also received permission in January 1984).[42] It was at this time, in the thick of an extended period of oil price weakness, that the 15-Day Brent market really took off, and we will shortly learn about this market.

Although staffed in their Supply and Trading Division by highly respected and well-liked industry professionals, many of whom, such as Richard Johnstone and Liz Bossley (known to their colleagues as Dick and Betty from Sales)[43] went on to have stellar careers in oil trading, the BNOC traders had no chance. Famously referred to by the Sunday Times as the 'Pin Striped Sheiks of Bolton Street,[44] selling long-term fixed, forced to buy short term in a falling market and constrained by a U.K. government taking care to not offend OPEC, the end came on the 13th March 1985 when finance trumped ideology and BNOC was abolished.[45]

The last word is best left to ex-BP senior executive, Basil Butler: '*I think BNOC would have been a splendid idea if Britain had been a banana republic*'.[46]

One winner from the whole ten- or so-year journey was BP. They had successfully obfuscated, spoiled, and filibustered at the time of the inception of BNOC,[47] cutely managed to dispose of unwanted Iranian oil to BNOC via their Participation agreement and, in the end, were able to buy in 1988 Britoil, the already publicly floated production arm of BNOC. The company had lasted a mere nine years and, apart from the positive effect on house prices in Helensburgh and Balfron where staff who were relocated from the Home Counties of London to the Glasgow headquarters preferred to live, there was little to commend the whole exercise.

The biggest winner however was the spot market which, without the BNOC surplus, would never have developed as it did. Brent/Ninian/Forties trading at sellers' option,'15-day' forward Brent, the Dated Brent market, and the many layers of associated derivatives and attempted copycat contracts are a legacy of the U.K. governments ideological stubbornness. The fumbling of the Department of Energy, pushed and pulled by their strategically inadequate political masters, the inadvisable exercise of Participation options by Frank Kearton, the absence of downstream assets as a safety net for unsold barrels and an ill-conceived taxation regime helped too.

The basic canvas was in place, but it needed the self-interest motives of companies and people identifying the opportunity to generate trading profits to develop all this into the active and remunerative milieu that it became. This is another interesting story.

Let's step back a moment though to understand the seminal events of the late 1970s across international geopolitics which also impacted on the development of trading.

Notes

1. Throughout the book, we claim that acquiring free or cheap optionality is the best way of running a trading business.
2. In those days, heavy gas oil was primarily used as heating fuel.
3. 'However, in 1970, the United States production peaked anyway… The United States had no longer any spare oil capacity.' See Imsirovic (2021), page 111.
4. Ibid.

   Nixon issued Executive Order 11,615 (pursuant to the Economic Stabilization Act of 1970), imposing a 90-day freeze on wages and prices in order to counter inflation. See: https://www.cato.org/commentary/remembering-nixons-wage-price-controls
5. Kraft, J and Rodekohr, M: Crude Oil Price Controls-Their Purpose and Impact 56 Denv.L.J.3I5 (1979).
6. The consequences were discussed in Chapter 1.
7. For a good timeline, see: https://www.cfr.org/timeline/oil-dependence-and-us-foreign-policy

8. https://www.energypolicy.columbia.edu/publications/the-1973-oil-crisis-three-crises-in-one-and-the-lessons-for-today/
9. Razavi (1986), page 17.
10. There were other events linked to the higher oil prices. For details, see Imsirovic (2021), 'Panic of 1979: Everything that Could Go Wrong, Went Wrong', page 125.
11. Razavi (1986), page 27.
12. One of the authors was personally involved in negotiating and lifting of oil in such countertrade deals.
13. Razavi (1986), page 24.
14. See chapter six for processing deals in Asia.
15. See Imsirovic (2021), page 126. This whole section is based on the material from the book.
16. Roeber 1979.
17. Roeber 1980, Page 33.
18. From Interviews with Nigel Whiteley on 5/9/2024 and 23/1/2025.
19. More on ANS: ttps://dec.alaska.gov/spar/ppr/response/sum_fy06/060302301/factsheets/060302301_factsheet_PB.pdf.
20. https://www.aoga.org/industry-history/
21. https://www.congress.gov/bill/96th-congress/senate-bill/737
22. The Act made crude from the US exclusively subject to the shipping under the American flag:
    https://www.law.cornell.edu/wex/jones_act#:~:text=The%20Jones%20Act%2C%20also%20known,see%2046%20USC%20%C2%A7%2050101).
23. Hoopes, Stephanie 1994, p. 177.
24. Kemp, Alex:2014, p. 236.
25. Kemp, Alex: The Official History of North Sea Oil and Gas Routledge p 236.
26. Eventually North Sea oil found its way to the US. The first cargo of Forties, for example, was bought by Ashland Oil for $12.85 in July 1979 and was shipped to their refinery in Louisville, Kentucky.
27. Declassified telex from the American Consul in Edinburgh to the American Embassy in London 18/12/1975.
28. A UK Act of Parliament dealing with oil industry matters as they related to, amongst other things, the production and transportation of oil in the UK. It also covered the establishment of the UK state owned entity, The British National Oil Corporation. https://www.legislation.gov.uk/ukpga/1975/74/contents

29. J B Dykes wrote the words for the Seafarers' hymn, 'Eternal Father Strong to Save'.
30. Authors recollection of a conversation in Aberdeen with Britoil Upstream Head, Jim Hay.
31. The first oil futures exchange in the 1980's: https://www.cmegroup.com/company/nymex.html
32. Parra, Francisco: Oil Politics a modern history of petroleum I.B.Tauris 2010, p. 274.
33. Noreng, Oystein: The Oil Business and The State Routledge 2022 p. 98.
34. The following section is based on the author's personal recollection.
35. Amongst them, Peter Ross, Robin Atkins and David Myring.
36. See Chapter 1.
37. Interview with the then BNOC Head of Pricing, Stuart Saint 20/03/2024.
38. Europ-Oil Prices (London) 27/10/1978.
39. Odell, Peter, in Staerck G: The Development of North Sea Oil and Gas. Institute of Contemporary British History p. 43.
40. Staerck, Gillian 2002, p. 42.
41. For example, see Hansard Volume 34 14/12/1982.
42. Europ-Oil (Prices) London 30/11/84 p. 3.
43. BNOC were referred to by Neste Oy trader, Rod Gavshon, as 'Statoil with a sense of humour'.
44. Sunday Times Business Sect. 06/02/1983.
45. Hansard–House of Commons Vol 75 13/03/1985.
46. Butler B in Staerck, Gillian: The Development of North Sea Oil and Gas Institute of Contemporary British History 2002, p. 45.
47. Note the prediction of Europ-Oil Prices (London) on 27/10/1978 "BNOC will be in trouble and will have to be rescued… by BP".

Bibliography

Dykes, J.B.: 'Eternal Father Strong to Save'–Scottish Psalter and Church Hymnary-Hoopes, Stephanie (1994): The Privatisation of UK Oil Assets 1977–1987 LSE PhD Thesis.

Kemp, Alex (2012): 'The Official History of North Sea Oil and Gas', Routledge.

Imsirovic, Adi (2021): 'Trading and Price Discovery for Crude Oils', Palgrave.

Longhurst, Henry: 'Adventure in Oil. The Story of British Petroleum', Sidgwick and Jackson, 1959

Noreng, Oystein :The Oil Business and The State–Routledge 2022Norman, James R: 'The Oil Card', Trine Day, 2008

Roeber, J: The Rotterdam Oil Market Petroleum Economist month? 1979

Roeber, J: The Evolution of Oil Markets: 'Trading Instruments and Their Role in Price Formation.' Royal Institute of International Affairs, 1993.

Razavi Hossein, (1986): 'The New Era of Petroleum Trading', World Bank Technical paper number 96.

Staerck, Gillian : The Development of North Sea Oil and Gas ICBH Witness Seminar 2002

5

The London Crowd

(Spot) Revolution

Back in what was rapidly becoming the 'old world' of OPEC and international oil geopolitics, events were unfolding that would go on to shape the traded markets of the near future.

In early January of 1979, U.S. ally (or so they thought) the Shah of Iran fell on his sword. The revolution had been coming for many months, and even by July 1978, strikes and disturbances had caused a collapse in oil exports and a consequent increase in prices.[1] By Christmas of that year, Iran was exporting no oil at all. If the embargo of 1973 was all about control of supply, the Iranian revolution and its aftermath were about an explosion in prices. '*Spot crude prices had risen to over $40 a barrel at times, from levels of well under $15/b prior to October 1978*'.[2]

In this environment, all a trader needed to do was to find someone to sell him some oil, wait for a day or two, and then resell it at a colossal gain. After that: '*Eat, sleep, repeat*', and tremendous fortunes were being made with ease, if one had the right contacts. Of course, the likes of Phillip Brothers and Marc Rich + Co. had all the contacts they needed, as did a plethora of other entities founded on the oil price bounty.

Perhaps, the most important development at this time was the response of the producing states to the rise in spot prices which had risen to a level considerably in excess of 'posted prices'. This encouraged the producers to unilaterally abrogate long-term contract obligations and instead sell on the spot market. They sold to Independents and traders and through state-to-state deals, and much of the volume found its way onto the spot market

A. Imsirovic and C. Bryce, *The Rivers of Money*,
https://doi.org/10.1007/978-3-031-91806-3_5

as everyone who owned oil discovered the easy profits to be reaped from a rapid onward sale. Combined with the loss of volume from Iran, this led to panic in the markets as end-user buyers competed with speculators to secure supply at any cost. This was to presage the end of the fixed price long-term contract as buyers realised that they could not rely on the security of supply from their traditional sources. Several spot contracts would be seen as a better disseminator of risk than would be one large-term deal.

And so, the new market leaders began to think '*spot*'.

Although the crisis was extended by the commencement of the Iran–Iraq War in 1980, the seeds of a change in market direction had been sown even if the lifting of price controls in the United States in 1981 was to stoke up prices for a little longer. Iran was back onstream and had been selling up to 300,000 barrels a day on the spot market, Dubai was selling its 100,000 barrels a day state share in the same way and Qatar was holding monthly auctions.[3] Even Kuwait had an increasing taste for spot prices. But inventories were increasing across the globe, non-OPEC oil was adding to supply and, perhaps most importantly, there was a global demand reaction to high prices. Demand would decline very significantly over the first five years of the 1980s. Oil industry observer Philip Algar noted a fall in demand of 3 million barrels per day between 1980 and 1985.[4]

OPEC's last price rise of the period would be in October 1981, and by the following year they had abandoned the fixing of prices altogether. By this time, Iran was already basing their term contract off a spot price, and they were to be followed in this in 1984 by Statoil and in June 1985 by Mexico. By mid-1986, all the producer states were doing the same thing. This was a five-year period of great difficulty for OPEC, for the U.K. Government, and for BNOC, but a wonderful opportunity for the middleman and the many new and colourful characters who emerged who eyed the fortunes up for grabs. And with the BNOC surplus just around the corner, the honeypot relocated to the North Sea and to London in particular.

Forward or '15-Day' Brent

Texas Monthly of October 1984 ran a lengthy article on the new and somewhat secretive competency of oil trading. Traders were referred to as '*Financial speculators, con artists, impoverished aristocrats, former tennis pro's, ambitious young college and B school grads looking to make their fortune as fast as they can*'.[5] Alongside these were serious professionals, well-compensated and focussed on finding ways to grow this burgeoning industry. Then there were those whose charm, polished social graces, a dashing pocket square, and impeccably shined shoes blurred the line between appearances and substance.

In contrast, individuals from Science, Technology, Engineering, and Mathematics (STEM) backgrounds—now highly sought after—were once viewed as decidedly unremarkable. With their short-sleeved shirts and pencil-filled top pockets, they were deemed anything but 'clubbable'. Some even wore lab coats!

Initially, it was in the upscale West End of London where the new opportunities began to take shape. Chez Gerard at 31 Dover Street in London's Mayfair was right in the heart of oil trading territory. Just up the street from Sun Oil and PVM, round the corner from BNOC in Bolton Street, and within shouting distance of many others, the faux French brasserie was a favourite meeting place for senior trading types. Long lunches at this trader's cafeteria would be attended by the likes of broker PVM's head honcho, David Hufton, Player Edwards of Conoco, the formidable Doris Balzer of Rhein Oel, Mike Watson of Nova, Jerry Brennan of BP, Urs Reider of Marc Rich and Maurizio Martins da Silva of whichever company he happened to be with at the time. The restaurant kindly provided two open telephone lines—this was prior to the age of the portable-sized mobile phone—so lunch could carry on (and on) without the diners having to return to the office.

There were many other similar 'offices' throughout upmarket Mayfair that served the prandial needs of the oil trading community, among them the Red Lion in Duke of York Street, The Grapes in Shepherds Market, Langan's Brasserie in Stratton Street and Cecconi's in Burlington Gardens. One was never far away from a lunching and gossiping oil trader in Mayfair.

It was at Chez Gerard that a new 'Brent' market was conceived by the folks mentioned.[6]

The initial iteration of the market was the so-called 'B/N/F market', named after the North Sea crude oil streams: Brent, Ninian, and Forties. A B/N/F contract would be sold without specifying the exact grade of crude to be delivered, which would only be confirmed 15 days prior to the lifting date. In this market, the seller held the option to determine the loading tolerance. Over time, this system evolved into what became known as '15-day Brent'.

Whether this new trading vehicle was invented because integrated companies had wised up to the concept of tax arbitrage through 'spinning',[7] or whether it was because Saudi Arabia had recently clamped down on trading of their Arab Light grade by re-enforcing existing destination restrictions,[8] is not clear.

It may have been conceived simply as a result of Player Edwards' Conoco having an extra cargo of Ninian crude oil over and above its refinery needs, and this was a flexible way to dispose of that small surplus while encouraging trading.[9] Shell, along with Esso as major equity holders in the Brent field, displayed some interest in the emerging market, though Esso chose not to engage at that stage. BP, holding a majority stake in the Forties and Ninian fields, took a keen interest, and their involvement proved pivotal to the success of this nascent trading instrument.

From 1981 and for approximately the next eighteen months, the B/N/F market dominated North Sea oil trading. While the focus remained on these key grades, individual cargoes of lesser known streams such as Montrose, Argyll, and Beryl were also traded. Additionally, spot trades of non-UK grades were recorded during this period, including Norwegian Ekofisk, Ecuadorian Oriente, Angolaan Cabinda, Russian Urals, and several Nigerian streams such as Bonny Light and Forcados.[10] There was also a 'BBQ' spot market, referring to a basket of Nigerian crude grades: Brass River, Bonny Light, and Qua Iboe.

With the growing awareness that the differential tax rates levied on the integrated companies' upstream and downstream businesses (Petroleum Revenue Tax (PRT) and Corporation Tax (CT)) offered the possibility of a tax arbitrage in the United Kingdom, the volume of spot contracts of the North Sea grades began to steadily increase. As PRT was levied at a higher rate on oil production than CT, which was levied on oil companies' downstream operations, if equity oil could somehow be taxed at CT rates rather than PRT, the overall gains to an integrated oil company were substantial. That is what spinning was all about, and 36 cents in every dollar could be saved by the levy of CT rather than PRT.[11]

The big kicker, as we have already heard, came in mid-1983 when Shell and Esso were granted permission by the U.K. Oil Taxation Office (OTO) to 'spin' not only their equity oil but also the oil, which was sold to BNOC and then sold back to the companies under the 'Participation agreements' (BP gained the same permission in January 1984).

In the mid-1980s, BNOC was struggling with a surplus of oil. In a falling market, BNOC was setting the quarterly prices at which they would buy from producers at levels in excess of the spot market. A result, they were on-selling oil at a loss in the spot market. In an effort to try to appease those who were buying BNOC oil at the BNOC quarterly price and in an effort to reward them for continuing to do so, the 'spinning' concession was granted. This proved to be a massive mistake as the effect was to significantly increase the 'spinnable' volume which simply added to the downward pressure on spot prices as well as tax revenues.[12]

And so, the trade volumes exploded and the forward, '15-Day Brent' market was born. Shell UK and its trading manager, Peter Lane, assisted by his senior trader Peter Hugill, are credited with writing the initial trading contract and progressing the activity.[13] It was clearly in Shell's interest to do so and they would take a central role in the further development and policing of the 15-Day Brent market in later years through their highly regarded trading manager, the lugubrious Peter Ward.[14]

According to Petroleum Argus, Brent deals reported to their publication in 1981 had numbered a mere 23 trades. This number rose to 221 in 1982, 725 in 1983, before a huge increase to 2,656 in 1984. Deals for delivery in future months also rose from zero in 1981 to 2,650 in 1984, representing the first indication of liquidity in the forward market.[15]

Argus reported their first 'spread' forward trade in February 1984 when March/April forward Brent was traded at a 25-cent premium.[16] Backwardation and contango were new terms for the crude oil traders and referred to the premium or discount respectively of near-period prices to later-period prices. So, the forward Brent market became the oil industry's own forwards market'.[17]

Assessing the Market Prices

As trading grew in importance, greater price transparency emerged, with Price Reporting Agencies (PRAs) becoming the primary sources for oil price assessments across the trade sector. These agencies evolved into a critical link in the growing ecosystem surrounding the 'free' markets. Their role transcended mere importance, eventually becoming indispensable for market functionality.

The origins of PRAs trace back to the early days of the oil industry and the advent of spot trading in the United States. One of the earliest recorded price reports appeared in Derrick's Handbook of Petroleum.[18] The first publications dedicated solely to oil prices and assessments were pioneered by Warren Platt, who founded National Petroleum News in 1909 with the explicit goal of fostering industry transparency.[19] This initiative coincided with the breakup of Standard Oil two years later, creating a pressing need for reliable price information.

In 1923, Platt introduced Platt's Oilgram, a concise daily newsletter focussed exclusively on the oil market and price information. Its influence grew rapidly as its assessments became integral to the oil majors' calculations of the 'Gulf-Plus' formula. Today, Platts Oilgram continues to publish prices under the ownership of Standard & Poor's Global.[20]

The growth of non-OPEC oil production such as in Alaska and the North Sea was a major spur for the development of price discovery.

1976, Tony Benn, Secretary of State for Energy, introduced the Petroleum Revenue Tax (PRT), which was specifically designed to tax profits from oil and gas extraction in the United Kingdom. '*This change in taxation regime in the UK was a major incentive to discover market prices – as it directly led to the level of tax paid by oil company to the government*', says Adrian Binks, the CEO of Argus Media.[21]

In 1978, Platts launched the Crude Oil MarketWire, while that same year saw Argus (now Argus Media) initiate daily reporting on the emerging spot crude market through the renowned Argus Telex. These developments were soon followed by the introduction of the London Oil Report in 1980 and Japan's RIM Intelligence in 1984.

Concern within European governments about the growing influence of the spot market and the veracity of spot market prices eventually led to a call for an interventionist policy to control speculation, and even earlier in 1980, consultant Joe Roeber had authored the European Commission Market Report, better known as the COMMA report.[22] While European companies CFP, Fina, ENI, Veba, and Elf kicked up a fuss over spot prices, others felt that the free markets offered a 'marginal price', which was truly representative of trade value at the time.

Price reporting has enabled the evaluating and pricing of hundreds of distinct types of oil. As discussed in the previous chapter, the Aramco partners adopted pricing formulas anchored to the most frequently traded oil grades: Brent, WTI, and Dubai.[23] These widely recognised grades, known as benchmarks, serve as foundational references, and all other types of oil are evaluated in reference to their prices. PRAs continued to assess benchmark values daily, ensuring the smooth operation of global oil markets.

If we turn to examine what was developing in the United States in the wake of the abolition of price controls in the United States, it is to futures rather than forwards that our attention is drawn.

New York Mercantile Exchange (NYMEX)

As far back as 1972, a securities broker, E.M. Whitlock, had mooted the creation of a crude oil futures contract. In 1975, the New York Cotton Exchange listed oil futures with delivery in 100,000-barrel parcels at

Rotterdam. While unsuccessful, it was not to be very long before in 1978, the Harrison Street-based, New York Mercantile Exchange (NYMEX) successfully introduced a heating oil contract based on New York Harbor delivery. This was followed in 1981 by unleaded gasoline and then in 1983, by the hugely influential West Texas Intermediate (WTI) crude oil contract.[24]

While OPEC and the Seven Sisters inadvertently played a role in the development of oil trading, today's traders might owe an unexpected debt of gratitude to the humble potato. In 1976, the flagship Maine Potatoes contract on the NYMEX collapsed in default, leaving the exchange with limited activity and dim prospects. Regulatory restrictions further compounded the problem, as they prohibited the listing of new contracts, pushing the exchange into a precarious position.[25]

Fortunately, the exchange had listed Heating Oil and Residual Fuel Oil contracts in 1974, though both had initially languished in dormancy. However, regulators had not prohibited a relaunch, and NYMEX seized the opportunity to revive these contracts. A pivotal figure in this effort was Michael Marks, a 28-year-old Princeton economics graduate hailing from a family of potato traders. Marks became the Chairman of the Exchange during its formative years and remained in that role until stepping down in 1987. His vision and leadership were instrumental in building an organisation that would exert a profound influence on oil markets for at least the next 30 years.

First up was a heating oil contract, followed by gasoline in 1981, and then the banner WTI crude oil contract in 1983. 'Nobody in the industry wanted it—least of all the majors',[26] commented Thomas McMahon, a NYMEX trader from 1981 through 2001, referring to the WTI contract. Arnold Safer, an advisor to the exchange and an Irving Bank oil economist, wrote the contract, and trading took place by open outcry in a crowded pit on the NYMEX's 9th-floor home in the World Trade Centre.[27]

Unlike their sophisticated counterparts in London's emerging trading crowd, the NYMEX types were somewhat more earthy. Variously described as 'baboons, cheeseburger-for-breakfast-eating, foul-mouthed, uneducated bums'[28] and 'New Yorkers without pedigree', there wasn't a lot of blue blood in the commodity pits.[29]

The atmosphere of the pits themselves was variously described as '… a cross between Goldman Sachs and a maximum-security prison'[30] or 'middle school with money'.[31] It paid to be tall so as to be seen when bidding or offering into the cacophony, and it paid to be loud, albeit with a ready supply of throat lozenges.

Jobs were handed out to friends and acquaintances, and if they could deal with the noise, aggression, and claustrophobia of the workspace, they got hired, provided they could also think on their feet. Rough and tumble Brooklyn Italian-Americans were much in evidence as were those members of the Jewish community for whom hustling commerce was a second nature. They also had to be able to drink. Exhausted traders and their clerks would retire to Suspenders Pub on Greenwich Street or P. J. Clark's on the Hudson,[32] name badges and colourful jackets removed for another day, and they would drink like a Glaswegian.

Of course, not all fitted the caricature—not be any means. Future Chairman Vinnie Viola had been a 101st Airborne Division, West Point, and New York Law School graduate before hitting the pits. Chairman from 2001 to 2004, he guided the exchange through the early period of competition with the newly formed Inter Continental Exchange (ICE), and through the establishment of the exchange ClearPort, a Clearing technology.[33] Viola, who was the founder of Pioneer Futures, would subsequently become a billionaire by founding Virtu Financial.[34]

NYMEX prices were driven by the liquidity provided by floor traders, known as 'locals'. These traders risked their own capital but typically avoided holding positions overnight. Whether formally educated or not, they needed the confident insouciance of a poker player, the sharp instincts of a fox, and the predatory drive of a wolf to thrive. But over time, major financial institutions and independent traders began contributing to the market's liquidity, ensuring price visibility for everyone.

This was unlike the Brent market across the water which relied on daily surveys by the Price Reporting Agencies (PRA's) to reveal what had traded. Unlike OPEC, NYMEX set prices but did not try to control them. This was a transparent, competitive, and open market that was accessible and trustworthy. The whole industry came to trust it very quickly, and there is little doubt that throughout the period from 1983 until the end of the twentieth century, it was the key market acting as a barometer to gauge the price of oil.

NYMEX led the way in price discovery for crude oil on a minute-by-minute, daily, and longer term basis. '*The Crude Oil pit at the Merc set the price of oil*'.[35] Brent prices moved after NYMEX, even if Brent was to become the more frequently used global oil benchmark. The U.S. market was 'the' oil price leader.

Moving with the times is important, though, if a business wants to retain its competitive advantage. This is what NYMEX did not do and that led to its ultimate downfall. Daniel Rappoport had been the Exchange Chairman from 1993 until 2001. In 2000 he rebuffed an approach from ICE to merge the exchanges (ICE acquired the International Petroleum Exchange instead in 2001) and an earlier effort in 1998 to pursue a link up with the IPE had been dropped after a vote at the NYMEX board.[36]

ICE was electronic and was an anathema to the 'locals' who, with equity invested in their exchange 'seats' that needed to be protected, viewed open outcry as the only feasible method of profitable trading for themselves. Rappoport famously quipped, '*Our floor will be fitted with the latest in technology—humans!*'[37] Unfortunately, for him and his peers, electronic trading ultimately prevailed.

Despite NYMEX's attempts to adapt, their efforts were too little, too late. Their electronic platform, Globex, showed promise but was only accessible outside regular floor trading hours, limiting its impact. As a result, NYMEX lost its competitive edge and was eventually acquired by the Chicago Mercantile Exchange (CME), which shuttered all trading pits in 2016. Meanwhile, ICE continued to evolve rapidly, as we shall explore further.

Forward Brent and NYMEX WTI were perfectly complementary. Traders could arbitrage them as a spread, capitalising on the freight differential between the two and the differing market conditions in the U.S. compared to international markets. Liquidity in one market supported liquidity in the other, and both benefited from this interconnectedness. The synergy between them made the whole much greater than the sum of its parts. This symbiotic relationship played a crucial role in establishing transparent, actively traded spot oil markets.

The London Crowd

It was back in London that the international side of oil trading markets would find their home and there were some just as equally idiosyncratic characters to be found there as in the NYMEX pits. London became the centre of the forward markets and the home of physical oil trading.

Why then London and not, say, Houston or Rotterdam?

In contrast to the sweltering heat of Dubai and Singapore, where ceiling fans were once the only relief before air conditioning, Houston offered the comfort of proper A.C. cooling. Houston is an exotic city, even for many Americans. With no sidewalks, just muddy ditches and small levees, it's a place defined by its car culture—cars everywhere, often with a glimpse of a shotgun resting on the rear shelf as they drive by. Walking to work is almost unheard of, unless one enjoys sweating like an oarsman. Yet, Houston is a sociable city. Texans are famously friendly, and any business visitor is unlikely to leave without having attended a rodeo or gone on a turkey shoot.

While home to many oil companies and some domestic oil trading, Houston's true specialty lies in the upstream sector—tools, pipes, and machinery, the everyday equipment used by petroleum engineers. Think of companies like Halliburton and Schlumberger and you'll have a good sense of what oil in Houston is all about.

International oil trading in the United States was historically an East Coast thing and, most especially, a midtown New York business. Almost all the majors had their foreign trading offices there. There have always been oil traders based in New York, and the Wall Street Refiners, who we will learn about in due course, were all there. If less well connected with the 'good ol' boy' community than Houston, the New Yorkers tended to be more commercial than the folks that met regularly at the River Oaks Country Club in Houston. Nowhere in New York though was there more trading activity than on NYMEX, as observed by Jan Nasmyth in Petroleum Argus in 1984: '*… the location of the New York market is on the floor of the NYMEX*'.[38]

Nasmyth went on to comment that: '*The London market is spread all over the world*'.[39] This is much the same as comments made ten years earlier about the Rotterdam spot market. Rotterdam is no London though. Picturesque from a distance, its only 'bright lights' are refinery flare stacks and gaudily illuminated, round-the-clock-churning petrochemical plants.

The 'bright lights' of London's West End shine with much greater appeal and it is a much more sophisticated and interesting place to be. It is in London that international oil trading found its natural habitat. Vendome or the Guinea Grill for lunch, Morton's in Berkeley Square for after-work cocktails followed by Marks Club or Les Ambassadeurs (clubs for those who didn't qualify on breeding grounds for the proper men's clubs of St James) for supper. Members of even lower echelons might then end up in Tokyo Joe's nightclub or, horror upon horrors, the Dover Street wine bar or the Stork Club on Aire Street. Rumours, an establishment in Covent Garden, was also popular. Ex Bank of America foreign exchange trading supremo Rob Eades recalls, '*The forex boys would be sitting around with their pints of warm beer while over in the corner you just knew it was a crowd of 'Johnny-come-lately' oil traders because they thought they were the height of sophistication drinking Blue Lagoon cocktails*'.

Wives were happy too: Knightsbridge offered the latest in fashion, Harrod's Food Halls, the freshest of oysters from most parts of the world, and Scalini's, Signor Sassi or Toto's were convenient spots to meet over sophisticated Italian cuisine. All the while the kids were educated in pretty much any international school one's heart desired. English was the language of oil and international trade and one that everyone had to be either fluent in or learn as quickly as possible.

The trading company offices were shoehorned into a square mile or so in London's Mayfair and St James, or WC1 as it is known. To the North and South of Piccadilly, the elegant townhouses were fronted by gold nameplates identifying the lucky folks working in considerable comfort. Avant, backed by Mitsui; Bomar, created by ex-Phillip Brothers trader Vin Boemio; Coastal, Oscar Wyatt's company; Michael Linehan's Delaney Petroleum and it's forerunner Carey Petroleum, owned by a former New York Mayor Ed Carey's brother, and many more took up residence there.

And so, London, with its contiguity of people, a trusted legal system, and a strong capitalist attitude towards contractual obligations and free markets in general, was the place to be. And it was on the doorstep of the North Sea and the home of Shell and BP.

The daily routine of a London oil trader typically began around 9:00 am (it wouldn't be until the first Gulf War that trading started earlier) with a review of overnight telexes from Platts Oilgram Service and Europ-Oil Prices. This was followed by a couple of hours spent on the phone with brokers and counterparts, gauging the market's appetite. Lunch, often accompanied by generous amounts of alcohol, was followed by a quiet period, where traders tried to regain their composure. Occasionally, a deal might be struck (with the word 'done' signalling the completion of a trade) before wrapping up for the day with a visit to the pub on the way to the train, a copy of the London Evening Standard tucked under one arm, and a generally empty briefcase in the other.

Of course, this is something of a caricature—though not entirely inaccurate. Many in the oil trading world approached the job with seriousness and purpose, lasting the course and eventually securing the best positions. These traders also reaped significant personal rewards in a business that offered ample opportunities for those capable of navigating its complexities.

The companies that entered the trading scene in the early 1980s were a diverse group. The majors were primarily represented by BP and Shell, with Mobil and Chevron also showing interest in the emerging market, while Gulf (whose trading arm became Gotco in 1984 after Chevron's acquisition) got involved as well. Even Texaco, under the leadership of Willis R. Buck, granted greater authority to their traders in response to the evolving market conditions.

The Japanese Shoshas, including Idemitsu, C. Itoh, Kanematsu, Toyo Menka, all large trading houses, were also active players,. A Kanematsu trader, Kibe-san, was known for his boldness and appetite for risk in trading Brent.

Other Shoshas generally acted as intermediaries for companies that, often due to credit issues, were unable to trade directly with each other. In return for this 'sleeving' service, they earned a modest commission. Typically led by an expatriate Japanese individual, these Shoshas would often hire seasoned London traders familiar with the market dynamics.

While the banks were yet to arrive on the scene, and most particularly the Wall Street Refiners, there were plenty of independent traders such as Vitol, Phibro (the re-named Phillip Brothers), Patrick de Barros's trading vehicle Sigmoil, Tradax (an arm of Cargill), Greek-backed Nova and John Deuss's Transworld Oil. Statoil, BNOC, and Neste of Finland were the primary state players. France's Elf and CFP were active, but from Paris rather than London. There was a presence of U.S. refining companies, producers, and Independents—some like Conoco, Koch, and Sun who had been around forever, and some newer faces like Crown Central, Amerada Hess, Texas Eastern, Kerr McGee, and others took up townhouse residency. All these types were topped off by the growing presence of an oil broker community—an important group at this juncture and who we will hear more of later.

Neste is a prime example of a company that was active across the board during this period and remained so for many years afterwards. It might seem surprising that it was the typically reserved Finns (sometimes humorously referred to as 'po-faced') who would go on to create a bold and successful trading firm in those early days. However, in trading, success can largely be attributed to the people behind the company—after all, it's often the initiative and drive of individuals, rather than company structures, that paves the way for the most lucrative opportunities.

Female Leaders

Eija Malmivirta, a young and talented engineer, served as the General Manager of Neste's International Trade Department, with the primary responsibility of supplying the company's refinery in Porvoo. Historically, Neste had cast a wide net to secure oil supplies for the plant, maintaining strong relationships with major producers like Iran, Saudi Arabia, and other large state-owned entities. Malmivirta was a protégé of Vice Chairman and Trading CEO, Kai Hieterinta, and was credited with convincing him to expand their trading efforts based on their natural position as a refiner. Hieterinta, who enjoyed the perks of international travel and the privileges that came with his status, was easily persuaded.

Malmivirta recognised the potential of the growing spot markets in London and saw an opportunity to get involved. Operating from the company's existing office in St. James, she hired two seasoned traders from Houston Oil Refining, a company affiliated with former Phibro trader Vin Boemio, which was on the verge of going under. The two traders, John Hughes and Ron Gray, brought valuable experience to the team. Gray, a former professional soccer player who had played goalkeeper for Hibernian, a Scottish football club, was a veteran of Phillip Brothers from the post-Marc Rich era.

Hughes, an alumnus of Gulf Oil, whose brother David also worked in oil trading specialising in LPG, was an especially cultured individual. For many years, he and Gray offered gourmet and classical music weekends in the English Lake District to their counterparts. Their invites to sample celebrity chef John Tovey's exquisite fare at his Miller Howe hotel were much prized. Hughes also chaired the London City Ballet troupe whose Patron was the late Princess Diana, and it was a role that was to prove handy for him in another matter. Former colleague Charlie Tuke recounts that Hughes had wanted to join the prestigious Wentworth golf club in London's select Surrey suburbs but had encountered a stumbling block. The waiting list was some 20 years, and unless one had an especially acceptable escutcheon or knew the creme de la crème, a rapid ascension up the waiting list was unlikely to be forthcoming. But John felt that treating the Wentworth Club Secretary—a particularly stubborn fellow—to a fine lunch at Green's Oyster Bar might somehow convince him of the merits of his candidacy. It was all to no avail and the lunch was about to end on a sour note when the door of the restaurant opened and in walked Diana, Princess of Wales. Seeing John, she immediately approached and warmly embraced him and they chatted as the Wentworth Club Secretary looked on in awe. Not entirely surprisingly, a courier arrived at Neste's office with John's membership papers for the Wentworth golf course, not 20 years later, but on the very next day!

Over the succeeding years, Hughes and Gray assembled a strong team of popular and skilled traders around the new Neste trading ideology. Californian Tom Leaver (later to be CEO of the Dubai Mercantile Exchange) joined in late 1983 and structural geology graduate, Rod Gavshon, joined from Player Edward's Conoco Nursery in 1985. With Bev Atkins from Tampimex and, at a later stage, Wall Streeter Charlie Tuke, who we shall hear from later, they had a formidable lineup to trade Brent, physical oil from the North Sea, the Middle East, and Africa, along with participation in the growing spot markets of Dubai and Oman.

Neste had an interesting method of training their new employees- or not, as the case may be. While these days, new traders undergo serious induction processes, such as the week-long Citadel Securities programme where newbies take maths classes and perform trading simulations, back in the day things were not quite like that. Gary King was a young Neste geologist who spent his day colouring-in, as geologists do, on the floor above the traders. When a junior trader role opened up, he was taken on by Hughes and Gray. Shown a desk with a telephone on his first day, he was told just to answer the phone when it rang. The trading secretary duly put a call through to the ingenue, young Mr King. 'Where are you for Brent?', enquired the voice at the other end of the line. 'Where are we for Brent?' Gary repeated to the Neste trading floor. 'Twenty Sixty', shouted Hughes. 'Twenty Sixty' repeated Gary to the fellow at the other end of the line. 'Done' the caller said and with that, the phone went down. Gary's new colleagues were impressed and were quick to congratulate him on his first deal. 'Who did you sell to', said one of them. To this, there was no reply as, in fact, Gary had no idea who was on the other side of the trade nor who was now in possession of almost $11 million worth of Neste's oil. Of course, it ended well as the trading secretary had recognised the voice on the end of the line that she had put through to Gary. Wouldn't be allowed to happen today though!

Rhein Oel was one of the earlier and more active members of the London Crowd and their trader, Doris Balzer, was her nation's daughter. She preferred uncluttered efficiency when it came to the organisation of the office. The Germans like things to be ordered, or 'ordnung'. Crisp, clear, clean. Doris had gone to considerable lengths to purchase a set of expensive, beautifully finished teak desks for her trading staff, a small group of British males. After a short time, Doris had become concerned that her desks were not being kept with the Teutonic cleanliness that she expected.

Arriving one morning at the Rhein Oel offices, her trading staff discovered a feather duster and a note from Doris protruding from each of their personal pigeonholes where their mail would normally be collected. The note commanded that the duster was to be used to keep the desks ship-shape. Unfortunately, when she subsequently arrived, Ms. Balzer encountered her staff reclining in their chairs with their feet on her prized new teak desks, polishing their shoes with the feather dusters.

It is likely that this was very much the canvas intended to greet Doris, carefully planned by the overgrown schoolboy traders. They were most amused at their little prank. Doris was not amused.

The question is—would they have acted in this way to a similar request to keep their desks tidy if the instruction had been issued by a male? Was this a disrespectful gender-associated act or something else? A jibe at Germanic sensibilities perhaps?[40] It was a normal German practice after all for Doris to refer to her boss Helmar Schank as Herr Schank, while he referred to her as Balzer.

Some women in the oil trading industry have risen to success through sheer hard work and strength of character. Ingeborg Srenger is one such example. She unexpectedly inherited her father's trading business at Petraco as a young graduate, fresh out of university. Despite several setbacks, her determination and 'can-do' attitude helped her turn the company around.

One particular occasion perfectly illustrates her relentless drive and versatility. While travelling to a meeting with oil producers in the former Soviet Union, the author accompanied Ms. Srenger on a three-hour bus ride to the hotel and meeting venue. Throughout the journey, she was almost constantly on the phone. First, she spoke in her native Italian with a trader from her Milan office about an oil shipment. Then, she switched to fluent Russian while discussing matters with her Moscow office. Later, her CFO called from Petraco's Swiss office in Lugano, and the conversation continued in French. For the remainder of the trip, she effortlessly chatted with the author in Croatian.

At one point, the author noticed a fellow passenger sitting directly behind them, shaking his head in disbelief—no doubt amazed by her linguistic prowess and work ethic.

In their book on commodity trading, Blas and Farchy write that: '... *on the issue of gender diversity... the trading industry is one of the most backward in the Western world*'.[41] There is little doubt that the 'industry' was and remains backward on issues of gender. A recent study by McKinsey[42] establishes that while in 2024 48% of entry-level employees in a corporate role were women, only 29% were women at the top executive level. Some progress has been made though as 10 years ago the latter representation was a meagre 17%. The 1989 trader contact list of these authors contained just under 10% of women while the Texaco Crude Oil Personnel Directory of 1993 had roughly the same share of female names.

Whether the oil industry is better or worse today for women is perhaps a question for future research. What is clear, however, is that the experience of women in oil trading has historically been far from ideal. The challenges they faced stretch back decades. A striking example comes from the 1960s, when Oil Light, a Pennsylvania magazine, referred to the renowned and pioneering female oil journalist Wanda Jablonski as 'William'. Known professionally as W. Jablonski, the magazine simply assumed she must be male, highlighting the pervasive gender biases of the time.[43]

When in the early 1980s one employee of BNOC was sent to Iceland to prospect for new business opportunities, his trip report included the observation that 'the girls were very accommodating'.

In the same era, British oil Major BP published a monthly magazine, BP Shield. One of the most awaited features was the 'Dolly of the Month', consisting of a usually flattering photograph of a young lady and a matching write-up.

Rick's Cabaret in Houston, Scores in New York, and Stringfellows in London were all venues where a woman would feel at the very least uncomfortable. But all were frequented by male traders, all bonding and entertaining clients. The exclusion of women would certainly have implications for their client relationships relative to male attendees.

The need to be 'extra sociable'[44] to break into the 'good old boys' network or to act like 'a man in a frock',[45] or drink and carouse until the wee small hours were extra pressures put on women in an already highly pressurised industry. Of course, for some women, this way of operating and this type of work mode was welcomed. They were likely a minority though. Perhaps this is why women 'worked harder—they had to'.[46] '*Why*', asks a head-hunter Trish Collins, '*does it take adversity and the woman's response to it to bring about success*?' Clearly adversity is a barrier for some. And for others, the response is to seek to group together with other women, formally or informally, an action which enhances the sense of 'otherness' and, in the opinion of Collins, is an '*admission of failure*'.

The other side of the coin though is that many women encountered no problem at all in their career progression or in their daily conduct of business that could be associated with gender. Lourdes Rodriguez, who advanced to the top echelons of Spanish company Repsol, says: '*I had no problem, ever*'. In fact, it is interesting to note that from as far back as the mid-1980s, the Spanish oil companies were unique in the number of front-line women traders that they employed. It is especially surprising given the traditional view of Spanish culture of that era as being extremely macho, misogynistic even.

Matters may have improved somewhat over time. For at least 20 years, lap-dancing and striptease clubs have been out of bounds for employees of public companies at least, and there seems, qualitatively, to be a greater number of women in trading seats than in the early days, reflecting trends in society and in the workplace.

Yet, when one looks back, there are a plethora of top female names that come easily to mind as standout successes in the man's world of the time. Among the industry shapers are Neste's Eija Malmavirta, Bridie Tobin, and

Nancy Kropp who we have already encountered. In the United States, names such as Phibro's Tammi Danner, Robin D'Alessandro of Vitol, futures pioneer Mary Bergonia (Ross) of EDF Man, and Rosemary McFadden of NYMEX were important contributors as the business developed.

In Europe, Liz Bossley was the innovative Head of Trading and Marketing at Enterprise Oil before becoming a consultant and successful author on trading matters. Petraco's owner and CEO, Inga Srenger has ruled the 'niche' markets of Russia and the Levant for decades. Vivienne Cox at BP rose to the very top of that firm and will always be associated with her contribution to the success of oil derivatives markets as they established themselves. Shell's Christine Crossley was another important innovator in the derivatives revolution while popular American, Katrina Landis, played a key role at BP in London in that firm's inclusion in the equity partnership that founded the Intercontinental Exchange (ICE), an interest that would be cashed in for a figure in excess of $1 billion. BP, a firm with an enlightened diversity policy, recently had Carol Howle as their CEO of the trading business, BP Oil International.

Successful racehorse owner and breeder, Isabel Ealet, was a successful Head of Commodities at Goldman Sachs before taking up even higher order in her firm. Blythe Masters performed the same role at J. P. Morgan and Nancy King co-headed the Morgan Stanley business, having had a successful career as a trader in London and in New York while Shell promoted Stacie Pitts to replace Mark Quartermain as Head of Oil Trading in 2020.

Women often possess a natural aptitude for tempering the behavioural excesses of those they oversee. Perhaps this stems, at least in part, from the experience some—but certainly not all—gain in raising children. This role demands the ability to reason with the unreasonable, to deliver scolding with dignity, and to strike a balance between teaching and encouraging. Such skills, honed in personal life, can translate seamlessly into professional leadership.

Andy Hall

Back in the man's world, probably the most influential company in the new trading market was the successor to Phillip Brothers, Phibro, and their head trader, ex-BP and Oxford University graduate, Andy Hall.[47] Hall was to oil markets what the Bank of England was to financial markets in the United Kingdom—the dealer of last resort. Hall traded the biggest book in the market and probably took the greatest risks. He actively traded spot markets and forward physical markets as well as financial derivatives ('paper') and futures. Andy Hall always had a price at which he would sell or buy oil, and he was a friend to the distressed seller loading oil with no final destination. Many a trader caught out on the wrong side of the market when the Tuesday API 'stats' were issued,[48] after the close of NYMEX, would have Hall's number on speed dial to dispose of unwanted long or short positions.

While still at BP, Hall had been posted to work in their New York trading office on 42nd Street, and his abilities soon caught the eye of Phibro. As a big ticket in the business, he was in demand and was frequently invited to industry functions. Sun Oil held an annual party at the Henley Regatta, an elite event in the British social calendar, but having not received an invitation, Hall badgered Sun's Nancy Kropp for an invite. Kropp contacted the organiser in the London office, Tony Dillon, and an invite winged its way to New York. Hall arrived late and immediately took the launch across the river to the Leander Club, an exclusive rowing club, where he remained all afternoon before departing for the airport to return to New York. According to Dillon, Andy had met with Phibro executive, David Tobey and others in the Leander Club to negotiate his contract to join Phibro, having used his invitation to get BP's permission for the trip to London.[49]

Hall believed in picking a direction and playing in size such as when trading the 'six-pack', a clutch of six Brent forward cargoes (or at least 3 million barrels) on one phone call. Why buy one when you could buy six? Andy Hall was a 'bull'[50] who believed that demand was constantly underestimated, and he went on to make fortunes over the succeeding 20-plus years in a number of different guises by being 'long the market'.

Famous for his mind-boggling bonuses at the time,[51] he did not always have it his own way. During the 1990–1991 Gulf War, his position suffered a setback. In January 1991, Brent fell from over $30 to just over $18 a barrel.[52] Hall and his team in Westport, Connecticut were, of course, long. When your author asked his trading lieutenant Malcom Macavity how they managed the position, he said: '*We would come into the office in the morning, check the price, and it would not bounce back. Then we sat and played cards. This went on for a few days. Then prices recovered to over $20 per barrel and we sold our long position. We lost money, but it was not as bad as it could have been*'.[53]

Of course, this was just a blip, and his bullish attitude worked extremely well in the booming years of the 2000s when he received a $100 million bonus from his parent bank, Citigroup.[54] The issue of the bonus went all the way to the Treasury Department in Washington since Citigroup had received $45 billion in taxpayer aid to survive the 2008 Financial crisis.

It was not just the Treasury that was concerned. Andy Hall was very much running his own operation within Citi. One anecdote illustrates this well:

The head of commodity trading at Citi came to visit Singapore. '*This was back in 2005 or 2006. He told us how he and his two bosses, the heads of fixed income trading for Citi, decided to drive up to Greenwich to explain the Andy Hall that he worked for Citi, not for Phibro or himself. They would explain to him that he would have to work together with the Citi oil derivative traders, share information and cooperate on market views. Or else!*

As they moved north through Manhattan, they discussed Andy's role at Citi. Someone remarked that Andy had been their most profitable trader for the past five or six years, generating a few billion in income for the group. Comments such as: 'He made $500 million last year alone' and 'plus, he made only slight less than that the previous year.' …And "he's already up $350 million this year!' As they rolled north, they starting to discuss what would happen if Andy Hall chose 'Or else!' Suppose they startled him into losing his appetite? Suppose he quit and took his trading and profits elsewhere?

As the Town Car cruised up I-95 the executives reached a decision. They ordered the driver to take the next exit and head back to Manhattan. Andy was never given an ultimatum. The trip was never officially mentioned to him or anyone at Phibro'.[55]

Over time, the 'wait it out as we have deep pockets' style of trading has become an anathema to the concept of risk management, and without control of the probabilities while the market does its own thing, it is perhaps better categorised as gambling rather than trading. As we will see though, this method of approaching markets will come back into fashion 25 years or so later, as size and deep pockets can trump risk management in cyclical markets.

But if Marc Rich, Oscar Wyatt, and John Deuss are the other big names of the era, their businesses were more defined by their desire to do 'difficult things in difficult places', often controversially. Hall stayed closer to home, trading the more formal and transparent markets, realising that taking a strong stance in the market, being reliable, and being patient was a strategy that could return generous profits corporately and personally, and he was the master of doing just that.

Notes

1. Yergin, Daniel 1993, p. 63.
2. Parra, Francisco: Oil Politics a modern history of petroleum I.B. Tauris 2010, p. 224.
3. Europ- Oil (Prices) London various 1979 and 1980 issues.

4. Algar, Philip in Talking of History- Pipeline Magazine May 1986.
5. Hurt, Harry: Feasting on the Oil Glut Texas Monthly October 1984.
6. Discussion with David Hufton on 24/04/2024.
7. See Bossley, L in Imsirovic, A (2023) ed. pp. 27–41.
8. Comment by David Hufton 24/04/2024.
9. Conversation with Tony Dillon 07/11/2023 who recalls that the first B/N/F cargo was sold by Conoco to Ron Gray at HOR.
10. Europ-Oil (Prices) London. Various issues 1982 and 1983.
11. Weekly Patroleum Argus 10/04/1983, p. 1.
12. Petroleum Argus 01/01/1985.
13. Personal recollection of the author.
14. Very well liked, Ward was usually to be encountered in his private Shell office shrouded in cigarette smoke while dispensing wisdom and a voice of reason all round.
15. Petroleum Argus 1/1/1985.
16. The spread price means the premium of the front month relative to the second-quoted month.
17. Ravazi, Hossein: The New Era of Petroleum Trading. World Bank Technical Paper Number 96 1989.
18. https://www.loc.gov/item/06017920/
19. Johnson (2018, p. 43).
20. They acquired the business from Platt in 1953: https://www.platts.com/IM.Platts.Content/AboutPlatts/Platts%20History-Full%20Summary_5-08-09Final_pdf.pdf.
21. From an interview with Adrian Binks on 7th December 2020 and subsequent discussions.
22. Roeber 1993, p. xi.
23. See Chapter 4.
24. WTI has been to the domestic US oil benchmarking world, what Brent has been to the oil markets internationally. It refers to crude oil gathered throughout an area approximating to Oklahoma and Texas and transported to the major storage centre in Cushing Texas.
25. Marks, Michael in Smarter Markets Podcast 06/03/2023.
26. Blinch, Russel: The Year Crude Oil Markets Embraced Something New Money 04/03/2023.
27. Marks, Michael in Smarter Markets Podcast 06/03/2023.
28. Dicker, Dan: Oil's Endless Bid Wiley 2011, p. 122.
29. McMahon, Thomas in Johnson, Owain: Routledge 2022, p. 192.
30. Attributed to former Shell and Phibro trader, Danny Masters.
31. Attributed to Mark Vonderheid.

32. Bloomberg Markets November 2006, p. 123.
33. https://www.cmegroup.com/clearport.html
34. Discussion with Jonathan Cowan, a former employee of a Viola company.
35. Burke, Paul: The Oil Revolution Texas Monthly May 1986.
36. Personal recollection of the author who was Deputy Chairman of the IPE at the time of the discussions in New York with NYMEX.
37. Meyer, Gregory: The Big Read. Financial Times 06/07/2016.
38. Petroleum Argus 13/04/1984.
39. Petroleum Argus 13/04/1984.
40. Doris's male boss, Helmar Schank referred to her as simply 'Balzer' while she referred to him as Herr Schank. However this is probably German hierarchical practice rather than a gender slight.
41. Blas J and Farchy J 2021, p. 326.
42. Krivkovic A, Yee L et al. 2024 Women in the Workplace 2024 10th Anniversary Edition McKinsey & Company 2024.
43. Rubino Ann 2008, p. 47 Pls add in Bibliography.
44. Discussion with Anne Summers 03/02/2024.
45. Discussion with Trish Collins 12/12/2023.
46. Conversation with Exchange Consulting founder Trish Collins 17/12/2023.
47. According to Tony Dillon, a Sun Oil trader at the time,
48. API weekly Statistical bulleting is a key source for petroleum industry data and information. https://www.api.org/products-and-services/statistics
49. According to Tony Dillon 17/09/2024.
50. Bull is a trader who believes that the price should go up and generally prefers long positions.
51. https://www.ft.com/content/9b924fda-56b1-11e9-91f9-b6515a54c5b1
52. Data from ICE Brent futures.
53. Author's recollection of the conversation with Malcom in the Phibro office a few months after the event.
54. https://www.nytimes.com/2009/08/02/business/02bonus.html
55. Interview with a former Citi commodity trader on 13/2/25. He wished to stay anonymous.

Bibliography

Algar, Philip: Talking of History- IPE Pipeline May 1986.

Blas, Javier and Farchy, Jack: The World For Sale Penguin Random House 2021.

Blinch, Russell: The Year Crude Oil Markets Embraced Something New. Money 04/03/2023.

Burke, Paul: The Oil Revolution Texas Monthly May 1986.

Dicker, Dan: Oil's Endless Bid Wiley 2011

Europ-Oil (Prices) London -Various Issues.

Export Administration Act 1979.

Hurt, Harry: Feasting On The Oil Glut Texas Monthly October 1984.

Johnson, Owain: 40 Classic Crude Oil Traders Routledge 2022

Marks, Michael: Smarter Markets Days of Futures Past Podcast 2023

McMahon, Thomas in Johnson, Owain: 40 Classic Crude Oil Trades Routledge 2022.

Meyer, Gregory: The Big Read Financial Times 06/07/2016.

Parra, Francisco; Oil Politics a modern history of petroleum I, B, Tauris 2010.

Petroleum Argus- Various Issues.

Ravazi, Hossein (1986) 'The New Era of Petroleum Trading', World Bank Technical Paper Number 96

Roeber, J (1979): 'The Rotterdam Oil Market', Petroleum Economist Publications.

Robinson, Silvan in Shell World October 1987.

Rubino, A (2008) Queen of the Oil Club, Beacon Press, Boston

Yergin, Daniel: The Prize The Epic Quest for Oil, Money and Power Simon and Schuster 1993.

6

The Industry in Which We Were Paid

New Faces in London

American oil company executives, tall and well-fed, were an increasing presence in London in the 1980s. The new government of Margaret Thatcher and her liberal economic policies led to major changes in the City of London. The so-called 'Big Bang' attracted a number of American and other banks and corporations looking for opportunities in finance.[1] Oil trading and broking were no exceptions.

One of these companies was Union Oil of California (Unocal). Trading Manager John Chapman had been, like Vinnie Viola,[2] in the 101st Airborne Division and so in his words: '*Unlike many of my contemporaries in the US, I had a passport so they sent me to London*'. Despite his efforts to spark Unocal's interest in using futures and forward markets for price risk management, John Chapman found such concepts were largely a mystery to the senior leadership back in California. It was only later, and to a limited extent, that Unocal dipped its toes into these markets.

Chapman's primary role, however, was to market Unocal's oil production outside the U.S. or to negotiate swaps for crude grades produced by other majors that better suited Unocal's refining needs. For instance, he would trade Unocal's North Sea Ninian crude for BP's Alaskan North Slope (ANS) oil, or exchange his Dutch Helder crude with Shell Nederland for Nigerian Forcados, a preferred feedstock for Unocal's refinery in Beaumont, Texas.[3]

In the days before the widely available technological provision of data, John's background in military intelligence had cultivated an enquiring mind and digging out correlations between PADD 2[4] diesel stocks and the price of

A. Imsirovic and C. Bryce, *The Rivers of Money*,
https://doi.org/10.1007/978-3-031-91806-3_6

Forcados or[5] the effect of the water balances in Japan on the price of Indonesian crudes was a speciality. In later years, that curiosity seems to have been passed on to his son Kurt, who would become a scion of trading in Brent, especially for Mercuria, one of the larger trading companies.

By the early part of the 1980s, the producer states were also setting up shop in London. Kuwait Petroleum Company (KPC) had been around for a while in St. James's, and the first African producer to arrive was Angolan Sonangol in 1984. Under the leadership of Jose Paiva, who had a direct line to the then Vice Minister, Desideri Ocosta, the mandate was clear: establish Angola's flagship Cabinda crude oil, along with Takula, Molongo, and Soyo, as recognisable and sought-after grades in the market. Buyers included major players such as Sohio and BP, as well as the notorious bargain hunters, Shell Nederland.[6]

Algerian state oil company Sonatrach did not, at that stage, have a major London presence.[7] Rather, their head commercial man, a Mr. Mahmoud, would come to London for a quarterly deliberation among the bright lights.[8] His regular fixture was lunch with BP at Signor Sassi's, a walking distance from their representative office in Knightsbridge. Calling these meetings about future crude supplies for BP 'lunch' was not entirely a correct description. Each visit followed a predictable pattern: lunch seamlessly transitioned into a prolonged session of post-prandial digestifs, which inevitably stretched into the dinner hour. At that point, the table would be reset, and dining would resume. Luckily, BP's esteemed senior executive, Jerry Brennan, was a seasoned participant in such rituals. A masterful imbiber, he could effortlessly carry on past midnight, ensuring the gathering maintained its momentum until the eventual parting of ways.

On one occasion, Mr. Mahmoud, having taken to one of Brennan's particularly attractive assistants, decided to call her, rather alarmingly, in the middle of the night, some hours after the meetings had finished. Concerned that, at the least, this was inappropriate, she called Brennan to seek guidance. The response, which was inappropriate by today's standards, was not: '*How awful, let me deal with him*', but rather: '*Oh really? Did he say how many cargoes we are getting next month?*'

In an era when the oil business was rife with misogyny, some unscrupulous operators exploited the charm of attractive young women to curry favour with clients. One such colourful figure was David Thieme, the controversial head of Essex Overseas Petroleum and sponsor of Formula 1 driver Mario Andretti and the Lotus team. Thieme, who resided in lavish style at the Hotel de Paris in Monte Carlo, began his ventures by acquiring Ras Gharib crude oil[9]—a particularly challenging grade—from Egypt and refining it at Saras in Sardinia.

For a time, he made waves in the oil markets, his flamboyant presence impossible to ignore. However, his fortunes ultimately crumbled. Among his most notorious acts was hosting an extravagant reception at London's Royal Albert Hall during the Institute of Petroleum (IP) week,[10] attended by clients and celebrities alike. Even in an industry known for its excesses, Thieme's display was a spectacle that stood out—before Essex Overseas Petroleum eventually went bust.

One trader, having travelled down from the North of England to attend a party held in a private suite at the Grosvenor Hotel on Park Lane, vividly recalls his surprise upon entering the room. He was astonished to find that the firm in question seemingly employed an unusually high number of stunningly beautiful and scantily clad 'lady traders'. In hindsight, it's likely he hadn't entirely grasped the true nature of the situation at the time!

This awkward encounter likely occurred during London's annual Institute of Petroleum (IP) Week, a glittering and frenetic February tradition that drew traders from across the globe for networking and no shortage of indulgence. Lavish entertainment was the norm, with firms vying to outdo each other in hosting extravagant events.

Park Lane became a playground for oil executives, who staggered from grand dinners to after-hours diversions in salons of varying repute. Mondays typically featured BP's lunch buffet atop the Park Lane Hilton or Mobil's equally popular affair. Monday evenings belonged to SITCO, hosting multiple dinners catering to the various facets of their business interests.

As the week gained momentum, Wednesday brought the marquee event—the official IP Dinner at the Grosvenor House Hotel—followed by Vitol's famously exclusive party at the Dorchester.

In between, the schedule was dotted with smaller, more intimate gatherings, such as BP's North Sea dinner, notorious for heavy drinking and its predictable after-party at Stringfellow's, or SUN Oil's lunch at Quaglino's, which often lasted as long as the supply of select wines held out.[11] By Thursday, recovery was required but little real work recommenced until the following week.

The United States had its own, more sober versions of IP Week. The American Petroleum Institute's (API) week took place in a different city each year and was more characterised by prayer breakfasts than night clubbing. Indeed, observing the Houston and Deep South habit of dining early, most activities were over by 8.00 pm and the delegates, or at least some of them, were tucked up in bed at an early hour.

The more recently established Cambridge Energy Research Associates (CERA) Week[12] takes the concept of industry gatherings to an entirely different realm. Departing from the orbit of socialising and revelry, it places a far greater emphasis on intellectual discourse and strategic engagement. A sure proof that things do not necessarily improve over time!

The French Connection

Away from London, but umbilically joined through the pursuit of identical trading business, were the French firms Elf and Compagnie Française des Pétroles (CFP).[13] Very different in outlook, CFP were the patricians of French commerce. Not necessarily all educated at a 'Grand Ecole', family pedigree played its part in securing a position with the company. Forced by the pricing policy of the French state to incur losses in the core refining and distribution business throughout the 1970s and 80s,[14] they were slowish to take to markets as they evolved. Sitting isolated from each other in their well-appointed private offices, there was little exchange of market information between CFP traders, and they were regularly caught off-market by their more alert counterparts.

Elf, in contrast, was both adventurous and astute. Formed from its various constituent parts in 1976[15] and eventually merging with CFP (later rebranded as Total) in 2000, Elf had a storied history of operations in West Africa. The French government had actively encouraged the company to pursue State-to-State business in the region, and Elf had honed a deep understanding of what it took to succeed in such challenging markets. Competing head-to-head with formidable niche players like Marc Rich in this demanding arena, Elf demonstrated a unique ability to navigate the complexities of the African political and oil landscape.

From 1983 onwards, Elf benefited greatly from having Bernard de Combret as its Head of Trading. A former civil servant and Grand École graduate, de Combret was an exceptional figure—more a sharp commercial strategist than the archetypal meticulous bureaucrat associated with French civil service. His forward-thinking and keen commercial instincts kept Elf at the cutting-edge of oil trading throughout his tenure, which lasted until 2002. Under his leadership, Elf cemented its position as a formidable force in global trading markets.[16] At one point, de Combret even contemplated acquiring Vitol, a bold idea that ultimately didn't come to fruition but reflected his ambitious mindset.[17]

In the Middle East and Africa during those years, 'commercial incentives' were often a key component in conducting oil business. As the seasoned and avuncular Elf trading veteran, the late Yves Gautrot, aptly put it: '*Crude oil is strategic*'. This concept was vividly demonstrated in a memorable oil trade. A former Elf executive recalls a tense negotiation between Gautrot and representatives from Qatar Petroleum regarding the renewal of a term contract. When Gautrot's initial proposal was rejected, he subtly reminded the Qataris of the potential challenges in securing spare parts for Mirage fighter jets—aircraft that France had supplied to Qatar. With this pointed remark, a quick and amicable agreement was soon reached.[18]

An Elf executive recalls his surprise at losing the renewal of a deal with the Nigerian National Petroleum Company (NNPC)—especially after setting aside $10 million to 'facilitate the renewal process'. The previous year, Elf had made a $100 million profit from a transaction in which they supplied Brazilian oil products to Nigeria in exchange for crude oil—a line of trade that would continue with notoriety for many years, involving numerous independent trading companies. Given the success of the deal, $10 million seemed like a reasonable price to secure the renewal. However, their shock only deepened when they discovered that the contract had instead been awarded to their French rivals—Total!

In the mid-1980s, major oil companies, particularly those with London-based commercial teams, intensified their focus on trading activities. Silvan Robinson, a proponent of traded markets, assumed leadership of Shell International Trading Company (SITCO) in 1983. Under his guidance, SITCO successfully reclaimed supply business from affiliates such as Deutsche Shell and Shell Nederland at least for a while. This strategic move not only restored Shell's competitive edge but also prompted SITCO to expand its trading staff to improve its risk management and capitalise on growing trading opportunities.

Private offices at Sitco gave way to, initially, six-sided desks. It was a communal space for the traders to quickly exchange market information. At the end of the room was a large, whiteboard where a tally of cargoes bought, sold, and available for sale was kept. Without the benefit of modern technology, it was left to SITCO trader Kevin Brown to control the content of the whiteboard. Most unfortunately, one morning the traders arrived to find that the board had been completely wiped by over-assiduous cleaning staff and that a record of that month's business had been completely lost. As a result, Kevin's day became a shade longer as each evening he was subsequently required to wait until the last trader left before taking a Polaroid photograph of the board in case a rogue cleaner got over-enthusiastic with a wet cloth.[19]

A bonus system was started in 1986 to reward, in Silvan Robinson's words: '*stress and long hours*', in a business: '*Fast moving between difficulty, disappointment and elation*'.[20] SITCO had got the joke too and followed the BP trading strategy, whose ever-changing bench of traders were the gold standard for other companies setting up their operations.

Over in the United States, there were also some interesting stirrings, none more so than the founding of Citizens Energy in Boston by the Kennedy family (of political fame) and placed under the leadership of Wilbur James. Set up as a non-profit venture to provide fuel to needy families in New England, they were backed by the Venezuelans who provided oil to Citizens, not at the official selling price but at the prevailing, and usually lower, spot prices.[21] At times, this oil was as much as $6 a barrel cheaper. The cheap oil was processed at the Commonwealth Oil Refining Company (CORCO) refinery in Puerto Rico, with petroleum products going to Venezuela, except the heating oil which was taken to New England to distribute it to 'the needy'.

Subsequently, the Kennedy family connections opened doors for deals in Nigeria and Angola, and Citizens became a significant presence in the global market. At times, the company operated via Morgan Stanley (who often disposed of the West African oil into Spain). At a later date, when markets became more 'complicated' in such difficult places, Citizens used Glencore.

'No Jerks' Rule

Marcus Green and David Hufton had been early BP leavers to Phibro and PVM respectively, and scores of others moved on in the succeeding years including the highly regarded Urs Reider who left for Marc Rich and the aforementioned Andy Hall who joined Phibro in 1981. BP was the fountainhead of trading talent and ended up populating the whole industry, although they would eventually become one of the most attractive and remunerative places to work after a generous bonus system was put in place in later years.

BP was not alone in trading traders with other companies, and there was a transfer market in traders long before footballers were the attractive commodities that they are today. The standard compensation on offer was to become, in due course, £100,000 (or £100k in traders speak), usually with a 'company car' and private health insurance thrown in to boot. As Andy Whitrow, who began his career at BP perceptively observed: '*Oil traders are like football managers—they fail but someone always wants to hire them*'. And so, it was and because there was little or no auditing of performance, one never really knew if someone was jumping ship as a failure or perhaps was head-hunted as a rainmaker.

One head-hunted individual was the popular Tony Dillon. Entranced by watching the U.K. television series 'The Troubleshooters' which was about the daring exploits of dashing oil executives, Tony had written to Shell looking for his first job, having decided not to pursue a degree in Computer Science at University in 1970. His lightbulb moment had come as he ambled past a Shell petrol station on his way into town. In applying to Shell, his ambition though was more Head Office than Forecourt and he was to strike it lucky when he was accepted for a job in Central Supplies for an annual salary of £950. Tony would cut his teeth at Shell before joining Conoco in a more senior role.

He had been quite contentedly trading at Conoco for a number of years when he received an invitation to join the head of Sun Oil's London office, Bruce Cross, for cocktails at the Inn on the Park (there was no need to check out the Labour Exchange or the job listings in this industry). Cross, who had cut his teeth with Murphy Oil during the 1970s, made Tony a very decent offer, and when he eventually threw into the bargain a BMW 7 Series, the deal was done.[22] Tony, who still runs the 'London Silver Tops' lunches for ancient, retired traders (they were to be called Old Timers, but an objection was raised that the name sounded like Alzheimer's) was to remain at Sun for the greater part of his career, before becoming involved in the price reporting business at the London Oil Report.

Not every Sun trading executive was as up to speed as Tony, however, and he recalls that in an attempt to show his understanding of the new trading lingo, his U.S. boss, instructed him on one occasion: '*Buy me some of those shorts*!'

Tony's lack of relevant educational experience was not necessarily a drawback in these early days. While Exxon may have preferred Geologists, Petroleum or Chemical Engineers, there was plenty of room for the Oxbridge PPE graduates, Classicists, Historians, and Economists, whose discipline was fairly new in the early 1970s.

Before joining City of London Options, a member and floor trading firm of the International Petroleum Exchange, Charlie Rankin graduated from the University of Glasgow with a degree in Botany. Eschewing the attractions of a career at a local garden centre, he began his professional journey as a casino croupier. He then transitioned to the emerging field of oil options trading, leveraging his strong mental arithmetic skills. His unconventional background did not hinder his ascent; he held a leadership position at a Wall Street bank for nearly two decades.

A different route into oil trading was via shipping operations or 'traffic' as it was known in the United States. Many alumni of the Kings Point Merchant Marine Academy found their way in due course into front-line trading. And there are many who believe that training in operations is a sine qua non for success as a trader, most especially in physical oil trading.

Fortunately, success in the industry isn't solely determined by academic credentials or prestigious institutions. Donald Porteus, BP's unassuming yet highly respected 'King of Cushing', exemplifies this. Despite attending the modest Napier College of Further Education in Edinburgh, he rose to the pinnacle of his profession, retiring with distinction in 2015. Regarded by colleagues such as Gene Grabinski as not only a '*good guy*' and by John Rodger as '*unassuming*', he made his money at BP at a time when the firm was under severe restrictions following a few brushes with U.S. authorities.

Street smarts and 'touch' matter. Shania Twain's hit single, '*That Don't Impress Me Much*' contains the most appropriate of sentiments in this connection: '*So you got the brains, but have you got the touch*'? Certainly, a threshold level of academic ability is necessary, but it is not sufficient. Former Barclays Bank CEO, Bob Diamond famously had a '*No Jerks*' rule when making hiring decisions.[23]

The traders and buccaneers of the early days had emotional intelligence to burn-gregarious, sociable, and clubbable (at least night-clubbable), and they could just as easily negotiate their way around the salons and restaurants of Paris and London as around a typical business problem of the day. Ambition, a will to win, intensity (also the key differentiator in sporting brilliance), self-belief, and a capacity for hard work took a trader a long way from then as now.

Coolness under pressure, humility that respected the fact that the market was always bigger than you, decisiveness and resilience are all key. Oil trading is a cyclical business and unemployment is commonplace. Witness the fate of the city of Houston in the mid-1980s when prices crashed to historic lows and engineers had to take to driving taxis. The joke at the time went along the lines of- '*What is the difference between an oil trader and a pigeon*?' And of course, the answer is that: '*At least a pigeon can put down a deposit on a Mercedes*!'[24] The need to be resilient in the face of such adversity is a required characteristic in trading oil.

In trading—a field where the odds of success start at 50/50 but are diminished by the detrimental effects of human behavioural psychology (let's generously estimate it at 40/60)—downturns are often self-inflicted. Founder of Exchange Consultants and long-time industry head-hunter, Trish Collins, observes that traders' performances tend to run in five-year cycles: '*Three average years, a stonking year and a fuck-up*!'[25]

Oil Brokers

Oil brokers took no risk as principals in markets yet collected a generous fee. In return they effectively directed business to and from their clients as they saw fit. Knowing who wanted to do what on a minute-by-minute basis, while being the trusted third party for market players, brokers occupied a position of huge influence. They were seen as a discrete sounding board for the rest of the market, and top brokers could extract information from even the most constipated of traders, information that they would not even have told their granny's. And their role as opinion-formers was not to be underestimated in importance.

Fretoil was the first by a long way in Europe, having been founded in 1938 in Paris. Eperon was another old hand in European markets. The Italian broking house Gambini was primarily a products broker, as was Phil Pollocks' Aspen Oil. In the United States, Bruggeman's and Commerce Oil were active early in New York. Some other brokers like Fearnoil came from a shipping background where brokerage had been part and parcel of the business for a long time.

In the early 1980s, oil brokerage firms paid well, and a number of high-class oil trading folks were attracted to that part of the business. Simon Cowie moved from BP to Max Bernegger's brokerage, First National, and Per Adler left Statoil[26] to join Fearnley's. Some others, such as the founder of Spectron Johan Frestadius, arrived from different backgrounds. Frestadius was an Electrolux salesman in Paris.[27] In the words of Phil Pollock, the highly regarded founder of Aspen Oil Brokers 'Broking wasn't that difficult as most of the competition were so poor!'[28]

PVM[29] was the premier oil brokers during some half a century. Eventually, the company was sold to a financial broking firm Tullet in 2014 for a hefty $140 million. This was a substantial sum to be paid for a company that had no assets, other than people working for it. PVM was founded in Fort Lee, New Jersey by Pat Mazzarulli who staffed the firm with high-quality individuals such as Tom Cain, Bill Emmitt, and David Hufton, who left BP to head PVM's broking business in London.

An articulate, precise, and down-to-earth fellow from the North of England, Hufton was, for many, the doyen of brokers during the rapid period of growth of North Sea oil trading. He actively cajoled and encouraged participation in the embryonic Brent markets. Over the years, David was known as a discreet middleman for many physical cargos as he was the trusted 'oil man' of the brokerage community with, arguably, the most senior corporate contacts at that time. As he pertinently comments: '*Autistic trading types needed the comfort of an intermediary*'.[30] Hufton's seminal role in the creation of traded oil markets is not to be underestimated.

Some broker-traders had to tread a fine line between their own interests and those of their clients. However, one who wasn't particularly concerned with that distinction was Marc Wolman.

During the 1970s, much of Iran's oil was making its way to a refinery in Bonaire in the Caribbean - a trade facilitated by Wolman. BP, which always had an oil surplus and was eager to offload difficult Iranian grades, struggled to understand how it was being consistently undercut in the Caribbean by Bonaire Petroleum. Eventually, they uncovered the reason: Wolman was back-hauling Mexican oil to Israel, a trade that most avoided. By doing so, he drastically reduced shipping costs, securing a major competitive advantage.

Wolman, a colourful character, was rumoured by some to have been a South African spy as his various entities played a significant role in sanctions-busting there and in Rhodesia.[31] Also active in Libya, Wolman acquired at one point a cargo of Sarir, a waxy and difficult to process crude oil from Libya. It was Urs Reider—a highly skilled trader and a BP 'exile' who then worked for Marc Rich—who was able to relieve Wolman of the cargo. Then, he used the PVM brokers to sell the cargo to Shell in Rotterdam.[32]

It was typical of the new type of business where newcomers, with the help of brokers, were finding interesting nooks and crannies to prise open. Wolman whose main occupation was '*stealing*', according to the South African newspaper, The Mail and Guardian,[33] came to a sticky end when his body was discovered in the boot of a car in the Strandfontein suburb of Cape Town in 1996.[34]

Legislative Arbitrage

In the late 70s through the 80s, the dark side or 'underbelly' of the oil trading industry was most commonly, if not transparently, associated with sanctions-busting. Rhodesia, South Africa, and Israel were either legally or morally sanctioned during the 1970s and 1980s.

This was an opportunity, which did not pass by the traders who specialised in '*doing difficult things in difficult places*'. The names of Marc Rich + Co.,

John Deuss's Transworld Oil, Gert Lutter's Marimpex, Mark Wolman's Tiger along with various Greek shipowners and many others appear in the records of oil embargo violations.[35] According to the popular South African Magazine, The Executive: 'Marc Rich has a soft spot for commodity dependent countries in trouble'.[36]

In the early years of Southern African sanctions from 1973 to 1979, it was reported that as much as 95% of the crude oil destined for ports in Mozambique and South Africa had originated in Iran. This is unsurprising in that the National Iranian Oil Company (NIOC) owned a 17% share of the National Refinery (NATREF) refinery in Sasolburg, South Africa. From 1971, despite sanctions, the two parties had a 20-year oil supply agreement.[37]

Arguably the activities of Marc Rich + Co. and others were no different from those of the South African affiliates of the oil Majors: Mobil, Caltex, BP, and Shell were all bringing oil into the region, including Lourenco Marques for shipment to Rhodesia, using various legal loopholes.[38] For whatever reason, it appears that a blind eye was turned to such activity.

Max Bernegger, the founder of the broking firm, First National, and a long-time consigliere to John Deuss, commented that the U.S. majors would sell Arab Light to Deuss's Transworld Oil who would in return supply other crudes to South Africa.[39] In their book '*Embargo- Apartheid's Oil Secrets Revealed*' Hengeveld and Rodenburg cite that from 1979 to 1983, of the 865 tracked shipments to Southern Africa in tankers of over 50,000 mt deadweight, 149 were linked to Marc Rich, 108 to John Deuss and, in the case of 465 of the cargoes, the names of the suppliers were unidentifiable.[40]

From 1981 onwards, Saudi oil sourced from allocations to 'princelings'—members of the extended Saudi royal family gifted oil by the Ruler—gained prominence, as did spot barrels from Brunei. Remarkably, even as late as 1985, Iran continued to exchange oil for weapons with South Africa. Notably, Philipp Brothers is absent from records of companies breaching sanctions during this era. This highlights another avenue for trading companies of the time to exploit the financial opportunities in the rapidly developing '*free markets*', often navigating a precarious legal line.

Regulating trading companies proved particularly challenging, as many were unlisted or family-run trading in physical commodities, an activity largely beyond the reach of financial regulators. Outside the oil industry, these companies were often little known, yet they played a vital role in the global economic framework.

Traders Behaving Badly

Back in the unregulated forward Brent market, standards of behaviour were falling. In March 1985, two trading houses successfully cornered the market for April 15 Day forward Brent deliveries. Between 20 and 25 of the 45 Brent cargoes scheduled to load were available for sale. By early March that year, after 10 more cargoes were sold to end users, only 10–15 cargoes were still available. Enter Gatoil and Phibro, two traders who then purchased around 15 further forward cargoes for April delivery, more than were available in the market.[41] This led to a sharp rise in prices as the shorts[42] were forced to cover late in the day.[43] Levantine trader Petroship, however, remained short four cargoes and defaulted,[44] causing a series of problems in the Brent forward 'daisy chains' as we shall later discover.

Daisy chains in oil markets had first appeared during the early 1970s in the United States when markets for 'old' and 'new' domestic oil were created, as we have seen in Chapter 2. They would form when the same traders would participate in a number of mutual purchases and sales of cargoes loading in the same month. Sometimes, if there was a perfect loop where a seller ended up as a buyer of the same month of loading oil, there was a 'book-out' or a financial settlement involving all the participants. After a book-out, nominations would not be made any more and there was no physical oil involved other than financial payments between buyers and sellers.

'Daisy chains' were always susceptible to complications, especially when the ultimate supplier was a speculator who had no oil! The North Sea Brent market was generally well policed by Shell UK, the primary Brent producer, and trader, and by PVM brokers' operations 'queen', Yvonne Fernandis. Both the producers and the brokers had vested interest in keeping the gravy train going. The oil producers needed a well-functioning forward Brent market to optimise their tax exposure and the brokers benefited from a premier position of middleman in a busy market greased by fat broking fees of up to 2 cents per barrel (although the more active players received discounts).

If any proof were needed of the personal and corporate profitability wrapped up in the Brent forward market boon, then the rapidity with which the 'issues' were dealt with by self-regulation demonstrates the strength of a desire to assure performance.

As issues with alleged squeezes, defaults, and other bad behaviour in the market began to become more common in the late 1980s, the intelligence provided by PVM's cargo tracking and the firm disciplinary and cleansing hand of Shell UK were to become important with growing frequency as we will discover later.[45]

Petroleum Products Markets Get in on the Act

In the rush to create more and new financial instruments, the markets in petroleum products were not about to be left behind.

In early 1985, Petroleum Argus reported that the Russian Gas Oil market in Northwest Europe was: 'The healthiest physical products market in the world'.[46] In the mode of Brent, it offered traders a marker price for gas oil predominantly sourced from the Russian Baltic Sea ports and, like Brent, it was a 'daisy chain' forward market with a healthy number of participants. There were around fifteen major traders, and they were involved in trading approximately 45 to 50 cargoes per month.

At times, there was an extremely high level of activity, such as in December 1987 when a chain consisting of 320 participants was created, considerably more than the usual 60 or so buyers and sellers, which was the norm at the time.[47] Although this was primarily a Europe-centric trade, occasional cargoes were shipped across 'the pond' to New York, usually in the depths of winter. It was the over-the-counter (OTC) cousin of IPE Gas Oil which had become a successful, heavily traded futures contract.

This gas oil forward market was soon to become known as the Russian Roulette. Whether that monicker is more or less interesting than the equally idiosyncratically named Boston Bingo (the spot market for crude oil in Boston; called 'Bingo' due to its chaotic, speculative nature, akin to the unpredictability of the game 'Bingo'), Swedish Sweepstake, and Littlebrook Lottery is a matter of judgement. The product traders of the time were clearly enamoured with games of chance.

Swedish Sweepstake was a short-lived, informal fuel oil market for delivery centred around the port of Gothenburg in Sweden. Like the other three, it developed in the volatile 1970s when petroleum products still traded on a fixed price basis. However, issues around the ability of suppliers to meet the strict viscosity and density requirements in Sweden caused the contract to be less used than it might have been, despite the increased import requirements for fuel oil into Scandinavia at the time.

A further fuel oil forward market, this time targeted at the Central Electricity Generating Board's appetite for the product in the United Kingdom, was the Littlebrook Lottery forward market, generally centred around the oil terminal in the United Kingdom with the same name. Like Russian Roulette, it divided the market into 2-week delivery periods but, like other forward markets of the time, it suffered mainly from the inability of shorts to cover their commitments at times. Also, there were issues around the expiry of the contract and passing of nominations down daisy chains.

However, the players were a respectable group such as Phibro, Anro (who in March 1988 attempted a rewrite of the contract to resolve the logistical issues), Cargill, Vitol, Elf, Mobil, Texaco, and others. At its peak, there were around 20 companies involved, trading cargoes of 20,000 tonnes at a time. In the long run though, the contract withered, as did an attempt by the IPE to list a similar fuel oil futures contract around the same time.

Boston Bingo was a No 2 Heating Oil[48] contract for forward delivery basis Boston. The 225,000-barrel cargoes allowed parties to buy size volume more quickly than on NYMEX.

The Bingo contract was for delivery via the Colonial pipeline[49] whereas NYMEX listed a New York Harbour contract. In addition, Venezuelan supply which was of a different quality than that accepted in New York, was ideal for Boston. Like other 'games of chance' contracts of the time, there were performance and logistical hurdles in this unregulated forum. The participants were on the one hand the big boys-Mobil, Chevron, and BP with marketing systems in the Boston area, and on the other hand, the local and international trader/marketers like Citgo, Cumberland, Global, and Northeast.[50] Over time, however, the regulated markets of NYMEX were to win out over the Bingo.

While none of these forward market creations were to have the longevity or influence of the forward Brent contract and it's evolved successors, another contract that would outlast the others is the 'Open Spec Naphtha'[51] contract. Envisaged as a hedge contract for the petrochemical industry, the contract was written by Theo Walti of Dow Chemicals.[52] With 17–25 thousand tonne parcels of open origin product, quality controlled with flexible delivery, the contract took off quickly. Stefan Clarkson, oil products trading manager at Scan Trading, was an early adopter as were traders from Vitol, Vanol, Phibro, and Koch. Jonathan Martland got Shell involved, and David Gale, ICI's naphtha man who was not allowed by his company to sell cargoes, managed to participate having introduced his management to the creative concept of 'reverse purchasing!'

When Morimoto San of Marubeni persuaded Aspen's Phil Pollock and Stephen Kneen from Marc Rich to go to Japan to sell the concept of a naphtha forward market to the Shoshas, there was a realisation that an East/West arbitrage could be traded and hedged. Of course, there were some different conditions to allow for the vast delivery area of the Far East. The contract quickly brought in the likes of Phibro and J. Aron to provide speculative liquidity. Although the contract committee, comprised of Dow Chemicals, BASF, and the likes evolved the terms over time, given their vested interests as consumers of the product, the problems with the expiry of the contract and volume tolerance abuse killed the market and it was replaced in due course by a swaps market.[53]

But big changes were afoot. In August 1985, Saudi Oil Minister Sheik Zaki Yamani spoke at the Oxford Institute of Petroleum Studies seminar in Oxford. There he talked of the pain being suffered by the Saudis as their production went into freefall while following a policy of being the swing producer in a falling market while other OPEC members cheated on quotas. He made it clear that patience was running out and went on to describe, for those who were listening, a form of pricing, which might be the response of his government.[54]

This was '*netback pricing*', where the overall price of crude oil would be based on the delivered value of refined products. When this pricing mechanism was introduced, all hell broke loose. Given an excess of refining capacity, the netback pricing guaranteed refineries a profit, and they ramped up their production to capture it. The more petroleum products the refineries produced, the lower their crude oil cost was. It was a refiners' Nirvana. Oil prices collapsed, producers went out of business and laid-off oilmen took to driving cabs.

But this event hid a more important legacy. It was to lead oil market practices to a further level of maturity, sophistication, and usability. This was a period of great personal benefit to those who were on the trading merry-go-round. Pretty much every company involved in the new oil markets came to realise that there was a river of money and that it was time to get rowing.

Despite all the lunching, carousing, golfing, and gossiping, an industry was developing with a rapidly increasing seriousness of purpose. It was an industry that would in future years become one of the most influential, yet one of the least understood by the outsiders. Oil trading would impact the global economy through the part it played in setting the price of oil. And it would make some people very rich indeed, mostly by honest toil but also, at times, by operating on the dark side.

Many can feel grateful for being part of the 1970s and 80s, a formational era of oil trading. As Neste trading executive, Rod Gavshon would say: '*This was a great industry in which we worked, or perhaps more correctly stated, in which we were paid*'.

It was to be Wall Street that would turbocharge a seriousness of purpose into oil trading and it is to there that we now turn.

Notes

1. https://www.bbc.com/news/business-37751599
2. An American self-made billionaire and a US Army veteran. See: https://www.forbes.com/profile/vincent-viola/
3. Discussion with John Chapman 01/12/2023.
4. The shortened name for the US Petroleum Administration District broadly covering the Middle West of the US. Stock builds of Crude Oil and Oil Products in this region were closely watched as they could determine market movements in especially, the price of WTI.
5. Swapping Unocal's Ataca crude for Cinta in advance of the market realising that a drought in Japan would lead to lower hydro-electric production and a rising demand for burning crude oils like Cinta, could offer up to a $4/barrel improvement in returns according to John Chapman, the Unocal trader at that time.
6. Details are from a discussion with Andy Whitrow, a former Sonangol employee.
7. Sonatrach had a small representative office in Knightsbridge with few executive powers.
8. Discussion with ex BP traders, John Rodger and Ron Davidson 26/04/2024
9. Very heavy (about 20 API) and very high in sulphur (about 3%) crude oil.
10. https://www.ieweek.co.uk/
11. Your author was given charge of organising and enduring the Quaglino's lunch.
12. https://ceraweek.com/about/#:~:text=CERAWeek%20History,advance%20the%20energy%20innovation%20ecosystem.
13. CFP was a French oil company that was founded in 1924 and later became TotalEnergies. See: https://totalenergies.com/company/identity/history/pioneers-hundred-years#:~:text=a%20Hundred%20Years-,TotalEnergies%2C%20pioneers%20for%20a%20Hundred%20Years,what%20would%20later%20become%20TotalEnergies.
14. Throughout the 1970s and 1980s, the French state used price controls and subsidies to 'mitigate' the impact of global oil price fluctuations on domestic consumers and industries. The state regulated fuel prices, often keeping them artificially low to 'prevent inflation' and ease the burden on consumers. These price controls led to losses for refiners and distributors, as their revenues could not match the high costs of

imported crude oil. For details, see: https://scholar.harvard.edu/hall/files/evolution_of_econ_pol_2001.pdf

15. Elf was formed by the amalgamation of Regie Autonome des Petroles, Societe National des Petroles d'Aquitaine and Bureau de Recherches de Petroles.
16. As a part of a new company, Total Energies.
17. Discussion with former Elf employee Marc Mourre 27/06/2024.
18. Discussion with former Elf trader, Marc Mourre 27/06/2024.
19. Discussion with ex SITCO employee, Steve Gutteridge 24/01/2023.
20. Shell World interview with Silvan Robinson October 1987.
21. Discussion with John Hunt, a former Citizens executive 09/02/2024.
22. Discussion with Tony Dillon 07/11/2023.
23. https://www.cbc.ca/news/world/no-jerk-rule-imposed-on-u-k-bank-employees-1.1066309
24. A joke attributed to Steve Gutteridge
25. Discussion with Trish Collins18/12/2023
26. Statoil was a Norway's national oil company, now renamed Equinor.
27. Discussion with Goran Trapp 05/02/2024.
28. Discussion with Phil Pollock 26/06/2024.
29. The name PVM comes from the initials of the founder of the company, Pasquale V Mazzarulli. https://www.nytimes.com/2006/06/22/classified/paid-notice deaths-mazzarulli-pasquale-v-pat.html
30. Discussion with David Hufton 24/04/2024.
31. https://atqnews.com/man-in-weahs-shadows-controversial-figure-from-tolbert-doe-taylor-era-resurfaces/
32. Discussion with David Hufton on 24/04/2024.
33. Mail and Guardian 19/12/1997
34. https://allafrica.com/stories/199711280068.html
35. Hengeveld, R. and Rodenburg, J: Embargo-Apartheid's Oil Secrets Revealed Amsterdam University 2006, page 221.
36. Hengeveld, R. and Rodenburg, J: Embargo- Apartheid's Oil Secrets Revealed Amsterdam University Press 1995, p. 138.
37. Ibid. page 271.
38. Bailey, M 1979, p. 140.
39. Mazur, Susan 2006.
40. Hengeveld R. and Rodenburg J. 1995, p. 273
41. In the forward Brent market, cargoes are bought and sold for loading in a particular month, without the loading dates (or 'nominations'). As a result, it was (and still is) easy to sell cargoes one did not have or to buy cargoes one did not need.

42. Shorts are traders that sold, but did not have the oil.
43. This was possible by negotiating with the traders who were long. In some cases, it is possible to buy the oil back from the refinery and supply alternative grades of oil.
44. Their way out was to buy oil from the 'long' companies (Gatoil and Phibro) at very high price and incur a large loss. For whatever reason, they deemed it easier to default and resolve the issue in courts. It would not be the first time for the company to be in court for similar reasons—see: https://vlex.co.uk/vid/avant-petroleum-inc-v-793474717, https://vlex.co.uk/vid/sohio-supply-company-v-793859209 and many others.
45. Shell UK would release extra cargoes into the market to counter squeezes and would refuse to trade with bad actors.
46. Petroleum Argus 04/01 1985, p. 3.
47. Petroleum Argus 29/02/1988.
48. No2 Heating Oil is the trade name for home heating oil in the US Northeast.
49. Colonial Pipeline is the main mode of transport for oil products from the US Gulf Coast refineries to the Northeast markets.
50. See Petroleum Argus 14/11/1988 for further detail.
51. Naphtha is a light hydrocarbon liquid, derived from crude oil refining or from natural gas condensates. It is a critical raw material for the production of petrochemicals—used in steam crackers to produce ethylene and other building blocks of the petrochemical industry. Open Spec refers to acceptance of various qualities (Spec is for specification) and origin of the material.

    It is also used in gasoline blending as an additive to increase the octane rating of fuel.
52. Discussion with Phil Pollock 26/06/2024.
53. Discussion with Phil Pollock 26/05/2024
54. Discussion with Paul Horsnell 26/02/2024.

Bibliography

Bailey, Martin (1970): 'OILGATE - The Sanctions Scandal,' Coronet Books.
Blas, Javier and Farchy, Jack (2021): 'The World For Sale,' Penguin, Random House.
Burke, Paul (1986): 'The Oil Revolution,' Texas Monthly May 1986.
Europ-Oil (Prices) London - Various Issues.

Hengeveld, R .and Rodenburg J. (1995): 'Embargo- Apartheid's Oil Secrets Revealed', Amsterdam University Press.

Mazur, Susan (2006): 'John Deuss - Oil Trader Max Bernegger Speaks', Scoop Independent News.

Petroleum Argus- Various Issues.

Robinson, Silvan (1987):'Shell World' October 1987.

7

Wall Street Warriors

Wall Street Warriors

Even in the days of ex-New York Crime-buster Mayor Rudolph Giuliani, strolling around that city's parks after dark was not to be recommended. Sympathise with J. Aron oil trader Tom Wolkoff who often covered London trading hours from New York and whose 2.30 AM journey to work at their Broad Street office involved a dark and dangerous walk through Battery Park.

Unsurprising then, when removing his jacket on arrival at his desk, he was seen to be fully holstered and 'tooled-up'. More surprisingly though, when he opened his briefcase, generally used by the investment banking types as a posh sandwich carrier, one encountered a serious armoury of items that would prove more than useful in the event of not just a skirmish on the way to work but a full-blown coup d'etat. Of course, it wouldn't happen today, not even in Texas.[1]

When Jan Nasmyth, principal of the Petroleum Argus news group, referred to the Investment Banks who had newly entered oil markets in 1984 as 'Wall Street Warriors', it is unlikely that he knew just how apt his description was!

These same entrants came to be known as the 'Wall Street Refiners' and although the source of that monicker remains elusive, it has stuck and became a much-used description, with its somewhat ironic undertone, given that they did precious little refining of oil over the years.

The emergence of this new group of oil market participants began in 1984 and their cohort was restricted to Investment as opposed to Commercial banks. In 1938, the United States passed into law the Glass Steagall Act.[2] This legislation provided for a separation of activities between the two

A. Imsirovic and C. Bryce, *The Rivers of Money*,
https://doi.org/10.1007/978-3-031-91806-3_7

types of banks and, although oil was not specifically mentioned in the Act, it was interpreted as being included in the types of commerce from which Commercial banks were debarred.

The Wall Street Refiners were Morgan Stanley, Goldman Sachs (via their wholly owned broker-dealer J Aron),[3] Drexel Burnham Lambert, and Bear Stearns, the last two being significantly less active participants.[4] The rise of Wall Street in oil trading can be traced to three coinciding developments.

First, by the early 1980s, Morgan and J. Aron were active in the precious metals markets, but these quickly became oversaturated with brokers and traders, leaving a pool of experienced but underutilised professionals seeking new opportunities.

Second, the New York Mercantile Exchange (NYMEX) crude oil contract began attracting significant interest from speculators. Like metals futures contracts, it offered opportunities as well as liquidity for investment banks, enabling them to trade on their own accounts or assist clients in managing oil price risks.

The third, and arguably most transformative, event was increased volatility, emanating from the collapse in oil prices following the Saudi decision to recover the lost market share of the cartel and the adoption of 'netback pricing' in the mid-1980s. This new pricing methodology dramatically impacted crude oil pricing in international markets, creating such significant volatility that companies exposed to oil price risks began actively exploring how to leverage emerging futures and forward markets for risk management.

Let's briefly revisit the oil market of the 1980's.

It proved to be a torrid time for OPEC. High prices following the Iranian revolution of 1979 and consuming government measures to reduce consumption dented demand. In the OECD area, demand fell from 41.8 mbd in 1979 to 38.5 mbd in just one year.[5] Between 1981 and 1983, Iran's production was recovering and increased by over 2 mbd, while global oil demand fell by about the same amount. A year later, U.K. production increased from 2.1 to 2.3 mbd and Norwegian production from 0.5 to 0.6 mbd.[6]

While Norway, the USSR, and the United Kingdom were selling at prices that would clear the market, most OPEC countries could not find buyers at official prices. In December 1984 the Norwegian state oil company Statoil offered its customers monthly pricing linked to spot market prices. Mexico soon followed.[7] Some OPEC countries started selling at discounts to OSPs.[8]

To stop prices from falling, the OPEC, at their conference in Vienna, agreed on a ceiling (so-called 'total allowable production') of 17.5 mbd.

They also agreed on maximum production quotas allocated to each individual country.[9] The 'would-be cartel' has finally realised they needed strict discipline to act as one.

In spite of OPEC dropping their OSPs, Saudi Arabia had to save the day by acting as a swing producer. The leader of the cartel was forced to cut production by 6.5 mbd in just four years. In 1985, the kingdom was producing only about 3.5 mbd! This was unsustainable and the Kingdom was not getting much support from any other producer, OPEC or not.

Nuclear Option: 'Netback' Pricing

Saudi Oil Minister, Sheik Zaki Yamani, addressed an Oxford Institute of Energy Conference in August 1985.[10] Had the wider trading community been listening, they would have heard Yamani first pleading with the United Kingdom to assist in production control and second warning the world that his government had run out of patience and were minded to act to recover revenues that they had foregone during the previous four years. It was the same message that Saudi's King Fahd had delivered to a gathering of OPEC representatives in Taif earlier that summer.[11]

Saudi Arabia quietly began signing contracts with the Aramco partners based on netback pricing. 'Netback' contracts provided for the price of crude oil to be determined *ex post facto* by deducting the cost of marketing, processing, and transportation and a fixed profit margin from the prices of products produced by refining the crude[12] This had the effect of indemnifying the refiners from having to bear any price risk, guaranteeing them a margin resultant from buying and refining crude oil. The clear incentive was for refiners to run their plants at maximum capacity, which they did, resulting in a downward cascade of oil prices led by ever-cheaper oil product prices.

'Netback' pricing was a perfect weapon for regaining market share. The Saudis offered their customers to convert to this formula early in 1986. At the time, there was excess refinery capacity across the market and since 'netback' pricing offered the customers a guaranteed refinery margin, incentivising them to process as much oil as they possibly could. They did not care about the falling product prices as their feedstock cost would drop as a function of the price of the products they produced. Their margin was guaranteed by the oil supplier no matter how much product they produced or how low product prices went! Any rational refiner would buy as much Saudi oil as he could.

By November of 1985, netback oil was hitting Europe, and by early January 1986, the price of Dated Brent fell below the price of forward Brent, signifying a desire on the part of refiners to not hold physical cargoes in an oversupplied market.[13] Iraq, Iran, and Nigeria rapidly followed Saudi Arabia's strategy and began signing netback deals with customers. Soon, all the other OPEC countries were at it.

In this context, it is interesting to note that OPEC members Kuwait and Venezuela had already been operating in a similar way through their interests in oil refining via partnerships with German company Veba and U.S. refiner Citgo. Effectively they were receiving a netback-like return for their own crude which they were themselves refining.

Over the succeeding four months, prices collapsed from the high $20's per barrel to single figures. Saudi production doubled from 2.2 to 4.5 million barrels per day, and they even added a sweetener by offering a $1 discount on their netback formula.[14]

Predictably, the Saudis and the rest of OPEC soon recovered their market share, but prices fell below $10 a barrel. Since the refiners with excess capacity were encouraged to refine as much as they could, they had to sell their excess products in the spot market, further helping its growth.

This lasted for about a year before the price pain became too great for all the producers, and OPEC members came together around a price target of $18 per barrel, backed up by lower quotas for each country. But this arrangement was to prove to be temporary, as the OPEC hegemony of the 1970s continued to be undermined by cheating from within the cartel, and free spot markets continued to rise in importance.

The impact of low oil prices on high-cost producers, such as those in the United States, was so severe that President, George Bush senior had to intervene. Of course, he had to intervene: '*Donations from oil and gas interests accounted for a substantial portion of the more than $800,000 raised by Vice President Bush's political action committee in its first two months, according to the committee's first report, made public earlier this month by the Federal Election Commission*', according to the New York Times.[15]

Eventually, this madness, driving oil prices towards zero had to stop. At the OPEC meet, in Geneva, on August 1986, the cartel agreed to substantially cut output, and prices soon started recovering. But what never recovered was the OPEC's pretence that they were in control of the market and prices. The cartel continued to play a significant role in the market, but the illusion that they could replicate the market power of the oil Majors' oligopoly was not coming back.

It was the market and traders that were setting the scene for the oil industry to follow. And oil was coming from new places, outside the cartel, offering further trading opportunities. Wall Street refiners were perfectly positioned to capitalise on these changes. While the rise of NYMEX and the influx of skilled trading staff provided the initial momentum, it was the sweeping effects of the netback pricing volatility that cemented a major role for Wall Street in oil trading.

Paper Refiners

Wall Street may not have received a warm welcome in the oil markets, but the volatility in oil prices—underscored by the netback pricing experiment—made it clear to anyone managing oil price risk that their presence was inevitable.

If Morgan Stanley was the first to establish a presence in the oil markets from their offices in the Exxon building at 1251 Avenue of the Americas in New York's Midtown, the seeds of change were also sown at Goldman Sachs. Bob Feduniak, then-head of the Floor Commission Merchants (FCM) business at Goldman, played a pivotal role. The FCM acted as a broker on various futures exchanges for clients, including investors and financial institutions, while also engaging in limited proprietary trading, primarily in metals.

Feduniak, a nationally ranked poker player, had the foresight from his position at Goldman's FCM to recognise that oil was entering financial markets. In 1981, Goldman tasked him with exploring the possibility of launching a commodities trading operation. However, instead of building a business from scratch, Goldman acquired J. Aron, originally a New Orleans coffee dealer with German-Jewish roots, in September of that year.

After the acquisition, finding himself redundant at Goldman, Feduniak joined Morgan Stanley, where Lewis Bernard, a senior executive, was closely monitoring the growing opportunities in commodities. Bernard saw Feduniak as the ideal candidate to spearhead Morgan Stanley's entry into metals trading and capitalise on emerging opportunities in the oil market. So while Goldman had paid \$150 million in cash and \$100 million in notes for J Aron, Morgan decided to build ab initio.[16]

During this period, several individuals who would later play significant roles in oil trading were just starting their careers. Steve Semlitz, initially working in the firm's technology department, was soon to lead precious metals trading. Meanwhile, Steve Hendel, a lawyer, joined the firm in 1981, and Gary Cohn, a future Goldman Sachs CEO, was gaining experience as a local trader on the metals futures floor of the Commodity Exchange (COMEX), though not yet affiliated with J. Aron.

J. Aron proved to be a breeding ground for leadership within Goldman Sachs. Many top executives, including Lloyd Blankfein - who became CEO of Goldman Sachs in 2006—began their careers at J. Aron as commodities traders following the merger. This integration not only bolstered Goldman's presence in commodities but also shaped its future leadership.

Neal Shear, the future leader of Morgan Stanley's commodities business, was not long out of Cornell University holding an MBA, when he joined J. Aron in 1979 where he spent three years trading metals. At various times he was the firm's representative on the futures floor while he also traded the arbitrage[17] between the COMEX silver market and the Chicago Board of Trade (CBOT) silver contracts. Shear recalls that the melting of silver and gold coin based trading was a big money spinner for J. Aron, and he was involved in both. Another arbitrage that was Neal's favourite was the spread in gold price between the Chicago Mercantile Exchange (CME) and COMEX. In due course, the CME would take over both COMEX and NYMEX..[18]

These individuals would go on to steer Morgan Stanley and J. Aron through some of their most pivotal—and, in Shear's case, most profitable—years. Feduniak wasted no time in recruiting Shear to Morgan Stanley, where he launched the bank's commodities trading operations in 1984.[19] While Shear primarily focussed on building the metals trading division, Feduniak quickly turned his attention to expanding the nascent oil business, actively hiring talent to lay its foundation.

Feduniak's first major move was to transfer Marc Crandall, the firm's youngest-ever Executive Director, from Financial Planning to his newly formed oil group. Crandall, a Comparative Religion major and son of the famously hard-charging American Airlines CEO Bob Crandall, brought a sharp intellect to the table. Unlike his father's outwardly combative style, Marc was known for his measured demeanour, but his keen analytical mind and curiosity set him apart as did his habit of sitting at his desk with a pouch of tobacco, rolling his own cigarettes.

Despite lacking a formal mathematics background, Crandall quickly mastered the complexities of options trading, which became his primary focus in the early days at Morgan Stanley. His thirst for challenge and adventure eventually led him to join Marc Rich + Co in short order. As we'll explore later, Crandall's contributions were pivotal in shaping the broader landscape of oil trading.

Then Feduniak did something that was to significantly shape the character of Morgan Stanley's oil business. He hired two seasoned oil company executives, Nancy Kropp and John Shapiro. Nancy Kropp had been known as 'The Queen' at Sun Oil in Pennsylvania.[20] Nancy was a natural charmer and the ideal person to assure her colleagues and competitors in the oil industry that Morgan Stanley was not just a flashy Wall Street firm with 'red braces and suspenders', but a serious player dedicated to addressing the industry's risk management needs. She worked tirelessly to ensure that Morgan Stanley earned its place in the 'oil club', gaining acceptance to trade as an equal among established industry players.

Around the same time, John Shapiro, a cerebral Princeton and Harvard graduate was tempted to leave his role with Conoco in Houston and join up with Crandall and Kropp. The Morgan Stanley team of the earliest days was completed by hiring three more individuals: a young English geologist Simon Greenshields, who was trading metals options at Morgan Stanley, Michelle Markey from Mapco, a Tulsa Oklahoma based oil firm, and a recent Arts graduate, Ann Summers from Cargill.

Greenshields, a particularly entrepreneurial figure, would later go on to co-head Morgan Stanley Commodities. Summers, a single mother of four children, became one of New York's most skilled and well-regarded oil traders. Ann specialised in managing the U.S. refining industry's crude oil import needs and also traded domestic crude. Her dedication was legendary—so much so that, during the final days of her pregnancies, she only agreed to start maternity leave when her growing baby bump made it physically impossible for her to reach her phone console!

Ann was friendly with the journalist Amy Myers Jaffe who would routinely cover OPEC meetings across the globe. When calling Ann to report whisperings from the sidelines of their conferences- information that might be useful to a trader—she and Ann would speak in a previously arranged code in case Amy was overheard. It was valuable information even if it came at a cost—Amy always insisted on 'calling collect!'

Morgan Stanley employed a similar strategy when launching their London office in late 1986 to manage business across the Atlantic. For their international leadership team, they recruited talent from France's Elf and the United Kingdom's national oil company, Britoil, reinforcing their reputation for hiring professionals with deep industry experience. This approach led to a strong emphasis on oil producers, refiners, and the physical oil business, consistently prioritising it over the 'paper oil' activities of financial trading. This strategy stood in stark contrast to that of their primary competitor, J.

Aron, and became a key differentiator for Morgan Stanley in the global oil markets.

In New York, the Morgan team would labour diligently during the trading day, only to unwind in style after the late-afternoon Nymex close. Their retreat of choice was the sophisticated ambiance of the Plaza Hotel bar, where they enjoyed a pre-dinner drink before venturing to the upscale Upper East Side and establishments like J. J. Mellon's bistro. A constant across oil trading circles, regardless of the era, is the penchant for conducting business in opulent surroundings.

In London, the Wall Street crowd transitioned from the West End to the equally luxurious Canary Wharf, replete with Parisian-style brasseries, chic Danish coffee houses, and high-end jewellers. Meanwhile, Houston's Galleria area remained the favoured spot for traders. In Tokyo, Marunouchi—with its distinctly international flair—served as the hub where traders worked and socialised. Here, the baseball and football idioms of the trading floor—like 'home runs' and 'stepping up to the plate'—faded into the background, only to resurface when the markets reopened the next day, kicking off the cycle anew.

Goldman and Morgan Rivalry

It didn't take long for J. Aron to recognise Morgan Stanley's strategy, prompting them to reposition key talent by transferring Steve Hendel and Steve Semlitz into their emerging oil business. To lead the team, Aron looked outside the firm and hired John Drewry, an Australian from agricultural giant Cargill. Meanwhile, Steve Scala, who was brokering oil at PVM in Fort Lee (when not acting as Maître D' in the family restaurant), caught Aron's attention. This connection was established when Pat Mazzarulli, PVM's founder, allowed Aron traders to observe operations at their Fort Lee office to learn the intricacies of the oil business.

David Solomon[21] already within J. Aron, transitioned to focus on oil options derivatives, adding further expertise to the team. This blend of internal talent and external hires positioned J. Aron to compete effectively in the evolving oil trading business.

J. Aron focussed heavily on trading big volumes and prided themselves as a market-maker, always providing a competitive price at which they would buy and sell. This market-making role put them in direct competition with Morgan Stanley, standing ready to deal on request.

An intriguing young Brit, Charles Tuke, was brought over from the silver desk, where he had been successfully collecting premiums by selling options on that metal. Tuke would go on to become the trading face of J. Aron, epitomising their bold approach as they carved out a reputation as risk-takers in the futures and forward oil markets. Tuke's focus was less about oil itself and more about the underlying opportunities, famously stating: 'We don't buy oil; we buy value'.

Charlie Tuke may not be well known outside oil trading circles, but he was astounded to realise that in Tom Bower's book on oil, 'The Squeeze',[22] he was cited on 58 occasions while the notorious Marc Rich received only 24 mentions!

Tuke, a farmer and stockman at heart, having declined a place at the London School of Economics and determined not to train as an Accountant, took himself off to Sardinia as a young man where he worked on building sites. From there he fell into some delivery work but when it became apparent that the deliveries were consignments of hand grenades, he hot-footed it back to London before matters got out of hand. He eventually joined the 'Wall Street Warrior' J. Aron in New York in 1980 and must have had much of mutual interest to discuss with Tom Wolkoff who we met earlier in this chapter![23]

Tuke focussed on trading forward or 15-day Brent, Brent against WTI, intermonth Brent and WTI spreads, along with a little physical oil with Steve Scala. Known for executing large volume trades, he was particularly adept at handling the infamous 'six-pack'—a trade involving six cargos of forward Brent, all concluded in a single transaction. Few traders would have the stomach to take on that level of risk in one go.

Perhaps, the only exception was Andy Hall, who had been commanding exalted heights at Phibro since the early 1980s. Occasionally though, Tuke could be caught out as was once the case when called by the dry Amerada Hess trader and man of few words, John Maher.[24] '*Where are you for August Brent?*' asked Maher with his usual verbal economy. Tuke gave him a price. *'Hmm, and September?*'. Tuke gave him a price. '*October…*? This went on through the months until January. Given the sixth price by Tuke, the unexpected and unusually verbose four-word response from Maher before putting down the phone was: '*I'll take them all*'.

Getting it wrong on the Aron floor was not to be recommended. Former derivatives trader and author, Terri Duhon, characterises the trading floor in a bank as '*a harsh place to work*'.[25] Charlie Tuke recalls the behaviour of his robust Dutchman boss, Mark Winkleman (who he describes as '*cold*'), remembering his favoured way of summoning the guilty to his office by shouting at them over a loudspeaker for all to hear, before screaming at them in his corner office in full view of the floor, only to send them back to their desks in shame.

At J. Aron, Steve Hendel was soon to usurp John Drewry whose role in education had become redundant. Steve Semlitz, who had taken to day trading (being neither long nor short overnight), joined him as co-head of J Aron Commodities.

At Morgan Stanley, there was a distinct sense of collegiality from the outset, a contrast to the more competitive atmosphere at J. Aron. While customers often appreciated the tone of their dealings with Morgan, it didn't prevent J. Aron from thriving. Aron's willingness to take on riskier business that the more cautious Morgan would pass on allowed them to prosper in ways that Morgan, with its more risk-averse approach, often could not.

Yet, Morgan Stanley was the clear winner when the clients were asked to vote on who were the best dealers. An example appears in the rankings of 'Dealers' voted for by clients in the publication Energy Risk. On the occasion of the 15th anniversary of the rankings, they published the tally of No. 1 spots in Oil over these years. Morgan Stanley led with 119 first places followed by Goldman Sachs on 78, with a gap down to 38 for Societe General.[26] Perhaps if Morgan were more popular, Aron would be more commercially aggressive,[27] and for a certain type of client, running with the fast guys was a badge of honour as opposed to working with the more staid and more conservative goody two shoes reputation of Morgan Stanley. If Morgan were Damon Runyan's Scarsdale Galahads, then Goldman would be more like Sky Masterson.[28]

Yet, over the years, despite differences in client perception of these two and despite their differences of focus, they have tended to end each year on roughly the same revenue as each other from their activities in oil markets. Perhaps, Aron was relatively more profitable in oil over the first 10 years of their life, to be usurped by Morgan for the next 20 years before pulling ahead again in the last 10 years?

In 2006, the research house Bernstein estimated that across the eight-year period from 1998 to 2005, overall Commodities Trading had returned a pretax contribution to Goldman of \$2.27 billion and to Morgan of \$2.07 billion. They estimated that, in the case of Goldman, 40% of that was contributed by oil—\$0.9 billion, while in the case of Morgan, the contribution of oil was 60%, at \$1.25 billion. In the years thereafter, up until the Financial Crisis of 2008, annual net returns for these two banks from the commodities business rose to in excess of \$2 billion per annum, with up to a half coming from oil.[29]

Perversely, it was Goldman who were first to get in on the act of employing physical oil assets in their business.[30] Early in the 1990s, they attempted, unsuccessfully, to purchase the Wilhelmshaven refinery that was being sold by Conoco. Jeremy Asher (having left Marc Rich + Co., along with partner Mark Voloshin), joined with French grain trader Louis-Dreyfus[31] and succeeded in completing the purchase. But it was not long before an idea was brought to J. Aron by the 40-year-old Dutch storage company, Van Ommeren (now Vopak),[32] to build a simple plant, the so-called 'splitter' on their land to refine a light crude oil known as condensate.[33] Only one such unit was engaged in this operation outside the United States, and that was in the United Arab Emirates. Condensate from Algeria was in ready supply as were new finds from the Sleipner oil field in Norway, so it seemed to be a reasonable proposition.

In 1987, Jonathan Martland, who had cut his teeth trading at SITCO, got hired by J. Aron to trade naphtha, which was to be the main product of the proposed plant. Jonathan was also put in charge of the commercial aspects of the plant. However, what had seemed a good idea turned sour as the price of Condensate began to rise due to the likes of BP, who would buy and combine it with very heavy crude oil to be run in their refineries instead of more standard and more expensive crude oils.

It was Morgan though who eventually triumphed on the physical side of the business and much of the credit for that goes to their Norwegian head of products trading, Olav Refvik. Refvik, a graduate of the Bergen School of Economics had been trading oil at Statoil since 1981, before joining Morgan Stanley in 1990. He became known as 'the King of New York Harbour' when, during the 1990s he instigated a strategy of leasing oil product storage tanks in places like New Haven, New England. Refvik would use the tanks to store heating oil which he purchased on the NYMEX as far in the future and at the lowest available price he could find. This gave him the option to sell it into the NYMEX heating oil contract as it approached expiry.[34] Refvik could use the storage to either buy or sell the product, depending on the market, and would always go for the more profitable option.

Morgan Stanley recognised at an early stage that owning physical storage should be viewed as a relatively low-risk trading option: It was like having an option on a time spread with the storage fee plus the cost of capital being the option premium.

Refvik's foray into futures/physical arbitrage, combined with Morgan Stanley's extensive geographical reach, positioned him at the heart of oil products trading in both the United States and Europe. His London team also focussed on arbitrage with the Singapore markets. As a result, Refvik's U.S.

team, working closely with the international team in London led by Swedish-born Goran Trapp, became a significant force in global oil products trading. Their business covered a broad range of activities, from gasoline blending and trading products on the Colonial Pipeline (which runs from the U.S. Gulf to the Northeast), to making markets in jet fuel.

But it was the Morgan Stanley purchase of the U.S. domestic distributor, TransMontaigne (TMG) that would underpin their hegemony among the oil traders of the day. The system served by TMG afforded Refvik what became known as 'a short'. A short is a reliable source of demand and a sure destination for the product for any producer. It offered the bank an opportunity to trade the product, always with the optionality of placing it into TMG or simply buying it on their behalf. Cheap optionality is always the best way to trade as it is profitable, without increasing risk.

Morgan went on to build on this activity in many ways such as becoming a leading provider of physical aviation fuel to airlines 'on airport', building on their groundbreaking deal to supply all of United Airlines physical jet fuel needs in the United States and becoming a leading credit enhancing partner to oil refining companies in Europe and the United States, by combining and packaging crude and product trading with financing.

Only in fuel oil markets was Morgan Stanley arguably usurped by Aron, especially during the years when well-regarded and highly profitable trader John Bertuzzi was running their fuel business.

While Morgan Stanley benefitted from the tendency of its senior staff to remain at the company for long time, providing a continuity to clients, Goldman underwent more regular changes. Hendel, who in his spare time is a Broadway 'Angel', having been involved in the production of the successful show 'FELA', and Semlitz, along with their senior Aron colleague, Guy Merison, went on to found Hess Energy Trading (HETCO) with support of the Hess family of Amerada Hess fame.[35] Eventually, the Hess share of the partnership was bought by Oaktree Capital Management LP and became today's very successful trading company Hartree.[36]

Aron's leadership passed through the hands of Americans such as Frank Brosnan, Gary Cohn, who went on to be a president of Goldman Sachs, Lee Vance, who retired at an early age to return to University to study Mathematics, and Rich Ruszica, a former futures trader. Europeans such as Dick Bronks (a derivatives expert and a masterly trader of options from the short side) and Isabel Ealet (a former oil products trader) also spent some time in charge of the shop. Bronks (or Bronksy to his friends) would retire early to dedicate his time to running a fly-fishing business in one of the shires of England. And in the true style of an English gentleman, he assumed the position of Chairman of the Salmon and Trout Association for a number of years.

Over at Morgan, after the departure of Crandall to Marc Rich and Kropp to retirement, the energy business continued to be run by Shapiro, who was reporting to Shear, now the Division head. They were a complimentary pair—with Shear's strategic brilliance and easy manner fitting well with Shapiro's focus on risk. Shear would go on to lead all of Morgan Stanley's Sales and Trading businesses. When Goldman passed the baton to a duo, Bronks and Rusika, Morgan did the same thing when Shapiro left in 2008, appointing Simon Greenshields and Colin Bryce, followed by Peter Sherk and Morgan's Commodity businesses first female head, Nancy King in 2015. In prior years, Nancy had excelled as a trader in London and New York across a number of different commodity markets.

The Legacy

The Wall Street refiners brought change to the business in many ways. Their work pattern was different and was driven by the timings of futures markets rather than the less regimented OTC, forward and physical markets. Lunch was taken at the desk and the intensity levels in the industry increased with their entry to the business of oil trading.

Where the traditional oil trading sector was often primarily a club, Wall Streeters were analysing and calculating machines, valuing their optionalities using Monte-Carlo methods and pulling a trigger only when the probabilities struck up in their favour.

Wall Street was unconcerned with absolute prices, recognising that flat price trading was too risky, as no one had ever consistently predicted future price levels accurately. Instead, Wall Street focussed on relative values or spreads: Is heating oil fairly priced compared to gasoline? Is the January heating oil price a good value relative to February? Is Dated Brent underpriced compared to forward Brent contracts? Is Singapore jet overvalued relative to Mediterranean jet, and so on? This approach allowed traders to capitalise on market inefficiencies rather than trying to forecast absolute price movements.

There are a multitude of relationships over time, across different geographical locations, and between different qualities of crude oil and petroleum products that display a natural and normal price difference. But markets can be dislocated, so that relationships move in and out of equilibrium. Identifying these temporary changes in relative values has been the core skill of the Wall Streeters. When they were asked to make a market, they would lay off any risk taken on in that transaction by finding the most correlated tradeable commodity, which they would use to offset risk. Alternatively, they would proactively seek out relationships in disequilibrium for their proprietary trading purposes or 'for their own book', as it was then known.

It is almost amusing to recollect that there were more than a few clients and competitors who truly believed that Wall Street had some kind of magic black box that would mysteriously enable them to outsmart everyone else and so pay their traders salaries, which at that time led the pack and were much sought after. Of course, there was no black box. Rather there was a fiercely disciplined approach to risk and reward, a seriousness of purpose, and an early willingness to learn from other more mature markets. And the superior personal rewards on offer were quite a motivator.

Interestingly, Phibro, who in 1981 had taken over the Wall Street investment bank, Salomon Brothers, was never considered to be a Wall Street Refiner. Rather, their earlier establishment as Philipp Brothers led to their classification as a commodities trader, albeit with an increasingly important oil operation relative to other commodities. Their later absorption into Salomon in 1984 did not change the categorisation.[37] Indeed, their lead trader and rising star of the combined firm, Andy Hall, would go out of his way to differentiate his firm from Aron and Morgan.

Two other banks, Bear Stearns and Drexel Burnham Lambert, did enter the business and participated in futures and forward markets. With less of a focus on offering clients oil price risk management service and with a seemingly less serious commitment to oil trading, their significance was not comparable to that of Aron and Morgan Stanley.[38] At a slightly later stage, JP Morgan, Deutsche Bank, and others came forward to join the club, also focussing primarily on the financial oil space.

Wall Street was to be the catalyst for a series of new forward, as opposed to futures, products that came to be core and central to oil trading and to the practice of oil price risk management from the mid-1980s onwards. But before we look at these products—Brent and Dubai Partials, Dated-to-Paper CFD swaps, OTC Options, and others, we must turn and look at how the traditional trade and traders were faring.

Notes

1. Discussion with Ex J Aron trader Charles Tuke 23/01/2024.
2. https://www.federalreservehistory.org/essays/glass-steagall-act

3. J. Aron & Company was a pioneering commodities trading company, initially focused on coffee trading, that expanded into gold, oil, and foreign exchange markets, particularly in the 1970s. The firm's expertise in these areas made it a leader in commodity and financial markets, and its 1981 acquisition by Goldman Sachs played a significant role in shaping Goldman's dominant commodities trading division.
4. Phibro, the commodities trading entity created out of Phillip Brothers and which combined with Investment Bank Salomon Brothers in 1981, were never considered to be one of the Wall Street Refiners. Their business model aligned more closely with the Independent Trader community given their primary interest in speculation. This is despite the fact that they had a far greater involvement in refining than the other Investment Banks and also despite the fact that they were leaders in promulgating new products based on oil price movements into wider financial markets (such as Warrants- and other option related products).
5. Hearing Before the Committee on Energy and Natural Resources (1983), page 29.
6. CIA (1986), page 1.
7. Razavi (1986), page 29.
8. Effectively, they all had 'official prices', but the three non-OPEC producers did not have to comply to any agreed prices. Sweet, high-quality North Sea barrels competed in Europe directly with the Nigerian grades of oil, and when the British National Oil Corporation (BNOC) dropped its selling price by $3 a barrel, Nigeria responded by an even greater cut of $5.5 a barrel below the OSP.
9. See Parra (2004), page 278.
10. Discussion with Paul Horsnell 26/02/2024.
11. Parra, F 2004, p. 283.
12. Parra, Francisco: 2004, p. 283.
13. Europ-Oil (Prices) London 13/01/1986.
14. Parra, Francisco: 2004, p. 287.
15. NY Times, August 19, 1985.
16. According to Neal Shear, Goldman also gave up 6 Partnership places to J Aron- a significant number in these days.
17. In this instance, Shear would buy or sell one market while doing the reverse on the other- a so-called arbitrage.
18. https://investor.cmegroup.com/news-releases/news-release-details/cme-group-inc-completes-acquisition-nymex-holdings-inc-expands

19. Feduniak, Shear and another hire, Cedric Foster, closed the deal to move to J Aron over a 6 hour lunch at Wilson's on 2nd Avenue having answered a Financial Times jobs ad strategically placed for them to see. No allegation of poaching could then be levelled.
20. Discussion with Tony Dillon 07/11/2023.
21. Not the same David Solomon who was a CEO at the time of writing.
22. Bower, Tom: 2009.
23. This is based on a discussion with Charles Tuke on 23/01/2027.
24. Between Maher, his boss Bernie Deverin and Leon Hess himself, there were few words to pass on a phone call with any of them.
25. Duhon, Terri: 2012, p. 37.
26. Energy Risk July 2009, p. 75.
27. During the mid-1980's, Aron acted for a time in the Brent markets as an agent for Repsol charging them a fee of 7 cents per barrel to enter deals and the same to liquidate, according to a former Aron employee of the time. As a comparison, the standard brokerage fee at that time was 2 cents per barrel on crude oil. Perhaps there was more in that relationship than meets the eye to justify such level of fees?
28. Referencing a line from Broadway writer Damon Runyon that occurs in the musical Guys and Dolls.
29. In 2010, Oliver Wyman estimated that the MS oil business had returned $0.99 billion to the firm.
30. In fact, Morgan Stanley had, in 1986, leased tankage at Cushing, Texas from ARCO-tankage that had lain dormant for two decades. They filled it with oil and executed possibly the first cash and carry trade undertaken in the petroleum business. Second nature to former metals dealers, Feduniak and Shear, John Shapiro, who had arrived from Conoco, also had a hand in conceptualising the deal.
31. https://www.ldc.com/who-we-are/about-us/heritage/
32. https://www.vopak.com/who-we-are/our-history?language_content_entity=en
33. Condensate contains mainly light hydrocarbons (primarily naphtha) and does not need a sophisticated refining system. A splitter is a simple distillation column that uses only heat (no catalyst) to split the main, light factions of crude oil.
34. It was a physical delivery contract and long contract holders had to either take delivery or close the futures position.
35. https://www.hess.com/company/hess-history. More on this later on in the book.

36. See: https://www.reuters.com/article/world/europe/oaktree-closes-hetco-deal-trader-renamed-to-hartree-partners-idUSKBN0LG33I/
37. Despite their focus away from the Wall Street refiner business, Phibro was the first company to introduce options on crude oil to the general public when, in 1985, they issued an offering of warrants for the investor community.
38. Two of the employees of these firms at the time were Doug Dickie and Ron Deal. Given the English slang meaning of "a dickie deal"- best translated as "a suspect transaction", these gentlemen were up against it at the start trying to convince potential clients of their veracity as counterparts!

Bibliography

Bower, T. (2009): 'The Squeeze-Oil, Money and Greed in the 21st Century,' Harper Press

Duhon, T. (2012): 'How the Trading Floor Really Works', Bloomberg Press

Parra, F. (2004): 'Oil Politic A Modern History of Petroleum', I.B. Tauris

Razavi, Hossein (1986): 'The New Era of Petroleum Trading' World Bank Technical Paper Number 96

8

Troubles with Brent

Troubles with Brent

Khalil Gattas was a modest, unassuming Lebanese former chicken farmer. Like many oil traders of the mid-1980s, he enjoyed a quiet afternoon nap, though in his case, it wasn't due to recovering from a particularly indulgent trading lunch.

Gattas became a notorious figure in forward oil market circles for two key reasons. First, his company, Gatoil, defaulted on contractual obligations in the Brent market in early 1986. Second, he played a covert role in the oil trading fraud that engulfed the German industrial giant Kloeckner two years later.

Gatoil's alleged misbehaviour in February 1986 was not the first instance of a problem arising in the unregulated forward Brent market. That honour belonged to another Levantine entity, Petroship.[1] In March 1985, Gatoil and Phibro purchased more April forward Brent cargoes than were available for delivery outside of the equity producers' commitments.[2] This resulted in Petroship needing four cargoes (known as being 'short') just as the market rose from just over $26 a barrel in early March to almost $30 a barrel in mid-April, when the contract was expiring.

Gatoil and Phibro were successful, and the tactic was to be repeated on a number of occasions in the succeeding years.

While in the context of the price volatility seen in the 2020s the absolute amount of this price move seems ordinary, in the early days of oil trading, especially prior to the volatility caused by the Saudi netback pricing, this was a big thing. And it was an especially big thing for a small, undercapitalised

A. Imsirovic and C. Bryce, *The Rivers of Money*,
https://doi.org/10.1007/978-3-031-91806-3_8

trading company. Those with original Brent purchases from Petroship had to replace them with purchases of alternative barrels at a much higher cost.[3]

It was not long before Gatoil themselves hit the headlines after defaulting on obligations in the forward Brent market in February 1986. The unfortunate events of that month were the result of a significant fall in prices between November 1985 when the contract was first traded and the contract expiry in February of the following year. During that three-month period, Saudi Arabia and other OPEC members embraced netback pricing which resulted in a fall in prices of almost $12 per barrel over three and a half months. Some companies such as BP, Britoil, and Conoco saw the writing on the wall and closed out[4] their February positions early.[5] Those that didn't found themselves in long 'daisy chains' of forward Brent which would turn into physical cargoes of North Sea crude.

One other company with Brent exposure to Gatoil was Morgan Stanley, and on hearing the rumours of a default, they bought an equal amount of WTI from Gatoil (Houston) for negotiating leverage. Morgan's Nancy Kropp then travelled from New York to Geneva and turned up at Gattas's office opposite Geneva Airport. '*I refused to leave until we had an assurance of performance. Gattas was most polite and welcoming and we had supper in his kitchen and I caught the midnight flight out to Zurich as there was an OPEC meeting taking place in Geneva and I couldn't get a hotel room there*'.[6]

With a great deal of money at stake, the chains broke down as false dates were passed from one company to another, resulting in Gatoil receiving seven nominations for cargoes loading in the period 26–28 February. As there were only two shipments scheduled at Sullom Voe in this date range, it was clear that artificial nominations had been created.

The rules of the forward Brent market required a buyer to be notified of the date range of his purchase by 5.00 PM, 15 days prior to the loading range (hence the name 15-day Brent). In a weak market, if a buying company received nomination just before 5.00 PM and was unable to pass the date to another buyer, it was said to have been '5-o'clocked'. The company was obliged to hold the cargo which then became a 'Dated Brent' cargo (a Brent cargo with loading dates). In weak markets like February 1986, the company would have to sell physical cargo that was not wanted by end users and incur a massive loss. And so, renegade chain participants simply changed the dates to dates which not exist in the original loading programme of the Brent operator.

Gatoil issued a telex to relevant parties on the evening of 11th February notifying all that they intended to accept only one of the seven 26–28

February nominations they had received, a cargo they had bought from Statoil.

Perhaps the most interesting aspect of this early saga of misbehaviour is that it was not all Gatoil's fault, which was the conclusion that many took from the event (in fact, there were clearly multiple incidents of misbehaviour across the daisy chains).[7] That the situation was so rapidly resolved (the main Brent players met on the following Sunday evening to 'tidy up the mess)'[8] indicated the importance of protecting this unregulated market from disrepute. Indeed, the market did continue to thrive.

At the time, the Pin-Striped Sheik, Don Miller, was asked to produce a study to determine the way forward, and a variety of fixes were proposed, ranging from the creation of a clearing house to margining of positions, but none caught the imagination of the main players. The preferred fix was the unspoken understanding among the major players that Shell would act as the informal regulator of the market. Of course, this was not on behalf of the miscreants but rather on behalf of the 'spinners', the Major oil companies who were minting money out of the forward Brent market by optimising their tax exposure. Their traders were being amply rewarded for the effort, playing the legal tax arbitrage. Self-interest, corporate and personal, was a strong motivator to keep the show going and the 'rivers of money' flowing.

Traders Behaving Badly

If the Gatoil business was dealt with satisfactorily and swiftly, another situation arose that was to take more time and cause more angst. Transnor was a small Bermuda-based trading company that was caught 'long'[9] when oil prices cratered from late 1985 through March of 1986. On 3rd March, they issued a writ in the Southern District Court in New York alleging that BP, Conoco, Esso, and Shell had manipulated the price of Brent, causing it to fall against the interests of Transnor.[10] Their Counsel successfully argued to Judge William Connor in the U.S. District Court in New York that the Brent market should be considered to be a U.S. market falling under U.S. rules. As such, it was an unregulated futures market, declared the judge![11]

Of course, NYMEX considered the forward Brent market to be a major competitor to its futures contract in West Texas Intermediate (WTI), and a demise of Brent would have suited them just fine.[12] And the author recalls murmurings at the time that NYMEX was minded to add fuel to the fire and hasten the end of Brent as a contract.

Although this stance of a major U.S. District Court forced a number of participants to relocate their Brent trading activities outside of the United States in order to avoid coming under the aegis of U.S. law, and some even left the Brent market altogether, the forward Brent market survived the shock. It took, though, until May 1990 [13] for a judgement to be issued nullifying the Connor findings (after significant diplomatic pressure exerted by the U.K. Government on their U.S. counterparts).[14]

However, the ruling would ripple for decades and become the main reason for the 'new' Brent contract, augmented by the inclusion of WTI Midland in 2023, to have a contractual transfer of title outside U.S. territorial waters.[15]

All the while Mr. Gattas was beavering away, not front and centre, but deep in the shadows. Unable to attract counterparts to trade with Gatoil in Brent, he set up a behind-the-scenes, unauthorised trading operation with Wolfgang Zeschmar at Kloeckner, a German-based international metal conglomerate.[16] This diversion was to end badly, as indeed had involvement in oil trading at other German industrial companies such as Voest Alpine, Metallgesellschaft (MG), and Merx.[17]

Kloeckner used the brokerage services of Stardust, a Monte Carlo-based firm, to allegedly help conceal trading losses for nearly two years. They did this by arranging off-market transactions designed to delay the realisation of losses, hoping the market would recover. The losses stemmed from Gatoil buying Brent oil contracts through Kloeckner, often using Stardust as a broker, and suffering from a long position as oil prices fell.

To hide their losses, they struck deals with various counterparts to sell their contracts at close to the purchase price—higher than the prevailing market price—before the contracts expired. In exchange, they agreed to buy new contracts for later delivery (usually the following month) from the same counterparties at above-market prices, plus a fee. This tactic temporarily hid the losses, deferring them month by month in the hope of a market rebound. However, as prices continued to drop, losses accumulated. Eventually, the counterparties refused to participate, even with generous fees, forcing the losses to be exposed.

The rubber hit the road for Gattas and Zeschmar as losses, first estimated at $450 million, were discovered and both men were subsequently incarcerated. In the meantime, there was quite understandable panic in the German industrial and financial circles. Deutsche Bank stepped in to calm the market by providing the funds to cover the losses, took over the company, and subsequently converted it into a stock corporation. They turned to Nancy Kropp, a retired Morgan Stanley trader, for help. In doing so, they lucked out.

Nancy's gregarious and enthusiastic persona hid an astute awareness of what was going on in the markets to which she paid attention. And her iron fist, albeit hidden inside a velvet glove, came in handy in the rough and tumble, male-dominated oil trading world. She had spent four years at Morgan Stanley after her arrival from Sun Oil, enough time to set the bank on the right road, having carefully recruited a team of amiable and capable staff.

In the departures lounge at London airport and about to check-in with her husband Thomas Galdy to fly to Los Angeles to begin a life of retirement, an important telephone call came for her. Thanks in all likelihood to a recommendation from her friend, Rhein Oel trader Doris Balzer, she found herself talking to the chairman of Deutsche Bank, Dr Alfred Herrhausen.[18]

Herrhausen, who was later to lose his life in a bomb blast targeted at him by the Red Brigade terrorist group,[19] commanded Nancy to abandon her thoughts of Santa Monica beach and to get herself instead to downtown Dusseldorf.

Kropp was appalled at what she found.[20] In her assessment, fraud had been committed, and it was likely enabled, directly or indirectly, by several well known oil traders and corporations. Later, Kropp attempted to document her experiences in the oil markets, including this incident, in a book titled Oil and Money. However, despite the book being written, advertised, and slated for release, it mysteriously never became available—likely suppressed by legal intervention from unknown parties.

In any event, Kropp closed the trading positions for Kloeckner, reduced the loss to somewhere in the region of $300 million, took a cut of the savings, and happily retired.

Back in the Brent market, the alleged squeezes continued. But they proved to be a misguided way of behaving in a market populated by companies and individuals whose interests were otherwise relatively aligned.

The names of John Deuss and Transworld Oil appear writ large in the alleged squeezes of 1987 and early 1988.[21] A very large premium for forward Brent, in the absence of a major supply problem or a geopolitical event, usually signifies the presence of a squeeze in the forward market.[22] In 1987, the April premium in forward over Dated Brent was $1.14, in May it was $0.37, while in January 1988, it was $2.83.[23] All these months were likely squeezed, as can be seen from the premium of the next month's paper contract over the prompt physical cargoes.

In the last of these alleged squeezes, Shell Trading Manager Peter Ward decided to teach the squeezers a lesson.[24] He arranged for additional cargoes to be released to the market to traders who were short.[25] This left Transworld

Oil with a reported 40 or so physical Brent cargoes to dispose of at a significant loss. It is believed that Deuss was forced to sell his refinery on the U.S. East Coast to pay for the losses. Rod Gavshon, a Neste oil trader is quoted as saying: 'Transworld Oil traders Pat Stamford and Mauricio Martins da Silva could walk all the way from Sullom Voe to the U.S. Gulf on the decks of their vessels needed to load the Brent'.[26]

Perhaps, traders with an ego were emboldened to attempt to squeeze the Brent market just because they could. Yet, it was a dumb strategy. It was short-termism that rarely worked, ran the risk of being countered by a large Brent producer, and for some traders, resulted in a pariah—like status in the market.

The 1980s were a period of the Brent market reaching maturity, eventually resulting in a successful futures contract in crude oil being launched on the International Petroleum Exchange of London (the IPE). After the middle of that decade, falling prices certainly helped that process with participants looking for a way of managing the increasingly volatile prices. But it also meant that being squeeze quantity long was not a way to make money trading Brent. Attempts to squeeze the market were a particularly good way to bankrupt a trading company.

Eventually, the bad actors were black-balled and those who should have known better desisted. We will learn though that attempts to influence the price of Brent and other instruments by exploiting loopholes and weaknesses in the system are an ongoing saga, albeit primarily in the business of attempting to influence the prices set by Price Reporting Agencies (PRA's).

'Locals' and Bad Practices

Over in the World Trade Center, NYMEX was far from immune from the desire of stakeholders to profit at any cost and in any way. In a market where CCTV was not present on the trading floor, those traders and brokers who wanted to misbehave had little to stop them: 'The traders were free to collude with each other sharing inside information about customers and trades that allowed them to anticipate big moves and profit from them'.[27] This was an era where, allegedly, front-running, spoofing, and bullying markets were almost required activities for floor traders.

Front-running refers to the practice of a floor trader trading futures for their own account before placing a customer's order in the marketplace—especially if the customer's order is a large one, likely to move the price. In doing so, the floor trader is assured of risk-free profit, resulting from such a move. The customer had no way of knowing what was going on and was likely to end up buying or selling at prices above or below what they should otherwise have been.

Spoofing is a practice of entering small buy (or sell) orders in the hope that the market responds by rising (falling), before a larger personal order is placed at the spoofed price level. So, the trader would pretend to be a buyer, when he was really a seller—and the other way round.

Bullying is a practice more normally associated with large volume traders 'upstairs'[28] where large orders are placed in succession to frighten off those who want to trade the market in the opposite direction.

Over time, all these and other practices have been made illegal.[29] But not before some floor traders made small fortunes. It would also explain the reluctance of the NYMEX 'members', floor traders who had shares and votes in the exchange, to follow the technology and make the exchange electronic.

Inherent in many of the questionable strategies that were allegedly commonplace on the NYMEX floor is the existence of what was called '*dual capacity*'. This is where a brokerage house is able to trade for their own account as well as on behalf of customers. The conflict of interest and illicit profiting opportunities are not hard to imagine. Not all firms would tolerate this conflict of interest and some, such as Michael Marks' brokerage, would not allow his firm's brokers to trade for their own account or for the house.[30]

Back in the world of physical contracts and forward physical markets, the most successful one was Brent, and it was going from strength to strength. Importantly, the perceived quality of the participants was improving as real oil companies became increasingly aware of the opportunity to manage their firm's exposure to oil prices using the Brent market.

Statoil[31] had been set up by the Norwegian government in 1972 with a very clear mandate—'*…to acquire and hold participation rights and direct licences in the industry*'.[32] At the same time, a separate regulator body, the Norwegian Petroleum Directorate was created. This was a different approach from the one in the United Kingdom, where BNOC was envisaged to be both a commercial entity and the regulator of commerce.[33]

Besides their clearer strategic imperative, the Norwegians also invested in becoming significant equity holders in successfully explored licences, initially through a system of carried interest.[34] This made Norwegian operations significantly more profitable than BNOC or the U.K. Exchequer, albeit having risked public money.

And what's more, 'the explicit goal was a fully integrated company'.[35] '*The decision to enter the downstream was an early priority for Statoil believing that vertical integration would add value and diversify and protect revenues*'.[36] And so, unlike BNOC, Statoil got into refining, storage, distribution, and the retail markets.[37] Later to arrive on the scene in the Brent complex, they appeared in the mid-1980s and were typical of the newer, better-capitalised entities that would populate the market from that time forward.

Their relative lateness to traded markets was probably due to the different taxation regimes in Norway relative to the United Kingdom. The Norwegian tax was based on what was referred to as 'Norm Prices'. Set ex post, the Norm price was intended to reflect the price at which petroleum could have been bought and sold over a period of time by independent parties in a free market. It was set by the Norwegian Petroleum Price Board after they had taken account of actual transactions.[38]

Statoil became interested in using the Brent and spot physical markets to try to 'beat' the retroactive Norm price and avoid being taxed in excess of their realised sales returns. To that end, they set up a small trading team in London headed by Paul Haynes, a former BNOC senior trader.

However, it was Oystein Berentsen, a young Norwegian who came to be the face of crude oil trading at Statoil (Olav Refvik and Elizabeth Roll were the oil products faces of the firm). Berentsen had spent some time learning in the active trading offices of Conoco, Statoil's equity partner in the Statfjord Oil Field.[39] Statoil chose well in seeking Conoco's help as they had one of the most active and professional operations of the time, run by a wily but well-liked Player Edwards.[40] Mr. Berentsen became very successful at his task: '*He was very disciplined and trusted by Statoil's Stavanger management*', and he was soon given authority to trade speculatively and to recruit a larger team. [41] By 1990, they had become the third most active trader of 15-Day Brent after J. Aron and Phibro with a close to 10% market share.[42]

A number of other oil companies became active in the London market around this time such as Pertofina, Elf, ICI, LSMO, Repsol and even some commercial banks began to participate. As a consequence of financial lending transactions, Lloyds International Trading, a British bank, ended up supplying oil to Gamex's 26,000 barrel per day oil refinery in Mobile, Alabama in the U.S. Lazard Brothers and S.G. Warburg ended up having exposure to oil prices through the activities of their commercial loan officers. However, when they became more familiar with the risks involved, they quickly exited the market. In years to come, various banks would come and go as oil traders and providers of derivative products.

Perhaps the most relevant reason for the enhanced participation of oil companies in the Brent market was the growing prevalence of formula pricing for physical oil as well as growing price volatility. One of the great benefits of hedging is that by using liquid markets, a buyer or a seller is able to separate the timing of supply from the time when the price must be set. So, trades were not concluded at a fixed price at the time of the deal, but rather at a price to be agreed by a pre-set formula in relation to an observable benchmark price.[43] For example, Exxon may agree to buy a cargo of Nigerian Bonny Light from Shell with the price to be set at a $0.30 a barrel premium to the Dated Brent price assessed during a five-day period around the date of loading.[44] Or perhaps, a form of formula pricing known as 'trigger' pricing could be employed.[45] For example, BP may purchase a cargo of Norwegian Oseberg from J. Aron, a trading house, and agree that the cargo can be priced in five separate and equal segments on any day between the date of the sale and the date of the lifting and, at a pre-arranged premium or discount to Brent. BP could then choose to call J. Aron when they wanted to fix the price, in line with the prevailing market.

A small industry grew up around the teaching of hedging techniques to the oil trading community. Such courses were those of Farnham and Bentley (F&B Trading) run at St. Catherine's College in Oxford by former Shell and Vitol trader, John Dobson and the Oxford-Princeton programme run by ex-BP hand, Robin Burley.

Providers of trigger and other pricing services were usually the market-making, Wall Street banks.[46] These entities would run their own educational sessions for the prospective clients in the hope of winning market-making business on which they could earn a margin set by the bid/offer spread. For banks, this was a natural extension of business activities in financial markets such as foreign exchange. They were also in the forefront of developing new products to address the price risks that they found to be specific to oil markets.

Brent 'Partials'

In the years immediately preceding the successful listing in 1988 (at the third attempt) of a Brent Futures contract on London's International Petroleum Exchange (IPE), companies keen to take advantage of the newly popular trigger pricing methodology for buying and selling physical oil found they had a problem. Market-makers would need to hedge their own exposure. They were companies such as BP, ELF, Shell, and Phibro along with the Wall Street banks.

Hedging was far easier when they used WTI as their price reference. The well-established NYMEX light crude oil contract was quite liquid even for large hedging volumes. But most international crude oil was being priced at a premium or discount to Dated Brent, yet Brent was only tradeable on forward markets in full 500,000-barrel cargo sizes.[47] Hedgers had a poor choice of either hedging their price exposure to North Sea or West African oil with North American, inland and pipeline-delivered WTI or with a wrong volume of forward Brent.

The Wall Streeters stepped in to resolve the problem. It was not only about helping the market participants, in general, but also about minimising their own price risk. It was also about translating the language of financial markets into oil-speak. In 1987, in a windowless back room in New York's Midtown, Morgan Stanley traders were enduring their annual traders meeting where strategy, staffing, and expansion plans were discussed. The issue of basis risk in the Brent market was also on the agenda. Simon Greenshields, an especially entrepreneurial trader came up with a solution: creation of a market in partial Brent.[48]

Morgan Stanley would make markets on request for any volume of Brent of less than 500,000 barrels. However, by the expiry of the given Brent contract, customers would be required to either increase the volume up to full, physical, forward Brent cargo or reduce the outstanding volume with the bank to zero.[49] The success of this concept would rely on the customers trusting Morgan Stanley not to 'squeeze' them at expiry. This could have occurred as the counterpart was totally reliant on the good grace and practices of the provider, MS, to exit the transaction.

Within days of the meeting in New York, Morgan's U.K.-based traders wrote and then marketed the 'partial' Brent contract. The concept caught on very quickly, and smaller players such as Conoco, Imperial Chemical Industries (ICI), LASMO, Petronor, Unocal, and many others began requesting price quotations from Morgan Stanley for even the smallest daily volumes they needed to hedge. This contract also appealed to traders of oil products such as naphtha and gas oil, as their volumes would better match the smaller volumes of petroleum products.

Morgan's competitor J. Aron quickly joined the Brent partials trade and the market swiftly took off. The need for a liquid futures market, reflecting the forward, cargo Brent market became obvious. In its first week of operation in June 1988 and, supported by Imperial Chemical Industries (ICI) and Morgan Stanley, the International Petroleum Exchange (IPE) Brent futures contract began its journey on the road to the massive success it is today.

Oil Goes Financial

Not many years before, and on the back of the successful launch of a WTI options market on NYMEX, J. Aron and Morgan Stanley began promulgating an over-the-counter market (OTC) in crude oil options.[50] Oil options, which confer the right but not an obligation to buy or to sell at a certain price at a certain time in the future, were ripe for OTC markets. Oil is a heterogeneous product—there are many different types of crude, many time frames over which deals might be concluded, and many differing geographies involved. Options can be constructed in a complex form to enable market users to align the specific risk coverage they require with the bespoke option available to them. And OTC markets do this better than the more homogeneous, albeit more liquid and transparent futures venues.

David Solomon at J. Aron and Marc Crandall at Morgan Stanley went about creating and popularising this market. The Wall Streeters viewed options exposure in their books from the perspective of the volatility valuation—a key component of the price of an option. They would run computer simulations to assess their exposure to the movement in absolute prices, the rate of movement in price, in volatility, and in the time left before an option expired. These complex models produced what was known as a 'Death Matrix', updatable in real time, informing the market-maker how many futures contracts were to be bought or sold at any point in time to keep the bank price-neutral. Of course, the option trader could choose not to remain neutral and speculate within approved limits of the overall position.

Generally, users of options viewed things rather differently from their providers. An oil producer might believe that the oil price was about to fall and might want to buy the right, but not the obligation to sell at a certain price level. There would be no management of volatility, just the success or failure of the hedging strategy.

Some participants were indifferent to volatility and others to price. This created a 'win-win' situation where both parties could profit from the trade. This concept of 'mining the indifference of others' or buying free or cheap optionality was to become a bedrock of long-term, profitable trading businesses.[51]

The 'derivatives revolution' of the late 1980s would lead to a growing interest in oil as a financial product. In this context, options and swaps[52] would become the building blocks of complex risk management and proprietary trading strategies. It would presage the widespread participation of banks as providers of complex products to those companies with a need for tailor-made, price risk-mitigating strategies. It is a subject to which we will return after first finding out what was going on in the Far East.

Notes

1. The bankruptcy of Charter Petroleum in April 1984 had caused only minor waves in the Brent market prior to the Petroship incident.
2. Petroleum Argus 07/05/1985, p. 3.
3. Author's recollection while trading at Britoil, a UK national oil company.
4. Closing out a position means covering short (buying oil for a prior sale) or selling a long position (selling oil previously purchased), resulting in a volumetric net zero position.
5. Authors personal recollection.
6. Conversation with Nancy Kropp (Galdy) 22/12/2025.
7. Horsnell and Mabro in their 1993 book, Oil Markets and Prices cite Marc Rich and Co as one of the companies who 'changed' date ranges as they were passed through the chains.
8. Petroleum Argus 14/02/1986.
9. They had purchased cargoes which they had been unwilling or unable to resell as oil prices collapsed. In any case, selling 'long' cargoes purchased at a high price would have caused them massive losses.
10. *'By mid-February 1986, the price of Brent blend crude oil declined by approximately $15 per barrel allegedly because of a conspiracy among defendants to manipulate the Brent market in order to establish trading prices at lower levels. The purpose of the alleged manipulation was to take advantage of certain provisions of the tax laws of the United Kingdom that affect defendants as producers of Brent blend crude oil and as European refiners.'* See https://law.justia.com/cases/federal/district-courts/FSupp/666/581/2151144/
11. 'Defendants assert that the tax spinning transactions were not responsible for the decline in oil prices thereby defeating Transnor's manipulation claim for lack of causation. Defendants submitted testimony that the drop in oil prices resulted from the actions of OPEC, particularly its decision to compete for market share. However, where "multiple causes of an artificial price … can be sorted out, and [defendants] are a 'proximate' cause of the artificial price, a charge of manipulation can be sustained.' https://law.justia.com/cases/federal/district-courts/FSupp/738/1472/1972253/

12. More enlightened operators viewed the NYMEX and 15-day Brent contracts as complimentary rather than competitive.
13. https://casetext.com/case/transnor-sdny-bermuda-ltd-v-bp-north-amer-petro
14. For a detailed coverage of the Gatoil and Transnor debacles, see Mabro and Horsnell 1993, pp. 138–145.
15. 44.1 Subject to section 44.2, the risk and title in the Crude Oil will pass to the Buyer immediately after the Vessel carrying the Crude Oil leaves the waters comprising the exclusive economic zone of the United States of America (USA) or the territories of the USA.' https://www.shell.com/business-customers/trading-and-supply/trading/general-trading-terms-and-conditions/_jcr_content/root/main/section/simple/call_to_action/links/item0.stream/1677248184495/0a921882c6b596fdb3641757dab1b1c83f59b17a/stasco-bfoetm-2022-version-1.1.pdf
16. https://www.kloeckner.com/en/
17. There was a view at the time that the strict requirements of the hierarchical culture in German industry precluded individuals whistle-blowing on the actions of superiors to higher levels of their company. It was the role of one's boss only to communicate upwards.
18. There are conspiracy theorists who believe that Herrhausen was assassinated by the 'Deep State' as a result of his dovish view on Third World debt forgiveness. See Henderson, Deal: Big Oil and their Bankers in the Persian Gulf Bridger House Publishing 2005.
19. https://www.britannica.com/money/Alfred-Herrhausen
20. This author travelled to meet her in Germany the very next day to assist in the quiet liquidation of Klockner's positions.
21. Petroleum Argus 14/12/1987.
22. Such a price difference would suggest that the physical market, as reflected by physical Brent or Dated Brent was balanced, while the forward Brent indicated a shortage of the 15-day deliverable, forward cargoes.
23. Petroleum Argus 22/02/1988.
24. Authors personal recollection.
25. Additional cargoes can be 'released' in several ways: Operational storage at the terminal can be brought to a minimum and cargo loadings can be moved from previous and subsequent months into the current month.
26. Stated in an e mail from Rod Gavshon to the author in 2022.
27. Goodman, Leah McGrath 2011, p. 146.

28. Upstairs refers to the offices of the users of futures exchanges where a company's traders work from.
29. For example: https://constantinecannon.com/practice/whistleblower/whistleblower-types/financial-investment-fraud/market-manipulation-trading-violations/
30. Goodman, Leah McGrath 2011, p. 147.
31. Now re-branded as Equinor: https://www.equinor.com/
32. Parra, Francisco 2004, p. 274.
33. Denmark also had a different take to the UK. The Danes prioritised the diversification of supply sources by focussing on wind power in addition to oil. They also acted to promote energy efficiency. On the oil side, they took participation oil into a State company, DONG, negotiated processing agreements with local refineries, risk managed to operation and sold products.
34. Carried Interest, which was considered but not pursued by the UK government at the time, refers to a methodology whereby the Norwegian State via Statoil did not pay any exploration costs until oil and gas were found to be economically viable. They would pay for and take up a pre-arranged equity share in the find only when it was found viable.
35. Noreng, Oystein 2022, p. 98.
36. Gordon, R and Stenvoll, T 2007, p. 28.
37. Of course, Norway did not already have a BP which made entry across the spectrum less controversial.
38. https://www.regjeringen.no/en/topics/energy/oil-and-gas/petroleum-price-board-and-the-norm-price/id661459/
39. https://www.equinor.com/energy/statfjord
40. Many 'names' graduated from Players Conoco nursery over the years.
41. Discussion with Goran Trapp 05/02/2024.
42. Horsnell, P and Mabro, R 1993, p. 98.
43. Actively traded markets such as Forward Brent or NYMEX WTI serve as such benchmarks.
44. The first recorded deal of this type is reported significantly ex post in Petroleum Argus of 02/05/1988 and was a sale of an August 1986 cargo of ANS priced by reference to July WTI. In the same edition, Petroleum Argus cite that in the 1st Quarter of 1988, 232 such deals had been reported.
45. A technique known as price fixation trading in agricultural products markets.
46. An example of a Morgan Stanley trade is where Angolan Cabinda crude oil would be purchased on a formula price set for the 5 days

around the date of loading but the cargo would be shipped to China at a fixed price with MS hedging the freight and price exposures.

47. The 'standard' Brent size has changed over time from 600 to 500 and then to 700,000 barrels.
48. For more on this see Bryce, C. in Imsirovic, A (ed) 2023, p. 52.
49. By design of the contract, the customer was required to either buy or sell additional volume from the bank.
50. A shorthand expression for a forward, non-standardised, bilateral market.
51. A term first encountered by the author at a lunch in 1989 when used by Justus Van Der Spuy, an expert in valuing and trading in oil storage products from his time at the South African sate company, SFF and at the trading company, Masefield.
52. A swap is essentially a bet on a price outcome over an agreed period of time and for an agreed volume. It is a perfect hedging mechanism for market participants who wanted to change their 'floating' price exposure (Dated Brent over five days of pricing, for example) into a fixed price or vice versa.

Bibliography

Barrera-Rey, F. and Seymour, A. (1996): Oxford Institute for Energy Studies (OIES) paper.
Duhon, T (2012): How the Trading Floor Really Works Bloomberg Press
Ford, J (2016): Depression, Oil Trading and A Mind At War With Itself Chipmunk Publishing
Goodman, Leah McGrath (2011): The Asylum William Morrow
Gordon, R and Stenvoll, T (2007): Statoil-A Study in Political Entrepreneurship James A Baker Institute for Public Policy of Rice University
Horsnell, P and Mabro, R: (1993) Oil Markets and Prices Oxford University Press
Imsirovic, A (ed 2023): Brent Crude Oil- Genesis and Development of the World's Most Important Oil Benchmark Palgrave McMillan.
Noreng, Oystein (2022): The Oil Business and the State Routledge.
Parra, Francisco (2010): Oil Politics A Modern History of Petroleum I.B. Tauris.

9

The White Guys in Tokyo

The White Guys in Tokyo

In the 1970s Asia, rivers of money were flowing through Tokyo. As Japan emerged as the world's second-largest economy and a major global manufactured goods exporter, its government began to loosen restrictions on capital flows.[1] This led to an increase in trading activity, attracting both domestic and international finance. Multinational corporations began setting up regional offices and sending expatriate personnel to manage operations in the booming Japanese market.

White men (yes, they were pretty much all men) became common in public places, especially bars and restaurants. '*The market would drink everywhere, especially in Roppongi. Popular bars there were Motown House, Gas Panic, Mogambo…*', says Michael Sarosiak, a foreign exchange (FOREX) broker in Tokyo at the time. '*In some of them, you would get kicked out if you did not have a drink in your hand! Lunches were had at the Imperial Hotel. You would stand at the bar, skull beers and order steak sandwiches. It was truly a banker/broker two-hour lunch-time hang out*', reminisces Michael with a dose of nostalgia.

'*There were way more establishments where one would meet*', adds Junichi Kasahara, who was a trainee operator at the commodity trader Phibro at the time. '*Ginza and Shibuya were also popular, especially Omotesandō avenue with trendy cafes and shops. The white guys would go to French restaurants. There were no Italian or other Western restaurants at the time*'. His personal favourite drinking hole was Copacabana in Akasaka.

Junichi joined Phibro in 1980 and was quickly assigned to the company's New York headquarters to gain hands-on experience in shipping and precious

A. Imsirovic and C. Bryce, *The Rivers of Money*,
https://doi.org/10.1007/978-3-031-91806-3_9

metals operations. Upon returning to Tokyo, he remembered Marcus Green joining Phibro from BP as the head of oil trading, which was, at that time, part of the company's '*Miscellaneous Commodities*' department.

But in the booming 1980s, Tokyo was becoming very expensive. *'The white guys' were renting expensive apartments and office space and prices were rocketing. So, they started thinking about moving elsewhere'*, said Kasahara-san. Phibro decided to split its Tokyo operations between Europe and Singapore. Marcus Green moved back to London, and Junichi ended up in Singapore[2] where Peter Rogers headed the company office. The move out of Tokyo was led by trading companies such as Marc Rich, Phibro, Gotco, Trans World Oil, and they were joined by oil Majors, banks and even Japanese trading houses.

Japanese trading houses, or Sogo Sosha, such as Mitsubishi, Mitsui, Sumitomo, Marubeni, Itochu, and others were at the forefront of the country's economic boom. They supplied the export-oriented and growing domestic industry with pretty much every commodity the resource-poor country needed. They were more than happy to see the foreign traders go—Sogo Sosha preferred to retain the 'special relations' with the Japanese end users tightly wrapped to themselves.

To an outsider, it was a strange relationship. For example, Japan Energy (JE) loved buying cheap but hard-to-process crude oil from the Neutral Zone[3] in the Middle East. They knew very well that Texaco was the main supplier of that particular kind of crude oil.[4] But Japan Energy would never talk to Texaco directly, even though they knew the management there very well. Instead, they kept on buying it through Mitsubishi, who negotiated with Texaco on their behalf and charged a fat commission for the privilege.

The exodus of commodity traders from Tokyo could have had different destinations. British Hong Kong was one obvious location. And why not Perth, the resource-rich capital of Western Australia? Both were located in the same time zone, and English as the official language. But from 1989, Singapore had something that always attracted the profit-seeking community—low tax. From January of that year, Singapore introduced the Approved Oil Trader (AOT) scheme – and it charged the approved oil trading companies only 10 per cent tax, a significant improvement from the usual (and not unreasonable) 27 per cent. Later, under the 'Global Trader Programme', the tax could be as low as 5 per cent.[5]

Singapore was already a refining hub with an active trading environment in physical petroleum products. The Majors such as Exxon, Shell, Mobil, and BP were already in Singapore with active physical trading teams. One of the earliest traders and refiners in the Lion City was Shell.

Shell and Singapore

The history of oil in Singapore is closely linked to that of Shell.

In 1891, when the Samuel brothers (Marcus Samuel and Samuel Samuel) arrived in Singapore, they were expanding their family business,[6] which had started as a trading company in London in the early nineteenth century. Initially, the business dealt with antiques, textiles, and decorative shells, hence the name 'Shell'.[7]

Marcus Samuel saw an opportunity in the fast-growing oil trade and began focussing on the transportation of cheap kerosene from the Caspian Sea and, later, crude oil from the Middle East to the Far East. Their strategy was to create an infrastructure for transporting and marketing oil in Asia, a growth region for energy.

They commissioned ships to carry oil in bulk, instead of barrels, which was far more efficient and reduced costs. In 1892, one such ocean-going tanker, the Murex, loaded in Europe discharged 2,500 tonnes of kerosene at Pulau Bukom (Singapore), the very first ever delivery of bulk petroleum to Asia.[8] A year later, eleven vessels were regularly shipping kerosene through the Suez Canal to Asia.

In essence, the arrival of the Samuel brothers in Singapore laid the groundwork for what would later become Shell Transport and Trading Company, founded by Marcus Samuel in 1897.[9] The company expanded by adding bulk storage and a tin factory for packaging the product for the retail market. Facing stiff competition from Standard Oil Company, Shell joined Royal Dutch and the Rothschilds (who supplied the bulk of the kerosene) to form the Asiatic Petroleum Company (APC) in 1903.[10] The success of APC led to the eventual merger of Shell Transport and Trading and Royal Dutch in 1907, forming Royal Dutch Shell [11] as a major competitor to Standard Oil and laid the foundation for Shell's future role in the oil industry.

In 1961, Shell built their first refinery in Pulau Bukom, Singapore.[12] Initially, the plant was primarily built to supply petroleum products to the Japanese market. However, the rest of the region was experiencing economic growth as well. In particular, the war in Vietnam was a spur to petroleum product exports from Singapore: '*Petroleum exports to South Vietnam quadrupled over 1965–1969 and in 1969 at S$394 million constituted 42 per cent of total petroleum exports from Singapore. This has made South Vietnam, second only to West Malaysia in the ranking of countries of export destination*'.[13] Following Shell's lead, three more refineries were built on the islands off mainland Singapore: Esso, Singapore Refining Company (SPC), and Mobil Oil.[14]

Another company, closely linked to Shell was to make a mark on the Singapore oil industry: Van Ommeren. Back in 1910, Henri Deterding, chairman of Royal Dutch Petroleum, the forerunner of Royal Dutch Shell, nagged his friend Philippus van Ommeren to enter into the tank storage business.[15] In 1980, the Van Ommeren company explored locations for a deep-sea terminal in Singapore.

The feasibility study of the storage facilities was being carried out by one Dr Fereidun Fesharaki,[16] who will come back into our Singapore story later. In the event, the island of Pulau Sebarok, south of Singapore, was identified as a convenient location. On 31 August 1983, Van Ommeren opened the first independent, deep-water oil terminal in Singapore. The initial capacity was 484,000 cubic metres; later, the terminal would be expanded to more than 1.2 million cubic metres.[17] Following the 1999 merger of Pakhoed and Van Ommeren, it would continue to operate in the city under the name of Vopak.[18]

An Accidental Trader

Following the end of the Vietnam War and especially after the second oil shock, demand for oil began to fall.[19] Between 1979 and 1983, oil consumption in Japan fell by 20 per cent, following the government's efforts to reduce dependence on the Middle East oil.[20] Suddenly, there was a massive overcapacity in refining in Asia, which hit Singapore particularly hard, forcing major oil companies to offer their facilities for third-party processing. Sudden excess refining capacity in key hubs such as Singapore supported the refineries' willingness to 'lease' a share of their plants to others for a fee.

Given Singapore's strategic position as a hub in Southeast Asia,[21] this was a perfect opportunity for trading companies to seek arbitrage opportunities by supplying oil to one of the underemployed Singapore refineries and taking petroleum products to various niche, consuming markets in the region. In so-called 'processing deals', long-term arrangements(usually for a year at a time) were made where the refiner received delivered crude oil, and in return for a fee, supplied an agreed volume (and quality) of petroleum products.

For a trading company, this provided flexibility (in trading lingo—optionality) both in sourcing crude oil from the least cost locations and choosing the highest revenue destinations for the final products. Processing did not just involve traders. National oil companies facing booming demand and long lead times in building new refineries such as Indonesia's Pertamina were keen processors in Singapore. Being one of the largest global ports and thus a huge bunkering hub[22] with an ambitious government looking to grow the service sector in the tiny island nation,[23] Singapore had all the ingredients for developing into a major global trading centre.

Excess supply of crude and breaking down of the Majors' control of the oil market led to a boom in spot trading from the beginning of the 1980s onwards. Some OPEC countries such as Iran almost exclusively used the spot market for their sales as they could achieve prices well above the official OPEC prices.[24]

After two years of working with Natomas Co. in San Francisco,[25] John Driscoll was sent to Asia to scout for space for a trading office there. In 1984, the market was challenging, and the main outlets for Natomas' Cinta and Arjuna crude production dried up. John had to set up an office in Asia and find alternative outlets for almost 200,000 barrels of company's Indonesian production.[26] Japanese oil traders, the Shoshas, did not want John in Tokyo. They could handle the imports on behalf of the Japanese end users themselves and buy the oil via their offices in Singapore. For young John Driscoll, a third-generation oilman from California,[27] Singapore offered not only the place from which to market the oil throughout Asia, but also the option to process it in one of the local refineries and find outlets for petroleum products. Exchange trades where John supplied Arjuna crude into Pertamina's new Cilicap, Java refinery for other export grades like Minas, Duri, and Arun Condensate generated additional trading opportunities and arbitrages. Ultimately Diamond Shamrock was attracted by the offshore oil production that Natomas had in Indonesia and bought the company.[28]

'*The most aggressive processor in Singapore was Shell, led by a young crude oil trader, Ian Taylor*', says John, mentioning a Shell trader who would later become the legendary CEO of Vitol. 'Ian *was pretty straightforward*', continued John, '*He explained to me that in a processing deal, we would get screwed anyway… but he would screw us less than the others*'.[29] So, John took him at his word and started a crude processing arrangement with Shell in 1984, which made Exxon very unhappy to see a U.S. oil producer working closely with a European refinery. Driscoll did a '*lot of processing*' with Mobil as well, especially after Ian Taylor left and joined Vitol in 1985. In the deal with Mobil, he inked a processing deal where he agreed to sell the petroleum products back a day later—they ended up with Mobil at a price, thus making the deal essentially a '*netback*' sale of crude oil. This elicited a call from Mobil's New York trading boss Brian Williams claiming this netback deal should be negotiated in the United States, not Singapore. As the internal politics played out, John continued to deal with Mobil Singapore—a firm he later joined in 1997.

Another early processor in Singapore was Kuo International, founded by the late Peter Fu Yun Siak, a timber and wax trader in the 1960s.[30] Kuo developed a close relationship with the Indonesian national oil company, Pertamina, and soon started selling the country's flagship crude oil Minas as well as some petroleum products from the country's refineries. In the early 1980s, the world was reeling from the second oil price shock, following the Iranian revolution; Japanese sogo shoshas were queuing up in front of Kuo offices: '*Begging for barrels at any price*'.[31]

Weimin Yuan was an accidental oil trader. Trained to be a historian, angry at his supervisor for not bothering to read his work, he left his PhD course in Modern East Asian history at Harvard in 1974 without a degree. His Master's Degree from Korea was plenty of education at the time anyway. Like many Harvard dropouts, Weimin Yuan ended up with a splendid and colourful career. He joined the Chase Manhattan Bank graduate training programme in New York and became a banker. China was opening up and banks were hiring young Asians from Singapore, Malaysia, Thailand, and other places, with good command of English and ideally, with a Western education. It helped that Weimin spoke fluent Mandarin, Cantonese, and his native Shanghai dialect as well as English, Japanese, and Korean. In the early days of physical commodity trading, being multilingual was more important than having a good university degree.

David Ban was a university friend of Weimin Yuan, and by coincidence, his uncle was Peter Fu Senior, the chairman of Kuo International, then a prominent regional trading company. Recognising Weimin's exceptional language skills, Kuo International soon enlisted him, and he joined the company in 1982 in Singapore. After successfully navigating the Indonesian oil market, Kuo International turned its focus to China, and it was Weimin Yuan who was tasked with spearheading this new venture.

Black Cat, White Cat

Peter Fu Yun Siak knew well that China was opening up. The Chinese oil industry was growing and had little idea of how the outside world market operated. Peter's trading sense was telling him he should get involved.

The Chinese reforms of Dec 1978[32] and Deng Xiaoping's ideas of market socialism quickly translated into the creation of Special Economic Zones.[33] In 1979, there were only two major energy bodies in the country: the Ministry of Petroleum and China National Chemicals Import & Export Company or Sinochem. In 1982, China National Offshore Oil Corporation

(CNOOC) took offshore interests from the Ministry of Petroleum, and in 1983, most of the country's refineries were sold to Sinopec.[34] But, for the world outside China, Sinochem was the main player and the face of the Chinese oil industry in the outside world. '*Sinochem imported and exported everything under the sun*', says Mr. Yuan. China badly needed to earn foreign exchange and one of its first oil exports was Daqing crude oil, soon followed by poor-quality Sheng Li oil from Shandong province.

Weimin was typical of his generation of traders: the business was built on relationships, and relationships thrived on communication. He modestly attributed his success to luck, noting that he was older than most of his peers, though still slightly younger than the senior management at Sinochem, who were in their mid-50s, lacked knowledge of international oil trading, and spoke no English. '*They saw me as their peer and spoke to me in their own language or dialect, often seeking my advice, "he explained." I spent a lot of time in Beijing, and they felt at ease in my company*'.

One morning in 1984, the General Manager (GM) of Sinochem Trading called him. Given the high cost of international calls at the time and the fact that Sinochem typically waited to be contacted, Weimin was taken aback. Mr. Lee, the Sinochem GM, had an unusual request: '*Could we fax them the Platts Oil Report every morning? They couldn't afford it themselves…*'.

Later, younger graduates at Sinochem came in and asked if Mr. Yuan was able to help them check calculations in a demurrage claim (they had no idea how to do it!). Of course, favours would be returned. So, the relationship developed.

Trading with China was a part of the deliberate government policy in Singapore. The '*Speak Mandarin Campaign*' was devised to encourage the Chinese Singaporean population to speak the official Mandarin Chinese (other Chinese dialects were commonly spoken in the island city). The campaign was launched back in 1979 by Prime Minister Lee Kuan Yew and organised by the Promote Mandarin Council, with annual events promoting the use of Mandarin.[35]

Kuo International was far from the only trading company processing crude oil in Singapore. Phibro, Marc Rich, and others were doing it as well, and products were sold all over the region. Stephen Chow was the go-to guy for processing at the Mobil refinery in the city-state. A young Taiwanese, educated at Columbia University and trained at the Mobil state of the art (at least for an oil Major) trading department in New York, Stephen quickly gained the confidence of the mainland Chinese as well as the local, Singaporean Chinese. '*The first time I went to Bei Jing, they realised we were not devils they thought we were and* vice versa. *We quickly 'clicked'*, Says Mr. Chow.[36]

Mobil kept most of the refinery capacity for its own system, but some spare capacity, perhaps 50,000 barrels a day, was offered to third parties at a fee. The main customers were Sinochem and Kuo, Malaysian Petronas, Taiwanese CPC, and Korean Yukong (later a part of SK Energy).[37] Petroleum products were exported to Taiwan and China, but after the Tiananmen Square massacre, Stephen had to put his business development hat on and look for buyers elsewhere such as the Indian subcontinent.

> '*The trading community was divided into roughly four groups,*' Says Stephen Chow. '*There were Westerners, usually working for the Majors and some trading houses. There were the Japanese, almost exclusively working for Sogo Shoshas such as Mitsui, Sumitomo and others. Then there were the local traders such as Kuo, Astra and Hin Leong. Lastly, there were the mainland Chinese – in the early days it was only Sinochem, headed by Mr. Chen, a stern, former People's Liberation Army officer. The mainland Chinese never went out to socialise - they could not afford it*'.

There was also a minority of Malay Chinese traders, who were not easily slotted into any group. One of them was Kho Hui Meng who joined John Driscoll at Natomas (later Diamond Shamrock) in 1986, after being poached from trading-averse Exxon. Mr. Kho was quite an asset to the company as he was a bright chemical engineer with '*deep understanding of petroleum product specifications*'. More importantly, Kho Hui Meng spoke fluent Bahasa as he was a Chinese who grew up in Malaysia, where the Malay form of the language was spoken.[38]

John Driscoll and Kho Hui Meng would go to Jakarta every Tuesday for 'upstream' meetings in the Pertamina offices with all the Indonesian oil and gas producers such as Caltex (a joint venture between Chevron and Texaco), Mobil, Total, and others. However, the participants of the meeting had little knowledge that Kho and John were given mandates by the new owners, Diamond Shamrock, to market, process, and even trade their Indonesian oil (and petroleum products processed from it) since the company did not need it. 'Hui Meng was a trading dynamo' said Driscoll, 'his instincts and knowledge were ahead of the curve'.

Getting all the loading schedules and inventory reports was a major advantage in trading the Indonesian barrels, and they were getting them from the very source, from the unsuspecting producers. Kho Hui Meng would not tell anyone he was fluent in Bahasa, and he could get a lot of information from the informal comments the locals would pass on between them, not suspecting the foreigners to understand them. As a major treat when visiting the Pertamina busy headquarters, the duo was entitled to use the 'executive' lift that did not stop at every floor, but went straight up to the fifth, where the foreign market offices were housed.

Kho Hui Meng was at Diamond Shamrock only for a year, but having excelled both in products and crude trading, moved to Vitol where he had a long prosperous career, eventually earning a Malay royal title 'Dato' (Sir)[39] and becoming the President & CEO of Vitol Asia.[40]

Another Chinese immigrant to Singapore, Lim Oon Kuin, known to most as OK Lim, began with just a fishing boat that he used to supply diesel fuel to other small boats. This business grew into a Singapore-based trading company, Hin Leong. More at ease speaking his native Hokkien than English or Mandarin, he was one of the first traders from outside China to start doing business with the mainland, sending fuel to southern Chinese provinces in the early 1980s.[41]

Hin Leong grew along with the port of Singapore and the increasing demand for diesel and fuel oil, which were the main products of his trade. As China's economy grew over the following decades, more ships stopped in Singapore to refuel, and Hin Leong became a major player in the industry, owning an oil terminal and tanks that could hold millions of barrels of oil. OK Lim was sourcing the fuel in the local Singapore refineries and 'blending' it.[42] At first, OK Lim had no tanks and blending was done under dubious conditions, on ships. Hin Leong was always challenging to deal with, but way too important to ignore.[43]

OK Lim was unpopular with the Majors, especially with their finance departments because he would show up with bags of cash to pay for the fuel.[44] But, he was massively popular with the Singaporean oil folks, probably for the same reason.

Hin Leong's became so dominant in the island state's diesel and fuel oil market that anyone who wanted to start a ship fuel business in Singapore: '*...should get an "OK" from Mr. Lim*'.[45] In spite of his big and bold trading strategies, often involving pricing of diesel and fuel oil at the market settlement, he was known as a '*humble businessman who stayed true to his roots*'.[46] Weimin remembers Mr. Lim as: '*Very hard working and smart*'.

In the late 1990s, Hin Leong became a Singapore institution not only as one of the biggest bunkering suppliers in one of the busiest ports on the planet, but also as a key product supplier in Southeast Asia and countries such as Indonesia and Myanmar. Much later, OK Lim's gambling instincts prevailed, leading to his company's demise through speculative losses and fraud, following the price collapse caused by the Covid-19 pandemic.[47]

By then, Singapore grew into the biggest oil trading hub in Asia and one of the biggest and most important trading centres on the planet.

Hardship Posting? Can Lah!

Junichi Kasahara moved to Phibro Singapore on a full-time basis in 1987. He worked for Peter Rogers, an ex-Shell employee who ran the shop '*with a very colonial British style, very plumb in mouth*'.[48] Another junior trader/operator was Ling Kok Ming, who later went onto Texaco and eventually became a part owner of Star Supply brokerage.

It was not unusual for a trader to end up in the business of broking. Peter Rogers also ended up looking after fuel oil at PVM[49] for a while, before setting up his 'talent search' business on the island. PVM Singapore (and elsewhere) was home to some legendary figures in broking: Aron Loh (later the Singapore office head); Scott Brown,[50] who left New York to spend a long broking career in many corners of the world; Paul Clausen, perhaps the busiest Dubai broker in the early 2000s; and Lawrence Ho, a local Singaporean who would join Junichi Kasahara in a formidable trading team at Phibro in the 1990s.

Early oil trading was about long chats with customers, looking for common interests, asking for indications, and trying to find the ones that made commercial sense. '*You would get an offer for a cargo of Arab Light from a major at, say $35 a barrel. This is before futures markets, CNN, Bloomberg and Reuters, and prices would not change very much. You would ask for this price indication (it was not a firm offer, but firm enough to work with it), call the New York office for their opinion and approval and the next morning, if it came through, you would trade. The fixed price idea was just what 'you and me' believed to be the value. The Majors kept their oil supplies roughly 90 per cent on long-term deals and about 10 per cent on spot basis. They would buy and sell oil, depending on refinery runs. This also depended on seasonality and products demand, so they would optimise the crude oils they wanted to process. Indonesian (Minas, Duri) and Malaysian (Arjuna, Tapis, Labuan) all traded fixed price. Asian Petroleum Price Index (APPI) came in later, following the switch from fixed to formula or floating prices. Then Brent and Dubai became reference prices. Malaysian Tapis became a reference for lighter grades in the region*', explains Kasahara-san. He should know, as his trading prowess eventually made him the head of the Phibro office in Singapore in the 1990s.

By 1990, Singapore had become the central hub for crude trading. The country's favourable fiscal regime and the government's generally positive stance on trading were likely the most significant factors. History, geography, and a bustling port also played important roles. However, the '*soft power*' that most effectively attracted the trading community could perhaps be best described by the wives of traders (who, at the time, were still predominantly men). Singapore was a clean, safe city with excellent international schools, luxurious, marble-clad accommodations in newly built condominiums, complete with gyms and swimming pools. Its bars and restaurants, which mirrored those of any major Western city, also contributed significantly to making Singapore an attractive place to live and work.[51]

The entire family enjoyed the comforts of top-tier international schools—British, American, German, French, Canadian, and just about any other global institution one could wish for. Leisurely lunches could be spent in the relaxed atmosphere of Holland Village or the busier vibes of Orchard Road. A great meal could be found at one of the hawker stalls in places like Newton Circus Market, where 'chili stingray' was a popular favourite. Seafood dinners featuring pepper and chili crab, along with other fresh seafood delicacies on the East Coast, were always a treat.

Saturdays typically had a slow, relaxing pace, spent by the condominium's swimming pool or at one of the expatriate retreats like the British, American, Cricket, or Tanglin clubs. The first two were family-friendly affairs, while the latter required smart attire, where children were expected to be 'seen but not heard'. The week would usually close with a traditional free-flow Sunday lunch at one of the luxury hotels like Shangri-La, Fullerton, Pan Pacific, or Ritz-Carlton, followed by a hangover and an afternoon nap to recover for the coming week.

'*I remember oil traders gathered at Da Paulo, Italian restaurant on Club Street almost every Friday, especially after the 1st generation heavy mobile phones were introduced. We were all trading from the restaurant on Friday afternoons over endless procession of bottles of white wine*', Reminisces Junichi Kasahara.

Among the Asian traders, karaoke was a big thing. Probably because the local, Singaporean version of karaoke was a lot more a party-like affair. But others quickly caught up on the gig when they learned that karaoke bars sometimes offered a lot more than just singing. The bars would suddenly spring to life in the evening around Orchard Road, but also around some less familiar places. Such entertainment was expensive, and that was where having a good broker came in handy. Such friendly partners in business would make sure that alcohol and food were well supplied and they were always discrete about any excess, paying the bill whatever was being charged on the tab.

Not all the traders surrendered to alcohol and parties after hours. Weimin Yuan, the 'accidental trader', did not drink, smoke, or party. But he liked tennis. Fortunately, there were plenty of tennis courts on offer in condominiums, clubs, and on the East Coast of Singapore. To keep up with his passion, he organised the Singapore Oil Traders Tennis Association, a group of like-minded traders who would plan tournaments and play singles and doubles over lunch breaks and in the evening. The 'healthy lot' included the likes of John Lloyd Davies who was heading the trading office of Texaco Singapore, Len Williamson of BP, Paul Ying of Elf, Stephen Chow and George Hawthorn from Mobil, John Driscoll from Maxus Energy (the successor to Diamond Shamrock), Ren Xinzi from Sinochem, Kenny Lim (OK Lim's younger brother) from Hin Leong Trading and many others.[52]

China Awakens

By the early 1990s, Southern China was opening up. Places like Port of Amoy (sometimes called Port of Xiamen) along the Southern coast all started importing diesel and gasoline. Kuo International Trading Company was selling 73 RON[53] gasoline to small traders (tank owners) there. '*The cheaper, the better', says Mr. Weiming.*[54] *Their storage was very limited and they stored all the gasoline in the same tank, regardless of quality!*' Kuo would source the cheapest, lowest quality gasoline from their good friends in Indonesian Pertamina and ship it on tiny 5,000-tonne vessels to Amoy. '*Roads were muddy and in poor state. It took five or six hours to cover the distance you now do in less than an hour. Meeting customers was a nightmare. There were no rules and pollution was everywhere*', remembers Mr. Weiming.

The boom was temporarily interrupted by the Tiananmen Square events in 1989, but from the trading and profit point of view, it was '*the best time to get in*'.[55]

Other traders were also enjoying the boom and Junichi Kasahara also brought to Phibro new people such as Lawrence Ho from PVM and Kuroda-san[56] from Cosmo. Phibro metals trading closed in Singapore, only for oil to survive. It was a small shop, but made good money. Phibro traded naphtha, kerosine/ jet fuel, fuel oil, gas oil, low sulphur waxy residue (from waxy Indonesian oil), and crude oil. Saudi crude was popular with Japanese refineries. Dubai trading was very active. Phibro had a long-term Dubai contract, started by Marcus Green during his Tokyo days. They were selling Dubai on a long-term basis into Taiwan.

Japanese traders, Sogo Shoshas, were slow to enter the world of oil trading, outside the 'back-to-back' supply to the local refineries. Itochu was the first to start taking physical positions around 1985. The main Itochu trader was Nasu-san. Kanematsu (KG) probably came into Brent forwards trading in and around 1986. The key trader was Kibe-san. Then, an avalanche of companies followed into the market: Cosmo, Nippon Oil, Idemitsu,

Showa Shell, Kashima, Tonen General, Nippon Mining, Mitsubishi Oil, and others.[57]

Phibro's direct Dubai crude oil contract with the ruler of Dubai (the contract was handled by Peter Abenz from Phibro Zug office in Switzerland) was highly praised given the information content such a contract entailed,[58] and was referred to as a '*God's cargo*'. Dubai traded at fixed prices and in 1987/88, few brokers were working in the crude oil physical market in Asia. Deals were mainly done directly with refineries in Korea, Japan, Sri Lanka, China, India, and with the Majors in Singapore.

> '*After 1988, I believe Phibro was the company that introduced Dubai partials and we were trading 60 Dubai cargoes every month. We had Malcolm Macavity in Greenwich, Connecticut; At first, the Swiss office was handling the Dubai contract and operations from Zug, and Singapore was actively involved in trading it. Then I took it over since I started to talk to Jim O'Connell, who was the point of contract with the Ruler of Dubai. Conoco was the Dubai terminal operator but sometimes we worked together especially for VLCC loading operations. Other companies that joined the Dubai partials market were the Japanese trading houses, Japanese and Korean refiners, oil Majors and banks: J. Aron and Morgan Stanley*'.[59]

It was not just the Asian companies that traded in Dubai. European companies such as Repsol had roughly two equity cargoes they produced each month (their upstream company had five per cent of the production). They actively traded on a forward basis, although not in big volume—perhaps, no more than twice their production.[60] The company never processed Dubai in its own refining system and never used it to hedge its own crude oil purchases. Dubai seldom came to Europe unless the Brent/Dubai spread was very wide, making the grade very cheap there, according to Repsol's trader at the time, Lourdes Rodriguez.

'*Jim O'Connell sold the ruler's share. Shell trader Mike Muller was very active, but he was a pain to deal with, insisting on using only their [Shell] GT&Cs. The Japanese, Morgan Stanley and J. Aron were also very active. The main Dubai brokers were PVM and Amerex*',

Other European traders tried their luck in the Dubai forward market, but they soon found out that it was a rather specialised market and a bit of a club. Texaco Trading was one of those companies, but quickly gave it up, realising they were out of depth in this market.[61]

Physical trading shifted not only from Japan to China, but also to India, Korea, Philippines, and Thailand. Hin Leong started using very large crude carriers (VLCCs)[62] to move gas oil to Asia, with Singapore serving as the bulk-breaking location.[63]

In 1989, Argus introduced the first formula prices for gas oil. By 1991, there was an equal number of fixed price deals, and by the mid-1990s, there were roughly twice as many formula deals.[64]

In highly regulated Asian markets with dominant government control in many countries, some very unusual pricing methods developed. The Indonesian Crude Pricing (ICP) was a good example of this. It used a 52-week moving average of prices of a basket of crude oils and it was so complicated that was impossible to hedge. Paul Horsnell, an astute market observer, described it as: '*lacking any internal logic*'.[65] A veteran of derivatives trading at Morgan Stanley, Dennis Kongsiri, who worked alongside Gary King (they both reported to Jim Moonier) said: '*We decided to start trading ICP Minas… It did not go so well!*'.[66]

Half of this ICP or 'official price' was based on the Asian Petroleum Price Index (APPI), which was produced by 'Seapac Services' in Hong Kong.[67] Astonishingly, this was a trading and marketing company, but it did not worry the Indonesian government that there may be a conflict of interest! It seems that the franchise for this pricing service (which was paid for) was acquired by Perta Oil Marketing Limited based in Jakarta, Indonesia.[68] The managing director of both companies was Roger Osborne, a graduate of the Colorado School of Mines.[69] But, it seems that there were other partners in the company, including a former governor of California Pat Brown, a former U.S. Lieutenant General George Benson and Manuel Rojas, an actor.[70]

The APPI price was published twice a week and was calculated on the basis of market assessments made by a panel of market participants, who had to pay for the 'membership' on the panel. It mainly consisted of traders, oil Majors, and refiners. The calculation was a simple average of the submitted price assessments by the panellists, after removing the 'outliers', or prices outside one standard deviation from the mean.[71]The problem with the APPI price was simple: Everyone on the panel wanted low prices: '*The only company that wanted higher prices would be Pertamina, and they only had one vote!*' says John Driscoll: '*Traders, refiners and brokers would probably talk to each other, submitting buying ideas that were favourable to them, but the one company/one vote structure favoured them. One of the key APPI price assessments was for Malaysian Tapis which was linked to the price of many regional Asian crudes. One enterprising trader was so skilled in influencing the APPI assessment he was nicknamed 'Captain Tapis'.*

Needless to say, this was a highly imperfect arrangement, but it lasted for decades. Eventually, it was replaced with Platts Dated Brent, a pricing concept that was perhaps fairer, but equally unsuitable for the Asia–Pacific crude oil market.[72]

Another result of the move to formula-based pricing was that the Dubai swaps market developed as a means of converting floating to fixed and vice versa. '*I believe then Morgan Stanley introduced Dubai paper trading to the market, if I remember correctly*', says Phibro's Singapore boss of many years, Junichi Kasahara. Since most of the Asian pricing was based on average price quotations during the month of loading, Dubai swaps also started trading on a monthly basis (for example, average January, February, and so on). The explosive growth of WTI and Brent futures markets also helped the price discovery for these derivative instruments.[73]

Notes

1. https://www.bis.org/publ/bppdf/bispap15h.pdf
2. Junichi Kasahara first went to Singapore temporarily, substituting for an operator who was doing his obligatory military service. Later, the Tokyo office was closed and he moved to Singapore on a permanent basis. From discussions with Kasahara-san on 7/6/24 and subsequent communications.
3. Disputed territory between S. Arabia and Kuwait.
4. It was Ratio crude.
5. For details, see: https://singapore-academy.org/index.php/en/education/research-consulting/singapore-companies/item/233-singapore-s-global-trader-scheme
6. Horsnell P. (1997), p. 136.
7. https://www.shell.com/who-we-are/our-history/our-brand-history.html
8. https://www.nlb.gov.sg/main/article-detail?cmsuuid=93a29125-66aa-46c6-8ca3-9b9b0f65ab8d
9. https://www.willesdenjewishcemetery.org.uk/life-stories-listing/marcus-samuel
10. https://www.shell.com.cn/en_cn/about-us/who-we-are/shell-history-in-china/_jcr_content/par/textimage.stream/1468531404098/71ba96f4fb7485cc77b7c388e7b015b5f330c699a976f6a99b5e57fac91cb601/shell-story2004.pdf
11. https://www.shell.com/who-we-are/our-history/our-brand-history.html
12. https://www.nlb.gov.sg/main/article-detail?cmsuuid=37c6a7dd-c7de-4378-819e-e2407839f8d5#:~:text=Article&text=Singapore's%20oil%20refining%20industry%20started,awarded%20by%20the%20Singapore%20government.

13. https://www.nlb.gov.sg/main/Book-Detail-Page?cmsUuID=638f7f12-1658-4ca6-8105-5ed4a8179c44
14. https://www.nlb.gov.sg/main/article-detail?cmsuuid=ad9dd6c3-782d-474c-a632-92d57ba9e1e3#:~:text=Between%20the%20late%201960s%20and,Mobil%20Oil%20on%20Pulau%20Pesek.
15. https://www.vopak.com/who-we-are/our-history?language_content_entity=en
16. According to Dr Fesharaki.
17. Ibid.
18. https://www.vopak.com/
19. For details, see: https://www.oxfordenergy.org/wpcms/wp-content/uploads/2018/02/A-Review-of-the-Evolution-of-the-Japanese-Oil-Industry-Oil-Policy-and-its-Relationship-with-the-Middle-East-WPM-76.pdf
20. For policy details, see: https://www.jstor.org/stable/45316064
21. https://www.trade.gov/energy-resource-guide-singapore-oil-and-gas#:~:text=The%20country%20has%20a%20strategic,day%20(bbl%2Fd).
22. Bunkering is a term for fuelling ships, normally (at the time) with cheap, low quality fuel oil.
23. https://www.sg101.gov.sg/economy/growing-our-economy/1986/
24. 'While officially hostile to the spot markets, some OPEC members effectively facilitated its creation. In a remarkably short time, the share of spot trades rocketed, from less than five percent, prior to January 1979, to about a quarter, by November of the very same year.' (See Imsirovic (2021), page 127.
25. Natomas was soon to be taken over by another American company Diamond Shamrock. See: https://www.upi.com/Archives/1983/05/31/Diamond-Shamrock-and-Natomas-to-merge/2706423201600/
26. https://www.upi.com/Archives/1982/08/30/Natomas-Co-said-Monday-it-has-begun-operating-the/2377399528000/
27. Also, a third generation Stamford graduate. Just like his father and grandfather.
28. https://www.upi.com/Archives/1983/05/31/Diamond-Shamrock-and-Natomas-to-merge/2706423201600/
29. Interview with John Driscoll on 08/09/24.
30. https://www.forbes.com/profile/peter-fu-chong-cheng/
31. From the interviews with Weimin Yuan on 3/9 and 4/9, 2024 and subsequent correspondence.

32. The reforms briefly went into stagnation after the 1989 Tiananmen Square protests and massacre, but were revived after Deng Xiaoping's southern tour in 1992. See: https://www.scmp.com/news/china/politics/article/2173020/inside-story-propaganda-fightback-deng-xiaopings-market-reforms
33. "*It doesn't matter whether a cat is black or white, as long as it catches mice*." This is taken to mean that as long as the economy works, it is a good economy. For a great essay on the topic, see: https://www.chinadaily.com.cn/a/201808/02/WS5b728ae4a310add14f385b4a.html
34. Horsnell (1997), page 42.
35. https://www.languagecouncils.sg/mandarin/en
36. Interview with Mr. Chow on 09/09/2024.
37. https://www.upi.com/Archives/1987/01/13/Yukong-Limited-South-Koreas-second-largest-oil-company-has/1774537512400/
38. A common language in Malaysia and Indonesia. See https://asiasociety.org/education/bahasa-indonesian
39. Conferred the title "Dato" by the Sultan of Pahang, Malaysia on His Royal Highness' 74th birthday. https://www.smu.edu.sg/about/board-trustees/dato-kho-hui-meng
40. https://theorg.com/org/singapore-management-university/org-chart/kho-hui-meng
41. https://www.livemint.com/companies/news/how-an-epic-gamble-exposed-the-rot-inside-oil-empire-of-hin-leong-11587472769925.html
42. Blending is simply mixing the product to achieve an acceptable (usually lowest acceptable) quality.
43. Personal experience of one of your authors who was dealing with Hin Leong.
44. The source preferred to stay anonymous.
45. https://www.straitstimes.com/business/companies-markets/how-an-epic-gamble-exposed-the-rot-inside-o-k-lims-hin-leong-oil-trading
46. Ibid.
47. https://www.spglobal.com/commodityinsights/en/market-insights/blogs/oil/092420-after-hin-leong-collapse-of-a-singaporean-oil-prodigy
48. Interview with Paul Clausen, 31/10/24 and subsequent correspondence.
49. PVM comes from Pasquale Vincent MAZZARULLI, a founding member and a former Director of the company. https://find-and-update.company-information.service.gov.uk/officers/81e8BMGw8PB6vlZP_MFWqcHIYhs/appointments

50. In a typical 'no filter' comment about Peter Rogers, Scott Brown says: 'He was a tiny ineffective employee who I almost fired in his first month of work for claiming new eyeglasses on his expense report! The pink-eyed rat spent most of his time in the British Club!' Correspondence with Scotty Brown on 31/10/24.
51. In 2002, your author was interviewed by the Financial Times about the attractiveness of Singapore as an oil trading hub. My comment was: '*You should really talk to my wife.*' Unfortunately, the journalist did not get it.
52. Rough recollection of Weimin Yuan.
53. RON (Research Octane Number), numbers indicate the level of pressure generated during fuel combustion within a vehicle's engine. Also, serves as an indicator of fuel stability.
54. From the interview with Weimin Yuan on 3rd and 4th September 2024.
55. Ibid.
56. Kuroda san will later end up in Morgan Stanley.
57. Junichi Kasahara interview, 7/6/24.
58. Being first in the chain entails direct contacts with the producer.
59. Junichi Kasahara interview, 7/6/24.
60. From an interview with Lourdes Rodrigues, a trader at the time and later the head of trading of Repsol. Interview was on 12/06/24.
61. At the time, one of the authors traded for Texaco, focusing largely on the North Sea and Brent. Having successfully traded forward Brent, the team decided to try their luck trading forward Dubai. In the summer of 1994, they sold a forward or cash Dubai spread versus Brent (they bought Brent and sold forward Dubai). A couple of weeks later, one of the Dubai players called the author and asked him when they were going to buy back their Dubai short! Texaco eventually covered that short, lost some money and did not return to the Dubai market for almost a decade.
62. VLCCs on average carry 2 million barrels crude oil. On per barrel basis, they are far cheaper than smaller vessels.
63. Large cargoes had to be broken up into smaller ones to fit into numerous ports with shipping restrictions throughout Asia.
64. Junichi Kasahara interview, 7/6/24.
65. See Horsnell P. (1997), page 269.
66. From the interview with Dennis Kongsiri on 12 November 2024.
67. Ibid, page 396.
68. There is very little information about the company, other than: https://abc-gcc.net/companies/All/398051

69. https://www.linkedin.com/in/roger-osborne-777a4561/?originalSubdomain=hk
70. According to John Driscoll, interviewed on 08/09/24.
71. See Horsnell P. (1997), page 369.
72. S&P Platts PRA did an excellent job marketing Dated Brent as an Asian sweet benchmark. Your author always argued that it made no sense for a North West European benchmark to set prices for crude oil in Asia. What is more, it sent wrong signals – when Brent basket crudes moved to Asia and made the Asian market weaker, the benchmark would actually increase in price, making regional grades of oil even more uncompetitive relative to Brent!
73. The First Gulf war (2 Aug 1990 – 28 Feb 1991) was a major catalyst for this.

Bibliography

Horsnell, P. (1997): 'Oil in Asia', OIES, Oxford University Press 1997.

Imsirovic A. (2014): 'Oil Markets in Transition and the Dubai Crude Oil Benchmark', OIES, https://www.oxfordenergy.org/wpcms/wp-content/uploads/2014/10/Oil-Markets-in-Transition and the-Dubai-Crude-Oil-Benchmark.pdf

Imsirovic A. (2021): 'Trading and Price Discovery for Crude oils', Palgrave.

Imsirovic A. (2024): 'International Oil Markets in the Age of Climate Change', Palgrave.

10

China is Back

Abstract This chapter concerns with the resurgence of China's influence in the global oil markets, particularly through its evolving trading strategies and structural reforms. It traces the rise of key players in Singapore's oil brokerage industry, detailing how early pioneers like Shogun and PVM shaped the market. The narrative follows the expansion of China's oil companies—Sinopec, CNPC, and CNOOC—and their transition from passive price-takers to dominant price-makers, ultimately redefining benchmark pricing in Asia. The chapter also examines the role of Singapore as a crucial trading hub, the emergence of paper markets, and the competitive dynamics between Western traders and their Chinese counterparts. Through historical accounts and industry insights, this chapter highlights the transformation of China's oil trade from a controlled, state-driven system to a sophisticated, market-driven force with global implications.

Singapore Brokers

Probably, the first oil broker in Singapore was Shogun, owned and run by an Irishman, Patrick McKiernan around 1988. Originally, Patrick was the head of Platts, a price reporting agency (PRA), based in Tong building on Orchard Road, Singapore's main street, conveniently close to pretty Emerald Hill with great bars and cafés. At Shogun, Patrick and his lieutenant Derek Potter were broking only products.[1] Patrick later sold his shares in the brokerage to Geoffrey Collier, who later became infamous as the first person to be convicted of insider trading at Morgan Grenfell, following the 1986 Financial

A. Imsirovic and C. Bryce, *The Rivers of Money*,
https://doi.org/10.1007/978-3-031-91806-3_10

Services Act.[2] Around 1993, PVM bought Shogun, with Derek as the head of products in the new, bigger company.

It was 1988 and Scott Brown left Platt's and joined a small, boutique oil trader called Petraco in New York. That year, Inga Srenger, the head of Petraco, set up a new, plush N. York office in the General Motors building with a $1 million credit line for trading. She hired Scott Brown with instructions that he made lots of money, and she promptly left for the Milan HQ. Sadly, the credit line did not last long and Scotty blew a million bucks speculating in oil futures contracts on NYMEX.

Fortunately for Scott, a friend at an oil brokerage house, Fearnoil in New York, needed some help. Along with most of the oil industry, they were closing their Tokyo office and hoped to set up a shop in Singapore. Scott Brown promptly went to the Japanese capital, closed the office, and together with the office furniture, shipped himself to Singapore where he started broking crude oil. He was probably the first broker to do so in the city-state.

In 1991, Scott Brown was hired by David Hufton of PVM London to set up a shop for PVM in Singapore. So, he left Fearnoil to start PVM Eastern Services with a small office in a Chinese shophouse on Amoy Street, conveniently located between the Singapore business district and popular bars and restaurants on Boat Key.

Scott's big break came at the start of the First Gulf War in 1991, with a Chinese trading house, Sinochem. As the war started, he thought that was a great opportunity for a big player to go long and make money. So, he picked up the phone and called the President of Sinochem, Mr. Jiang Yun Long in Beijing. He explained that the market was going up and it was a good idea to buy some oil. The President obliged and with Scott Brown's help, bought five full cargoes of forward Brent. Mr. Jiang Yun Long and Sinochem made lots of money. At $5,000 of brokerage commission per each Brent cargo,[3] so did Scott and PVM.[4] With subsequent hires of Aron Loh and then Paul Clausen, PVM-Shogun became the most dominant oil brokerage in Singapore.

Lawrence Ho considered himself very lucky. He joined Fernoil just before the First Gulf War. It was a fortunate timing and business quickly took off: '*It was pretty crazy in those days,*' says Lawrence. Staple business was Dubai partials, which would either be accumulated to a full cargo (of 500,000 barrels) between two parties, or the trades would be 'booked out' (financially settled) between the parties by the end of the month.

Lawrence Ho (often called LoHo and sometimes LoLo by his friends) became Junichi Kasahara's favourite broker. When the first opening came at Phibro, Kasahara-san offered Lawrence an opportunity to trade with him and he readily took it.

Around that time, Marco Dunand and Daniel Jaeggi joined Phibro[5] in London and the two teams developed a good and friendly relationship.[6] Aside from Dubai, Lawrence and Junichi traded Oman crude, which at the time, transacted either on a basis of the official price, called The Ministry of Energy and Minerals or MOG price, or on a Dubai-related basis, which is how refineries preferred to buy it. To convert one price to another, an MOG/Dubai swap market developed where refiners would hedge their MOG price risk, while traders would offer liquidity by speculating on the eventual Omani government decision regarding the retroactive Oman price.

Paul Clausen came to Singapore from Perth, Western Australia, to work with a small Aussie company financing property deals. The company went bankrupt and he was left destitute in the Lion City with no money even for a return ticket. According to Paul: '*The manner of doing business at the time was informal and appears rather amateurish today, if not outright funny*'.

A good example is the way Paul Clauson got a job with PVM, following an interview with Peter Rogers: '*They operated out of a little shop house on Club Street… That would have been 1993–94. My employment interview was crazy*', says Paul Clauson. '*Peter Rogers sat me down and ranted for about 25 minutes flat, about how horrible the brokers he had were and how terrible the market was, how no one knew how to make money. They were all lazy he said, and on and on in that fashion… Then, he finally looked at me and said—now Paul, if you think you can do a better job than any of those arseholes, the job is yours. At this point the only thing I had said was my name and it was nice to meet him. His first offer was S$3k a month and 10 percent commission… and I walked out of there with 6k and 20 percent commission for the first two months, and if I made it to month 3, it would go to 9k per month plus 30% commission… The rest is history*'.[7]

Paul started working long hours, covering some of the traders who preferred quieter, evening shifts such as Alf Salti, a market-maker in fuel oil swaps at Morgan Stanley. Alf was doing big volumes and appreciated having Paul staying behind the office late in the evenings to broker deals for him. Soon, Paul became well-received by Junichi and Lawrence and became one of the key brokers in the forward Dubai market.

Amerex, one of the pioneers of the Dubai forward market was in Singapore too, and oil was handled by Phil Jump. United Brokers briefly had an office with oil handled by David Scott, who later moved to Coastal, and then to Glencore.[8] There, David spent most of his time working with Simon Waters, covering Glencore's customers in China and elsewhere.[9] He tragically died just before the Glencore initial public offering in 2011, which would have made him very rich.[10] So, it was a double tragedy.

Other brokers were Tullet, Prebon, and ICAP[11]—all three were money brokers that became involved in oil after the Forex trading liquidity dried up, following the Asian Financial crisis in 1997.[12] Much later, in 2014, all of the mentioned brokerage firms would end up under one roof and form the world's largest commodity broker, the TP ICAP Group.[13]

'*At the crude desk, the biggest prize was cash Dubai—due to size [the commission was charged on per barrel basis]*', says Paul Clausen, '*We were always working out who had the physical cargoes and where they were going. Then you knew who needed to trade swaps. This helped us to decide who to call. The most curious thing was observing twenty Dubai players always doing the same thing, pushing each other around in the marketplace, while staying civil at the end of it all!*'

What did soothe the pain of trading were long lunches. The favourite hangout continued to be the Italian restaurant, Da Paolo on Club Street. This culinary heaven in Singapore is a storied institution. [14] Suffice it to say that a lot of oil broking profits were spent there. Particularly frequent customers were the Phibro guys, but Glencore traders Simon Waters and David Scott often visited the restaurant too. PVM's Paul Clausen did his best deals there and his colleague Scott Brown started calling him 'Paolo'. '*He would have a bit of fun asking if I was going out to lunch there again by saying silly stuff like Paolo, Paolo, "de Paolo," Paolo*?' Says Clausen.

Singapore Paper

With almost all the physical crude oil contracts moving to 'floating' or formula pricing, using one of the price reporting agencies (PRAs), the paper markets seriously took off. This was supported by the Singapore government. In the early 1990s, finance was by far the fastest-growing sector of the economy.[15] The government restructured the old Gold Exchange of Singapore into a new Singapore Monetary Exchange (SIMEX), strengthened by the 1987 legal framework in the form of the Futures Trading Act.

SIMEX launched two oil contracts: A high sulphur fuel oil (HSFO) contract in 1989 and a Dubai futures contract a year later. The former lasted for a while, while the latter never really took off. One of the reasons was the volatility of the First Gulf War which focussed traders' attention on the already existing and liquid contracts on NYMEX and the IPE. The Dubai contract was still traded from London, and Asian national oil companies (NOCs) had very little need to hedge their price risk—the cost was generally passed on to the consumer. Tax regimes in Asia were also retrospective and impossible to hedge using derivatives contracts.[16] Finally, Singapore was a cargo market with a large number of different specifications traded across the continent, making a standardised contract difficult.

However, the lack of transparency and over-the-counter (OTC) nature of trading suited many traders who enjoyed good margins and low taxes in the city. One such informal and unregulated market was the 'open spec naphtha' forward market which we have previously encountered.

In the mid-1980s, Japanese demand for naphtha picked up, prompting increased imports from Singapore, but also from other parts of the world. This coincided with greater price volatility and the increasing willingness of Japanese Shoshas to speculate on oil prices.[17] Over the next decade, a forward market for physical naphtha from various sources such as the Middle East, Algeria, and even Europe, and delivered into Japan (C&F Japan) developed. It worked along the lines of a Brent forward market, where chains would develop and unwanted cargoes resulted in 'five o'clocking'.[18] The market especially grew in popularity in the mid-90s when increased spread trading and growing involvement of the Korean players added to the liquidity.

Swap markets also developed around Indonesian Minas and Malaysian Tapis crude pricing.[19] 'Paper oil markets' in Asia were coming of age and they were more varied and complex than their equivalents in the Atlantic basin. This complexity, lack of sophistication of the state-owned actors, and growing volatility started to attract an increasing eco-system of players.

Fereidun Fesharaki was a young academic with a PhD from Surrey University in the United Kingdom, a home to some of the leading energy economists of the time.[20] Due to circumstances, instead of a promising career as an energy economist in the government of the Shah of Iran, Fereidun found himself in self-imposed exile in Honolulu, Hawaii. There, he organised a conference on the evolving trends in the global oil market, but Honolulu was hardly a hub for the oil industry.

Then, a friend and later lifelong mentor, S.R. Nathan,[21] invited Dr Fesharaki to organise a similar conference in Singapore. The conference would not only serve as a vital gathering for those in the Asian oil markets, but it would also help establish Singapore as the key regional trading hub. As Dr Fesharaki recalls: '*Up until then, there was no real oil market in Asia worth mentioning. Everything was government-controlled and regulated. There was little need for experts or consultants*'.

Determined to make the idea a reality, Fesharaki set to work, launching the Asia–Pacific Petroleum Conference (APPEC). The inaugural event in 1985 attracted just sixty attendees. However, by the time Fesharaki stepped down as chairman in 1990, the conference had grown to over a thousand participants.

'*Clearly, there was a need for the global oil community to connect*', he says. '*The Singapore Economic Development Board, recognising the conference's potential, actively promoted and invested in its growth*'.

'*The first place I opened an office was in Singapore,*' Dr Fesharaki notes. '*The government made everything so easy. Changi Airport—still the best in the world—was only forty minutes from my apartment when I landed. Everything worked seamlessly*'.[22]

For the next four decades, the APPEC conference would become a cornerstone event on the calendar of anyone serious about the global oil markets.[23]

But before addressing the flood of new entrants into the Singapore oil market, mention must be made of another key development—the restructuring of the Chinese oil sector.

New Kids on the Block

Chinese economic development always faced a paradox in the form of two opposing forces: state centralism with its domination over the market and the need for greater autonomy of the companies for greater economic efficiency.

The roots of the reform were in the early 1980s when the China National Offshore Corporation (CNOOC) was established to control offshore production, previously under the Ministry of Petroleum. A year later in 1983, control of most refineries was moved from the ministries and moved into a new company, China Petroleum Corporation or Sinopec. In 1989, the Ministry of Petroleum was abolished and onshore production was given to the China National Petroleum Corporation or CNPC with some control functions given to the Ministry of Energy. [24] Then, in 1992–93, the Ministry of Energy as well as the Sinochem import—export monopoly was abolished.[25]

Sinochem started a fight for survival by forming two joint ventures: China Oil (a JV between CNPC and Sinochem) was formed to export Chinese crude production.[26] Then Unipec (a JV between Sinopec and Sinochem) was formed to import crude oil and trade petroleum products.[27] In 1993, both CNOOC and Sinopec opened Singapore offices. In November 1995, China formally requested to accede to the WTO and relaxed the state control over trade. Everything looked set for a major expansion of trade with China.[28]

PVM's Scott Brown remembered: '*The Chinese government appointed Mr Jiang Jun Long to start Unipec. We all went to Beijing for a big ceremony at the Great Hall of the People and had a ball!*'.

A big change in the oil market out East was coming.

In 1993, Chinese economic growth led to the country becoming a net oil importer.[29] While Chinese oil trading 'Majors' (Unipec, China Oil, and Sinochem) remained price-takers on the sidelines of paper trading, their flows of oil outside the South East Asia significantly increased. Another important government policy was diversification of crude oil imports: they were looking for the cheapest source of oil from as many different regions as possible in order to maximise their security of supply. In particular, imports from West Africa gained momentum, growing from 5 per cent in 1992 to 26 per cent in 2005.[30]

West African crude is normally traded on the basis of Dated Brent, while the Chinese refiners used Dubai as their benchmark.[31] This was significant in terms of the oil market flows for two reasons. First, big players in West Africa (Nigeria and Angola in particular) became very important for China. In fact, China even started buying some North Sea oil in the late 1990s. Later, South American crude gained in prominence. Second, Chinese importers had to convert a Dated Brent-related price into a Dubai-related one on which their refineries were buying most of the oil.[32]

So, the Majors such as Shell and BP, but also traders such as Vitol and Glencore saw an increasing role for their Singapore trading teams. For example, the Glencore traders, Simon Waters and especially David Scott spent most of their time in Bei Jing and Hong Kong, the main Unipec office outside China, placing West African (WAF) barrels.[33]

Vitol was no different. '*Placing WAF into Asia was a major money-making business for Vitol*', says Dennis Kongsiri, who moved there from Glencore in 2001 and worked for Koh Hui Meng. At the time, Ian Taylor was the global head of oil trading in London. Vitol's best agent in Indonesia was Nasrat (Naz for friends) who was also friendly with the Quaddaffi regime in Libya. Naz was so successful that he eventually started up his own trading company in Singapore, Concord Energy. At one stage, Concord was planning a major investment in Singapore, building a condensate splitter costing at least $200 million.[34] Nobody quite understood where he made so much money. One rumour was that he handled the private sales of Quaddaffi's own allotment of oil production, and after the dictator's execution in 2011, he sold a cargo and simply kept the money![35]

Because the number of WAF cargoes moving to Asia was growing, the volumes of Brent-Dubai exposure they would generate were becoming large too. This normally required laying off the pricing risk with one of the market-makers, usually banks, Majors, or trading companies. The crude oil sellers such as the Nigerian National Oil Company (NNPC) and Angolan Sonangol did not hedge their prices, so there was no natural offset for such price risk in the market. Ultimately, someone had to end up holding the price risk.

In the Brent market, this was not a problem. The market was divided between price-takers such as NNPC and Sonangol and price-makers such as Shell, BP, Phibro, J. Aron, Morgan Stanley, Elf (later merged with Total), and others. The price-makers would hold the risk and get actively involved in setting the price for Dated Brent,[36] effectively defending their overall position in that market. In the 1990s, it became increasingly obvious that the same would happen in the Dubai market, as demand for liquidity in that pricing market was growing exponentially, with few natural takers.

Steve Williams was employed by Gulf Oil, one of the more adventurous commercial oil Majors with its trading arm—Gotco. However, after Chevron acquired the company, trading activities were phased out (Chevron never quite understood trading as a business)[37] and Steve took up consulting. He managed to get a major gig, advising the Caltex President of Manufacturing, Supply, and Trading, Leo Lonergan. His timing was perfect—refineries across Asia were suffering from overcapacity and Caltex plants in Singapore, Korea, Japan, and Thailand were losing money.

'The *Caltex organisation was full of old, fat expatriate Americans living in luxury accommodation, with kids in international schools, costing the company a fortune, but bringing in very little money*'.[38] Steve advised that Caltex needed to adopt a more commercial approach in their supply operations driven by a proactive stance in trading activities within this rapidly growing region. In other words, it was to be a more flexible system in which traders would be telling the refiners what crude oil to buy rather than the old system in which the refineries would simply order traders what to procure oil for them. With limited alternatives, Leo agreed, and Steve immediately set to work recruiting key personnel to drive the initiative forward.

Mick Conway was a young and talented crude oil trader at Texaco London. He began his career in the company as an analyst, and gradually worked his way up to the trading floor, where, under the leadership of the highly commercial, trade-savvy, Brian Savino, he quickly became a star trader. Before Brian's arrival from Texaco's White Plains, New York office, rewards for success on the trading floor in London were sparse. In one particularly profitable year, the team's manager, Gene Nemanich, gathered everyone together for a meeting. After delivering a long speech praising the team's impressive overall results and acknowledging Mick's standout contributions, he ordered pizzas for the whole team and handed Mick a Texaco pin as recognition. In any decent trading outfit such as Phibro or Glencore, the prize would have been a six-digit cash bonus.

When Brian took over as trading manager, things improved significantly, and the team began receiving small but appreciated bonuses. This was enough to attract experienced traders like José Miguel Orti from Repsol and retain the senior trader Chris Glaas, who was considering leaving the company. However, other companies were offering even higher compensation for experienced traders[39] and Mick had already caught the attention of Statoil (now Equinor). At the same time, he was sought after by Koch Supply & Trading (KST), a dynamic trading arm of Koch Industries, owned by the infamous Koch brothers. In fact, both companies made Mick such enticing offers that he might have accepted them both.[40]

Around the same time, Steve Williams was discussing his ambitious plans for Caltex with Brian Savino, and Brian fully supported the idea. It fitted well within a new company mantra 'The Power of Three', which encouraged cooperation, rather than competition between Chevron, Caltex, and Texaco. The strategy proved a good indicator of the forthcoming merger between the two Majors.

Having an actively trading sister company in the rapidly growing Asian market would have been a major asset for Texaco, which, alongside Chevron, was a half-owner of Caltex. At the same time, Brian was desperate to retain Mick, but Texaco's rigid pay structure left no room for that kind of concession. Steve Williams had more flexibility when it came to salary and bonuses, and Mick would have been an ideal addition to the Caltex trading team. This presented a perfect solution for both Brian and Steve. In 1997, Steve extended an offer to Mick to join Caltex that was so compelling Mick couldn't refuse. Along with him, Mick brought Steven Lim, a talented Singaporean trader from Caltex. Steven had been seconded to Texaco's London office to gain experience in the Western markets.

'*I wish I could say I had a foresight that Asia was the place to be*', *says Mick.* '*Asia was just interesting, but there was not much going on there at first… It was a diverse place with every country very different. Asia was a cash [physical] market with few players and there were only about 12 cargoes of Dubai at the time. The Platts window was not even in the Singapore time zone—Dubai was, settled at the same time as Brent, in the London time zone. Swaps market just got going and Brent-Dubai arbitrage became a big deal. Most players did not understand it and knowing the Brent benchmark was a big advantage for me. Banks such as J. Aron and Morgan Stanley just got into the game and started offering margin hedging to the local refiners desperate to lock in some profit. Suddenly the excitement was there and you could feel that change was in the air. Between 1997 and 1999, there was a huge growth in Dubai swaps*', remembers Mick Conway.[41]

By the late 1990s, Caltex had become the dominant player in the Dubai oil market and they expanded into other more globally orientated trading where there might be an 'Asian' edge. In 1998, Mick Conway made a bold move by selling two VLCCs of Brent crude oil to Unipec for delivery into China. With the availability of Brent crude dwindling, this trade sent shock-waves through the Western oil market, catching several trading houses short of oil for the benchmark. While the transaction eventually led to a financial settlement ('book-out'),[42] it was a clear signal that China's rapidly expanding oil imports would fundamentally reshape global oil markets.

Asian Brent

A brand-new approach to trading crude oil was coming to Asia. Rather than focussing on the differential relative to the benchmark at which oil was trading, it was the benchmark itself that became the focus of trade. Most players in the London Brent market have been aware of this for quite some time. But moving to Asia and actively seeking market-making as well as price-making in the underlying Dubai risk was revolutionary - and it changed the Singapore oil market forever.

Dwindling production of Dubai and growing oil imports into China increased leverage—greater and greater volumes of oil were priced on the basis of fewer and fewer barrels of Dubai crude oil. The Singapore trading community was caught off-guard in December 2000, when Caltex moved most of the Dubai programme into their own refining system. '*The front Dubai spread widened by two to three dollars a barrel*', says Dennis Kongsiri, who was at Glencore at the time. 'I was short two Dubai cargoes and there were none available for sale. *I managed to get one cargo which was going into the Mitsui system and give them some other oil*', remembers the Glencore trader. '*Then John Calvert, a trader for Conoco who operated Dubai terminal, helped me "roll" one cargo from November into December using the terminal storage facility. We lost a lot of money, but it could have been a lot worse if it had not been for Mitsui and Conoco helping', explains Dennis. Even in the cut-throat world of international oil trading in the early 2000s, people and relationships were still crucial.*

Originally, the Platts Dubai 'window' or the assessment period was in the Western time zone, clearly indicative of where the Asian price benchmark was set. '*First it was in the New York time-zone, which made no sense. So, I made it a bit earlier to be during London time, and then I moved it fully to Singapore time, at 6,00 pm. Then 5,30 PM and the 'whoosh' to 4,30 PM, which was fought quite hard by some-hard core Brits who didn't want to go into the office early,'* says Jorge Montepeque, a Platts employee who devised the oil 'pricing window'.[43]

It was Jorge Montepeque, who arrived in 1991 from New York to head the Platts office in Singapore, who revolutionised the Dubai (and later, following the same pattern, Brent benchmark) price assessment. Jorge originally worked for the Venezuelan national oil company, PDVSA in New York. 'After losing his job in PDVSA, he worked as a doorman/ bouncer in a city's night club in a very bad neighborhood at the time. Lots of junkies and bad people were trying to get into the club! He joined McGraw Hill Platts and with them came to Singapore. Jorge is from Guatemala, so we used to say he was a dictator and the oil market was his Banana Republic,' says Chris Brown. The key problem was that trades were done in different time periods and were not comparable—having two deals separated by half-an-hour was like comparing apples and oranges. People would sometimes report deals which could not be verified by the other counterparty and it was not unheard of for fake deals to be reported too. It was probably Neil Barry Franks from Glencore who told Jorge to: '*Ask traders to put their money where their mouth was*', by trading on a platform visible to Platts.

A lot of money was at stake and traders would regularly complain about assessments being either too high or too low: '*We needed systems and technology. Everything needed to be collected and recorded, including dates, times, and prices. If anyone wanted to audit us, I wanted to be able to show what we did and why. The only way to do it was to store it electronically*', said Jorge. '*We first used ICQ, but it did not have proper time-stamps, so we moved on to Yahoo Messenger. At first, companies did not want to use these systems, but we insisted and somehow, magically, they ended up using them*', added Jorge. Companies would bid and offer and even agree to trade—electronically. All the information had to be taken from Yahoo and entered into the Platts electronic system. *'Soon, it became clear that Yahoo was not good enough. We tried other systems, but they were never "real time. At the end, we moved to the Intercontinental Exchange (ICE) platform. As an exchange, they understood the importance of time. It took several years, but they delivered. There was a lot of internal fighting to get the right technology. At the end, I prevailed. Singapore was the first office to get linked'*.[44]

In order to increase the volume of oil available for assessment of Dubai and following the introduction of Oseberg and Forties crude into the Brent contract, Platts also introduced Oman crude oil into the Dubai contract in 2002.[45]

In a later and very fortuitous move, Mick left Caltex just as a trading disaster was going to strike the company. A fuel oil trader, G.S. Teh, who Steve Williams pinched from J. Aron to trade the key shipping fuel in Singapore, managed to lose tens of millions of dollars trading options,[46] wiping out any chance of trading bonuses for quite some time.

In 2004, the trading duo of Marco Dunand and Danny Jaeggi left Sempra[47] and set up a new trading company, Mercuria.[48] With them, they took Lawrence Ho. Also came the inevitable, old Sinochem Chinese duo of Han Jin and Zhu Hong, who were originally hired by Marco Dunand in the late 1990s, recognising the growing role China was playing in the international oil markets. Your author recalls playing one of the regular tennis games at the Paddington Recreation Grounds with Marco Dunand, when Marco broke the news that he hired Han Jin (Zhu Hong came as an inevitable extra), in order to break into the Chinese market. It was a gamble, but one that paid off handsomely. Much later, over lunch in Singapore, Han Jin explained how Mercuria made massive progress in China and how he arranged for Marco to meet with Xi Jin Ping in Davos. The company had certainly come a long way!

Left without a senior trading team in Singapore, Phibro's Malcolm Macavity then hired Mick Conway, (who also took with him Steven Lim). Mick was at the top of his game and immediately produced a stellar trading year in Phibro. Shortly after, they hired from Masefield a young, outgoing, and popular South African trader, Michael Livingston. Michael did a great job marketing and developing the business, and in the process, probably saved Mick's liver (there was always a lot of drinking involved in meeting customers and seeking new business).

Caltex worked hard on hiring a substitute for Mick. They brought Ken Leask, an experienced oil trader who cut his teeth at Mobil but joined Caltex London a couple of years before.[49] Ken came to Singapore in 2001, followed by another hire from Shell London, a 'Great Dane', Thomas Andersen. The duo would keep Caltex as a major player in the Dubai market for years, until they moved on to do the same at major Wall Street banks.[50]

The Caltex trading team had a pretty hard division between the 'sour' (Dubai) and 'sweet' (regional grades of oil) crude oil books in more than one way. The 'sour' book was run by former London traders in an aggressive, price-making style, while the 'sweet book' was run by local Singapore hands, Meng Tong, Chan, and Kong in a more 'traditional style' of trading, based on differentials versus a benchmark.

The obvious question is: Why did it take Caltex to introduce 'modern' trading to Singapore? Why not one of the majors such as BP, Shell, or Elf?

According to Ken Leask, the answer is in the nature of rotating talent in the Majors. BP had amazing trading talent in London at the time with the formidable trio of Jimmy Dyer, Wolfram Thummel, and Chris McAleese[51]. However, the Singapore trading rotation would usually come from the Asia–Pacific region, rather than London. For example, BP brought to Singapore Richard Massim, a very popular and charismatic employee from BP's Marsden Point refinery in New Zealand.[52] Shell brought an equally charismatic and very capable manager, Australian John Dimech. But they ended up learning on the job in Singapore, rather than bringing new trading techniques to the region.[53]

Fortunately for the majors, they had a deep pool of excellent talent, who were quick learners and benefited from the extensive market information of their companies. In BP Singapore, they were Yee Meng, Chu Said Thong and Ruddin Dhilawala. Yee Meng would later head Unipec trading efforts from Hong Kong, Ruddin would try and introduce more commercial sense into the biggest Major, ExxonMobil, and Chu would trade for BB Energy.

Probably the strongest BP trading team in Singapore at the time was their fuel oil desk, a staple commodity of one of the biggest ports in the world. The key trader there was a Brit Andy Parsons, who later moved to Vitol and eventually headed Vitol's global fuel oil trading team from London.

Shell would have the likes of Yuan Dong and Tarek Al Hassan, the latter staying on as a long-lasting crude trading head at Stasco.[54] Shell also had Steve McBain trading Dubai, but he moved early to Glencore in 2004 and would be replaced by John Dimech who was moved from Australia.

Other important players in the Asian market were J. Aron with their formidable customer flow handled by a 'naphtha' trader Arun Murthy and Koch with Jim Hamilton, who joined from their London team. Representing the French was Stephane Degenne who quickly learned the ropes and became a big player in the Dubai market. Much later, he would end up as a co-head of trading and a board member of Gunvor.

Initially, Jim Hamilton found the market hard and was struggling, before he grasped that the Dubai market was often driven by flows, rather than fundamentals. However, for a while at least, J. Aron and Koch were major players alongside Phibro and Caltex.

'*Vitol and Glencore were perhaps the most knowledgeable Singapore traders in terms of the regional flows, companies and contacts. They had an enormous amount of knowledge that the rest of us could not match. But they were niche players with a different business model*' says Mick Conway.

Dennis Kongsiri, a derivative trader who left Morgan Stanley for Glencore, and later Vitol confirms it: '*In places like India and Indonesia you had to have people on the ground, with strong offices and a network of agents. You could not operate there without it. At one stage, we managed to place nine out of twelve available Dubai cargoes into Indian Oil Corporation (IOC)*'.

But even in India, the oil industry was undergoing a process of change with liberalisation starting in the mid-1990s and finishing around 2002.[55] '*The driving force behind these changes was Dr Vijay Kelkar, the Secretary in Ministry of Petroleum & Natural Gas at the time. The old system of government monopolies in which all the actors received a guaranteed return was grossly inefficient*', said a senior manager at Reliance.[56]

Hoping for a soft landing in a country long used to stable oil prices, a phased approach of liberalisation of petroleum prices and opening up of the refining sector to private investments was undertaken. This resulted in the creation of a number of private companies, Reliance Industries' Jamnagar refinery[57] being the most prominent example of a commercially driven industrial unit both for domestic and export markets.

Back in Japan, Shoshas remained as cautious as ever, sticking to their niche business and close relationships with the Japanese end users. When venturing into new markets, again caution prevailed and to that end, they liked to use joint ventures (JVs). A good example was Mitsui who provided the trading capital for a JV with a Swiss trader, Arcadia, originally set up by the former Phibro oil trader Marcus Green. Hiromichi Kaburaki was the Mitsui trader in Singapore, following the joint trades involving South American, West African, East African, and Asian markets. His Arcadia counterpart at the time was Stephen Gibbons, a colourful former Shell and Elf trader and an expert in working in 'difficult places' and new markets.[58]

Poachers Got Poached

Throughout the 1990s, the Chinese traders sat quietly watching the market and taking the PRA price assessments and exchange settlements as given. In the early 2000s, they started taking active interest in the price-making process. Due to ballooning imports, the Chinese exposure to Brent and WTI kept increasing.[59]

It was the Golden Age for Dubai traders, with Phibro standing as the dominant force in the market. On one occasion, Shell was an aggressive seller in the 'Platts window' with Steve McBain offering a number of Dubai cargoes through PVM brokers. Phibro was a buyer. Shell kept selling whole cargoes and Phibro kept buying them. After about thirty full Dubai cargoes, Shell had nothing left to offer. But Phibro kept bidding, driving the price higher.

'*You do not bring a flick-knife to a gun fight*', said Mick Conway about the event.[60]

The company's success was annually celebrated each spring when Phibro organised an extravagant long weekend in Hong Kong, coinciding with the Rugby Sevens—one of Asia's most popular sporting events. Attendees were pretty much 'who is who' of the Asian crude oil community with a few international guests thrown in. From premium seating at Hong Kong's Kai Tak Stadium to an endless flow of alcohol from the early morning hours, personalised rugby shirts, exquisite Chinese and Japanese dinners, and aperitifs on yachts, these events were highly coveted. They not only generated massive goodwill for Phibro but also reinforced their image as a dominant player in the Asian oil market.[61]

Back in Singapore, the wining and dining scene also evolved. It gradually shifted from Da Paolo, located at the base of the city's hilly street, to L'Angélus, a French establishment at the top. An all-afternoon Friday lunch at this joint was a regular feature, with Phibro's Mick Conway, Steven Lim, Michael Livingston, Morgan Stanley's Alf Salti, Ken Leask, and Thomas Anderson of Caltex (and later Morgan Stanley and J. Aron respectively) and others as frequent guests.[62]Paul Clausen, who had by then transitioned to Amerex Brokers, was typically the sponsor. L'Angélus was his favourite restaurant, where he was such a valued patron that he had his own private table, and the owners even named a dish in his honour![63]

Other traders stuck to venues close to their offices. In general, banks favoured restaurants on Boat Key, close to the business districts. Glencore's den was Bice, an Italian restaurant in the Goodwood Hotel, close to the office. '*We were there almost every day*', Says Dennis Kongsiri.

Asian traders typically favoured their home cuisines, and Junichi Kasahara (often accompanied by Lawrence Ho) was a loyal patron of Shiraishi, a Japanese restaurant at the Ritz-Carlton. As a regular, Kasahara-san was usually offered a private room. After an especially satisfying lunch washed down with lots of sake, Junichi would return to the office, murmur a few trading instructions to Lawrence, then lean back, prop his feet on the desk, and drift off to sleep. True to good Japanese custom, as the boss snoozed, the rest of the trading floor remained respectfully quiet, careful not to disturb his nap![64]

Chinese restaurants quickly learned that big margins were to be made by selling quality wine. To encourage wine drinking, it was common for them not to remove empty wine bottles from the table. For Western traders, this could be rather embarrassing as a long lunch could leave many empty bottles on the table![65]

As the volumes of Dubai pricing risk continued to balloon, it became increasingly difficult to offload them. At the same time, it became impossible for Chinese importers to continue being passive price-takers in the Dubai market. Within a decade, the trading arms of the Chinese majors, ChinaOil and Unipec, had evolved into price-makers. With their size and financial power, the two quickly became central players in setting the price for Dubai crude—and, by extension, for much of the market east of Suez.[66]

In 2015, the Financial Times reported: 'In *August ChinaOil, whose parent company is PetroChina, bought more than 90 per cent of all the Oman, Abu Dhabi and Dubai cargoes available in the price assessment process run by Platts…*'[67] Shell, one of the dominant players in the market, complained: '*There need to be safeguards to prevent the risk of distortion and to ensure the Dubai benchmark price mirrors true market supply and demand fundamentals*'.[68]

Did the poacher just get poached?

The writing was on the wall. It was just the beginning of the process in which the two Chinese majors would end up dominating the Asian benchmark.[69] Most western traders threw in the towel. Mick Conway took an early retirement from Phibro in 2012.

Back in the centre, in London and New York, no one was taking early retirement. New opportunities were opening up as the 'Derivatives Revolution' took hold.

Notes

1. Chat with Scotty Brown on 4/11/24.
2. https://www.nytimes.com/1987/07/02/business/british-insider-fined-40000.html
3. This is just for one-way trade. Sinochem had to sell the cargoes as well!
4. According to chat with S. Brown, 05/10/2023 and subsequent communication on 04/11/2024.
5. 'Beginning their careers together at Cargill International, they both subsequently moved to trading roles at Goldman Sachs's J. Aron trading unit, Salomon Brothers and Sempra Energy before founding Mercuria in 2004.' https://mercuria.com/about-us/our-history/
6. Interview with Lawrence Ho on 26/9/23.
7. From the interview with Paul Clausen on 19/10/2023.
8. Junichi Kasahara interview, and subsequent correspondence: 7/6/24.

9. Denis Kongsiri was covering the paper markets. Dennis left Glencore early, in 2000 and missed on the IPO windfall as well.
10. https://www.reuters.com/article/world/glencore-11-billion-ipo-to-make-billionaires-of-bosses-idUSTRE7430EF/
11. The first two respective brokers merged in 2001 and ICAP was acquired in 2006: https://tpicap.com/tullettprebon/history
12. https://www.federalreservehistory.org/essays/asian-financial-crisis#:~:text=July%201997%E2%80%93December%201998,and%20Eastern%20Europe%20in%201998.
13. https://tpicap.com/pvm/about-us
14. https://cnaluxury.channelnewsasia.com/people/da-paolo-dempsey-italian-restaurant-singapore-181761#:~:text=It's%20been%2030%20years%20since,Paolo%20HQ%20along%20Club%20Street.
15. Horsnell, P. (1997), page 230.
16. Ibid, page 234.
17. Ibid, pages 183–195.
18. See chapter 8 on Brent.
19. For details, see Horsnell, P. (1997), pages 268–269.
20. Fesharaki thesis supervisor was Colin Robinson, who, together with his wife Eileen Marshall was one of the architects of the energy market liberalisation policy in the UK, pushed forward by Margaret Thatcher in the 1980's. From the interview with Dr Fesharaki on 10th July 2024.
21. Sellapan Ramanathan, later serving as the sixth president of Singapore between 1999 and 2011.
22. Your author, who traded in Singapore for 13 years, wholeheartedly agrees.
23. In 2025, S&P marked 40 years of the conference: https://share.vidyard.com/watch/3kMHCa2RdMaLp3nwNsttRy
24. Ibid, page 42.
25. https://www.tandfonline.com/doi/full/10.1016/j.polsoc.2008.10.007
26. http://www.chinaoil.com.cn/chinaoilen/gsgk/gsgk_index.shtml
27. http://www.sinopec.com/listco/en/about_sinopec/subsidiaries/subsidiaries_joint_ventures/20161109/news_20161109_398174095866.shtml
28. https://www.wto.org/english/thewto_e/acc_e/s7lu_e.pdf
29. See https://www.sciencedirect.com/science/article/abs/pii/S0301421509007927
30. See: https://www.iaee.org/en/publications/proceedingsabstractpdf.aspx?id=1408

31. Majority of imports, at 50% came from the Middle East with Dubai-based pricing. See Ibid.
32. The price basis is a common dominator, enabling price comparison.
33. From the interview with Dennis Kongsiri, 12/11/2024.
34. https://www.energyintel.com/0000017b-a7aa-de4c-a17b-e7eafe0b0001
35. It is important to stress that this was a rumour with no evidence to support it.
36. In the Platts window. For details of this process, see Imsirovic (2001), the 'Brent' chapter.
37. The same thing happened after they bought Texaco in 2001.
38. Interview with Ken Leask, 9/11/24.
39. At the time, your author left Texaco for another US refiner who doubled his salary.
40. Recollection of one of the authors.
41. Interview with Mick Conway on 3/10/23.
42. Your author was in the middle of it, procuring the pre-sold Brent cargoes.
43. Chat with Jorge on 10/11/24.
44. Interview with Jorge Montepeque, November 2020. Also, see Imsirovic (20s1), pages 162–163.
45. Ibid.
46. A well-informed source, who would not be named, talk of anything between $40 and $100 million in losses.
47. Marco & Danny, Han Jin & Zhu Hong, Junichi & Lawrence and your author worked for a while together at Sempra, then a Fortune 500 company, specialising in gas and gas trading.
48. A lot more on this in chapter 13.
49. Caltex London was based in Texaco London offices, benefiting from the market information of a big team and nominally reporting to the author.
50. Ken Leask moved to Morgan Stanley and later J.P. Morgan while Thomas Andersen moved to Goldman's J. Aron.
51. Ron Davidson, a long time BP and elsewhere senior trader rates McAleese as the best trader he encountered.
52. It was closed in 2022 and turned into a fuel import terminal.
53. John Dimech subsequently became a trading manager for the US Shell team. https://www.businesstimes.com.sg/companies-markets/energy-commodities/shell-earns-us-1-billion-year-us-crude-trading-court-filing-shows

54. Tareq is a good example, having come to Asia from the WAF and Med-trading background, rather than Brent/ North Sea trading.
55. https://www.brookings.edu/articles/how-india-reformed-its-petroleum-sector/
56. Interviewed on 17 November 2024, but wished to remain anonymous.
    'Production of oil/gas and coal was on a downward trend; the public distribution system for subsidised kerosene and LPG had become a sieve for black marketing and the administered price differential between naphtha, petrol, diesel and kerosene had created incentives for distributors and dealers to adulterate transportation fuels.' https://www.brookings.edu/articles/how-india-reformed-its-petroleum-sector/
57. https://www.ril.com/businesses/energy/refining-marketing
58. From the interview with Kaburaki Hiromichi on 11/11/24. For example, Steve was handling a term contract for crude from Yemen.
59. This was the main driver for the oil price explosion of the early 2000's, culminating in Brent at $140 a barrel.
60. From the Interview with Ken Leask on 9/11/24.
61. Recollection of the author.
62. Your author was often there too.
63. *'I would order a salad with ribeye steak cut into strips covered with mustard/mayo dressing. So very quickly the staff started saying "do you want the Clausen salad, Mr Clausen? "I would reply with something to the effect of "of course I will, it's the finest dish on the menu" or " well you can show me the specials.... but I'll still have the Clausen salad. It was a bit of fun and then of course other patrons would here this and ask about the Clausen salad. Then one day I rolled up there and with great pleasure Philippe the owner presented me with the menu showing "Clausen Salad" for all to order...'* In conversation with Paul on 7/11/24.
64. Author's personal experience working with Junichi and Lawrence at Sempra, Singapore.
65. After one particularly long, Friday lunch with one of his favourite brokers, your author was astonished to see five empty bottles of red on the side table (provided by the restaurant staff). Common sense prevailed, and he went home rather than venture back to the office.
66. Ibid, see Fig. 3. They were third and fourth biggest players after Shell and Vitol by 2014.
67. https://www.ft.com/content/44bf3818-a4d4-11e5-a91e-162b86790c58
68. Ibid.
69. Imsirovic A. (2024), page 174, Fig. 11.1.

Bibliography

Horsnell, P. (1997): 'Oil in Asia', OIES, Oxford University Press 1997.
Imsirovic A. (2014): 'Oil Markets in Transition and the Dubai Crude Oil Benchmark', OIES, https://www.oxfordenergy.org/wpcms/wp-content/uploads/2014/10/Oil-Markets-in-Transition-and-the-Dubai-Crude-Oil-Benchmark.pdf
Imsirovic A. (2021): 'Trading and Price Discovery for Crude oils', Palgrave.
Imsirovic A. (2024): 'International Oil Markets in the Age of Climate Change', Palgrave.

11

Market Astrology

Derivatives Revolution

The action was most definitely in Europe and North America, in very liquid instruments such as Brent and WTI. Increasingly, the oil trading community was turning its attention to the world of financial products and the risk management requirements of consumers bearing oil price risks outside the oil industry, such as airlines, freight companies, and other industries.

The overwhelming reason for the beginnings of derivatives trading in oil was volatility. 'Volatility brings me out in hives....in fact I've been treated many times for volatility' comments one radio broadcaster rather appropriately.[1] So, the 'derivatives revolution' was about to begin, and it did so contemporaneously in London and New York in 1986 although take-off in significant size did not begin until 1989.

Along with options, a market began to develop in 'swaps' the other building block of complex, bespoke derivative products that were to become so important in consumer price risk management and equally as important for the profit line in the accounts of a new (and old) breed of oil trader.

A 'swap' is defined as a transaction where one party—the provider say—will guarantee another party a fixed price for a volume of oil at a set time in the future. In return for this, the provider accepts the risk of price changes during the term of the transaction. So, a floating price has been swapped for a fixed price.

Financial markets, particularly fixed income (bonds) and foreign exchange, had been long-time users of swaps. Therefore, the technology was familiar to Wall Street as well as other commercial banks[2] already present in the oil

A. Imsirovic and C. Bryce, *The Rivers of Money*,
https://doi.org/10.1007/978-3-031-91806-3_11

markets. There was an avalanche of new entrants - Societe General, Paribas, Barclays Capital, CRT, Chase Manhattan, JP Morgan, Chemical Bank, and a host of other names of the era.

An example of the efficacy of a swap might be to consider the situation of a ship owner. The owner is given the opportunity to quote a client for a voyage say from Singapore to Japan 30 days hence. What price does he quote? That becomes a less tricky conundrum if he knows that he can execute a Singapore fuel oil swap with a provider at a fixed price which will then expire on the same day as he refills his vessel with fuel oil. His physical delivery and his swap will net off at the same price on the day he takes delivery of his fuel oil and he is then left with his fixed-price contract. The price certainty from the swap allows him to quote a freight rate to the customer without having to build in an extra risk premium for the uncertainty of price movement and thus be at a competitive advantage vis a vis other competitors' quotes.

Similarly, fuel can make as much as half of the total operating cost of an airline. Holidaymakers often book their favourite destinations many months in advance. Airlines can use price surcharges to protect themselves from jet fuel price rises, but these are highly unpopular with their customers. Therefore, fixing the cost of fuel as soon as tickets are sold is a sensible strategy for any air carrier.

Similar logic can easily be extended to bus and cab companies, cement makers, glass manufacturers, and almost any other industry where fuel constitutes a significant proportion of operating costs.

A special case was oil refineries. They would buy oil early, often a month or two before crude is delivered.[3] It could take a good month before this oil is processed and the petroleum products sold. While the refinery profit is simply the difference between the price of petroleum products and delivered crude oil (minus processing cost), the price difference between the acquisition of oil and the sale of products can fluctuate wildly. Stabilising and 'fixing' the refinery profits became a whole new line of business, and required increased liquidity in both oil and petroleum products markets many months forward. Young BP trader Louise Murray did much to promulgate and popularise this refinery margin swap business.

On 6th October 1986, Chase Manhattan intermediated[4] a swap between Koch Industries and Cathay Pacific Air. A four-month long, 25,000 barrels a month swap saw Cathay hedge against a rise in jet fuel prices by paying a fixed price per barrel and Koch taking the floating leg of the deal.[5] At the time, there were no liquid markets in jet fuel, so the swap was indexed to the WTI crude oil contract. Although Cathay retained the basis risk between jet fuel and crude, they hedged the bulk of their petroleum price risk overall. It is believed that this was the first oil swap ever executed.

Early growth in swaps, most especially in the U.S. was '... *hindered by the ambiguous stance of the Commodities Futures Trading Commission (CFTC)*',[6] who seemed inclined, possibly with some lobbying help from NYMEX, to view swaps as futures contracts and which would come under their jurisdiction.

This pushed the swaps action to London where the OTC derivatives such as swaps were not regulated. At the time, financial markets in London were undergoing major changes, especially following the 'Big Bang' reforms of 1986, which deregulated and modernised share dealing at the London Stock Exchange.[7] This favourable regulatory environment led to London becoming a global centre for trading swaps and other derivatives.

Only in 1989, the CFTC offered an opinion to the contrary,[8] resulting in a boom in the derivatives business in the United States. The CFTC-induced interregnum in the United States had served to give London a head start and it was there that the individual who was arguably more responsible than any other for galvanising the Derivatives Revolution was getting the business going.

Honorary Group Captain Paul Newman is an aerobatics addict. He was also a nationally ranked youth chess player, a Russophile, and a jolly and clubbable intellectual. Looking every inch the Tory 'Squire from the Shires' in his immaculate and loud pin-striped city suit, he was as comfortable passing the port in the right direction as he was discussing foreign exchange strategy and the economic imperatives of the G6 countries.[9]

A close ally of the founder of the broking firm Intercapital, Michael Spencer, Paul was described by the Financial Times as 'a key figure in making the City of London a hotspot for global commodity trading'.[10] He became associated with the development of jet fuel hedging. Initially, the key customers were holiday companies who were reacting against public displeasure when price surcharges were levied on package holidays as a result of oil price increases. In short order, the mainstream airlines came to the party, including British Airways, Lufthansa, Aer Lingus, Alitalia, Air France, Iberia, and United Airlines.[11]

As an intermediary, operating for a brokerage fee, he needed the other side of the transactions and so he set about charming the banks and oil companies. It was a new market and nobody was quite sure what they were supposed to do. According to Christine Crossley, a trader at Shell and the doyenne of early oil derivatives markets, '... my first trade was brokered by Paul Newman. It was like the blind leading the blind'.[12]

Some of the early names in trading jet swaps were Christophe Siat at Elf, Edouard Neviaski at Societe General, Nick Calabrese at Phibro, Paul Ford at Midland Bank (normally 'fronting' for BP for a fee, before Vivienne Cox and Alan Hayward brought BP into the game of trading jet on their own account), Chris Mason at Credit Lyonnais (known humorously by market participants as 'Debit Lyonnais') and Mike Hampton at Chase Manhattan bank.

In the early days, documentation pride—an insistence on using contracts drawn by their own lawyers was always an issue. Shell would only use their terms; BP would insist on using theirs and so on. Thankfully, the International Swap Dealers Association (ISDA) got involved and a common wording of the contract was established. The subsequent involvement of the airline body, The International Air Transport Association (IATA)[13] boosted interest in that business.

Even as the oil folks encountered the different culture of the bankers—and there was indeed resistance at the outset—the 'evangelist for derivatives', Paul Newman, pulled people together and played a considerable role in getting the trade going.

The derivatives revolution opened up new competencies and job opportunities in banks, trading houses, and oil companies. The marketer and salesperson became, as in other financial markets, a necessary role. Some of the 'dyed in the wool' physical commodity traders called them 'an expense' rather than a competency and the trader/sales interface has forever been a challenging one in provider companies.[14] Steve Jones, a head of sales at a Wall Street bank for many years made a comment that '*sales is as much about internal selling as external selling*'.[15]

Salespeople were natural networkers. Charles Tuke recounts an amusing incident in the lobby of Dubai's Burj Al Arab hotel. Goldman marketing executive Andrew Stewart, vaguely recognising a man and forever sniffing out a deal, approached him and asked, 'Do I know you from somewhere?' The man extended his hand and replied, 'Eubank'. Stewart responded, 'Oh, I haven't heard of New Bank—are you based in Canary Wharf?' It turned out he was speaking to the famous boxer, Chris Eubank. Such misunderstandings were bound to happen in the eager-beaver world of oil derivatives marketing!

In addition to salespeople, companies began to feel they needed 'originators'[16] to invent and promulgate products and tempt clients, 'structurers' to dress them up, and in later years, 'quants' to do the complex maths required to value the most esoteric derivative products. As much of what was peddled to clients was beyond the bounds of human comprehension, it was important that there were people who understood the fine, quantitative detail.[17]

During the 2008 Financial Crisis, a glaring lack of regulatory understanding became evident. In the years leading up to the crisis, the author, who was managing an international fixed-income business, was shocked to learn in a meeting with a Deputy Governor of the Bank of England that he had no grasp of the risks associated with complex, multi-layered credit products that were widely promoted despite their dangers. However, it is highly likely that regulators had a clearer awareness of the advancements in oil derivatives at the time.

But development of the hedging technology inherent in swaps and options was a godsend for corporate risk managers. They enabled company Treasurers and CFOs to plan and budget in an environment of volatile prices. Derivative products would not only reduce price and revenue risks, but also their costs of capital, while avoiding unanticipated financial distress. Oil derivatives were and are unquestionably socially and economically useful.

This makes it all the more difficult to understand why more oil-producing Sovereigns, reliant to varying degrees on oil prices for national budgetary considerations, have not embraced hedging through the use of derivatives.

Mexico has been the poster child for Sovereign hedging of this kind and that country has hedged in most years since they began the process in 1990. The Mexican Finance Ministry known as the 'Hacienda' regularly buys put options to guarantee a minimum price for their sales of oil. Consequently, lenders to Mexico are able to offer significantly improved terms given the security associated with the country having protected itself from a fall in oil prices.

It has typically been the large banks who have sold the put options to the Hacienda. While the deal offered by Mexico is complicated by the fact that they insist on using the price of their little-traded Maya stream of crude oil as the basis for the quote, the banks have generally been able to price enough risk premium into the deal to protect themselves from volatility changes and changes in the price basis between Maya and WTI/Brent. The operative word is 'generally'. Given the size and basis risk, along with the fact that the market knows the dealers are going to be short volatility post transaction, not every bank has chosen to be involved every year. Probably Barclays and Goldman Sachs, whose staff members assisted in the creation of Mexico's programme in the early days, have been the most consistently active.[18]

Other Sovereigns have mulled the idea of a Mexico-style hedge but have pulled back before dealing. While running the Goldman Sachs oil trading business in the Middle East, Taraneh Azad made 15 trips to Baku with proposals for an Azeri sovereign hedge. Eventually rebuffed she recalls being told 'we are not Mexicans- we went to Harvard you know'.[19]

There have been some minor instances of Sovereign hedging such as Jamaica in 2015 when the country hedged its oil consumption locking in 6 million barrels for 15 months at a price of $66.74. In 2013, Morocco also hedged consumption spending $50–60 million buying call options for European diesel from Barclays, Citibank, and Morgan Stanley. Ghana executed a small hedge of production at $107 in 2011 to stabilise budget revenue and other examples occurred in Panama, Brazil, Ecuador, and Egypt.[20]

None of these was market moving or earth-shattering, however, rather toe in the water stuff. There is little reason for the finance officials of Sovereign states to put their heads above the parapet and execute hedges as there is plenty of room for criticism and more if the hedges go wrong. It is bad for them if the market rallies well beyond the price at which oil production has been hedged and there is no reward if hedges go well and protect and stabilise the national budget. Which comes back to the matter of self-interest. As we have seen, the Brent market that grew up in London in the 1980s prospered, at least partly, because the people involved were able to secure jobs in companies that were trading these markets and that were offering high personal rewards. Self-interest is a hugely important factor in the direction of development of oil markets over the last fifty years and self-interest in the case of Sovereign hedging is to keep one's head down and do no harm.

Derivatives markets in oil have only continued to grow despite the scepticism in certain sectors and it is hard to imagine these days an oil trading world without swaps, options, and their combination in the wider business of oil-indexed financing and investor-targeted products. Many loans embodying interest rates that are set by reference to oil price movements have been extended over the years to oil producers and producing countries by Majors and increasingly by independent traders backed by Commercial banks.[21]

Contracts for Difference (CFD) Swaps

If options were instruments towards the financial products end of the oil trading spectrum of the day, another product created at the time was designed to further fine-tune the management of risks borne by physical oil traders. There is some contention over who invented the 'Dated for Paper' contract-for-difference (CFD) market and it might have well originated in more than one place. There was certainly a widespread need for producers and refiners to convert their 'floating' price into a fixed one and vice versa, or to move the pricing from one time period to another.

Some suggest that first up were Mobil traders who asked the Wall Street refiners for a price quotation for the spread between the two indices—Dated Brent and 15-Day Brent. Mobil were active hedgers of their crude oil production as well as the oil they were buying for their refineries globally. Many of them, such as the Nigerian types of oil, were priced against the published Dated Brent prices.[22] While Brent futures and partials enabled them to hedge the outright price risk, they were still exposed to a change in the differential between forward and physical Brent with loading dates or 'Dated Brent'. There was a need for a swap that would mitigate this basis risk, which could amount to several dollars a barrel.

A more likely possibility was that the swap emerged with Shell International Trading Company (SITCO),[23] the Shell 'in-house' trading entity, tasked with buying crude oil from government entities on behalf of affiliates, and also trading for profit.

In the mid-1980s Shell was very far from having a centralised trading operation. Each operating company such as Shell Netherlands, Shell UK (SUKO), or Deutsche Shell would buy their own oil and SUKO would sell their own sizeable Brent production. Even the SITCO trading floor was pretty decentralised. '*Traders were assessed based on individual financial performance and your biggest competitors were the guys sitting near you*', says Chris Evans, a SITCO trader and later the head of crude oil risk in the company. '*There was little incentive to share information and the database we had to share information was usually empty. It was even hard to gather all the deals done in a day on a single deal-sheet. J. Aron would trade a "SUKO/SITCO arbitrage"*[24] *where they would buy from one entity and sell to the other company for 5 cents profit. The deal-sheet was a wad of paper that was being passed around the SITCO trading floor, but it was often getting lost. I asked Russell Newton, a young computer wizard, to adapt the information database to do it and he did a stellar job—that is how he came into trading*', Remembers Chris.[25] '*There was little training and people would move to other jobs every three years*'.

Russell Newton recalls the time he joined SITCO as '*very fortunate*'. With a degree in experimental psychology from Cambridge, Russ had very little idea what he wanted to do. His early interest in computer programming helped him get into the Shell IT department in 1986, where he quickly got poached by Chris for a trading job at his 'futures and forwards' desk. '*I was very lucky with the timing and a great boss*', recalls Russell; '*It was an incredible time to be in oil trading with a lot of new ideas floating around and massive intellectual property developing*'.

However, the execution of Brent deals in SITCO was eventually centralised around one trading leader and most of the other traders in SITCO and affiliates would come to Nico Engelen, who was running the book at the time. Just like the 'Wall Street Refiners', Nico would offer to buy or sell Brent partials to entities that were normally pricing a cargo over five days. '*Most of the trades would internally cancel out, and the more volume we did, the less risk we carried on our books. As there was no futures Brent market at the time, any outstanding risk was hedged with WTI on the NYMEX exchange*', says Evans.

As Nico moved on to Shell Indonesia, Chris Evans took over the book. '*What was blatantly obvious was that most people wanted to hedge Dated and not forward Brent price risk. People wanted to fix the price difference between one pricing period and another, usually both indexed against Dated Brent. So, I started making internal markets in Dated Brent pricing periods, in the form of a price swap. Just like with [forward] Brent partials, much of the exposure would 'wash out' internally. After a trader-led reorganisation, all of the crude oil pricing risk in SITCO was centralised under my control. Later, all of Shell's crude oil trading was also centralised in an initiative led by Paul Skinner, the President of SITCO at the time*', says Chris.

Russell Newton recalls a '*collaborative effort*' over the 1987–1990 period in which Mike Treanor and Steve Gutteridge, and later Chris Evans tried to flesh out all the issues and ideas about the workings of the Brent market during lunchtime and evening seminars they organised at SITCO. '*Some traders were struggling with the idea of owning a physical cargo and associated pricing exposure because being long a long physical oil involved being short Dated Brent exposure. People were regularly getting it back-to-front! From our seminar discussions, it appeared natural to have an appropriate contract to hedge it. And Chris Evans was leading the effort*', says Newton.

At the time, the seminars also included other formidable talents such as Iain Lawson, Mike Muller, Steve Mawer, Danny Masters, and others, all of who would all, in their own right shape the future of the oil market.[26]

'The *word about Shell Dated swaps spread and there was more and more pressure, especially from younger traders who covered the third-party accounts to offer them externally. At the end, our legal team sat down and developed a simple 'contracts for difference' (CFD) contract, probably mimicking a similar one in financial markets. It was an instant success and other players got onto the game, crushing the premiums*', concludes Chris Evans.

It is quite possible that a number of players recognised the need for a dated swap around the same time. This '*Dated to Paper*' or Brent CFD market took off quickly with the help of brokers such as United and First National. It would become a major market instrument for hedging and speculation right up to the present day and other markets would try to emulate it.[27] In 1989, one Chevron trader (Rich Shelton) received a company award '*for his contribution to the development and industry standardisation on the Dated Brent to forward Brent spread*'.[28] One can only imagine his pride in receiving this honour!

Heavily marketed by providers, one bank's sales literature commended the product as being: '... *able to lock in a margin, assist in transferring a floating price to a fixed price, partially hedge backwardation, allow players to short the market without being physically short and more accurately hedge existing risks*'.[29] Quite the thing then![30]

It also proved to be a new source of income for the oil brokerage community. Steve Paice and Nigel Harris at First National, Liz Newton at PVM, Kevin Kitson-Jones at Petroder, and Sandra Carr at United became the most active brokers in the early days of the CFD swap.[31]

Less happily, the CFD market had gained a reputation for being susceptible to manipulation. It was the Platts Head of Market Reporting, Jorge Montepeque, who tried to take the business by the scruff of the neck. An important figure, Jorge was' the de facto arbiter of a largely unregulated physical market'[32] He created the system known as the Platts Window, a short end-of-day period when prices would be assessed in reference to trades concluded in the 'Window'.

The Platts assessment was summed up by former Vitol trader, Peter Smith as 'a casino'.[33] If a firm happened to be pricing an especially large volume of oil by reference to a certain day's price, the temptation to trade a significantly lesser amount of oil in the 'Window' at a price that would be advantageous to them was often too great to ignore. Although Platts vigorously rules out any trades that they are in any way suspicious of, a comment by ex-Rhein Oel trader, Rowan Bainbridge that '*traders regularly pulled the wool over Jorge's eyes*' would resonate with many across the business.[34] Notwithstanding these possible issues, important though they are in oil being priced globally at its correct market value, the contribution of Platts and Montepeque to that price-discovery process was noteworthy.

Perhaps more important was the relationship between large Brent players in this regard. While there was an intense competition by price-makers over the final assessments and large amounts of money at stake, the differences were usually settled in good humour. For example, in 1999, STASCO held an unusually large position in Brent and kept a large number of cargoes resulting in a very high Dated Brent price as well as the front-month spread. Some trading houses were seriously hurting under the circumstances. The whole affair coincided with a PVM golf outing on the beautiful island of Islay in

Scotland, an annual event, which all the key Brent traders would attend. A senior STASCO trader, Mark Quartermaine was there too, and during one of the rounds, while picking up a ball from the heather, he got bitten by a snake. Mark ended up in hospital with a serious case of septicemia. Having recovered somewhat, Mr. Quartermaine received a phone call in hospital by one of the traders who were very short Brent: 'What? It did not kill you?' He said.[35]

At the end of the day, it was always the major players in Brent such as Shell and BP that had to either initiate or support any significant change in the pricing methodology. For example, following an alleged squeeze of the benchmark in 2012 by the trader Mercuria, the companies caught short the oil and eventually had to deliver high premium oil such as Oseberg and Ekofisk in order to avoid a default. '*People were delivering great oil to Mercuria*', commented a trader.[36] Shell responded by amending its SUKO 90 terms, which govern how forward Brent (BFOE) works, by introducing a quality premium for Oseberg and Ekofisk.[37] Very soon, BP backed up Shell's plan[38]and, eventually, Platts incorporated it into the methodology for its Dated Brent price assessment.[39]

Clearly, understanding the likely positions and views of peers and competitors was essential. This further reinforced the social aspect of trading—long boozy lunches in particular. Of course, there was always a minority of traders that worked in small shops or even alone, thus generally starved of information. Such poor souls probably had more incentive than anyone to socialise as much as possible.

One such group was a club of single-trader shops in London, simply named the 'Singles Club'. The idea of such a club was the brainchild of Kurt Chapman, a trader in the London office of Ashland, an American oil company.[40] At an industry function, Kurt suggested the idea of forming the club at your author,[41] and he loved it. Soon, a number of traders were invited such as Robert Martin of Ultramar, Jim Rintoul of Louis Dreyfus, Jimmy Straughn from Arco, and others. The Singles Club held monthly lunches organised and paid for by the members in turn. Going back to the office was a rare occurrence after these affairs, but the exchange of information and market view was precious!

Market Astrology

As traders struggled to manage increased price volatility, a new form of analysis emerged in the oil markets. Known as 'Technical Analysis',[42] this approach was based on the belief that future price movements could be predicted by studying past price patterns. By analysing historical charts and applying principles from behavioural psychology, Technical Analysis sought to identify trends and market signals that could guide trading decisions.

And so, moving average analysis,[43] 'retracement' expectations,[44] 'candlestick' analysis,[45] reversal signals,[46] and other numerological 'tools' (Fibonacci sequence, in which each subsequent number was a simple sum of the previous two numbers as proposed by a famous Pisan mathematician, featured prominently in such analysis)[47] bred a whole new cadre of instant experts who saw something special in the newly discovered astrology of the oil markets as displayed on charts. The only thing they didn't do was colouring-in, a technique still remaining in the realm of the geologist community (and pre-school kindergartens).

Nonetheless, the daily reports focussing heavily on technical analysis and produced by PVM's Robin Bieber[48] were much read across the industry and could, at times, move markets.

While Elsewhere…

Brent and WTI were not the only shows in town. A heavily traded forward market was developing along the Colonial Pipeline, a gasoline common carrier pipeline owned by Unocal, Amoco, Citgo, and other big oil industry names, carrying the automobile fuel from the U.S. Gulf Coast, up the East Coast, and towards the New York market. With each month divided into three ten-day cycles, up to 2 million barrels a day of physical gasoline and gasoline price swaps were being traded.[49]

Over time, trading flows in gasoline in the U.S. markets and the success and failure of forward and futures contracts were to be dependent on environmental legislation as well as changes in the constituents in the blends that became gasoline (including ethanol).

While Colonial brewed up a storm, so did Naphtha in the Far East. With the fall off in the production of paraffinic naphtha in Japan in favour of gasoline production allied to an increased demand for the product for ethylene production, Japan sought imports which came increasingly from the Arab Gulf. The growth in trade benefited the forward market even if there was a wariness about taking on business in Japan which was traditionally dominated by the Shoshas. Shell, BP, Vitol, Vanol, and Phibro were the main international players at this time and, as in the North Sea Brent market, daisy chains developed along with active trading.[50]

One region though where liquid forward or physical markets failed to develop was in the Mediterranean, an influential, global export refining centre in the earliest years of trade. This was due to the lack of a stable and reliable regional source of crude oil, logistical complexities of the supply of Russian products, and the individual country-by-country import and quality restrictions. Price transparency in the Mediterranean was so opaque that in 1989, Petroleum Argus could only report 148 spot crude oil deals across the whole year covering nine different crude oils from six different countries.[51] Consequently over a five-year period, processing crude oil for third parties declined by 29 per cent across a region where the processing of oil for traders and others was perhaps the only driver of openly traded contracts.[52]

The Gulf War

Back in the traditional trading world of forwards, futures, and physical oil, one event interrupted the growing sense of comfort that participants felt in understanding, managing, and utilising these markets.

No one involved in oil trading at the time will forget one word uttered from Geneva by U.S. Secretary of State, James Baker on the evening of 9th January 1991. 'Regrettably' was the word that began the countdown to the action to remove Iraq from its illegal occupation of Kuwait.

Between July 1990 and the late winter of the same year, oil prices had doubled from the mid-teens to the mid $30's per barrel as anticipation built around Iraq's likely action, the pre-invasion negotiations, and the invasion of Kuwait itself. It was the short-term volatility in the oil price around the time of the final negotiations between Baker and Iraqi emissary, Tariq Aziz, that caused the most pain to some traders while making it a time to remember in a positive way for others. That day the price started and ended at $28 a barrel, but what happened during the day was quite dramatic. As the Baker/Aziz talks went on way longer than anybody expected, giving the impression that they were reaching agreement, the price steadily dropped to around $20. However, when Baker uttered the word '*regrettably*' in his news conference, the price went back to $28.

Every trading firm had their 'deep throat'—someone strategically placed at the end of the military runway in Dhahran or somebody who knew somebody who might have been around the same place. The danger of reliance on such contacts to provide useful trading guidance is well illustrated by Charlie Tuke's experience at Neste. One J. Robinson West was Neste's 'deep throat' and he confidently whispered to them that Baker would prevail in talks with Aziz and that the Iraqis would pull back.[53]

Tuke sold and then sold more in the sure knowledge that prices would collapse. And then Baker said 'regrettably' and oil prices 'roofed',[54] to use the language of the trading floor. It was to be Tuke's biggest-ever loss in his career.

Indiscriminately across the oil trading world, profits and losses were encountered as traders speculated on the outcome. Nigel Saperia, a well-respected trader at the time took the opposite view and 'bought every waterborne cargo he could get his hands on'.[55] In fact, if Charlie Tuke had waited and followed the age-old 'buy the rumour and sell the news' tactic, he would have lucked out as prices crashed within a day or two of the whipping of Iraq by the Coalition.

Andy Hall's Phibro was predictably long but stayed long when prices collapsed. They would come to the office, check the market, and then play cards—until the position improved and they got out, taking a hit, but not as bad as it could have been.[56]

Some weeks later, the actual start of the shooting was initiated by U.S. planes bombing Baghdad. *As Chris Evans says 'News of this hit us at about 10 pm London time and we had a strategy of selling into the expected price rise. I was at home but on the phone to Mike Muller and Ian Lawson in the office. It tested the transatlantic broking and telephonic setup. We offered a cargo at $28* via *a London broker who was talking to Phibro* via *his colleague in New York. Phibro were delaying when we received a bid at $29 from another broker. We told our broker in London to pull our offer to Phibro at the same time that Phibro told the NY broker they accepted our $28 offer; a very difficult situation for the brokers. There was a bit of a standoff and in the end I told the guys to take the $29 bid and to do the deal with Phibro at $28 so that we could get on with selling more. In the event the bids soon died down. I was very relieved when we bought back the next morning at $23! I think (but don't know for sure) that this was the time that Phibro went very long and had to wait a while to recover. That was a very difficult night for Jorge to set an end of day price!'.*[57]

It is easy in hindsight to suggest that this time was one where the outcome would be settled without massive upset. In fact, back in New York and London, oil traders were going to great lengths to position themselves to be first in line for information on what was then a very big deal with unknown consequences.

In London, one American trader and graduate in Electrical Engineering took the short trip from his office near Oxford Street to the electronics hub of Tottenham Court Road where he purchased a satellite dish. Picking up some sandbags from a building site, he set up a receiving station on the roof of his office and accessed CNN, the television channel at that stage unavailable in the United Kingdom. CNN's appropriately named correspondent, Wolf Blitzer, was a lead news correspondent, reporting from the Middle East. He then made a bed for himself under his desk and camped out in the office, watching CNN and hoping for a head start, which indeed he got as his company was able to position themselves fortuitously at times during the crisis period.

There were to be few long-term implications for the progress and design of trading markets in oil as a result of the Gulf War. It merely caused a short-term price upset. There were some odd consequences however, such as when one entrepreneurial trading company allegedly arranged to mop up oil spills and waste oil in devastated Kuwait, load the mixture onto a tanker, and sell it to Zambia, where it almost ruined the refinery that attempted to process it.[58]

But now, we must turn back to see what Phibro's once-estranged protégé, Marc Rich, was up to.

Notes

1. Jane Garvey comment on Times Radio, the broadcast arm of the Times newspaper, 20/01/2025.
2. Commercial banks were debarred form physical oil trading but allowed to trade financial instruments such as swaps.
3. Asian refineries, loading oil from the Middle East would typically buy oil a couple of months before it is delivered.
4. Essentially, they brokered the trade.
5. EnergyRisk.com 2009.
6. PIW December 1990 p 8.
7. OTC markets relied heavily on self-regulation, with counterparties establishing their own terms and assessing credit risk individually. The International Swaps and Derivatives Association (ISDA), founded in 1985, played a key role in developing standardized documentation and

promoting best practices to reduce counterparty risk. https://www.isda.org/about-isda/

8. See The Policy Statement was adopted by the Commission on July 21, 1989: https://www.cftc.gov/sites/default/files/opa/press98/opamntn.htm#:~:text=The%20Policy%20Statement%20was%20adopted,Commission%20on%20July%2021%2C%201989.&text=It%20provides%20a%20safe%20harbor,currencies%20considered%20to%20be%20cash.
9. In the 1970s, the club of developed countries included the United States, France, the United Kingdom, Germany, Japan, and Italy. Hence, the G6, rather than today's G7.
10. FT 02/06/2018.
11. Discussion with Paul Newman 23/05/2024.
12. Energy Risk.com July 2009 p34.
13. https://www.iata.org/en/about/
14. Traders like to think they are the profit centre and that salespeople look after their clients more than their own firms. For further explanation, see Duhon, T pp191-211.
15. Conversation with Steve Jones on 21/01/2025.
16. Essentially business developers.
17. A major failing of Bank management and Regulators in the 2008 Financial crisis. This author, running an International Fixed Income business a few years prior to the crisis was astounded to discover in a meeting with the Deputy Governor of the Bank of England that he had no idea of the risks involved in the popular at the time and dangerous multi layered credit products being widely traded. To many, these products were beyond the bounds of human comprehension.
18. See Blas, J Uncovering the Secret History of Wall Street's Largest Trade Bloomberg 04/04/2017.
19. Discussion with Taraneh Azad.
20. Information on Jamaica, Morocco, Panama and Egypt derived from internal Morgan Stanley research.
21. BP were an early provider of oil indexed loans to Angola and their state oil company, Sonatrach.
22. Dated Brent is physical cargo of Brent with loading dates.
23. SITCO later changed to STASCO (Shell Trading and Supply Company).
24. Your author remembers selling oil to Deutsche Shell only to be told that the deal is strictly private and confidential (P&C), but under no circumstances it could reach SITCO!

25. From an interview with Chris Evans on 10/08/202024.
26. Mike Muller, a Cambridge graduate would become the head of Shell trading and a head of Vitol for Asia. Steve Mawer, also a Cambridge graduate would become a Chairman of the Board for Calumet, a renewable fuels company, Danny Masters, a graduate of Imperial College London would later join Phibro, lead J.P. Morgan's oil business and eventually become an Executive Chairman of 'CoinShares,' a crypto-business; In both latter functions, he would work closely with Rus Newton. Iain Lawson would work for a number of banks, BP and eventually settle at EY in Singapore.
27. WTI Midland Houston market has been trying to develop a swap market for different 'decades' (ten-day windows) of loading the oil.
28. Awarded to Rich Shelton, London based Chevron trader.
29. A Morgan Stanley sales document from 1989.
30. For a full discussion of the Brent CFD market see Barrera-Rey, F. and Seymour, A 1996. Also, Ford, Jonathan 2016 pp 81–84.
31. Please forgive the author's recollection of some of the surnames: Liz married Russell Newton from Shell (Liz was a forward Brent operator there at the time) and Sandra married John Carr from Phibro (and later, Arcadia).
32. Hume, N and Sheppard, D: Financial Times May 6 2015.
33. Discussion with P Smith on 20/01/2025.
34. Discussion with R Bainbridge 24/06/2024.
35. From a chat with Mark Quartermaine on 27/2/25. Your author was present at the outing. The caller was Kurt Chapman.
36. The source wished to remain anonymous.
37. 'Royal Dutch Shell has unilaterally amended the rules of one of the important components of the North Sea Brent market…' reported Reuters: https://www.reuters.com/article/world/refile-update-1-shell-changes-rules-of-bfoe-oil-market-platts-takes-stock-idUSL5N0BB2H1/
38. https://www.brecorder.com/news/4070907/bp-backs-shell-in-response-to-platts-on-brent-reform-201303091161295
39. https://press.spglobal.com/2013-03-15-Platts-Introduces-Quality-Premiums-to-Boost-Liquidity-of-Worlds-North-Sea-Brent-Oil-Benchmark
40. Later bought by Marathon, another American oil company. Kurt Chapman also worked for: Morgan Stanley, Elf, Koch supply and trading, Sempra, Mercuria, Levmet…

41. At the time, he was the only trader for the American refiner Sun Oil in London.
42. https://www.investopedia.com/articles/active-trading/102314/top-technical-indicators-commodities-investing.asp
43. https://corporatefinanceinstitute.com/resources/equities/moving-average/
44. https://corporatefinanceinstitute.com/resources/career-map/sell-side/capital-markets/fibonacci-retracements/
45. https://corporatefinanceinstitute.com/resources/equities/candlestick-patterns/
46. https://www.cmegroup.com/education/courses/technical-analysis/technical-patterns-reversals.html
47. https://www.bbc.co.uk/bitesize/articles/zm3rdnb
48. Robin was a Director of PVM Associates and popular author of this very influential report.
49. Even though only around 400 kbd of physical gasoline was being shipped by the pipeline.
50. For more details, see chapter 8.
51. Petroleum Argus 21/11/1988.
52. Petroleum Argus 11/05/1989.
53. Discussion with C Tuke on 23/01/2024.
54. Price 'went to the roof' – went very high.
55. Discussion with Kevin O'Reilly on 22/03/2024.
56. From author's conversations with Andy Hall and Malcom Macavity in 1991.
57. Conversation with Chris Evans on 22/2/25.
58. Ford, J (2016) P121.

Bibliography

Duhon, T (2012): How the Trading Floor Really Works Bloomberg Press.
Ford, J (2016): Depression, Oil Trading and A Mind At War With Itself Chipmunk Publishing.
Goodman, Leah McGrath (2011): The Asylum William Morrow.
Gordon, R and Stenvoll, T (2007): Statoil-A Study in Political Entrepreneurship James A Baker Institute for Public Policy of Rice University.
Horsnell, P and Mabro, R: (1993) Oil Markets and Prices Oxford University Press.
Imsirovic, A (ed 2023): Brent Crude Oil- Genesis and Development of the World's Most Important Oil Benchmark Palgrave McMillan.

Noreng, Oystein (2022): The Oil Business and the State Routledge.
Parra, Francisco (2010): Oil Politics A Modern History of Petroleum I.B. Tauris.

12

An End and Two Beginnings

In Marc's Footsteps

For most normal mortals, a position in the Oil Trading Department of a Wall Street Refiner would have been thought to be pretty exciting. Not exciting enough though for Marc Crandall. Marc had been the insider of the Morgan Stanley oil leadership triad of himself, Nancy Kropp, and John Shapiro. By 1988, these three had proven the concept of oil trading to the banks' bigwigs, hired a cadre of staff commensurate with the perceived opportunity, and were starting to see decent bottom-line results.

And then Crandall left—'*for a bit more excitement!*'[1] or so he claimed. In fact, Crandall was seeing Nadia Voloshin, whose brother Mark was a trader at Marc Rich, and he was being constantly badgered about how much more money he could make at Marc Rich as opposed to straight-laced and stuffy, old, white-shoe Morgan Stanley.

Even to this day, Crandall's day-to-day life would not be described as ordinary. Living for half the year in his beach house in Uruguay's' 'right-on' Playa Del Este and the other half in Istria, on the Croatian coast on the Adriatic Sea, a typical schedule might find him travelling to places as esoteric as Mauritania or as distant as Indonesia. This way he looks after the companies he founded: sometimes on business for CWP Global,[2] a successful renewables developer, and sometimes to oversee the sawmills in Uruguay, supplying his lumber business in that country.

Marc is a modern-day international entrepreneur and one of the few non-household names that have really walked the walk when it comes to innovation and carefully managed risk-taking. What is absolutely not widely

A. Imsirovic and C. Bryce, *The Rivers of Money*,
https://doi.org/10.1007/978-3-031-91806-3_12

known, is the crucial role he played in the founding of Glencore and, more directly, in the founding of trading behemoth, Trafigura.

In early 1991, long-time Marc Rich cohorts, Pincus Green and Alex Hackle retired. Rich bought back their shares and so owned 85 per cent of the company bearing his name. At the same time, there began the germs of unrest among his most senior colleagues who were keen to understand succession and future ownership plans.

Crandall on gasoline, Danny Dreyfus on grains, Billy Strothotte[3] on metals (minus aluminium, which was under the leadership of Manny Weiss), and Claude Dauphin on oil (having replaced Jim Daley) were, in their own minds, the senior successors to the 'King'. At the time, Rich was a fugitive and was undergoing a messy divorce.[4] '*He was a lonely figure*' according to Crandall. There was particular tension between Rich and Strothotte 'who was the polar opposite of Marc and '*didn't work too hard*'.[5] Thinking that Strothotte wanted him out, and hearing confirmation to that effect from an old Madrid friend, Max Mazin, Rich got in the first blow and fired him. Crandall characterises the following two months as being akin to '*Florentina at the time of Machiavelli*'.

At around the same time, Claude Dauphin's father passed away, prompting a significant shift in his life. Having dropped out of school at sixteen, Claude had joined the family scrap metal business in Caen, France, but his father's death led him to make a major decision.[6] He chose to leave Marc Rich & Co. to return to the family firm.

This decision, however, caused confusion within the company. Manny Weiss, mistakenly believing that Claude had been fired along with Billy Strothotte, also resigned in solidarity, unaware that Claude's departure was voluntary and driven by personal reasons.

As a result, Crandall, who was focussing on gasoline trading and on highly profitable business in Argentina and Mexico, was made the head of oil. Crandall was asked not to occupy Dauphin's office as Marc was worried about the reaction of others, but he took the office anyway. That move earned him Rich's respect: '*Standing up to Marc always worked*', says Crandall.

By early 1993, Rich had appointed his disliked lawyer, Bob Thomajan as COO and the successor-level folks were becoming ever more restless. At a Zug company offsite, Crandall raised the succession question publicly. Having again been brick-walled, Crandall resigned: '*I put a spark to the flame but there was already gasoline on the floor*'. Despite resigning, Crandall was asked by Danny Dreyfus to negotiate a deal for succession and the future with Marc Rich. So, Crandall and Rich sat down in Zug, and over a bottle of Black Label, worked out a deal: what the net asset value of the company was, who would get what shares, when the successors would get control of the company, and when they could change the company's name. For Rich, price was fine with no premium, but he baulked at changing the name.

That weekend, the seniors met at a brunch organised by Claude Dauphin. Graham Sharp wrote up a term sheet to memorialise the deal that was to happen three weeks later. Crandall was to be President and he and a finance wizard, Eric de Turkheim (Paris-educated and a former Vice-Commodore of the Royal Ocean Racing Club) agreed to buy into Claude's family scrap firm.

Then Rich asked to renegotiate the whole thing. '*He was famous for this and it was always the most hated thing about him-he always tried to renegotiate*', recalls Crandall.

When Dauphin declined the offer, the deal was off. Undeterred, Crandall, Sharp, De Turkheim, and Dauphin, along with Antonio Cometti and Dan Posen, set their sights on building something new: Trafigura. The initial seed capital was $20.35 million, which included $7 million from the scrap business that had begun operating in Romania and Bulgaria. Dauphin took a 30% stake in the new venture, while the others each held 10%. The remaining 30% was set aside for future hires.

Dauphin was initially cautious, avoiding high-risk oil trading. He believed in a more conservative approach. However, over time, he was convinced that expansion and new talent were necessary for Trafigura's growth.

Crandall's strategic vision for the company was simple yet bold: to trade as broadly as possible across geographies, product qualities, timeframes, and markets, as long as they weren't losing money. As he often put it: '*Changes in the world create re-optimising opportunities*', and by capitalising on these shifting conditions, Trafigura could generate profits through '*monetising free optionalities*'.

Crandall's extensive network in Argentina and Mexico proved invaluable in those early days. One of his key contacts, Santiago Soldati from Argentina, helped them form Interpetrol, giving him a 10% stake in Trafigura. By late 1993, the company leveraged established contracts in China, tapping into a rapidly growing market, and soon they were trading oil in significant quantities. As with many successful ventures in oil trading, relationships were the cornerstone of their success. '*Trafigura would never have gotten off the ground from a standing start otherwise*', Crandall reflected.

And, thus began the rise of a company that would eventually become one of the top three commodities traders in the world.

Turning back to mid-1993 and the Sharp term *sheet*, it lay dormant for some months until Manny Weiss and Billy Strothotte took it back to Marc Rich with some amendments and finally, they closed the deal. The new company was to be called Glencore—yet another of the top three traders today.

While Rich is most remembered as the fugitive, tax fraudster that eloped from the United States in disgrace, his contribution to the development of oil trading has his substantially influential fingerprints all over it. Glencore, Trafigura, and Clarendon in the United States are three well known offspring of Marc Rich + Co. There have always been rumours across the market that graduates of Marc Rich + Co over the years have been able to set up their own firms with his considerable assistance.[7] From the earliest days in Madrid, his name has been synonymous with oil markets.

'*Marc didn't judge deals, he judged the people who brought them to him*', claims Crandall. This was a clear example of the dominance of the qualitative over the quantitative approach in these founding days of oil trading. And, to that end, Crandall was unsurprised to watch the exiled Rich patronising many charitable causes: '*He was a very nice man*'.

New Opportunities

In a relative sense, oil markets experienced something of a great moderation between the end of the Gulf War in early 1991 and mid-1996. Traders who had feasted on volatility and the growing interest of consumers in oil markets and associated derivative products and an array of banks providing liquidity, began to start twiddling their thumbs.

In search of alternative opportunities, some players alighted on the markets for natural gas and electricity. In the United States, trading natural gas begun to appear in the mid-1980s as the Federal Energy Regulatory Agency (FERC) mandated changes in the transportation and sales of gas. The agency introduced a series of regulatory reforms, liberating and fundamentally transforming the natural gas industry from a tightly regulated sector into a competitive and market-driven one.[8]

Then, the 1989 Natural Gas Wellhead Decontrol Act phased out federal price controls on natural gas at the wellhead.[9] Producers could now sell gas directly to buyers without being tied to long-term contracts with specific pipelines. This made gas markets more liquid and encouraged the growth of a spot market, which quickly emerged and on 3rd April 1990, NYMEX launched a gas futures contract based on delivery at the Henry Hub in Louisiana.[10]

In the United Kingdom, the government commenced a process of market deregulation in 1994 by forcing the monopoly gas company, British Gas, to 'release' volumes of product in order that other suppliers might emerge. This promulgated a spot market for gas which grew over time and eventually operated in tandem with other gas markets in Europe.[11] On a global scale, It became increasingly obvious that the LNG trade was liberating the gas trade from the shackles of the government-to-government pipeline trade. LNG became the marginal gas supply thus setting the global gas prices.[12] Gas trading and its price determination were gradually resembling the global oil markets[13]: Emerging gas market-equivalents of WTI Cushing, Brent in London, and Dubai in Singapore were Henry Hubb in Texas, Title Transfer Facility (TTF) in the Netherlands and Japan Korea Marker (JKM) in Asia.[14]

Although it would not be until the mid-1990's that electric power would become tradeable in the United States, when deregulation commenced, already there was an active market in the United Kingdom and in the Australian state of Victoria, both of which the author was involved in trading in.

Eventually, these markets would develop into huge centres of spot market liquidity and the source of significant profits for trading companies and many oil traders moved across to try their hand at power and gas at this otherwise quiet time.

Tights-for-Oil: From Soviets to Russia

Standing stalk-like and tall in the lobby of the Mezhdunarohdnaya Hotel in Moscow in the early 1990s was an absurdity—a cuckoo clock gifted by Russophile Dr Armand Hammer (he of Oxy fame), to the Russian state. Every hour, a wooden bird would appear from a housing atop this wonderful example of full Soviet kitsch and howl loudly, disturbing all the spies gathered in discreet conversation with each other in the lobby.

In the earliest days, the authorities attempted to direct all the prospecting foreigners to this one hotel from where they could keep an eye on them. Very soon, however, the visiting businessmen discovered the much more elegant Metropole Hotel which became the oilmen and bankers favoured haunt. It was a good place, in quiet moments, to play the favoured game of 'spot the one who is not a spy'.

Russia, then, was the other opportunity to which some traders turned their temporarily idle hands in search of easy pickings. With the collapse of the Soviet Union, the oil industry in Russia and the former Soviet Republics fell into a period of considerable difficulty and that meant opportunity beckoned.

The commercial end of the oil industry in Russia had been characterised by centralised control. A number of production companies, primarily in Siberia, had been ineptly flooding oil wells in an effort to meet centrally mandated volumetric production targets. Oil was then distributed domestically at a price many multiples below international prices or it was sold overseas by the state monopoly, Soyuzneftexport, having been transported to loading points (mainly Ventspils and Novorossiysk) by a state monopoly, Transneft.

Soyuzneftexport had a particularly important role as it was a generator of foreign currency and much-needed imports (in barter deals), and was usually staffed by the best people the ministry could find. As oil prices became volatile, long-term contracts had to be renegotiated more frequently, and, in the 1980s, such meetings were normally held on a quarterly basis.[15] Soviets were master negotiators, and meetings were normally started by one of the Soyuzneftexport senior technical staff, familiar with all the necessary statistics—volumes, prices, revenues, late payments, demurrage claims,[16] and other such details.

One of the most remarkable individuals in this realm was Ljudmila Tumarkina, a sharp and formidable woman who exuded the authority and discipline of a headmistress at a prestigious English public school. Affectionately (though affection was usually not reciprocal) known as 'Ljuda', she had a signature style of negotiation that was as effective as it was intimidating. Meetings under her watch began with a relentless critique of the customers' shortcomings—delays in loading, unacceptable ships, unpaid bills, and more. By the time lunch rolled around, most opposing negotiators were thoroughly battered and often ready to concede.

That was precisely when her boss, Yuri Harlamov, would make his grand entrance, bringing a dramatic change in tone. With a warm smile, hearty bear hugs, and an invitation to lunch, Harlamov would charm the beleaguered customers. The lunches, always paid for by the guests, were lavish affairs that stretched on for hours, featuring vodka served in tea cups and frequent toasts. These toasts began with lofty themes like the enduring friendship between nations but quickly descended into jovial celebrations of personal camaraderie among the attendees. This routine would play out over several days, with Ljuda and Yuri masterfully alternating pressure and charm until the customers inevitably relented and accepted Soyuzneftexport's terms.

This whole Soviet oil structure started falling apart with the ascension of Mikhail Gorbachev and his attempts to restructure a flailing Russian economy.[17] There then ensued a ten-plus year period of wild west-like events in Russian oil matters.

Miodrag Stanic was heading a tiny representative office for Petraco, an Italian oil trader, in Moscow. He just had a call from Raznoexport, a Russian state-run, import–export company, asking for help. They needed to find and import fifteen million pairs of tights! Urgently! Being headquartered in Milano, Italy the Petraco head, Branko Srenger had no problem finding some quality garments, which were promptly supplied and shipped to Moscow. '*Payment was not a problem, as a payment undertaking document from some of these big, state-run companies was a gold standard, better guaranty than the banks at the time*', says Ingeborg Srenger, Branko's daughter and later the CEO of the company.

But, the deal was closed just before the Soviet Union started to collapse. The payment for fifteen million tights was not forthcoming. Branko got to work and after endless meetings, a year and a half later, he was awarded an allotment of oil to pay for the goods. Soon, many Italian companies with similar problems started calling Petraco for help. '*That is how it all started*', says Inga.

It was her dad's last deal as he was suffering from terminal cancer. But, Ms. Srenger built on the existing relationships. '*As the Soyuzneftexport export monopoly collapsed, there were all these employees of the company around the world with no mothership telling them what to do. But soon, they started doing what they do best—travelling around Russia and collecting barrels that could be exported. They became "Nafta Italia", "Nafta Belgium" and so on... They were good and professional suppliers of crude oil and products, kept their word and we went along with them*', *says Ingeborg Srenger*.

Sensing an opportunity to capitalise, a number of Western oil companies began catching the Monday morning flight from London's Heathrow to Moscow's Sheremetyevo airport. The same folks would return every Friday evening and stand drinking in the galley of the British Airlines (BA) flight, exchanging war stories. There were successes and there were failures!

The 'upstream'[18] end of the Russian oil industry hosted 32 production associations (PA's). They were part of the Ministry of the Oil Industry but were run by powerful General Directors as local fiefdoms. Only one has survived the passage of time, Surgutneftegaz, run by Vladimir Bogdanov. The others have been assimilated into groupings over time, the most important of which these days are Lukoil and Rosneft.

Lukoil was an early beneficiary of both having the right connections and the most intelligently entrepreneurial leadership. Valery Grifer, who until his recent passing, was Chairman of Lukoil. In the early post-Soviet days of confusion, the popular and avuncular 'Grifer' was something of a kingmaker. It is likely that, as a former Oil Minister, he was behind the scenes at the creation of Lukoil. Three PA's, Langepas, Urengoi, and Kogalym came together under the leadership of Vagit Alekperov to form the company that he still runs today and which has significant international reach and vertical integration.[19]

Rosneft, which acquired many of the other PAs, took longer to settle into its dominant role in the market. Their rise to prominence began with a successful IPO in 2006 followed quickly by their adoption of international accounting, most especially Generally Accepted Accounting Principles (GAAP).[20]

Then, they got international, inking a long-term 2011–2030 supply deal with China, buying 50 per cent of Germany's Ruhr Oel from Petróleos de Venezuela, S.A. (PDVSA for short—Rosneft has always been close to Venezuela) and, in 2013, taking over TNK-BP. Boasting an international Board of Directors with such as BP CEO Bob Dudley, Wall Street legend John Mack, and Glencore's Ivan Glasenberg, they were mixing it with other large global integrated behemoths.

Rosneft's purchase of a majority shareholding in the Nayara refinery in India in partnership with Trafigura in 2016 gave them a share in that country's largest processing plant and they were careful to appoint internationally recognised oil traders to oversee its activities. Former BP big-wig Tony Fountain took the Chair while Russophile Andrew Balgarnie took a Board seat. Mergers and Acquisitions (M&A) banker Balgarnie was one of a handful of special advisors to Igor Sechin. Referred to colloquially as 'platoks' which is Russian for 'handkerchief', they sat behind the executive table in the weekly management meetings where Sechin gathered his ten Vice Presidents and the Finance Director each week.[21] Perhaps the 'handkerchiefs' were there to wipe away any mess that the execs may have created!

As their international interests increased, trading was handled by ex-BP executive, Didier Casimiro. A polyglot, suave Belgian with an impressive silver-grey mullet, he needed to have stamina to burn as he was dragged around the globe with the 'Boss' and called on at all times of day or night. Keeping up the BP connection, Casimiro relied on Marcus Cooper and Brian Chesterman, seasoned former company executives, to handle day-to-day trading.

Rosneft were on a roll but their wings were clipped and more when sanctions on the company and on individuals were levied in the wake of Vladimir Putin's invasion of Ukraine.

Lukoil has also made a significant impact on the international oil trading scene. In 2000, Swedish trader Christian Gleisner established Litasco in Geneva, though his untimely and mysterious death in 2005—allegedly due to a rare autoimmune condition—raised questions. He was succeeded by Gati Al-Gebouri, and in 2012, the company appointed former BP senior executive Tim Bullock as CEO. Litasco has since expanded into upstream ventures, particularly in Iraq, where it secured oil flows from the West Qurna field and other sources. The company also established offices in Dubai and New York, while cultivating substantial business relationships with clients across Latin America. Today, Litasco is led by Inna Dariy, but its operations have consistently relied on the approval of Valeri Subotin, a trusted adviser to Lukoil's founder, Vagit Alekperov, based in Moscow.

Despite Russia's vast oil reserves, a sizable refining industry, robust domestic and export markets, and encouragement from Western business interests over time, no traded oil markets have emerged inside the country. The absence of rewards for improved performance through the use of traded markets, combined with the severe consequences—such as blame or worse—for unfavourable outcomes, has created a strong disincentive. At every level—personal, corporate, and national—there is little motivation to take risks or stand out. It is probably the opposite—the less transparency and murkier the markets, the more chance there is to 'milk' the system and make money on the side.

That is not to say that the BA travellers of the 1990s all wasted their time though. The most successful from a financial point of view were the traders who were experts in doing tricky things in idiosyncratic places. An early favourite was sourcing dirt-cheap domestic oil and finding a way of exporting it to international markets where it was sold at world prices. One might easily imagine how producers, transport companies, export port authorities, and other miscellaneous inspectors might have been 'squared away' with more than just the price of a vodka or two. In fact, the streets of NefteYugansk, Nishnevartovsk, and Tyumen began to host the key local officials preferred gold-coloured Mercedes 500s in almost the same numbers as might be encountered in the upmarket U.S. suburb of Greenwich, Connecticut.

Dishonesty was a hugely profitable type of operation, much mined by a certain class of oil traders for a few years until Russian organised crime began to poke its nose into affairs and the traders felt it necessary to desist.

Other companies, BP, Mobil, Phibro, and Amoco among them, went to Moscow and on to Siberia with the somewhat more noble aim of helping restore production, joint venturing in the proceeds of improvement being the aim. They met with mixed success over time.

Wild West

In the period immediately following the collapse of the Soviet Union, the Western Siberian city of Tyumen was where it all happened. Militant 'oil generals' and the regional government led by Yuri Shafranik were busy fighting Moscow for control of 'their' oil in the business and political vacuum of the time.[22]

It was a city which was at the same time both very foreign to the Westerner and yet oddly familiar. This author was summoned from London for a meeting in far-away Tyumen by none other than Yuri Shafranik.[23] It proved to be an interesting journey. An uneventful flight by the, then, reliable British Airways to Moscow's Sheremetyevo airport was followed by a three-hour journey to the opposite side of the city where the very different domestic airport, Domodedovo was situated.

On arrival, and through a haze and smell of Turkish tobacco and smouldering wood, it was interesting to see the groups and families with goods and chattels alongside them, sitting around in circles on the concourse enjoying an al fresco lunch of sorts.

Most airports at the time boasted a restaurant or two, even if it was just a Wimpy Bar.[24] They also featured standard amenities like departure boards and check-in desks. But not Domodedovo—not in those days. The trick was to navigate through the lunchtime crowd on the tarmac, find the right plane, board it, and hope it was actually heading to your intended destination. It was a matter of chance, really. One such instance saw a landing on a dark winter evening in Tyumen, where the plane touched down through the snow after a last-minute go-around. As for whether the landing gear was downwell, maybe not.

The author was then taken to a city centre bar—restaurant for a beetroot, tomato, and apple salad while listening to a live band playing Status Quo songs.[25] Overnight was spent in a Sanitorium outside the city before news was passed along that Yuri had, in fact, departed on the previous evening for Moscow. Perhaps, he had been summoned there and perhaps, as we might later learn, he was summoned by Grisha and Slava, the principals of J&S and part founders of Mercuria,[26] who had managed to tie up Siberian oil exports at the time.[27] This was nothing out of the ordinary though as Russian politicians and aspiring oligarchs had a reputation for lateness, although they usually turned up eventually.

As the banking and oil company pioneers began to get an understanding of the lay of the land when it came to finding their way to the provinces, the delights of private charters became the commonplace mode of transport.

Even if a take-off from Vnukovo airfield close to the centre of Moscow was delayed while the co-pilot applied the full force of a hammer to the tail fin or when, hoping to arrive quietly at a far-flung city, the air traffic controllers switched the lights out on the runway as the flight had not been 'approved', the thrill of such adventures wholly outdid the rigours of the commercial, if it can be called that, option.

One trader recalls being summoned from Nishnevartovsk where he was stationed, along with his boss, who travelled from New York, to meet Prime Minister Victor Chernomyrdin (apparently a name which translated to 'black muzzle' in English). Unable to find a commercial flight, he was forced to hire the only private plane available in that far-flung region. This was a gas pipeline sniffer plane but, as it was unpressurised, he had to endure a six-hour flight as the plane ascended and descended following the contours of the ground as it was unable to operate at any great height.[28] One understands that he ran out of sick bags.

On a more recent occasion, the author encountered another challenge stemming from the relaxed approach Russian executives often take to punctuality. Offered a last-minute meeting with Igor Sechin, head of Rosneft and a close advisor to Vladimir Putin, the author managed to secure only a one-day tourist visa to visit Rosneft's headquarters along the Moskva River, with its striking view of the Kremlin. Despite the tight schedule—a 6:00 PM meeting and a 10:40 PM flight back to Munich (the very last of the day) it was decided to go ahead with the trip.

As expected, Sechin kept his guests waiting in his ante-room, where an ever-growing crowd vied for his attention. When the author was finally ushered in at 7:30 PM, the visa constraints were explained, and an escort through Moscow's infamous traffic to the airport was requested. Sechin's blunt response: 'Nyet'. Yet, when the meeting concluded an hour later, an escort was indeed provided. With flashing blue lights, a bit of luck, and a conveniently delayed Munich flight, a return trip to an unwelcoming Siberian locale for breaking visa laws was narrowly avoided. Of course, in those days, a few dollars discreetly placed in the right hands could have resolved any such complications just as effectively.

Trading companies that were quick on their feet and were in the right place, at the right time did very well and their kind mushroomed in Russia. The arbitrage between low, government-fixed domestic oil prices and high international prices was huge and profitable and very much resembled the 'tax arbitrage' in the United States in the early 1970s discussed in Chapter 1.

Anyone with good contacts in the oil regions and the bureaucracy in Moscow worked this 'arb'. Nafta Belgium morphed into Urals trading under

Andrei Pannikov, and a handful of former government officials who set up Balkar trading grew into one of the major exporters[29] of Russian oil in the 1990s.[30] For Western traders, such companies were a godsend, especially in the early days, when navigating the Wild West of Russian legislation and politics was impossible without a domestic partner. While these Russian traders captured most of the 'export arbitrage', there was still a lot of money to be made. Petraco had a large, 300,000-barrel contract with Balkar for Russian Export Blend or Urals crude for several years. When Mobil trading stepped in and paid over a dollar more per barrel for the very same contract, they still made '*very good money*'.[31]

Western traders such as Vitol and Glencore owe their current size and status to a not inconsiderable extent thanks to early entry into Russia. Glencore developed a mutually profitable relationship with Mikhail Gutseriev, an Ingush-born businessman and a deputy chairman to the State Duma. Gutseriev insisted on upfront, cash payments for oil, which he sourced through his contacts and facilitated export permits for it.[32] But he delivered. Gutseriev used the profits to increase production and acquire more producers, under the 'umbrella' industrial and financial group Safmar, which included RussNeft, Neftisa, Russian Coal, several banks, and other companies.[33] As Mikhail Gutseriev's importance grew, so did Glencore's. At one stage, Glencore's Russian trading in office employed some 150 people!

Eventually, the symbiotic relationship '*... lasting two decades of investments which saw it trading millions of barrels of Russneft's oil*'[34] came to an end, following Putin's invasion of Ukraine.

In two decades, from the initial management buyout by a handful of traders[35] to the final takeover of Xstrata, one of the largest mining conglomerates in 2013, Glencore grew to become; '*... one of the world's largest natural resources groups, extending through more than 90 commodities from copper to barley and from oil to vanadium... employs roughly 190,000 people across 50 countries... market capitalisation of roughly $65bn, becoming one of the 10 largest constituents of the blue-chip FTSE 100 stock index*'.[36] Some industry insiders attribute this stratospheric growth to Glencore's relationships and investments by Mikhail Gutseriev, who always kept his side of the bargain.[37] But, if you read the company's official history, he is not even mentioned.[38]

Vitol's early entry into Russia started with a close relationship with a refinery in the city of Perm in the European part of Russia, on the banks of the Kama River in the Urals.[39] The trading company also made an early inroad into Kazakhstan, and exploited trading opportunities not only in oil, but all commodities in this mineral-rich country.[40] For some 25 years, the trading company had a virtual monopoly in the country and this relationship made '*Vitol, the king of oil in Kazakhs*tan even if at one stage their representative, Gavin de Sallis, was arrested and imprisoned for a short time on trumped up tax charges'.[41] It is unlikely that Vitol would be the company it is now without this long-term stream of revenues from the former Soviet Union.

Many other western traders made their money in Russia: Ben Polner's 'Taurus' had a close and profitable working relationship with Lukoil (before they established their own, trading arm, Litasco) for many years, something that his close associate, a Dutchman, Niels Troost allegedly continued through his company Paramount even after the sanctions were imposed on Russia.[42] A Swiss trader J&S[43] was one of the earliest entrants, when working at Tyumenimpex, a local company in the Tyumen oil region of Russia. Later, after they left, the company grew in stature and developed a close relationship with Surgutneftegas,[44] a Russian oil and gas giant created by merging several previously state-owned companies in Western Siberia and Transneft, the country's pipeline monopoly.[45]

Looking back to the early years, Siberian hosts saw foreign traders as facilitators of the illicit export of cheap domestic crude oil, Western engineers as cleaners of their degraded oil fields, and foreign bankers as walking wallets. Those who obliged, like Phibro-Salomon in their ill-fated White Nights joint venture with Varyoganneftegas, often paid a steep price. Local, regional, and state authorities expertly wielded bureaucratic tools such as tax disputes and export license delays to ensure the ventures left significantly poorer. Eventually, the Russian 'Mafia' got involved, a few throats got cut (literally) and, message received and understood, the foreigners slipped quietly away, at least for a while.[46]

Russia has been a disappointment for the trader with an interest in globalising the opportunity and there is no more free market business done in Russia today than there was at the fall of the Berlin Wall 35 years ago.[47] However, traders who were experts at doing 'difficult things in difficult places' thrived, making some of them industrial giants of today.

A new wave of traders are now profiting from Russian oil while operating out of Dubai. A series of obscure entities, often with complex ownership structures and opaque operations, have been drawn to Dubai—a welcoming hub at a time when sanctions restrict Russian oil business in many traditional trading centres. Whether fuelled by this influx or other factors, Dubai has become a hotbed for oil trading. Its low taxes, quality schools, sunny climate, and vibrant lifestyle are attracting a community that might once have favoured Switzerland, long known for its lenient stance on the shadowy practices that appeal to certain types of oil traders.

All the while some wise heads in the industry understood that, with proper transparency, the oil trading market could grow exponentially turning the lazy river of money into a torrent of riches. They set about creating an institution that would eventually prosper beyond all conception—The Intercontinental Exchange (ICE).

Notes

1. Discussion with Marc Crandall on 02/05/2024. Much of what follows in this sub-chapter relies heavily on Crandall's comments and insights during this interview.
2. https://cwp.global/
3. Generally referred to as 'Willy' rather than 'Billy', the latter is the name used by Marc Crandall in discussion on 02/05/2024.
4. https://www.nytimes.com/2013/06/27/business/marc-rich-pardoned-financier-dies-at-78.html
5. Discussion with Marc Crandall 02/05/2024.
6. The company was called ACCOR at the time.
7. Vickars, Marcia The Rich Boys 2005.
8. In 1985, FERC issued Order 436, which introduced "open access" to interstate gas pipelines. The pipelines, previously involved in both the transportation and sale of gas, were required to offer their transportation services to any gas producer, marketer, or consumer on a non-discriminatory basis. Essentially, pipelines were "unbundled," separating the transportation function from the sale of gas. https://www.gao.gov/assets/rced-87-133br.pdf
9. https://www.congress.gov/bill/101st-congress/house-bill/1722
10. https://www.cmegroup.com/articles/whitepapers/henry-hub-natural-gas-futures-global-benchmark.html
11. https://www.europarl.europa.eu/ftu/pdf/en/FTU_2.1.9.pdf
12. For an early paper explaining this process, see: https://www.oxfordenergy.org/wpcms/wp-content/uploads/2020/04/Insight-68-A-Comparative-History-of-Oil-and-Gas-Markets-and-Prices.pdf
13. See A. Imsirovic (2020): 'Gas readies for its oil moment.'.
14. In reality, the latter covers China and Taiwan as well: https://www.spglobal.com/commodityinsights/en/our-methodology/price-assessments/lng/jkm-japan-korea-marker-gas-price-assessments#:~:text=JKM%E2%84%A2%20(Japan%20Korea%20Marker,Assessment%20%7C%20S%26P%20Global%20Commodity%20Insights

15. Your author participated in several such negotiations.
16. These are claims by the shipper of oil for any additional time spent loading and unloading the commodity, over and above agreed period. They are very common in oil trading and extremely tedious (and sometimes controversial) to calculate.
17. See Gustafson (2012), page 41.
18. Exploration and production.
19. https://www.lukoil.com/Company/history
20. https://www.ojp.gov/sites/g/files/xyckuh241/files/media/document/GAAP_Guide_Sheet_508.pdf
21. Conversation with Andrew Balgarnie in 2022.
22. The 'oil generals' were the all-powerful leaders of the 32 Production Associations. Names such as Viktor Paliy at Nishnevartovskneftegas, Anatoliy Fomin at Chernogorneft, Vladimir Bogdanov at Surgutneftegas and Sergei Muravlenko at Yugansk were storied and remained so during most of the 1990's.
23. Shafranik was briefly to become Russian Energy Minister from 1993–1996.
24. Wimpy Bars were a brand of especially casual fare- hamburgers and the likes- that were popular with a certain audience in the UK.
25. Status Quo were a rock band well known for inventing a number of hits using only three chords on the guitar.
26. For details, see the next chapter.
27. Grzegorz Jankselewicz and Slawomir Smolokowski, two Polish businessmen.
28. A story attributed to Richard Shelton.
29. See: https://www.joc.com/article/crude-for-credit-barter-agreement-raises-hackles-of-russian-firms-5439490 and https://www.joc.com/article/unlicensed-traders-win-russian-oil-export-bids-5426343
30. https://www.energyintel.com/0000017b-a7a3-de4c-a17b-e7e31eb80000
31. Author's recollection of a lunch-meeting with a Mobil trader at the time.
32. From an interview with an industry insider who wished to stay anonymous.
33. https://russneft.ru/eng/news/13906/
34. https://www.reuters.com/business/glencore-may-sell-russneft-stake-founder-gutseriyev-says-kommersant-2022-02-16/
35. More on this in Chapter 9.

36. https://www.ft.com/content/9d355d82-b31a-11e2-95b3-00144feabdc0
37. From an interviewee who wished to stay anonymous.
38. https://www.glencore.com/who-we-are/our-history
39. Today, it is a Lukoil-owned refinery: https://www.lukoil.com/Business/Downstream/OilRefining
40. Also, it is rich in coal, gold, manganese, titanium, zinc, lead etc. See: https://documents1.worldbank.org/curated/en/099081823001539573/pdf/P17674501063760b08b290a4ae6547845d.pdf
41. https://stories.publiceye.ch/vitolinkazakhstan/index.html
42. https://www.ft.com/content/eb3b3ea1-5aaa-4136-8f02-01b76fc8f405
43. For details about J&C, see Chapter 15.
44. For a short history, see: https://www.surgutneftegas.ru/en/company/history/
45. https://rus-petroleum.ru/en/founder/36-pjsc-transneft.html
46. It happened to a finance director of a company you author was dealing with. Problems were more prevalent, but not exclusive to metals.
47. For an excellent summary of the early post-Soviet period in the oil industry, see Gustafson, T 2012. For a sense of the experiences of early hopefuls in Russia, see Bryce, C 'Night Flight to Siberia' in Johnson, O (ed) 40 Classic Crude Trades.

Bibliography

Vickars, Marcia (2005): 'The Rich Boys', Australian Financial Review, July 30.

Gustafson, T. (2012): 'Wheel of Fortune, The Battle for Oil and Power in Russia', Belknap Harvard.

Imsirovic A. (2020): 'Gas readies for its oil moment' in Petroleum Economist, 28 January 2020.

Johnson, O. ed (2022): '40 Classic Crude Trades' by Owain Jonson, Routledge.

13

Transparency and Trading Around Assets

Transparency—A Turbocharge to Liquidity

In Monaco, you can effortlessly have your Lamborghini valet parked at 2 AM—or even later—without a hitch. However, good luck finding a carton of milk or a Hershey bar at that hour. The Principality has no trace of the ubiquitous Korean grocers or Asian corner shops found elsewhere. Instead, corner stores are far more likely to showcase Gucci handbags than everyday essentials for the average person.

Monaco is a glitzy enclave, huddled on the steep, sea-side slopes of Mont Agel, crowned by the imposing French rock formation of the Tête de Chien.[1] It's a sleek, densely packed town, with winding roads lined by luxury apartments and, of course, the famous Monte Carlo marina. Once dominated by Russian-flagged superyachts, the harbour is now filled with vessels flying Maltese and Cypriot flags, just a convenient rebranding, with the Mediterranean islands standing in as temporary hosts.

In 1999, at the height of their success, Enron hosted an exclusive gathering in Monaco, inviting senior executives from their key partners—and future competitors. The event's purpose? To showcase Enron's bold vision for trading in power, gas, weather derivatives, credit products, and beyond.

The gathering was hosted by John Sherriff, the well-regarded head of Enron's London office, whose approachable demeanour was a far cry from the typical image of the aggressive, intellectually arrogant Enron employee. Attendees included top executives from the European divisions of J Aron, BP, Total, Morgan Stanley, Vitol, Shell, and a few others.[2]

A. Imsirovic and C. Bryce, *The Rivers of Money*, https://doi.org/10.1007/978-3-031-91806-3_13

For this author, however, the most memorable takeaway wasn't the cutting-edge ideas Sherriff's team showcased. It was a dinner conversation with John's top female executive—a discussion that would soon ignite developments profoundly shaping the future of oil trading.

Louise Kitchen had joined Enron about five years earlier, transitioning from a relatively modest role at the U.K. electricity company PowerGen. With her driven, no-nonsense attitude and unmistakable confidence, she quickly carved out a reputation for herself. Her assertive approach and relentless determination propelled her to lead Enron's power and gas trading operations in Europe. Kitchen's legacy is indelibly tied to the creation of the company's groundbreaking one-to-all electronic trading platform, Enron Online.[3]

The story, however, dates back to 1996 when John Sherriff initiated an internal study to assess the feasibility of an online trading platform. After selling the concept to Lou Pai, Enron's Head of Trading, the two convinced their superior, Greg Whalley, to green-light the project. [4] Fast forward to mid-September 1999 in Monaco, just five weeks before the system's launch on 26th October—and it was Louise Kitchen who brought it all to life.

The concept was straightforward: a cutting-edge electronic trading platform enabling third parties to trade directly with Enron, but not with each other.[5] While prioritising technology over liquidity—the true source of value—may have been a strategic misstep, the idea ignited a pivotal realisation for the Morgan Stanley representative at the meeting. That light bulb moment would ultimately eclipse Enron Online and lay the foundation for ICE, now the financial world's most influential global electronic exchange.

The light bulb moment was the realisation that the true value—the liquidity—in the oil market wasn't controlled by Enron, but by the most active oil traders of the era: J Aron, Morgan Stanley, BP, and Shell. The value resided with them, and allowing Enron to profit from it would have been a critical mistake. This insight reshaped the balance of power, ensuring that the major players in oil trading retained control over what was rightfully theirs.

After receiving swift internal approval from MS Commodities head Neal Shear, Colin Bryce and Goran Trapp arranged a breakfast meeting at their 25 Cabot Square office on a chilly December morning with their J Aron London counterparts, Dick Bronks and Isabelle Ealet. It didn't take long to sell the idea to Bronks and Ealet, and within five hours, they had successfully pitched the concept to their division head, Gary Cohn.

Recognising that securing liquidity guarantees from the major players was the essential—though not sufficient—factor for success, Bryce and Bronks hit the road. They presented the deal to Chris Moorhouse and Katrina Landis at BP, Graham Smith at Shell, Bernard de Combret at Elf, Francois Xavier Saint Macary, and Edouard Neviaski at Societe Generale. Agreements were struck, offering these firms equity in the platform in exchange for multi-year liquidity guarantees.

Not everyone within these firms embraced the idea right away. The OTC markets, particularly in oil products, had long thrived on opacity, and many key players believed they held the upper hand under the existing system. However, the oil markets were rapidly evolving. New competitors were entering the fray, trading margins were tightening, and the sharpest minds began to see the potential of an electronic system to enhance transparency and drive liquidity. As trading volumes grew, the largest and most sophisticated players would be best positioned to seize the opportunities created by this expansion. Rather than cannibalising the market, the shift promised to enlarge it, unlocking the greater potential for those prepared to adapt.

The Brent Exchange

And so, it was proved. The establishment of the Intercontinental Exchange (ICE) marked a watershed moment, opening the oil markets to non-traditional players such as hedge funds, Commodity Trading Advisors (CTAs), pension funds, and other asset managers.[6] Oil evolved into a fully recognised 'asset class', nearly 30 years after Gaddafi's challenge to the dominance of big oil set in motion the transformation of traded markets. This shift fundamentally reshaped the landscape, enabling a broader spectrum of financial entities to participate in and influence the oil market.

Yet, ICE's success wasn't solely due to the critical accumulation of guaranteed liquidity. The true driving force behind its triumph was Jeff Sprecher.

While the London team concentrated on locking in guaranteed liquidity from oil companies, Harold Kamins at Morgan Stanley's New York office was on a quest for the crucial ingredient for success—a dependable, state of the art technology platform. Fortunately, he had already scheduled a meeting with a cold-caller, none other than Jeff Sprecher. Sprecher had acquired a small Atlanta-based exchange, the Continental Power Exchange (CPEX), for just $1,000 and was collaborating with a group known as 'Firewire'. This group consisted of Enron imitators, spurred on by Wall Street equity analysts to either emulate Enron or face potential irrelevance.[7] Neal Shear recalls the meeting—'*I gave the platform a 5 or 6 out of 10, but Sprecher, as a business builder was a 9 or 10*'.

The group included companies like Cinergy, Dynegy, Mirant, and others entering the gas and power marketing and trading sectors, hoping to see their stock prices soar by copying the Enron business model. Naturally, this would later lead to turmoil when Enron's Ponzi scheme collapsed. However, in 1999, everything seemed promising, and Firewire appeared poised for success. They eventually reached their goals with the creation of the Intercontinental Exchange (ICE), but oil markets were the first to make strides. Kamins and Tim O'Neill from J. Aron finalised the liquidity-for-equity deal with Sprecher, and with a total investment of $4 million each from Morgan Stanley and J. Aron, ICE officially launched in May 2000.

An early success for ICE came in 2001 with its acquisition of the International Petroleum Exchange (IPE), the London-based platform that hosted the Brent contract. The IPE had been grappling with concerns that its IT system was inadequate for trading, and it had been exploring the ICE model as part of its strategy moving forward. At that time, the IPE was recovering from a setback: an effort by Chairman Richard Reinhart and CEO Lynton Jones to demutualise the exchange, transferring ownership to a group of industry companies and shifting from an open-outcry floor to electronic trading, had been rejected at an extraordinary general meeting in early July 1999 and the chair had passed to Lord Peter Fraser (formerly the Attorney General in the UK)

However, Fraser and Jones then resigned, as the IPE floor members continued to resist change, leaving the Deputy Chair Colin Bryce to address the regulator, the Securities and Futures Authority (SFA),[8] which insisted on finding a new chair swiftly. Instead of choosing from the usual pool of London's elite, Bryce turned to fellow Scot Sir Bob Reid, the former CEO of Shell UK and British Rail. Reid accepted the role, swiftly elevated IPE's Director of Marketing, Richard Ward, to CEO, and set about the challenging task of persuading members to embrace demutualisation.

There was no one better suited for the role than the tough yet well-liked Reid, who excelled at connecting with people and effectively executing strategies. The partnership with ICE on technology had been instrumental, in streamlining the acquisition of the IPE. Meanwhile, Sprecher worked tirelessly, securing backing from major trading firms. By April 2005, the IPE—now under ICE—had seamlessly shut down its open-outcry trading floor, completing its transition to ICE's electronic platform.[9]

ICE experienced remarkable success almost from the start, and within five years, the original equity holders selected by Morgan Stanley and J. Aron cashed out through a series of public sales, totalling around $1.25 billion each. It was undoubtedly one of the deals of the decade and beyond for everyone involved!

It's worth noting that NYMEX had its chance to get involved. Between ICE's initial conception in late 1999 and its first trades in May 2000, the founding group saw NYMEX's participation as a major win for both sides. This vision culminated in a dinner at New York's upscale San Pietro restaurant, where Sprecher, along with Shear and John Shapiro of Morgan Stanley, met with NYMEX's Vinnie Viola. By the end of the evening, they believed they had struck a deal for NYMEX to take an equity stake—only for Viola to call Shear the next morning with the unexpected news that there would be no deal.

In hindsight, NYMEX's decision proved to be a costly misstep. Despite resistance to electronic trading at the time, and the leadership's failure to convince members that a greater opportunity lay beyond their familiar system, the shift to electronic platforms was inevitable. Ironically, Viola himself would later build his fortune by founding Virtu Financial—an electronic trading powerhouse.

Jeff Sprecher dramatically expanded ICE over the years, most notably acquiring the New York Stock Exchange for $11 billion in 2013. Headquartered in Atlanta, where Chairman and CEO Sprecher resides, ICE now spans an extensive range of financial products. Despite its remarkable growth, the company has stayed connected to its oil origins, introducing contracts for Abu Dhabi's Murban Crude and Platts Dubai on its electronic platform. These initiatives are guided by the ICE Emirates CEO Gary King, who, as you may recall from Chapter 5, made his first trade at Neste.

Today, ICE, CME, and other oil exchanges play a key role in modernising the energy market by ensuring clarity in royalties and taxes, smooth trading, and transparent market pricing for crude oil. For oil-producing nations, exchanges provide a mechanism to align prices with market conditions, streamlining sales, and stabilising revenue streams. Beyond their transactional role, exchanges carry strategic significance, offering oil producers options to adapt or innovate in response to market constraints. Ultimately, merging one or more of the Middle East exchanges and expanding their capabilities could even lead to the ultimate crude oil benchmark.

For all these reasons, Sprecher is undoubtedly one of the few key figures who have profoundly shaped oil trading over the last 50 years. His work has transformed the market by improving transparency, driving financialisation, and enabling oil to be recognised as a genuine asset class.

Trading Around the Asset

It was late morning on 15 February 2007, when the dogs began barking in the quiet English village of Lyndhurst. They picked up on the faint whirr of helicopter blades long before the villagers did. Curious locals twitched their curtains, peeking out to see who might be arriving next at the global headquarters of the petrochemical giant, INEOS.[10]

Despite the company's prominence, there were no smokestacks or gas flares near Lyndhurst's idyllic landscape. This was where the senior executives operated, where deals were struck, and, crucially at that moment, where the company's considerable debt burden was being weighed.[11]

The helicopter's visitors were surely investment bankers,[12] and indeed they were. Bright ties and expensive suits were visible as they stepped off the chopper onto the lawn of INEOS HQ. The three senior INEOS partners, Jim Ratcliffe and his closest cohorts, John Reece and Andy Currie, most likely did not like what they were seeing as the group of bankers made their way across the garden towards the offices. It might be assumed that there and then the down-to-earth INEOS men decided against awarding any deal to that lot.

Ratcliffe, originally from Manchester in the Northwest of England, was a chemical engineer by training who had restlessly moved around the industry before founding INEOS in the late 1990s.[13] His strategy was clear: leverage debt to acquire undervalued assets from a petrochemical industry under pressure, then drive profits by finding efficiencies, synergies, and entrusting capable lieutenants to run the various parts of the business.

The men from the helicopter had come to pitch their credentials as potential partners, hoping to help monetise the opportunities presented by INEOS's recent acquisition of oil refining assets from BP.[14] INEOS had bought the assets, but in the world of asset optimisation oil trading, it was also about combining physical infrastructure with the application of the skills of the right people.[15]

That morning, a more restrained group of bankers from Morgan Stanley—many with a background in oil trading—had already driven to Lyndhurst. They had fine-tuned their pitch over breakfast at a roadside café and would ultimately secure the contract, while the 'chopper boys' left empty-handed.

Ratcliffe, a serial entrepreneur with a short attention span and something of an 'unworldly' bearing, was very much the 'supreme being' at INEOS. With a disciple-like staff around him, the sense was of something of a cult. If Jim embarked on a diet, the staff followed suit, and they all went running at lunchtime if Jim was running. The atmosphere of casual informality masked a regime firmly controlled by the boss.

One executive recalls hosting the closing dinner for the deal that had kicked off that morning in Lyndhurst, where ample wine, champagne, and a hearty supper were to be served. However, when the gaunt INEOS team arrived, it became clear that a diet craze had taken hold in the New Forest.[16] Panic set in among the hosts when they realised there was no tofu on the menu. Thankfully, all was well, as the hosts were more than capable of doubling up—clearing the plates and emptying the glasses. Despite their light appetites, the INEOS team, as always, proved to be excellent company.

What INEOS had needed was something that they already had but were about to lose. For a transition period, BP continued to buy the crude oil for the two refineries that were part of the deal.[17] BP also handled the sale of petroleum products, logistics, and the provision of the necessary working capital to run an industrial portfolio of this type.

However, INEOS's goal was to learn the ropes so they could eventually handle these operations on their own, without paying fees to intermediaries. To achieve this, they needed their team embedded with BP's specialists in the BP trading room. Unfortunately, BP couldn't secure regulatory clearance for this arrangement, and after the two-year transition period, INEOS sought alternatives.

They needed working capital support, hands-on training, and most critically, the enhanced profits that could be generated by optimising trading around their assets.

At this point, it's worth stepping back to explore the evolution of asset-based trading in the oil markets. BP plays a key role in this story, but before diving into their involvement, we must rewind to the 1980s and the then king of the trading world: Phibro.

In 1982, Thomas O'Malley became President of Phibro, stepping in after the exit of key dealmakers Marc Rich and Pincus Green. Under O'Malley's leadership, Phibro grew into a major player in oil trading. Although the firm's oil trading peak was still to come, O'Malley pioneered a new direction by venturing into oil refining—a move that would define both his career and Phibro's legacy over the next three decades.[18]

In 1983, O'Malley led Phibro into refining by acquiring Hill Petroleum, a small U.S. Gulf refining company. By the early 1990s, Phibro had expanded to own four refineries in the United States, capitalising on distressed sales, including assets sold by giants like Exxon at bargain prices. Before 1980, price controls had insulated U.S. refiners from the global challenges plaguing the industry, but that protection vanished in 1981. With margins collapsing, refining became a money-losing endeavour for many. Yet, Phibro saw potential where others saw liabilities, snapping up these unwanted refineries at steep discounts.

Phibro wasn't entirely alone in this strategy. John Deuss, owner of the trading firm Transworld Oil, also entered the refining game in 1986, purchasing Atlantic Richfield's 50,000-barrel-per-day Marcus Hook refinery on the U.S. East Coast.

The refining industry has always been infamous for its volatile profit margins. Much of the sector's troubles stemmed from excess capacity, much of it built hastily during the boom of the late 1960s and early 1970s. Making consistent profits from refining remained an elusive, intermittent pleasure for most players.

In 1985, net U.S. domestic sweet crude complex refining margins on the Gulf Coast were a slim $1 per barrel. While fortunes began to improve in the last four years of the decade, crude oil prices continued to struggle, largely due to Saudi Arabia's efforts in 1985–86 to protect their market share by increasing output. As a result, it wasn't until 2000 that refining margins returned to sustained profitability; a period of years between 2004 and 2009 became known as 'golden years' for oil refining margins.[19]

Neither Phibro nor Transworld Oil acquired these assets with the intent of optimising them as part of an overall trading strategy, as BP would later pioneer. Instead, their approach was more aligned with the traditional oil majors, the 'Seven Sisters', focussing on vertical integration across the value chain. This strategy was driven by the industrial logic of acquiring assets at bargain prices. At the time, many observers were puzzled—what did a trading company know about refining? Why buy into such a notoriously cyclical business?

Yet, it wasn't the end of trading companies acquiring assets during that period. J. Aron, aiming to enhance its basic trading capabilities, built a naphtha splitter in Rotterdam. Louis Dreyfus teamed up with a pair of entrepreneurs to purchase a refinery in Wilhelmshaven, Germany, and shortly after, Vitol entered the scene by acquiring the Come-by-Chance refinery in Canada. This marked a broader trend of traders stepping into physical assets, despite the inherent risks of the refining industry.

O'Malley emerged as the key figure who successfully acquired distressed plants and turned them around over time. His major move came in 1987 when he purchased the assets of Tosco Corporation for $300 million. This acquisition would pay off handsomely; in 2001, he sold Tosco to Phillips Petroleum for $7 billion. He later became involved with Premcor and PBF in the U.S. but ultimately faced challenges in 2011–12 with Petroplus, a private equity-owned company where he served as CEO.

While O'Malley's early ventures into the industrial side of oil were driven by a straightforward cost-versus-margin equation, his later efforts evolved to focus on a more sophisticated approach. He began to see assets as part of a network of optimisable value nodes that could enhance returns.

This complex concept, at least on the surface, is what BP introduced to the oil trading world. It was precisely this strategy that INEOS was exploring during the beauty parade in Lyndhurst, aiming to tap into the potential it offered. The same approach would later be adopted by Wall Street banks in the late 1990s, only to be ceded, under regulatory restrictions, to independent traders over the past 15 years. For these traders, this shift represented a significant opportunity and the foundation upon which considerable personal wealth could be built.

Clearly, this concept warrants further explanation.

The concept of asset-backed trading, and the resulting enhancement of overall returns, is grounded in financial options pricing techniques and the embedded flexibility within physical assets. This flexibility, when properly leveraged, can add substantial value. However, it's worth depends largely on the asset holder's ability to actively trade in forward markets and manage a complex 'book' of positions to maximise profits.

Firms with a broad array of physical assets such as production facilities, refineries, storage units, supply contracts, shipping fleets, and pipelines—are well-positioned to engage in asset-backed trading, provided they also possess the necessary culture, risk appetite, and trading expertise. For these firms, their assets form a dynamic platform that can be optimised based on market conditions. Those without natural asset positions, however, face significant challenges. To engage in this type of trading, they must first build a portfolio of assets, and scaling up is a formidable barrier due to the high cost and cyclicality of industries like oil refining. Acquiring assets at full market value can quickly become a liability, creating financial burdens rather than opportunities.

To circumvent these barriers, many firms start by acquiring 'near assets' or 'assets by contract' rather than owning physical infrastructure outright. For example, they may lease storage tanks, contract for oil processing at third-party refineries, charter vessels for long-term use, secure supply contracts in various locations, or gain the rights to purchase products in specific markets. This approach allows firms to access the benefits of physical asset flexibility without the upfront capital expenditure and risk associated with owning cyclical assets.

Marc Crandall's early vision for Trafigura exemplified this strategy. He believed that building a wide portfolio of break-even deals would create opportunities to monetise flexibility as market conditions and relative prices fluctuated over time and across geographies. In this approach, the 'strategic short'—the right to supply specific commodities to particular buyers—often emerged as one of the most valuable assets, since it offered firms the ability to capitalise on changing market conditions while minimising direct exposure to physical infrastructure risks.

Ultimately, asset-backed trading allows firms to unlock value from their operations by capitalising on market shifts, optimising asset usage, and using financial and contractual flexibility to generate profits beyond traditional margins. However, it requires deep market knowledge, an appetite for risk, and advanced trading capabilities. As we will see, banks with that combination of skills came to the party, both to help others and for their own accounts.

Only a select few firms have managed to establish a tradeable, monetisable asset base from the start, while others have had to creatively build their positions over time.[20]

The asset-optimisation technique described here stands in stark contrast to the traditional vertically integrated model of the Seven Sisters. While the same types of assets—such as refineries, pipelines, storage facilities, and shipping fleets—are involved, the approach to managing and optimising them is fundamentally different.

In the Seven Sisters' model, assets were tightly integrated within a closed vertical chain, with upstream production, midstream transportation, and downstream refining and distribution all controlled by a single entity. This vertical integration was designed to create stability and reduce risk by controlling every stage of the supply chain. Each division of the company—production, refining, and marketing—operated relatively independently within the firm's hierarchical structure.

In contrast, the asset-optimisation technique treats these assets more as interconnected and fluid parts of a broader market network. Instead of managing them within a rigid vertical structure, traders combine them horizontally, allowing assets to interact across geographies and time zones, with the primary goal of capitalising on market fluctuations. Human expertise in liquid financial and commodity markets plays a critical role, with traders constantly seeking to optimise the value of each asset by responding dynamically to changing market conditions. The assets are not locked into a singular value chain but are instead treated as flexible components that can generate profits across different markets.

British Pioneers (BP)

BP pioneered this approach in the early 1980s with the creation of its Oil Trading and Supply (OTS) group, a market-facing entity designed to optimise the company's refinery operations. OTS was intended to manage the market activities of BP's affiliates, such as BP Rotterdam and BP Sweden, and to aggregate and trade their production. At the same time, Shell developed its own central trading entity, SITCO, under Silvan Robinson. However, there was resistance from the affiliates, who often bypassed these central aggregators, reflecting a degree of internal fragmentation within the old model.

The key difference between the traditional vertical model and this new approach lies in the upstream. BP's upstream operations were forced to negotiate quarterly transfer prices with OTS, where the central trading group would acquire equity production. This arrangement led to tension within the company, as the traders frequently negotiated better deals than the market suggested from the upstream divisions, resulting in internal competition and conflicts over performance evaluation and strategic investment decisions. The complaint of BP's upstream negotiator, Alan McKay, about being regularly 'de-bagged' by traders during price negotiations highlights the friction between traditional asset operators and the market-driven trading arm.

At BP, it was Iain Conn, who had spent time at BP Italia and had seen the other side, who put an end to the internal issues. Conn, who would rise to the Board level in BP before leaving to become CEO of Centrica, set up a concept known internally as EUTRO in 1992/3 while running BP's oil products trading business. In return for retiring their own trading departments and allowing the BP central traders to conduct all the market-facing business, the affiliates would be given 50% of the profits from the trading 'uplift'. And so, yet another interesting set of transfer price negotiations was set up! In fact, any profits made were already being paid out as dividends to the affiliates and so there was a sense of 'bribing partners internally with their own money'. But it worked.[21]

This coordinated approach, initially focussed on refining, was eventually extended into BP's wholesale operations. One of the key figures in this expansion was the CEO of Air BP at the time, Andy Duff, who later rose to prominence beyond BP. After leaving the company, he became Chairman of Severn Trent Water in the United Kingdom, among other high-profile roles.

Like Iain Conn, who had served as BP's representative in a perilous Bogota during a particularly volatile period, Duff had also paid his dues as BP's 'Russia man', navigating the complexities of the Russian oil market.

Both men faced significant challenges early in their careers, but their experiences positioned them well for later success in the fast-paced, high-stakes world of oil trading. Unlike their earlier postings, oil trading presented fewer personal risks but offered immense opportunities for growth and reward, as the company's asset-backed trading strategies matured and expanded beyond traditional refining operations.

The motivation within BP evolved from simply optimising existing assets to increasing their footprint without the costly acquisition of new ones. This shift saw traders seeking third-party opportunities, leveraging external assets through contracts and partnerships to expand BP's influence in the market.

Vivienne Cox, a rising star within BP who would later hold prominent roles in the industrial world, played a pivotal role in this evolution. As oil markets embraced greater complexity and integration, Cox spearheaded efforts to consolidate BP's market-facing operations. She became the driving force behind creating a unified entity called International Supply and Trading (IST). Her vision was to bring together BP's disparate market businesses under a single umbrella, allowing them to operate more cohesively and efficiently.

Tony Fountain, another BP leader and enthusiastic equestrian[22] who later chaired the U.K. Nuclear Decommissioning Authority, added a key strategic layer. Fountain introduced the concept of a 'web' of value nodes, where each node represented an option value within BP's portfolio. His approach, developed through the early to mid-2000s, focussed on growing this web by identifying and expanding nodes—strategic assets, supply contracts, or third-party relationships—each of which could be optimised as part of the broader trading strategy.

The success of this asset trading approach underscored the critical importance of people in BP's operations. The company had not only the physical assets but also the leadership talent to drive innovation and capitalise on market opportunities. BP's leadership fostered a culture that encouraged creative thinking and allowed innovative leaders like Cox and Fountain to push boundaries. The external successes of these individuals after leaving BP demonstrate just how special and influential they were in shaping the company's trading strategies and overall market success.

This leadership-driven model, with a focus on expanding the company's asset footprint through third-party partnerships and strategic market moves, was a key factor in BP's continued evolution in oil trading, showing how critical human expertise and strategic vision are in such a complex and competitive industry.

Eventually, BP faced regulatory challenges as their aggressive trading strategies and dominant, well-located assets raised concerns of market manipulation. In particular, regulators in the U.S. scrutinised BP's use of oil storage at Cushing, Oklahoma, a key location for the delivery of NYMEX WTI contracts. BP had inherited these storage assets through their acquisitions of Arco and Amoco, and it was alleged that they had leveraged their position to illegally influence oil prices by trading heavily around their Cushing holdings.

This led to accusations that BP's trading activities were manipulative, prompting U.S. regulators to take a critical stance. At the time, Brian Gilvary, the head of BP's trading arm (who would later become BP's CFO), was heavily involved in addressing these allegations. Gilvary worked to assuage the concerns of regulators by implementing reforms to BP's trading practices and revising the company's trading rulebook, aiming to restore trust and ensure compliance with market regulations. The system gradually evolved to recognise the importance of assets to trading. This would result in a Commercial Supply and Optimisation system, which internally recognised the asset contribution to the trade and would pass on a share of the profit to the company entity owning it (after cost and traders' bonuses, of course).

Asset Heavy or Asset Light?

BP was the pioneer and undisputed leader of the asset-heavy optimisation approach among oil companies, leveraging their well-coordinated strategy to great effect. Shell, on the other hand, attempted a similar strategy but initially struggled due to internal inefficiencies. Known for its complexity, Shell was hampered by overlapping responsibilities, a bureaucratic decision-making process, and a more committee-driven culture, which contrasted sharply with BP's entrepreneurial approach. While Shell had been a significant player in trading since establishing SITCO, they lacked internal champions who could thrive and push boundaries both within the company and externally.

It wasn't until a major downstream reorganisation in 2012 that Shell started improving in this area, finally becoming better equipped to seize the trading and optimisation opportunities.

ExxonMobil, by contrast, remained largely uninvolved in the optimisation-through-trading strategy for a long time. With a culture dominated by refinery engineers, the company historically placed less emphasis on trading markets, perhaps feeling its sheer scale rendered such tactics unnecessary. Exxon's massive size and influence could have overwhelmed the markets if it had taken a more active role in trading. However, under CEO

Darren Woods, starting in the twenty-teens, Exxon has begun exploring a more coordinated approach to align its assets with market activities, putting the right people in place to make this work. Despite these efforts, it remains to be seen whether this strategy will become a significant and profitable venture for them.

Total, the other major oil conglomerate, which had absorbed Elf and Petrofina in the 1990s, has a distinct history shaped by the influence of its geographically diverse affiliates, often maintaining significant autonomy from the corporate centre. This decentralised structure created a dynamic where the affiliates had considerable power relative to headquarters. However, under the innovative leadership of Bernard de Combret, Total began to shift away from the more aloof, traditional stance of pre-merger Total, adopting some of the market-savvy strategies of Elf.

Despite this evolution, Total's trading arm, TOTSA (based in Geneva), has primarily succeeded as a standalone entity specialising in physical, forward, and derivative trading, rather than pursuing the full-scale system optimisation seen at BP. While they have become skilled traders, their approach has been more about individual market participation than integrating trading as a central mechanism for optimising their broader asset base across the company.

'Asset light' was the alternative methodology and among the non-oil firms, it was Morgan Stanley who led the way in conceiving and developing this way of mining a system of value nodes. They created it from scratch, and their Norwegian head of oil trading, Olav Refvik, known as the 'King of New York Harbor', was the original innovator.

Refvik had developed an ecosystem around trading the NYMEX futures contracts, the London IPE, renting storage in nearby New England, and looking for opportunities to ship oil products across the Atlantic. To this limited set of flexible 'contractual assets', he added over time the arbitraging of financial and physical products between Europe and the Far East, under the guidance of his London oil head, Goran Trapp.

Over time, the bank expanded its operations to include a gasoline blending business, an on-airport jet fuel supply network across the United States and Europe, and a strategic short position through its ownership of Denver-based wholesaler TransMontaigne. Additionally, it secured a lucrative contract to supply crude oil to INEOS—clinching the deal on the same day, without the need for a dramatic helicopter arrival in quiet Lyndhurst. Beyond supplying crude, the bank also financed INEOS's activities at the Grangemouth and Lavera refineries while selling the refined products with a keen entrepreneurial approach, maximising optionality at every turn.[23] The uplift from the venture which accounted for some $100 million per annum was shared 50/50.[24]

The profitability of INEOS's asset-optimisation efforts proved to be a lifeline for the company during a critical period. With a heavy debt burden and pressure from lenders to refinance, INEOS needed to find a way to monetise their refining assets, which were otherwise considered almost worthless, except for the approximately $100 million uplift gained through optimisation.

A significant opportunity arose when they negotiated the sale of 50 per cent of two refineries to PetroChina for $1 billion. However, to justify this high valuation and close the deal, INEOS required Morgan Stanley to allow an early exit from a contractual agreement. Morgan Stanley, graciously, agreed to this early exit, a pivotal moment that helped secure INEOS's financial footing. Despite the importance of this event in the company's turnaround, it is surprisingly absent from the books written by Jim Ratcliffe on INEOS's history.[25]

While it was ultimately the right decision to accommodate a client in need, Morgan Stanley's optimisation traders weren't entirely pleased with the loss of a steady revenue stream from this important node in their web when the INEOS exit was facilitated. After a tense negotiation between a demanding and uncompromising PetroChina representative, under pressure from his superiors in Beijing, and the calm, capable INEOS leader, Calum McLean, a seasoned Aberdonian, a deal was struck.

Meanwhile, in the broader oil trading world, significant developments continued to unfold, particularly in the financialised realm of oil trading and the physical and forward hedging on platforms like NYMEX and ICE. And as this asset-optimisation strategy matured, more traditional traders and institutions began to see its potential. Players from the banking sector, including J.P. Morgan and Citibank, became increasingly active, while independent traders like Vitol, Trafigura, Glencore, and Mercuria emerged as key participants.

At this stage, sovereign states and producer governments had not yet entered the second-order trading activity. However, in the future, state-owned entities like ADNOC, Aramco Trading, SOCAR, and OQ would become major players in this contested space. What followed was a significant shift in the world of oil trading, where banks lost their dominance, reminiscent of the decline of the Seven Sisters in the 1970s. This shift was precipitated by the Financial Crisis of 2008 and the resulting regulatory changes, which shrank the banks' influence and paved the way for independent traders to rise to prominence.

Notes

1. Tête de Chien rock rises 550 m above sea level and towers over Monaco.
2. Including this author on behalf of Morgan Stanley.
3. One-to-all in the sense that all trades were between a counterparty and Enron and not open to counterparty-to-counterparty trading. Enron saw and controlled all the liquidity.
4. McLean, Bethany et al. (2004) p. 98.
5. Even though the own, one-way platform gave Enron a big advantage, it was not always bad for other users. Martin Farr and Chris Heilpern were at Sempra Singapore, trading fuel swaps on the platform from the first days it started. At first they traded a few times "for fun" just to see how the novelty worked. Then they realized that the Enron trader was under-pricing 1% Fuel Oil Barge Swaps, so they kept buying. The Enron trader called them directly to ask why they kept buying; they explained they believed the price was too low and would continue buying. Enron stopped offering those swaps, and as far as Chris could recall, never offered them again. From a chat With C. Heilpern on 24/2/25.
6. It was the launch of the NYMEX WTI futures contract in March 1983 heralded a return of the oil exchanges to the US and the world. Timing of the launch was fortunate, as OPEC was struggling to control the market and set prices.
7. Kent, Phil James Magazine (September/October 2024), pp. 42–45.
8. Securities and Futures Authority was a predecessor to Financial Services Authority (FSA).
9. For a full description of the ICE/IPE years, see Peniket, D. in Imsirovic, A (ed) (2022), pp. 91–108.
10. INEOS stands for INSPEC-Ethylene Oxide and Specialities, a previous name of the business. See: https://www.reuters.com/lifestyle/sports/jim-ratcliffe-who-is-ineos-founder-bidding-manchester-united-2023-01-18/#:~:text=The%20name%20INEOS%20was%20derived,employs%20more%20than%2026%2C000%20people.
11. From personal recollection of one of the authors.
12. The author recalls asking an investment banker to accompany him to a meeting with an energy company in the UK, close to the banker's office. The banker expressed surprise and questioned the importance of his attendance given that 'we are not flying there'!
13. For a very full history of the firm, see Ratcliffe and Heath (2018).

14. Specifically, the oil refineries at Lavera in the South of France and Grangemouth in Scotland. In general, INEOS was born out of Ratcliffe's management buyout of the former BP petrochemicals assets in Antwerp, Belgium in 1995. See: https://www.thechemicalengineer.com/news/bp-exits-petrochemicals-sells-plants-to-ineos/#:~:text=Ineos%20was%20born%20out%20of,refinery%2C%20for%20US%249bn.
15. When we come to examine the development of asset-backed trading at the home of the originators and masters, BP, we will see how important people are in the process.
16. Lyndhurst is in England's New Forest, an area of outstanding beauty.
17. The INEOS purchase had been for Innovene, an entity created by BP in their desire to float off as a package, unwanted assets consisting of oil refineries and some petrochemical assets. Before flotation, Ratcliffe had swooped to buy the package for INEOS.
18. O'Malley may not have been the 'Aristocat' of the film who pulled the cat out of the water to safety, but he did pull more than a few cats out of the bag when it came to oil refining.
19. See Purvin and Gertz (2008), p. 142.
20. Ibid.
21. Discussion with Tim Bullock 18/10/2024.
22. One of your authors spent a week-end horse riding with Tony in Wales. This was back in 1990's. The day would start with a long run over the Welsh hills. Riding would start after breakfast by which time the author would be ready to go back to bed. Not Tony, who was peaking for a marathon. By the end of the week-end of hard riding through the beautiful Welsh countryside, the author had to take a following week-day off, due to utter exhaustion and sore legs. For the avoidance of doubt, it wasn't the stud-owning author being referred to!
23. Amongst other MS 'assets' were contracts to supply the PBF refinery at Toledo and to market oil products from the Paulsboro and Delaware City units.
24. INEOS's prior deal with BP had only returned 30% of the additional optionality profits to them.
25. Ratcliffe J and Heath U (2018) and Ratcliffe, Sir Jim et al. (2023).

Bibliography

Imsirovic, A (2023): 'Brent Crude Oil Genesis and Development of the World's Most Important Benchmark', Palgrave McMillan.

Imsirovic, A (2024): 'International Oil Markets in the Age of Climate Change', Palgrave, 2024.

Kelly, Kate: 'The Secret Club That Runs the World', Penguin 2014.

McLean, B and Elkind, P (2003): The Smartest Guys in the Room- The Amazing Rise and Scandalous Fall of Enron Penguin.

Ratcliffe, J and Heath, U (2018): 'The Alchemists The INEOS Story- An Industrial Giant Comes of Age'. Biteback Publishing.

14

Traders 1: A billion dollars is not what it used to be

Boom Time

Peter Smith embodies the ideal oil trader that any firm would be fortunate to have on their team. Recently retired from Vitol, his career as a middle distillates trader was marked by consistent profitability with minimal risk-taking. Beyond his trading prowess, Pete has been an exceptional mentor and role model to generations of young, ambitious professionals.

Hailing from Doncaster in northern England—a town only truly appreciated by the few—Pete began his career in metals trading in the 1980s. From there, he progressed through Morgan Stanley before joining Vitol, where he would go on to build a career of remarkable impact.

Pete's low-risk, steady-earnings trading approach has gradually been overshadowed at Vitol in the 2020s. With the rise of big data providing greater confidence in market positions and the firm's deep pockets—bolstered by years of extraordinary profits—Vitol embraced a more risk-tolerant strategy. The company is now willing to hold positions through mark-to-market losses, trusting in eventual gains. This shift in philosophy has unfolded under the leadership of the unassuming yet approachable billionaire CEO, Russell Hardy.

Like many in the industry, Hardy began his career at BP. A down-to-earth chemical engineer with a genuine passion for refinery operations, he joined

---

The title of the chapter is Traders 1: A billion dollars is not what it used to be attributed to the late Nelson Bunker Hunt, Texas Oilman who once tried to corner the silver market with one of his brothers only to see the move end in financial disaster.

A. Imsirovic and C. Bryce, *The Rivers of Money*,
https://doi.org/10.1007/978-3-031-91806-3_14

Vitol in 1993, rising through the company's power and gas divisions. In 2018, he became CEO when his predecessor, Ian Taylor, assumed the role of chairman shortly before his passing from throat cancer. While Hardy would later oversee the boom years of the 2020s, it was Taylor who truly defined Vitol's dominance in the oil trading world.

Vitol itself was founded in 1966 by two Dutchmen as a Rotterdam barge trading operation.[1] Now one of the few companies from that era still active in oil trading (Mabanaft being another), Vitol has not always been the industry giant it is today. Throughout the 1990s, the firm struggled at times to turn a profit and was considered relatively minor compared to Wall Street refiners and the trading divisions of BP, Shell, and Total. When the Intercontinental Exchange (ICE) was being formed, Vitol was even overlooked as a potential equity partner, deemed too insignificant.

However, the 2000s saw Vitol's fortunes rise sharply, with profitability reaching levels comparable to those enjoyed by the major banks and oil companies. By 2009, with net revenues in the range of $2.28 billion, Vitol was on a rapid trajectory to dominance.[2]

Much of Vitol's growth can be credited to the advent of asset-backed trading,[3] both leased and owned assets, which bolstered the firm's stability and reach.[4] Nevertheless, a large part of this success is also attributed to the visionary leadership of Ian Taylor. An Oxford graduate who started his career at Shell in 1978, Taylor gained significant experience in Singapore and Venezuela before joining Vitol in the mid-1980s.

Ian Taylor's career in oil trading is a testament to his exceptional work ethic, commercial acumen, and larger-than-life personality, and it is well-documented,[5] as he is one of the few oil trading leaders whose personal and professional story has been widely covered by both industry and mainstream media. Known for his openness, friendliness, and highly commercial mindset, he approached his work with remarkable dedication, taking on workloads that most would avoid. Taylor was the type of leader who didn't just meet challenges head-on—he sought them out.

One memorable example of his legendary drive took place during a dinner with clients along with his head of oil trading, Paul Greenslade, and then-head of power and gas, Russell Hardy. Taylor requested an early start at 6:30 p.m., which, while earlier than the norm in London, wasn't as early as would be typical in New York or Houston. When he reached for the bill at 8:30 p.m., he explained that he had a second dinner scheduled with Libyan partners at a Lebanese restaurant down the street—scheduled to start in just thirty minutes. This kind of back-to-back commitment was routine for Taylor.

Despite his focus on Vitol, Taylor found time for outside pursuits, including his influential role in rescuing the struggling Harris Tweed industry. When the historic Scottish textile faced decline, Taylor intervened with the help of his friend, politician Brian Wilson, providing essential support that allowed the industry to survive and thrive. This legacy of dedication—to both his business and the causes he cared about—cements Taylor's place among the most respected figures in the oil trading world.

Ian Taylor wasn't the only one to step in when the Harris Tweed industry needed support; He would tell the story of Yorkshire cloth maker Brian Haggas who also took an interest, although their approaches and outcomes diverged.[6] While Taylor revitalised the brand by introducing bold, contemporary designs—waistcoats, miniskirts, and vibrant colours like pinks and purples aimed at younger consumers—Haggas stayed true to tradition, producing classic blue, green, and grey tweed jackets. However, Haggas's approach proved less successful; it's rumoured that warehouses in Yorkshire still hold racks of unsold tweed jackets in these more conventional vintage shades.

When asked how he found time to support the Harris Tweed industry amidst his responsibilities at Vitol, Taylor famously replied, 'That's the job I focussed on from 4:00 until 5:30 pm on Sundays'. This response perfectly encapsulates Taylor's boundless energy and his ability to juggle numerous commitments with unwavering focus and drive.

And it was Taylor who saved Vitol from falling into the arms of Enron.[7] Having discussed merging with Elf, Morgan Stanley, and probably others, Vitol was close to selling out to Enron just prior to the latter's collapse in an all-cash deal. At the last minute, Enron sought to change the terms to an all-share deal. Taylor said no and in doing so dodged a big bullet.

In an industry typically guarded and cautious about public image, Taylor stood out for his willingness to engage with the media. However, this openness came at a personal cost: In 2016, he declined a knighthood to avoid the potential wave of media scrutiny that might follow, with the risk of unwelcome investigative attention on Vitol.[8]

Despite Taylor's strong leadership and accomplishments, Vitol's reputation has faced challenges. In 2007, the company pleaded guilty in a New York court to paying 'surcharges' to Saddam Hussein's regime to secure oil under the UN's Iraq Oil-for-Food Programme[9]—a low point in the company's history. Other legal entanglements over the years have left their own marks on Vitol's otherwise exceptional financial record. Taylor's legacy is one of remarkable achievements and resilience, albeit shadowed by some of the complexities inherent in global oil trading. He very clearly put Vitol—the company—in the litigation firing line when the Oil-for-Food debacle and a subsequent issue related to operations in Brazil arose, a decision he made to deliberately protect colleagues from facing possible charges.[10]

Operating in regions where standards of conduct can vary widely from those in developed nations, many trading companies find themselves navigating a delicate boundary between legality and illegality. Commercially, they often push this line, testing limits to stay competitive. However, Vitol's CEO, Russell Hardy, seemed to have drawn a firm line in the sand, affirming the company's commitment to compliance: 'We comply with all laws, regulations, prohibitions, and sanctions'.[11]

This stance underscores Hardy's focus on maintaining rigorous standards amidst the complex and sometimes opaque regulatory landscapes where global trading firms operate.[12]

However, Hardy acknowledges the reality of operating in a global market, remarking: '*If we only wanted to trade with countries that shared Western standards, we would quickly run out of energy*'. This candid statement highlights the inherent challenges for trading firms that must engage with diverse regions to secure energy supplies, often navigating varying ethical and regulatory norms in the process.

While Vitol remains committed to legal compliance, Hardy's words reflect the complex balance between adhering to Western regulatory standards and meeting global energy demands—a balance that requires flexibility and adaptability in a rapidly changing geopolitical landscape.

Despite Vitol's remarkable recent revenues, ranging from $13 to $15 billion annually, [13] the company faces pressing challenges on the horizon. A former employee notes that 'people' issues are surfacing as a significant concern. '*Many younger ones want to earn enough, leave, and live well—they don't want a career. Whether it's fear of regulation, lack of enjoyment, pressure, or simply seeing how dull it is to be promoted to management, who knows*'.[14]

He further observes that this new generation is less inclined to accept traditional demands. '*They'll tell you they won't be in at 8:00 a.m. because they're doing the school run at 9:00 a.m*'. This shift reflects a broader trend within the industry, where young professionals prioritise work-life balance and flexibility over the long, high-stakes career paths that once defined the oil trading world.

Today's trading rooms are marked by a calm, almost cathedral-like quiet—a stark contrast to the vibrant buzz that once fuelled creativity and the exchange of ideas. The environment now is more subdued, fostering a culture of anonymity that, while lucrative, lacks the energetic atmosphere that once inspired ambition and innovation.

This shift poses questions for Vitol's future growth. Without a new generation that matches the hunger and drive of past leaders like Taylor and Hardy, the firm—and potentially its competitors—faces a strategic challenge: who will have the experience and ambition to sustain outperformance?

Independent traders, including Vitol, now face a crucial question: how best to deploy the significant profits amassed during recent extraordinary market conditions. While the energy transition market presents an appealing avenue, it is riddled with uncertainties, particularly for traditional oil traders. For these firms, reinvesting in physical assets is tempting but risky. In an inherently cyclical industry, such assets can quickly become burdensome liabilities when market conditions shift. Vitol is especially familiar with this dilemma, recalling the precarious experience of the Come-By-Chance refinery in Eastern Canada. Acquired in 1995, the refinery nearly bankrupted the company over a volatile decade, until cyclical market conditions finally allowed Vitol to exit the investment profitably more than ten years later. It was a near-disastrous lesson in the risks of asset-heavy strategies—but one from which Vitol emerged stronger and more cautious.

It was also the first time in Vitol's history that the company's partners were able to be rewarded with equity, a remuneration which was to grow exorbitantly in the post-COVID-19 and post-Russia-Ukraine years. The lowest equity percentage offered to partners is 0.025 per cent and, in recent years, this has been equivalent to $10 million. No partner can hold more than 5 per cent, which distributes ownership in a much more disaggregated way than happens at Vitol's competitors such as Mercuria and Glencore.[15]

Despite the Come-by-Chance experience, Vitol didn't shy away from asset acquisitions in the years that followed. By the time they invested in African energy distributor Vivo and the energy transition venture Varo, they were taking a more strategic approach, focussing on assets that could enhance their network and offer trading optionality rather than isolated, high-stakes bets like Come-By-Chance.

Proprietary trading has also been an important part of Vitol's success. For many years in the 2000s, it was the gasoline business led by Denis Crema that was their most successful business. At other times, the crude oil business led by Paul Greenslade was the major contributor, with a particular emphasis on acquiring preferential rights to Nigerian oil through partnerships with local entities.

Vitol was nothing if not agile and its global coverage allowed it to react to geopolitical circumstances affecting the market. An example is their decision to maximise the amount of oil they held in tankers on the water at times when the market structure was in contango. Vitol was able to store oil, hedge it forward at a price that more than covered storage and cost of money, and at one stage, it had as many as 400 tankers on the water in this trading play.

A current employee of the company comments that '*The biggest problem we faced was the issue of the mental health of the tanker crews, stuck at sea for many months*'.[16]

If a succession of windfalls from Come-By-Chance, Crema's gasoline trading, Pierre Andurand's jet fuel book, Paul Greenslade's' Nigerian and wider crude oil business, the firm's asset-backed strategy, entry into the loan intermediation business[17] as a means to secure offtake and the 2008–9 contango play all contributed to growth of the firm up to around 2010, an especially successful area of interest for Vitol more recently has been trading a derivatives book. This was run by an especially talented young Chinese émigré, Yao-Yao.

He arrived in the United Kingdom from China as a young boy when his parents moved to Cambridge. When his father had to return to Wuhan, he was left being brought up by his mother. Yao-Yao won a scholarship to The Perse, an academic hot-house school in the town, and from there was accepted to read for a degree in Chemical Engineering at Cambridge University. After a time on the Goldman Sachs graduate entry scheme, he was hired by Peter Smith to join Vitol as a junior derivatives trader. It didn't take long, having been coached and mentored by Smith, before the 'junior' became 'head of' and his record of very significant profitability (believed in some years to be of the order of billions) made him a very rich man. By 2025, Yao-Yao was running the derivatives business from Dubai; he is characterised as being, like his boss Russell Hardy, very down to earth—'dressed at Marks and Spencer's but driving a mega car'.[18]

Perhaps though, one of the biggest issues they, and other large traders, face is the need to provide margin to hedging counterparts. When physical oil that traders hold rises in value, the hedges that are placed decline in value and they must post margin with their counterparts. This can severely strain the financial loan lines that these companies operate with. In Vitol's case, the 2008 Financial crisis was a near-death experience for margin call reasons—most particularly margin owed to Wall Street refiners. A Vitol employee relates that during the worst of the crisis, Vitol closed off a long corridor leading to their offices as they had papered and sellotaped to the walls their margin position, so complex was it to understand on a small computer screen that they had printed it out to better view it.[19]

Vitol's approach to leadership also reflects a uniquely effective model. The firm has operated with a public-facing 'managing partner' like Ian Taylor, supported by a core team of senior operators known for their expertise and autonomy. Figures such as Bob Finch, David Fransen, Chris Bake, Denis Crema, and Mark Couling embody this model, each taking ownership of their respective areas and managing their time and efforts independently. These leaders operate with urgency and precision, confronting issues directly rather than deferring decisions—traits that sets them apart in the industry. Their work ethic and intensity rival that of top athletes, demonstrating the commitment required to thrive in a high-stakes, fast-paced trading environment.

This intense, results-driven approach remains a key part of Vitol's DNA, even as they navigate new strategic choices in a rapidly evolving energy landscape.

In addition to competing with the trading divisions of BP, Shell, and Total, Vitol faces stiff competition from other independent traders, most notably Trafigura and Glencore. While Glencore is primarily known for metals trading and mining rather than oil, Trafigura has emerged as a major force in oil trading in recent years.

Rich Renegades

Trafigura, founded in 1993 by a group of former Marc Rich + Co. traders, has made a name for itself with a relatively open approach—something that sets it apart in an industry often characterised by secrecy. However, Trafigura has also courted controversy over the years, sometimes at great cost. Among its more notable controversies was the 2006 dumping of toxic waste in the Ivory Coast, which resulted in severe environmental and public health issues and led to the five-month imprisonment of CEO and co-founder Claude Dauphin.[20] The company has also faced bribery allegations, including cases in Brazil and alleged similar issues in Angola.[21]

While these incidents have marred Trafigura's reputation, they underscore the risks that independent trading companies often face when operating in complex global markets. For both Trafigura and Vitol, these challenges illustrate the high-stakes nature of energy trading, where the pursuit of market access and profits must be balanced against legal and ethical considerations that are increasingly under scrutiny.

When Claude Dauphin's health began to decline, Trafigura turned to Jeremy Weir in 2014 to lead as CEO. Weir, an Australian geologist with a background in metals trading, brought a strategic, refined approach to the role. Unlike the stereotypical trading-floor operator focussed on quick profits, Weir is viewed as more of a business-minded trader—thoughtful, deliberate, and somewhat reminiscent of Ian Taylor in his polished approach. Under his leadership, Trafigura has gained a reputation for greater openness and professionalism, essential for a company seeking to move past controversies while still maintaining financial success.

Weir's influence has helped restore Trafigura's reputation, a critical shift for a company that risked being defined by its past. The toxic waste incident in the Ivory Coast in 2006, Dauphin's imprisonment, and further bribery allegations in Brazil and Angola had all weighed heavily on the company's image.

In addition to oil, run for many years by Jose Larroca until his retirement in 2024, Trafigura has also made significant investments in metals, power, gas, and agricultural trading, reflecting a more diversified portfolio than Vitol. Like Vitol's Vivo, Trafigura's downstream energy distribution network, Puma Energy, operates globally in storage and distribution, adding stability to its core trading business. Yet challenges remain. Despite Weir's efforts to foster transparency and accountability, the company still faces legal issues, with former CEO Mike Wainwright convicted of bribery by Swiss prosecutors of criminal activity.[22]

As Richard Holthum took over as CEO in 2025, Trafigura stood at a crossroads. The firm's ability to balance diversification and reputational management while navigating legal obstacles would be crucial to its continued success in an increasingly scrutinised industry.[23]

Richard Holthum, the new CEO at Trafigura, arrives from the power and gas sector, a sign that oil trading is no longer the dominant focus at the firm.[24] This shift reflects the broader industry trend towards renewables and the energy transition, with power trading on the rise, while oil trading remains stagnant or even in decline.

With Trafigura's revenues approximately half of Vitol's, Holthum and his team will have their work cut out for them, not only striving to close the gap but also navigating the ongoing challenges within the company.[25] One significant issue is the $1 billion fraud uncovered in Trafigura's Mongolian oil supply chain,[26] raising serious questions about the effectiveness of their risk management systems and the complexities of overseeing such a broad range of operations under one corporate roof.

Meanwhile, Glencore, which entered the commodities trading scene in 1994, has evolved into a predominantly metals trading and mining company, making it the least focussed on oil of the major independent traders. One ex-employee describes it as: 'A mining company with a tiny oil business.'[27] For many years, it's oil business was run by ex-BP trader and billionaire, Alex Beard. The same ex-employee observes that Beard ran the business in a dictatorial fashion, being responsible for much of the decision-making. Another seasoned ex-BP trader commented that Alex Beard reminded him of Andy Hall, a famous Phibro (and also an ex-BP) trader: '*Utterly ruthless*'.[28]

Up until 2015, the crude oil business was run by Spaniard, Luis Alvarez, who reported to Beard. From a family steeped in the oil business, Alvarez' father was managing the trading arm of the Spanish refiner, Peromed.

At the time of writing, Glencore was headed up by a Swede, Alex Sanna, who had joined as a rookie trader after a summer internship at Masefield, and the company has made strident efforts to seek outside assistance in developing risk, conduct, and culture best practice. As a U.K. public company, the risk to shareholders and individuals of trading in 'difficult places' had become too great and they focussed on more vanilla physical oil activities.

Glencore, like its competitors, has faced its share of legal troubles relating to past activities. The company is embroiled in bribery allegations involving former oil division head, Alex Beard, and several of his colleagues.[29] These legal challenges highlight the persistent risks associated with operating in the high stakes world of global commodities trading, where even the most established firms are not immune to scrutiny.

In the meantime, having retired in 2020 in the small village of Rüschlikon in Switzerland, former Glencre CEO, Ivan Glasenberg paid: '… so much tax that every one of his 3,600 neighbours in the picturesque village overlooking Lake Zurich got a 7% tax break…'.[30] He continued his passion for sports and cycling in particular by establishing his own pro-cycling team as well as Q36.5, a cycling-clothes manufacturer, famous Pinarello bicycles maker[31] as well as a sports nutrition outfit, Amacx.[32] His pro-cycling team which included a British champion Thomas Pidcock raced under the banner of Q36.5.

As the trading landscape continued to evolve, firms would need to balance their efforts in traditional markets like oil with the demands and risks of new sectors, all while grappling with increasing regulatory pressures and legal issues. And for the individuals the propensity to turn a blind eye using the excuse that 'it's not me 'it's the company' while knowingly acting in questionable activities is a matter of conduct that can no longer be tolerated and might well be prosecuted. Being one step removed is no longer a defence. Indeed, the companies to whom oil traders on-sell the barrels sourced in unacceptable ways (the household name oil companies among them), may be two steps removed physically but they are, arguably, a good deal closer morally if they were to take time to reflect.

Unsubstantiated rumours have persisted in the oil trading market suggesting that Marc Rich was, at least until his passing, somehow tied up with the financing/funding of Glencore through its early life. It is not the only company about whom such rumours have persisted. The successful and agile trading company, Masefield, founded by ex-Marc Rich + Co. trader Jim Daley, has had to parry similar unsubstantiated rumours over time. However, one ex-employee comments: 'We did see Marc in the corridors'![33]

Masefield was a particularly intriguing company—small by the standards of giants like Glencore or Vitol, but still highly effective in its niche. Under the leadership of the well-regarded and highly capable Jim Daley, the firm also benefitted from the expertise of South African trader Justus Van Der Spuy. Widely regarded as one of the sharpest and most successful operators of the past 30 years, Van Der Spuy, drawing on his experience at South Africa's strategic reserve organisation, Strategic Fuel Fund or SFF,[34] revolutionised the way the market viewed storage in backwardated markets.

A major event was the Iraqi invasion of Kuwait as low price and contango became high price and backwardation and the different values of storage in different market conditions began to hit home.[35] While the concept of filling storage and selling forward in contango markets has become standard practice, Van Der Spuy introduced a novel approach: convincing holders of strategic storage—often sovereign states—to sell off oil at high prices in backwardated markets, purchase cheaper deferred oil as replacements, and share the savings with the sovereigns. This innovation was coined within Masefield as their 'Offshore Strategic Research' business. The company took this model global, deploying it in markets such as Germany and South Korea, while selling the oil to countries like Mozambique and Tanzania.

Mum and Dad

Mercuria may be a smaller player than Vitol, Trafigura, and Glencore, but it's backstory is just as intriguing, albeit over what seems a much shorter time span. Founded in 2004 by Marco Dunand and Daniel Jaeggi,[36] the company's early funding came from two Ukrainians, Grzegorz Jankielewicz and Slawomir Smolokowski, affectionately known as Grisha and Slawa. The duo, known as J&S, were key figures in the gasoline business in Poland and played a crucial role in supplying the country's largest refinery, PKN Orlen. At one point, J&S provided 90 per cent of Poland's oil imports.[37]

But the very beginnings of Grisha and Slawa were also very humble. Following the fall of the Soviet Union and the opening of Eastern Europe to market-driven economies, they saw an opportunity to trade goods to and from Russia. Some say that their early success might have come from exporting Russian musical instruments such as balalaikas, accordions, etc.[38]

These instruments were cheap, while well-regarded for their craftsmanship in places like Poland.[39]

But more importantly, Grisha and Slawa were in the right place, at the right time. Gorbachev's *Perestroika* (policy 'reset') and *Glasnost* ('openness') demolished the old, centralised Soviet monopolies, leaving few, if any alternatives. '... anyone who could get their hands on something exportable stood to make a fortune—if they could reach the border'.[40] Remote places like Tyumen imported everything, and as the centrally planned economy started crumbling, they struggled to obtain food and other basic necessities. With no functioning markets, producers were forced to barter their oil for basic amenities.

For the first time, there was 'independent' oil that could be obtained without talking to the government. With some financial experience and good contacts, this oil could be purchased cheaply in the local currency, Rubles. Some of this oil could be exported for hard currency, desperately needed in the country.[41] The decline in the value of the Ruble further exaggerated the gap between domestic and global oil prices, making these transactions exceptionally profitable.

At the time, Grisha and Slawa happened to be trading in household goods in Tyumen, Western Siberia, and embraced the opportunity. Imported goods and equipment were badly needed in the region, and it gave them access to oil from the most important Russian oil-producing region, the home of Samotlor, the second-biggest oil field in the world at the time.[42] Their partner was Vadim Linetskiy, a graduate of the Moscow Institute of Physics and Technology (FizTech), a mathematician, and a '*rocket scientist*' as he was called by those who knew him.[43] Vadim's job was to work out all the economics, including complex pricing formulae on which the oil was sold.

Pavel Pojdl, a Czech trader at Phibro London, was one of the earliest traders to get involved in this emerging Russian oil market. Pavel was handpicked by Peter Arbenz, the head of Phibro in Europe, to get into Eastern European oil flows. While some of the earlier Phibro projects in Russia did not go well,[44] Pavel kept on trading oil in this brave new world, selling spot North Sea oil to Poland,[45] Russian Urals to Hungary, and so on.

Pavel began his career as a trainee operator at Cargill, a Minneapolis-based company primarily focussed on food and agriculture. The company's trading division had a tumultuous relationship with energy trading, frequently entering and exiting the sector. During this time, Danny and Marco were actively trading middle distillates at the company.

Cargill was a great training ground for oil traders. The first generation of oil traders to emerge from Cargill were Ben Pollner, who went on to start up Taurus, a key trader of Russian Urals crude at a time (and a very controversial company that became embroiled in the Iraq Oil-for-Food scandal),[46] Anne Summer who went to Morgan Stanley in New York, Adri Vogel, Freddy Goetsch, and Miguel Araoz who founded 'Vulcan', a distillate and fuel oil trader in Geneva and many others.

A 'younger' crop of traders who 'graduated' from Cargill were Rex Steed, who would later become a well known Brent trader at Elf Geneva, and Dick Vibe Rheymer, who later joined Norsk Hydro. Another Cargill trader who would end up with Elf trading was Jean Mathieu Sternberg, who was a middle distillate trader at the time, and later joined Rex at the North Sea bench. 'Musical chairs' had characterised employment in the oil trading industry for the earliest days of the 1970s and that remains the case even today.

'*From the day one at Cargill, I could tell Marco Dunand was different. Simply put, he was the smartest guy in the room*', says Pavel. In Dunand's own words, he was always a trader. He was the kind of kid who went to elementary school in the morning with a broken toy and came home at the end of the day with a new bike, having traded his way through the school day.[47]

After one of Cargill's 'exit' phases from energy markets, Marco moved to Goldman Sachs' commodity trading division J. Aron, with Danny following shortly after. Pavel then relocated to New York, where he began brokering middle distillates, with Danny and Marco quickly becoming his primary clients.

Jonathan Martland, an ex-Goldman trader, recalls that when Dunand joined Goldman in 1987, he revolutionised the firm's approach to trading. Instead of focussing purely on speculation, Dunand shifted the mindset towards identifying arbitrages between various Brent benchmarks, both paper and physical. In particular, he utilised the emerging Dated Brent contracts for difference (CFD) swaps to convert fixed priced oil into a 'floating' (or Dated-related) price and vice versa.[48] Martland describes the duo as '*thoughtful*' and notes that they earned the respect of many of their counterparts at the time. Lourdes Rodriguez, former head of trading and refining at Repsol, includes Dunand in a select group of individuals who have made foundational contributions to the development of oil trading over the past five decades. Lourdes comments 'I admired his intellectual approach to the business'.[49]

After a bumpy period at J. Aron, Marco and Danny left for Phibro, where Pavel was already focussing on Eastern Europe. At the time, other traders at Phibro were a young ex-Shell trader (SITCO at the time) Danny Masters, who would later set up the energy trading business for JP Morgan, Christophe Gros (later trading oil at Elf and Lukoil), and popular Jorgie Kuntz (later trading for Petroplus). Some of these young guns were already doing well.

Danny Masters was in his mid-twenties and already owned a two-engine aircraft, which he flew as an accomplished pilot.[50]

After roughly a decade of successful trading at Phibro, Danny and Marco started to dream of a business of their own. '*Annual negotiations with Andy Hall over a bonus were tough, and one was always left screwed*'.[51] Initially, the idea was to set up an independent operation within an existing trading company as trading oil required large capital and good credit lines.[52]

Eventually, Sempra offered a deal with something along those lines. The trading 'duo' gathered several trusted hands around them and began trading both in Europe and Asia. In Geneva, the Brent traders were Wolfgang Thumell from BP and Kurt Chapman from Koch, while the Chinese market was being covered by Han Jin and Zhu Hong.[53] In Singapore, they brought their former colleagues from Phibro, Junichi Kasahara and Lawrence Ho.

Having settled in Poland and having received Polish citizenships, Grisha and Slawa went on to capitalise on their contacts in the Gdansk refinery and supply the Russian crude to the biggest plant in the country, PKN Orlen, on a long-term basis. They registered their company, J&S (from Jankselewicz and Smolokowski) in Cyprus, a favourite financial hub of Russian oligarchs, and using a special 'power of attorney' from their Polish friends, went on to source and supply as much as 90 per cent of the Polish imports!

Pavel met Slawa and Grisha in 1992 in Moscow, having traded some pipeline oil into Poland, on behalf of Phibro. As the J&S Polish business grew, it was Pavel who managed their hedging portfolio and pricing options related to such sales. '*It is then that I got to know them*', says Pavel. '*I invited them to the annual Phibro trip for top customers in Pamplona, Spain for the "Running of the Bulls" spectacle, which they hated!*' And when the 'Polish duo' set up a trading company in 1999, Pavel was keen to join.

When they joined forces, the J&S sway over the Russian pipeline monopoly operator 'Transneft' was such that the trader organised the supply of Russian oil from the TNK-BP joint venture as well as the Russian companies Surgutneftgaz, Lukoil, Slavneft through the Druzhba pipeline to Germany, Slovakia, and Hungary as well.[54] From Poland, Russian Urals crude started leaving for the rest of Europe and Pavel started supplying Exxon, Repsol, Petronor, and other oil giants on long-term basis.

However, the privatisation of the Gdansk refinery and sale by the Russian Lukoil brought the trading activities into the open. A scandal over the privatisation and supply of the PKN refinery, 'Orlengate',[55] broke out at the time when the PKN Orlen's Plock refinery was the main destination for J&S oil. In a messy and highly politicised process, the company was accused of monopolising the Polish oil market through corruption and even ties with Russian intelligence services.[56] Navigating these troubled waters was hard and J&S had to change.

In 2004, the duo established a new entity with an office in Switzerland, naming it 'Mercuria' Energy Group, after the ancient Roman god of commerce. The controlling stake at that time (of about a quarter each) was probably held by Slawa and Grisha. During this period, Linieckij and Pavel also had very small shares, but the key figures and main managers of the company appeared to be Marco Dunand and Daniel Jaeggi.

This relationship started with a tennis tournament in Warsaw, where Pavel invited his old colleague, Danny Jaegi. There, they met Slawa and the idea of setting up a company together was born. J&S were making good money, but Slawa and Grisha wanted to go from '*the Premiership into the Champions League*'[57] and they needed people who would take them there. For Danny and Marco, J&S offered far more than Sempra—they could finally fulfil their dream and have their 'own' trading company![58]

From these modest beginnings, Mercuria rapidly expanded, carving out a name for itself in the global trading world. Despite being younger and smaller than its competitors, the company's growth has been notable, with a diverse portfolio that spans energy markets worldwide.

The core of the Mercuria oil team was completed by bringing in the trusted buddies from Sempra, Han Jin and Zhu Hong, Brent expiry-expert and lieutenant, Kurt Chapman, and a former BP trader, Wolfgang Thumell. In the old tradition of Marco and Danny ('Mum and Dad' as the Mercuria traders affectionately called them), they focussed on arbitrage, initially with the Russian barrels. '*We had a lot of Urals and moved it everywhere – Europe, Trinidad and even Houston*', recalls Pavel.

In 2006, Mercuria opened offices in China and Singapore, and then in the United States, the United Arab Emirates, Nigeria, and Canada. Mercuria's big leaps into the major league of trading came in a series of acquisitions: in 2014 Mercuria bought the trading unit of J.P. Morgan Chase and Company for \$3.5 billion, in 2017, they bought Noble Group's U.S. gas and power business, and in 2019, bought the Aegean Marine Petroleum Network, which was reorganised as a wholly owned bunkering and maritime subsidiary, Minerva Bunkering.[59]

The duo of Han Jin and Zhu Hong were instrumental in opening the doors to trading in China and in January 2016 Mercuria sold 12 per cent of its shares to the largest chemical company in China, ChemChina. Today, Mercuria operates in over 50 countries across 5 continents.[60] Like its larger counterparts, the trading company has faced its own set of challenges and opportunities, but its rapid ascent in the trading world highlights the impact that smaller, more agile firms can have on the industry.

Like most successful duos in trading, Danny and Marco have complemented each other perfectly. Energy trading veteran Russ Newton encapsulates their partnership well: 'Dunand and Jaeggi have always been better together'. Despite the immense pressures of running a global trading firm, the pair have worked side-by-side for two decades without any external sign of discord, successfully guiding Mercuria to become one of the most respected names in the industry.[61]

The reward was a billion-dollar dividend payment in 2023: '*… marking one of the biggest paydays for any individual commodity traders in history*'.[62]

Hess and the Goldmans

Hetco, now known as Hartree after merging with private equity firm Oaktree, was established in 1997 as a joint venture between former Goldman Sachs veterans Steve Hendel,[63] Steve Semlitz, and Guy Merison, alongside Amerada Hess. The partnership combined the financial expertise of the Goldman alumni with the oil industry experience of Amerada Hess, allowing Hetco to make an immediate impact in energy trading. Despite facing challenging years in the mid-2000s, when a cyclical downturn affected revenues across the board, Hartree (formerly Hetco) has successfully grown into a profitable organisation. However, it operates more as a collection of independent individuals and businesses, all functioning under the Hartree umbrella. In a reversal of the usual sobriquet, they bank on 'the sum of the parts being greater than the whole'.

A key figure in their recovery and expansion was Jon O'Neil, the former Shell UK trading manager, who was instrumental in managing their operations outside the United States. Like other major independent traders, Hartree has significantly diversified away from its core oil trading business, expanding into gas, power, and renewables sectors. This diversification has helped the firm weather industry fluctuations and position itself for future growth in the evolving energy market.

The ownership and backing of Gunvor have long been the subject of speculation, with rumours suggesting that Russian government figures, including Vladimir Putin, may have had interests in the firm. Gunvor was founded by Gennady Timchenko (who had founded Krrishineftekhimexport in St Petersburg in the wild days of post-Soviet Russia) and Torbjorn Tornquist, a former

BP executive. While Russian interests are believed to have exited the firm, Gunvor is now thought to be majority-owned by Tornquist.

Although Gunvor does not operate at the same scale as industry giants like Vitol, Glencore, and Trafigura, the firm remains a significant player in the global commodities market. Its most recently reported gross revenues of around $127 billion place it in close competition with Trafigura, whose revenues were also reported at $130 billion, but still significantly behind Vitol's $400 billion and Glencore's $218 billion.[64] Despite this, Gunvor's position reflects its continued influence and growth within the energy trading sector.

Notes

1. For more detail, see Chapter 2.
2. Blas, J: Commodities: Tougher Times for Trading Titans April 14th 2013 FT Opinion.
3. This chapter discusses asset-based trading in detail.
4. They include 550,000 barrels a day of refining capacity in Asia, Australia, Europe and the Middle East; Oil production of some 70,000 bpd in West Africa and the US and some 7,500 retail sites globally. From https://www.vitol.com/solutions/crude-oil-products/.
5. For example, see Blas and Farchy (2021), pp. 153–156.
6. Discussion with Ian Taylor during the dinner mentioned above.
7. Your author's recollection.
8. Taylor was a staunch supported of the 'Remainer' camp in the Brexit debate. See: https://www.bbc.com/news/uk-scotland-scotland-politics-36960686.
9. For more details, see chapter.
10. Author's own recollection.
11. https://www.nzz.ch/english/interview-commodity-giant-vitols-ceo-on-oil-trading-in-the-energy-transition-ld.1762549.
12. Hosp Gerald: Commodity Giant Vitol's CEO on Oil Trading in the Energy Transition October 30 2023 https://www.nzz.ch/english/interview-commodity-giant-vitols-ceo-on-oil-trading-in-the-energy-transition-id.1762549.
13. Farchy Jack: https://www.linkedin.com/posts/jack-farchy-5a3a6723.
14. Discussion with ex Vitol employee on 15/12/2023.
15. Form a discussion with a current Vitol employee who wishes to remain anonymous.

16. From an interview with Peter Smith on 13/12/2025.
17. Vitol began, around 2010, to fund pre-payment loans for the likes of Rosneft in return for long term oil contracts. Vitol then syndicated these loans amongst investment banks including Goldman and Morgan Stanley whose oil trading departments had to stand watching while traders like Vitol, Glencore and others walked off with oil acquisition business which GS and MS would have liked to service themselves.
18. Discussion with Peter Smith on 20/01/2025.
19. From a Vitol trader who preferred to stay anonymous.
20. https://www.bbc.com/news/world-africa-10735255.
21. https://www.swissinfo.ch/eng/multinational-companies/trafigura-trial-company-fined-defendants-jailed/88808833.
22. https://www.bbc.com/news/articles/c2d3z87yn51o.
23. https://www.bloomberg.com/news/articles/2023-12-07/trafigura-bribery-case-the-once-powerful-executive-now-facing-charges.
24. Long standing Trafigura oil trading head, Jose Larocca, also retired in 2024.
25. Revenues of $7.4 billion were reported by the firm for 2023 by various press sources but the proportion resulting from oil is unknown.
26. https://www.ft.com/content/acc6a7b0-29a9-40d9-aa53-fea63579b59e.
27. The trader would like to stay anonymous.
28. From a lunch conversation with Ronald Davidson in January 2025.
29. https://www.reuters.com/markets/commodities/glencores-ex-head-oil-faces-2027-trial-uk-court-bribery-charges-2024-10-09/.
30. https://www.theguardian.com/business/2015/sep/07/glencore-ceo-to-shell-out-210m-during-restructuring-drive#:~:text=Glasenberg%20made%20so%20much%20money,a%20flat%20in%20London's%20Belgravia.
31. https://bikebiz.com/pinarello-nears-sale-to-billionaire-ivan-glasenberg-according-to-reports/#:~:text=It%20is%20understood%20that%20his,remain%20after%20any%20potential%20takeover.&text=Earlier%20this%20year%2C%20Pinarello%20announced,of%20other%20World%20Cup%20circuits.
32. https://amacx.com/pages/about-us?srsltid=AfmBOoouXoyaNYguICzHVlbEIkY6rb7JVvbReJcyyIIrdHSD3RSpyqtG.
33. The trader wanted to stay anonymous.
34. https://www.strategicfuelfund.co.za/company.
35. Discussion with Justus Van Der Spuy 05/06/2024.

36. https://mercuria.com/about-us/our-history/.
37. https://www.forbes.pl/przywodztwo/grzegorz-jankilewicz-slawomir-smolokowski-jak-powstala-mercuria/rlxw17w.
38. This claim came from a well-informed trader who wished to stay anonymous.
39. From an interview with a European oil trader who wished to stay anonymous.
40. Gustafson (2012), page 44.
41. Initially, it could only be done using joint-ventures with foreign oil-service companies. See Gustafson (2012), page 45. Later, this would be relaxed.
42. Samotlor was producing almost 3.5 mbd and the whole region almost 8.5 mbd in the late 1980's. Gustafson, T. page 40.
43. From the interview With Pavel Pojdl on 28/11/24.
44. https://www.nytimes.com/1993/02/27/business/company-news-phibro-says-export-dispute-imperils-russia-oil-venture.html.
45. In the early 1990's, Poland (Gdansk refinery in particular) started buying non-Russian oil on spot basis. Your author was one of the first traders to sell a cargo of North Sea Flotta to PK Orlen, the state oil company.
46. For more details, see the next chapter. As a general reference, see: https://www.cfr.org/backgrounder/iraq-oil-food-scandal.
47. From a conversation Chris Heilpern (chat with Chris on 24/2/25) had with Dunand at a Sempra traders offsite in the Bahamas in the early 2000's. It is not clear weather Marco's description was figurative or literal.
48. Having heard that your author was finishing a part-time PhD at London University, Marco exclaimed: '*I do not need that, I have a PhD in CDSs*!'.
49. Discussion with Lourdes Rodrigues 23/01/2024.
50. Your author met Danny and the others in the Phibro office in 1991, just after they moved from Zug to London. He spent some time with Danny at the desk and talked mainly about flying (your author was a keen glider-pilot).
51. A common view from several Phibro traders the author spoke to.
52. Your author was a party of one such discussion between M&D and Texaco oil trading in the late 1990's, while they were still at Phibro.
53. Your author joined Sempra in 2001 in Singapore, trading own crude oil book.

54. https://www.forbes.pl/przywodztwo/grzegorz-jankilewicz-slawomir-smolokowski-jak-powstala-mercuria/rlxw17w.
55. https://en.wikipedia.org/wiki/Orlengate.
56. https://en.wikipedia.org/wiki/Orlengate.
57. Pavel's analogy.
58. During a chat with your author in their Geneva offices, Marko admitted: '*The company is my life.*'
59. https://mercuria.com/about-us/our-history/.
60. https://mercuria.com/.
61. https://www.tradersmagazine.com/departments/options/duo-who-built-energy-trading-empire-set-sights-on-jpmorgan-unit.
62. https://www.bloomberg.com/news/articles/2025-01-10/mercuria-s-top-duo-shared-1-billion-payday-amid-energy-crisis.
63. Hendel is also known as a Broadway 'angel' having been involved in the successful production of FELE in addition to other shows. Not the only Wall St trader to engage with Broadway as Brenden Connellan of Morgan Stanley wrote, produced and performed in 'Kill the Bid' a play about a trading business.
64. Data sourced from consultants Energex. Partners. Notably these figures compare with BP's $40 billion figure although this would not include any non-energy component.

Bibliography

Blas J. and Farchy J. (2021): 'The World for Sale', Random House.

Gordon, J. (2006): 'The Accusations Against the Oil For Food Programme', Arab Studies Quarterly, Summer/Fall 2006, Vol. 28, No. 3/4, pp. 19–26.

Gustafson, (2012): 'Wheel of Fortune', Harvard University Press.

15

Traders 2: Arcadia is in Nigeria

Arcadia is in Nigeria

Arcadia was founded by Marcus Green in 1998. Green, a high flyer, had caused quite a stir when, some years earlier, he left his BP Tokyo job to join Phibro in the same city as a one-man crude oil trading operation.[1] Moving back to London, he subsequently set up an oil trading operation called 'Kaines', a company owned by 'British & Commonwealth'.[2] The company had two offices, one in London and onc in Geneva.

Following the collapse of Kaines due to an unsuccessful copper options play, Green assumed management of the company's London offices and, leveraging longstanding connections with Mitsui in Tokyo, established Arcadia Petroleum, an oil trading company, in 1988.[3]

Jean Claude Gandur, a former Phibro trader with the storied background of a 'deep Africa' trader, took over Kaines' Geneva operations and rebranded them as Addax Petroleum, later expanding into Canada with the Oryx Group. Jean Claude popped up in all sorts of guises in Africa and further afield and was Commander of the National Order of Benin, an Honorary Consul for the Republic of the Congo in Geneva, and a Senegalese passport holder.

Arcadia benefited from Mitsui's well-accepted Parent Company Guarantees[4] and Marcus's contacts and experience. One of their first deals was to supply Middle East crude to Tanzania but it was the Nigerian business, thanks to a relationship[5] with General Yakubu Dan-Yumma 'Jack' Gowon, a former head of the state, that was to make them stand out amongst the oil trading milieu.

A. Imsirovic and C. Bryce, *The Rivers of Money*,
https://doi.org/10.1007/978-3-031-91806-3_15

At the time, the key equity producers in Nigeria were ENI, ExxonMobil, Shell, Chevron, and to a lesser extent, Texaco.[6] BP was also a major producer until 1979, when its assets were nationalised due to the United Kingdom's Rhodesia policy.

Nigeria was one of the first countries to sell oil on a spot basis in the late 1970s, and since then it has been almost ubiquitously necessary to engage local consultants, in order to access Nigerian crude oil. One such consultant from the earliest days was Alhaji Tijani Dagazau. A pioneer of this business, he was a facilitator for Marc Rich + Co, Rhein Oel, and Shell.[7]

Dealing with people such as Dagazao was not always easy. Pete Bosworth, Arcadia's man on the ground in the country, describes setting up one of their early NNPC contracts: '*It was with a company called "Jet Stream", one of Dagazao's 'special purpose vehicles (SPVs), Nigerian entities, created to facilitate the contract. Alhaji also had a carpet factory in Lagos where I went to meet him. The problem was that I was in my 20's and, in Nigeria, age was important. Even though I explained who I was and I proposed a JV for the contract that Jet Stream was awarded, including a downpayment for the privilege, he simply ignored me. I went back to his office every day for well over a month and sat down on a plastic chair outside his office, in the unbearable heat of the city. There was only a parrot there. Every day, Alhaji just walked straight past the parrot and I, and never said a word. One day he called me into his office and allowed me to show him a million dollar check I already had prepared for the NNPC contract in my briefcase. It took another couple of weeks of me sitting there with the parrot (who might have learned a few swear words in the process) and I finally closed the deal with Dagazao. Later I understood that he was talking to Schwab and Co. an American finance firm about the same contract, but it never materialised (they were probably never there to finalise it)*'.

Another very influential name in the Nigerian oil market at the time was Mike Adenuga, one of the first domestic investors in the Exploration and Production (E&P) of oil in Nigeria with his company 'Conoil'.[8] Mike's first contract with NNPC was in the name of Conoil, and he on-sold to most traders including Arcadia. Today, Adenuga is one of the richest businessmen in Africa and owner of Globacom, a sprawling telecommunications empire.[9] Nigerian consultants used in dealings with NNPC were usually the first to get involved not just in trading, but also in the rest of the value chain. Good examples are 'Ocean and Oil' (O&O)[10] and 'MRS' (which stands for Mr. Sayu),[11] which are now major players in the country's oil business.[12]

Trading Nigerian oil had a major impact on the Brent market. NNPC marketed their oil on a price basis related to Dated Brent. According to James Gooder of Argus: '*We started quoting Bonny Light at a differential to Dated*

Brent on 2nd of January 1990, and we were reporting trades on that basis a couple of years before that'.[13]

NNPC began offering pricing options with pricing periods linked to loading dates, a move often credited to Jay Surrena,[14] the influential head of crude at Sun Oil at the time. Sun Oil was a major consumer of Nigerian oil at its Philadelphia refinery, the largest sweet crude processing unit in the world. As far back as 1982, Surrena had been sourcing Nigerian oil including at one time inking a contract with a Yugoslavian state oil company who had built a railway in Nigeria and received oil as payment and needed to find a refiner to take it.

Sun always had a large NNPC contract, consuming up to four cargoes every month. Surrena, a key figure in the industry, was seeking pricing mechanisms tied as closely as possible to the delivery of oil to minimise the price risk between the sale of refined products and crude oil delivery. As a major buyer of Nigerian crude, he advocated for a late-delivery pricing option in his contracts and eventually succeeded in securing it.[15]

This innovation introduced significant optionality for buyers, enabling them to capitalise on price differences in the burgeoning CFD Brent market. [16] Consequently, trading companies increasingly demanded greater optionality. This allowed the price of the same cargo to be set across as many as three different weeks, during which market prices could fluctuate significantly. Exercising this pricing flexibility typically involved paying a premium, but once paid, buyers could select the most favourable price.[17] This development significantly elevated the importance of Nigerian crude for traders engaged in Dated Brent and CFD markets.

After Sun Oil closed its London office in 1992, Marcus Green brought in the aforementioned Peter Bosworth to be their expert on Nigerian oil. In 1999, Green, the 'father' of Arcadia, died and Alister Gordon and Pete Bosworth were made joint heads of trading. Nigerian contracts and the flow of Dated Brent they provided reinforced each other, making for a very profitable operation.[18]

Arcadia thrived in the Nigerian market, although they were not the only ones. Traders such as Vitol and Glencore along with majors such as Shell and Chevron, were active in Nigeria, often via the facilitation of 'consultants'. Neither must one forget the French, who, in the form of Elf and Total were long-time players, especially in Francophone West Africa. Total were later to the West African game than Elf and were close to the Lebanese Chagouri family who themselves were confidantes of the Nigerian military dictator, Sani Abacha.

The flexibility in pricing terms was of enormous benefit to these companies in addition to their preferential access to barrels. Calson (Bermuda) and Hyson (Nigeria) are two companies, founded in 1988, who have at times been associated with Chevron and with Vitol. Both of these companies sourced significant volumes of oil via Calson/Hyson but, controversially in 2010, allegations were made that Vitol had received oil at discounted prices from these entities, an allegation which they denied.[19] Rumours and second-hand allegations of this kind were not at all uncommon when the subject of the sourcing of Nigerian oil came up in oil trader's offline discussions.

In 2006, Mitsui and Arcadia parted ways, and Peter Bosworth, by then the CEO of Arcadia, quickly tied up a similar deal with John Frederickson, a Norwegian ship-owning billionaire with Cypriot citizenship.[20] With Frederickson's significant financial backing, Arcadia began to expand into the United States. They hired ex-BP traders James Dyer and Nick Wildgoose to undertake this new business.[21] Dyer had operated as BP's lead on WTI trading and had developed a reputation as a skilled user of the advantageous position that BP possessed at the Cushing storage hub for that product. This position, derived by BP from their takeover of Amoco and Arco offered Dyer the opportunity to optimise his trading positions as a consequence of his ownership of the almost free optionality of his firm's storage.[22]

This proved to be personally advantageous for Dyer as by the early 2000s, BP was paying top-drawer bonuses to their most outstanding revenue generators. He chose to take early retirement from BP to begin a new life in Brisbane, Australia while his colleague, Wildgoose, also retired. The subsequent tenure of the two ex-BP stars in Arcadia and Arcadia's associated U.S. company, Parnon, proved to be short-lived and controversial.[23]

Arcadia's business was not solely focussed on Dyer and Wildgoose, and they were also especially active in Yemen whose high-quality Marib crude oil was attractive to a wide range of refiners. But controversy was again not far away with allegations appearing in the press that Arcadia had been accessing below-market price oil from Yemen as a consequence of the relationship with the local consultant, tribal leader Hamid al-Ahmar, an allegation that was firmly denied by Arcadia trader Stephen Gibbons.[24]

Whether by design or circumstance, oil traders have long specialised in navigating relationships with autocratic governments. Similar to the Mafia's influence in the boxing world,[25] dealing with an autocrat often means persuading just one individual to secure a favourable contract. In these scenarios, the driving force is always price. As a result, totalitarian regimes and the illicit behaviour of companies dealing with them are self-reinforcing.

However, some well-intentioned policies can also create fertile ground for misbehaving traders.

Governments that attempt to impose price controls or offer options often end up creating opportunities for traders and corrupt leaders to exploit. Whether it's keeping prices artificially low, as was the case in Russia or Yemen, or offering flexible pricing or loading schedules, like in post-Gaddafi Libya or Nigeria, any effort to bend the forces of the market leaves room for substantial profits to be made and shared among those involved.

One such misguided attempt to change the flow of the 'river of money' was the United Nations 'Oil-for-Food' programme established in 1995 following the first Gulf War to provide the Iraqi people with food and other humanitarian aid, bypassing the Iraqi government.[26] But a badly designed and executed programme coupled with individual greed resulted in money flowing to individual pockets and the regime of the Iraqi dictator.

Iraq Oil-for-Food

The illicit actions of different groups of players ranging from Houston-based cabals to independent trading companies, Parisien-based brokers and bankers, to Russian entities, and many others were brought into clear view by Paul Volcker, the Chairman of a U.N. Independent Inquiry Committee investigating manipulation of the programme.[27]

Volcker concluded that the affair was one where: '*Iraq manipulated the programme to dispense contracts on the basis of political preference and to derive illicit payments from the companies that obtained oil*'.[28]

The events surrounding this UN programme have been well investigated and a subject of numerous hearings,[29] so we shall briefly mention the points relevant to our discussion. The essence of the scam was that, for a period of time, the 'official selling prices' for the Iraqi oil were set deliberately low, making the contracts very profitable. Then, the oil contracts would be handed out to individuals and companies either supportive or willing to pass kick-backs to Saddam Hussein, the Iraqi dictator.[30] To make such dealings opaque, some 2,200 companies from 66 countries were involved, paying estimated $1.8 billion in kickbacks to Iraqi officials in exchange for securing supply contracts.[31]

Although the programme began in 1996, it was during phases 8 and 9, from late autumn 2000 over a two-year period, that the Iraqi government decided to impose additional surcharges on oil contracts. This marked a turbulent period, leading the major oil companies, which had been lifting

Iraq's oil, to scale back their involvement. However, it also created an opportunity for other companies to quietly step in and take their place.

Volcker identifies four companies: Bayoil,[32] Taurus,[33] Vitol, and Glencore[34] as being responsible for 60 per cent of the liftings during that period via Italian, Lichenstein, Swiss, and Malaysian intermediaries among others. That the four traders and others on-sold their Iraqi crude to refiners including the household name oil majors should cause these 'two steps removed' receivers to engage in some moral reflection.

The whole '*UN management of the oil-for-food "operated in an ineffective, wasteful, and unsatisfactory manner." It .... accused the former head of the program, Benon Sevan, of an "irreconcilable conflict of interest" because he helped a company owned by a friend obtain valuable contracts to sell Iraqi oil*'.[35]

The last point was an understatement. Benon Sevan allegedly took at least $150,000 in cash bribes. The UN procurement officer at the time pleaded guilty to accepting bribes from UN contractors. Another former Soviet member of the UN, Alexander Yakovlev, pleaded guilty to receiving almost $1 m in bribes, conspiracy, wire fraud and money laundering.[36]

The traders faced relatively few consequences for their actions. In the United States, Bayoil principal David Chalmers was sentenced to two years in jail,[37] and the storied Houstonian oil man and founder of Coastal States Petroleum Co, Oscar Wyatt, was put away for a one-year stretch.[38] Taurus's Ben Pollner managed to slip away from the United States just as the authorities were seeking to have a conversation with him.[39] Vitol, by overtly protecting employees behind the corporate shield, paid a fine of $17.5 million in the United States after pleading guilty to grand larceny.[40]

Not all commentators focussed on the allegations of corruption however, and academic Joy Gordon, writing in the journal Arab Studies Quarterly, emphasises that in enabling the provision of food to those suffering in Iraq, the end may have somewhat justified the means.[41]

Questionable activities of those operating in a certain segment of the oil trading world will continue, most especially in the sourcing of oil from Africa and Latin America,[42] places where underpaid officials have the ability to exercise preference in allocating barrels and do so for personal gain.[43]

As we shall see later, poorly designed and half-hearted sanctions on Russia, following Putin's invasion of Ukraine in 2022, would also result in many negative consequences, enriching shady individuals and Putin's regime, while achieving very little.[44]

As was the case in the early days of oil trading with the folks who accomplished '*difficult things In difficult places*',[45] through the sanctions busters to the Oil-For-Food bandits, there is, as in all large industries with similar characteristics, a cadre, at home in the penumbra, that emerges from time to time to extract illicit pickings.[46] As a result, government interventions in the market need very careful consideration. Well-functioning markets such as the global oil markets cannot be easily bent to government will. As will be discussed later in the book, seemingly easy-to-implement policies such as sanctions always have unintended consequences,[47] often creating a fertile ground for unscrupulous characters who will use such an environment to divert the flow of money into their own pockets.

Legacy of traders

Throughout the period of the rise of the independent traders, the banks were still plugging away, albeit much reduced. Goldman Sachs has maintained a stronger foothold in the commodities trading business compared to its peers like Morgan Stanley or JP Morgan, reportedly earning as much as $4 billion during the boom year of 2022.[48] However, other banks no longer generate such substantial revenues from this sector. While institutions like Morgan Stanley, Citi, Macquarie, and a few others still operate smaller, profitable commodities trading businesses, they have been well and truly overtaken by independent traders whose profitability in the 2020s has been at another level. The rivers of money have turned into torrents and tsunamis and these companies have been able to widely splash the cash.

The decline of banks in commodities trading can largely be attributed to regulatory overreach,[49] which reduced their operational flexibility. They lost valuable staff and key counterparts, particularly as the market shifted from over-the-counter (OTC) trading to cleared market exchanges. Additionally, banks struggled to compete with traders in the asset-integrated model and lost their traditional cost-of-capital advantages, further eroding their position in the commodities market. As a result, independent traders have surged ahead, while banks have seen their prominence in this sector diminish.

Not at all diminished were the trading arms of the oil majors, most especially BP, Shell, and Total. As long ago as 2005—a time when the fruits of asset-backed trading were beginning to come through—BP was reported to be making as much as $3 billion in trading.[50] More recently, Shell's energy trading business is reported to be responsible for 'about a fifth of the wider group's profits'.[51]

Trading houses have benefited from a significant increase in their balance sheets, largely due to the high earnings of recent years. For example, in 2015,

Vitol reported a balance sheet of $10 billion, but that figure has since almost quadrupled, with the vast majority of the growth being attributed to shareholder (i.e. employee-owner) equity. How they choose to employ these riches, perhaps in a quest for assets or for the recruitment of top people, will, as in the post-Iran Revolution period in 1979–80 and in the high priced period before the global financial crisis in 2008 when beneficiaries were able to splurge their winnings, define their futures.

One of the key advantages that traders now have over banks is their relatively lighter regulatory burden. Traders operate under less stringent oversight, allowing them more flexibility in their activities. Additionally, by domiciling their businesses in tax-advantaged locations, they benefit from lower tax rates, further enhancing their profitability. Unlike banks, which are often bogged down by layers of bureaucracy, such as new product committees, risk committees, and credit committees, trading houses can remain more agile and make decisions quickly, enabling them to 'turn on a dime'. This nimbleness has become a critical edge in today's fast-paced, dynamic markets.

The independent trading houses also face significant challenges though. One of the key concerns has always been succession—who will replace industry leaders like Ian Taylor, Jeremy Weir, Marco Dunand, and Daniel Jaeggi? However, the smooth transitions seen with Russell Hardy's rise at Vitol and the promotion of Richard Holthum at Trafigura offer hope that succession issues can be successfully navigated.

And the ongoing propensity of independent traders to court controversy remains a concern. The previously mentioned Mongolian fraud scandal involving Trafigura is just one example of the ongoing risk management issues these firms face. This raises questions about corporate culture and whether ethical lapses will continue to be overlooked or whether a genuine shift towards transparency will occur.

Arcadia is not alone in facing allegations related to acquiring oil in Nigeria or operating on the edge of legality in physical markets and their corresponding paper contracts. Numerous accounts highlight instances of 'legislative arbitrage' involving trading companies, major oil firms, and individuals exchanging favours in countries where influential elites hold decision-making power and leverage their positions for personal gain.[52]

While authorities in the U.S. have shown a propensity to prosecute individuals who they suspect of bribing foreign officials or individuals who they believe are manipulating oil markets, the United Kingdom and other jurisdictions have been less on the front foot. However, most recently, Swiss authorities, considered by many to be the least likely to open prosecutions, have done so in the case of an alleged bribery involving Trafigura and certain of its executives.

Traditionally, independent oil traders have been advantaged in the conduct of business away from open sight behind the 'Swiss Curtain'. Switzerland has thus been home to the parent companies of many of the names appearing in this chapter and in addition to the advantages of anonymity, the generous taxation regime of the country has been beneficial. It is informative to note that five of the top six revenue-generating companies in Switzerland in 2021 were not the likes of Nestle or Roche, but oil traders Vitol, Trafigura, Glencore, Gunvor, and Mercuria.[53]

In the United Kingdom, another jurisdiction that has been hesitant to prosecute oil trading misadventures, a bribery case has been opened against employees of Glencore in respect of alleged activities in Cameroon and Nigeria between 2007 and 2019. It is entirely likely that the threat of prosecution will serve to clean up parts of the industry that still present a stickiness when it comes to behavioural reform. Certainly, prosecutions in interest rate and foreign exchange markets have had just that effect.

As the Swiss authorities turn towards a propensity to prosecute, perhaps it will be to Dubai, a jurisdiction openly welcoming to the many, that will turn out to be the next most favoured domicile for those in oil trading who prefer opacity. Already, there has been a build-up of a coterie of new entities domiciled there specialising in the trading of Russian oil at a time when sanctions apply to aspects of Russian oil commerce in certain jurisdictions.

The legacy of oil traders (working for companies of all shades) in their business practices in the less developed world will undoubtedly remain controversial. For decades, the money that poured into the region caused injustice and inequality,[54] but also provided much-needed finance that would not be forthcoming from banks and similar institutions due to perceived country risks.[55] By tying up oil deals with funding, trading companies provided much-needed investment, albeit at the risk of enabling corruption. Of course, it is important not to tar all with one brush nor to assume that all operators behaved in a disreputable manner. They did not and do not but there has undoubtedly been a minority who have constituted the underbelly of the oil trading business, a place which, of course, also exists in other industries operating in similar places. There is no doubt that many more books and papers will be written on this subject.

The oil trading community has largely escaped significant public scrutiny, despite the immense influence of oil prices on everyday life—from the cost of goods and fuel to economic growth and inflation. If the public begins to believe that these traders are manipulating markets for personal gain, there may be a growing backlash. Oil trading firms often justify their lucrative earnings by claiming that they are essential in directing resources to where they are most needed, at the most efficient price. Yet, these arguments are difficult for the general public to fully grasp, especially when traders' contributions are hidden behind the complex nature of their business.

One might wonder if the high barriers to entry—requiring expertise, systems, funding, contacts, contracts, and physical assets—are enough to justify the high rewards. There may be a certain level of exclusivity to this line of work, which, for some, feels morally ambiguous. The public may not like what they see, but they may still support the industry because they find its fast-paced, high-stakes nature alluring.

As the trading landscape continues to evolve, firms will need to balance their efforts in traditional markets like oil with the demands and risks of new sectors, all while grappling with increasing regulatory pressures and legal issues. And for the individuals the propensity to turn a blind eye on the excuse that 'it's not me 'it's the company' acting in questionable activities is a matter of conduct that can no longer be tolerated and might well be prosecuted. Being one step removed is no longer a defence. Indeed, the companies to whom oil traders on-sell the barrels sourced in unacceptable ways (the household name oil companies among them), may be two steps removed physically but they are, arguably, a good deal closer morally if they were to take time to reflect. What, for the outside world, was once occluded, opaque and subjectively imagined is now visible and ripe for criticism.

Ultimately, the future of oil trading will likely be shaped by how firms respond to growing demands for transparency, the evolving regulatory landscape, and the increasing competition from the renewable energy sector, which is beginning to attract both capital and talent. It will be fascinating to see whether the industry can evolve in a way that addresses these pressures, or if it will continue to face controversy as it navigates an increasingly complex landscape.

The hegemony of the independent traders was about to be challenged as a new cadre got their teeth into oil. And they knew what they were doing having had years of experience in financial markets. Welcome to the instigators of the 'financialisaton' of oil markets.

Notes

1. From an interview with a trader who worked with him for many years, but would prefer to stay anonymous, on 24/12/24 and 31/12/

24. Much of this section is from this source, combined with publicly available information.

2. https://en.wikipedia.org/wiki/British_and_Commonwealth_Holdings In the 1980s, under the leadership of maverick entrepreneur John Gunn, B&C saw rapid expansion in financial services. See:
   https://www.theguardian.com/business/2000/oct/01/theobserver.observerbusiness10.
3. Previously, Mitsui had a trading company called 'Avant,' which '*was rubbish, and did not make any money,*' according to our source. Mitsui covered the trading activity with a Parent Company Guarantee and Marcus negotiated a very good share of net profits of about 30–35%. He rewarded his traders well ('much better than Phibro') out of that pool.
4. PCG is a guarantee that a parent company often issues for its subsidiary, to enable it to trade more cheaply, without incurring large banking costs (such as letters of credit and bank guarantees). In essence, the parent company guarantees the subsidiary's credit.
5. A fixer, 'consultant' or 'sponsor' would normally establish and maintain the relationship with the Nigerian National Petroleum Corporation (NNPC) on behalf of the company, in return for a fee.
6. Texaco only had an offshore production of Pennington crude. https://www.offshore-technology.com/marketdata/oil-gas-field-profile-pennington-conventional-oil-field-australia/.
7. https://www.quarefinery.com/promoters.
8. https://conoilplc.com/who-we-are-2/.
9. https://www.thecable.ng/glo-reclaims-position-as-nigerias-2nd-largest-telecom-operator/
   And https://dangote.com/our-business/oil-and-gas/.
10. http://www.oandoholdings.com/.
11. https://www.mrsoilnigplc.net/.
12. MRS is also a major company on the Nigerian stock exchange.
13. Discussion with J. Gooder, 9/1/25.
14. https://www.jnelsonrigbyfh.com/obituaries/H-Jay-Surrena-Jr?obId=27408858.
15. This is the story you author heard during his tenure as a trader at Sun Oil.
16. Brent CFDs are discussed in Chapter 11.
17. For details of the working and value of this optionality, see: https://www.oxfordenergy.org/wpcms/wp-content/uploads/2019/06/Contracts-for-Difference-and-the-Evolution-of-the-Brent-Complex.pdf.

18. In August and September 1999, Arcadia and possibly several other traders moved a large volume of Brent outside the North Sea, causing an alleged squeeze, causing Brent prices to increase substantially. A large volume of that oil ended up in storage in Saldanha Bay, in South Africa. The storage deal at Saldanha bay was originally brought to Marcus Green by Michael Hacking of Engen, South Africa, who had access to the caverns belonging to the South African Strategic Fuel Fund (SFF) with over 40 million barrels of storage. See: https://www.strategicfuelfund.co.za/.
19. Swiss Traders Opaque Deals in Nigeria: Berne Declaration 2013, pp. 5–6.
20. https://www.forbes.com/profile/john-fredriksen/.
21. They are an ex-BP WTI-trader Jimmy Dyer (who was, at the time, happily retired on a ranch in Australia and did not want to work full-time) as a consultant. This set-off a quick exodus from BP: Nick Wildgoose, Jimmy's former partner who was running the WTI desk in Chicago left BP and joined Dyer in Arcadia. On the very same day, Mark Cooling also left the same BP team to join Vitol.

    Dyer was sought after even in retirement—having perfected his Brent trading in BP's London office where he was working on the Brent desk with Chris McAleese and Wolfgang Thummel. Then, he moved to the company's Chicago office where he 'invented' the BP trading system for WTI, based on ample storage (and information it provided) in Cushing, Oklahoma where WTI was delivered and set the price of the benchmark. Following a merger with AMOCO in 2000, BP inherited a large storage in Cushing giving it a good view of the fundamentals at this key delivery and pricing point for the US benchmark. This led to an industry saying: 'If you need a WTI trader, hire someone with 'BP' on their CV.'.

    See: https://www.wsj.com/articles/SB949020744769401144.
22. This optionality is similar to the one Morgan Stanley had in US products—as explained in this chapter.
23. https://www.cftc.gov/PressRoom/PressReleases/6971-14.
24. See Brian Grow and Jushua Schneyer Reuters June 2 2011 'Arcadia may have rigged Yemen oil exports'.
25. https://uk.boxraw.com/blogs/blog/boxings-dark-history-with-the-mafia.
26. https://www.un.org/depts/oip/sector-food.html.
27. Volcker, Paul. A et al.: Manipulation of the Oil-For-Food Programme By the Iraqi Regime October 27 2005 www.iic-offp.org.

28. Ibid p1.
29. For example, by the Subcommittee on National Security, Emerging Threats, And International.

    Relations of the Committee on Government Reform House of Representatives One Hundred Ninth Congress.
30. See page 2 of the report: https://www.files.ethz.ch/isn/13894/ManipulationReport.pdf.
31. Ibid, also see: https://www.reuters.com/article/world/iraq-sues-companies-over-oil-for-food-kickbacks-idUSL29694675/.
32. See: https://www.justice.gov/archive/usao/nys/pressreleases/August07/chalmersdionissievbayoiloilforfoodpleaspr.pdf.
33. https://www.bloomberg.com/news/articles/2005-07-17/the-rich-boys.
34. https://www.ft.com/content/1f250dd4-47de-11da-a949-00000e2511c8.
35. https://www.cfr.org/backgrounder/iraq-oil-food-scandal.
36. http://news.bbc.co.uk/2/hi/middle_east/4131602.stm.
37. See: 'Texas Trader Admits Guilt in Iraq Oil-for-Food Fraud,' Feuer, Alan in New York Times (1923-); Aug 18, 2007.
38. https://www.reuters.com/article/economy/texas-oilman-wyatt-sentenced-to-year-in-prison-idUSN27516951/.
39. https://web.archive.org/web/20120708061937/http://www.businessweek.com/stories/2005-07-17/the-rich-boys.
40. Vickers, Marcia: The Rich Boys: Business Week 18/07/2015, p. 71.
41. Gordon (2006). Your authors find this view laughable.
42. https://insightcrime.org/news/oil-trader-bribes-latin-america/.
43. https://www.justice.gov/archives/opa/pr/justice-departments-investigation-international-commodities-trading-companies-foreign.
44. https://www.csis.org/analysis/russian-oil-price-caps-are-failing-key-test.
45. See Chapter 6 for early history of Legislative arbitrage in oil trading.
46. https://www.wider.unu.edu/publication/sanction-busting-through-tax-havens.
47. See: https://www.csis.org/analysis/oil-market-interventions-and-consequences.
48. J Macaskill: Macaskill on Markets March 2023. Much of the recent profits of the banks has come from offering margin financing to independent traders and others who are required to post margin to counterparts and exchanges in respect of hedges placed to manage their physical price risks across the commodities markets.
49. Authors are aware that 'overreach' may be an understatement.

50. Zdhannikov, Dmitry Reuters 16/10/2015.
51. Gosden, Emily: Shell set to bounce back after traders recover momentum The Times 07/10/2023.
52. See for example http://www.sfo.gov.uk/2022/05/24/serious-fraud-office-charges-glencore-with-seven-counts-of-bribery/.
53. https://www.publiceye.ch/en/topics/soft-commodity-trading/war-and-crisis-and-commodity-traders-are-making-record-profits.
54. https://www.blackpast.org/global-african-history/events-global-african-history/niger-delta-conflict-1990s/.
55. https://www.spglobal.com/commodity-insights/en/news-research/latest-news/crude-oil/071824-traders-gulf-banks-move-to-fill-financing-vacuum-in-african-oil.

Bibliography

Blas J. and Farchy J. (2021): 'The World for Sale', Random House.

16

Financialisation and the Great Recession

Financialisaton

With the transparency of the Brent market improved by the creation of ICE, the stage was set for a significant evolution in oil and other commodity trading. Until 1980, markets were entirely dominated by physical oil trading. Over the next decade, forward and futures oil trading began to take shape. Then, starting around 1990, a parallel trading track emerged with the introduction of derivative products like swaps and options.

While a further new development wouldn't gain momentum for another ten years, it marked the beginning of a fourth branch in the oil trading landscape. Known within the financial industry as the 'Investor Products' business,[1] it differed from existing operations in two main ways. First, the demand side was composed of institutional and retail investors rather than oil traders, corporations, or consumers. Second, unlike the derivatives market, this sector was staffed not by traders transitioning from oil markets, but by finance and banking professionals—often refugees from fixed-income and other capital markets.

Additionally, this new area lacked the colourful nature of traditional oil trading.

The fast-paced, reckless, and sometimes borderline legal practices of certain trading personalities that had prevailed until then were noticeably absent in this new landscape. The environment was largely characterised by rigorous mathematics and quantitative research, populated by individuals who were typically MBA graduates dressed in suits. There were hardly any botanists or

A. Imsirovic and C. Bryce, *The Rivers of Money*,
https://doi.org/10.1007/978-3-031-91806-3_16

geologists among the prominent figures in this emerging world of new oil trading.

Investors began to take an interest in oil, and as a consequence, so did the media outside the narrow oil world. The Wall Street Journal and the Financial Times (FT) began printing oil trading stories that didn't mention OPEC. Brent and WTI prices started to be discussed over cocktails and at weekends in the Hamptons[2] and the Lyford Cay.[3]

One of the first groups to establish a presence in the oil market were hedge funds—firms that mostly did not hedge at all.[4] Iconic names like George Soros, Julian Robertson, and Paul Tudor Jones led the charge. Hedge funds operated as collective speculators rather than true hedgers, typically with very short time frames. They tended to cluster in areas like St. James' Place in London, where they seemed to share similar ideas simultaneously, leading to a herd mentality that, unsurprisingly, influenced prices to move in tandem with their actions.

While speculators from Wall Street banks, futures floor locals, and independent oil traders provided crucial market liquidity, hedge funds utilised this liquidity aggressively for their own benefit. Unlike the often-collegial relationships between liquidity providers and the oil world, hedge funds operated on a different paradigm: 'What have you done for me today?' and 'Eat what you kill' defined their approach.

Hedge funds primarily targeted high-net-worth individuals and institutional investors, whereas another group, Commodity Trading Advisors (CTAs), catered more to wealthy retail investors, speculating on their behalf. Although CTAs were a step lower on the financial food chain, they still wielded considerable influence over price movements due to their volume and impact.

When Pension Funds were added to the mix—bringing a bit more patience and a longer term perspective, along with other Asset Managers, the stage was set for oil prices to be driven not by traditional supply and demand fundamentals, but by the whims of these financial players reflecting the fluctuations of the macroeconomic landscape.

Oil prices very quickly became financialised.

Always quick to seize profit opportunities, investment, and commercial banks swiftly entered the scene as key providers. They introduced a range of products, including Index Products, Exchange-Traded Funds (ETFs), Structured Products, and Structured Notes, among other attractive investment options.

Indices had been in existence for over 20 years, but the one that most significantly fuelled the rapid growth of investor interest in oil was the

Goldman Sachs Commodity Index (GSCI). Established in 1991 and later sold to Standard and Poor's in 2007, the index was heavily weighted in energy, with nearly 70 per cent of its composition based on oil.

Returns from total return swaps could be generated through three main mechanisms. First, profits could result from a direct increase in the underlying asset's price. Second, additional gains could be realised through 'roll yield', which occurred when the provider sold expiring contracts tied to the index and simultaneously bought next-month contracts at a lower price. The price difference between these contracts represented the roll yield, a strategy that proved effective when future oil prices were lower than current (prompt) prices. While this market structure called 'Backwardation', was often considered typical due to oil's inherent 'convenience' value as a commodity, it was not guaranteed to persist.[5]

In the early days of Investor Products, this relationship generally remained intact, bolstered by the tendency of oil producers—more organised and interested in hedging than oil consumers—to sell future month contracts in advance, which kept future prices lower relative to prompt prices. However, as we will see, this dynamic was destined to change.

The third source of return came from the interest earned on the collateral required for these contracts. Margin was not merely a cost; it could generate income. Thus, enhanced (total) returns provided a compelling reason for hedge funds and others to engage in index products. There were also other significant incentives to invest in oil.

One often-cited advantage of investing in oil (and commodities in general) is their ability to diversify portfolios primarily focussed on equities. Savvy analysts provided statistical evidence to support this claim, and marketing teams at investment firms produced extensive reports to share with clients.

More importantly, it was these funds that were setting the absolute price of oil (or 'flat price' as traders like to call it). As quantitative analysis carried out by maths wizards became the norm, it worked out that using oil in any fund portfolio was a pretty decent hedge against inflation and a weak dollar. Simply put, the odds of making money in a highly volatile commodity were worth the risk. As a result, they would go 'long' or 'short' millions of dollars 'worth of oil' their flow setting the price of the precious commodity. While the oil companies, refiners, and oil traders primarily engaged in hedging and therefore buying and selling spreads and swaps, derivatives at the front-end of the price curve, the financial community traded futures, setting the absolute price level.

While Index investing represented the largest segment of this market, Exchange-Traded Funds (ETFs) also played a significant role. Among them, the United States Oil (USO) fund emerged as the most notable, albeit with a reputation for only intermittent success. ETFs enabled investors to participate in oil markets without requiring the professional expertise needed to handle physical commodities.

Since these funds typically operated within the futures markets and, given that oil markets have a time dimension requiring positions to be reset monthly, the concept of 'roll' became crucial for the profitability of ETFs.

Long positions were held in futures contracts that would expire at the end of each month. This is because there was plenty of liquidity in the prompt months, compared to later delivery contracts. Before the expiry of the contract with prompt delivery, the fund would need to sell it and buy the next delivery month, both at the same time, in order to avoid taking additional risk. This sale of the expiring contract and purchase of the following month was referred to as a 'roll'.[6]

It didn't take long for astute observers to recognise that they could front-run the 'rolls' by these large funds. Although 'front-running' often carries connotations of illegality, one former dealer at a commercial bank, who wished to remain anonymous, remarked, 'Front-running was a strategy!'.[7]

So large and predictable in their timing were these 'rolls' that they often caused a reversal in the price structure of the oil market. The nearby prices would fall below the level of future prices—a condition known as contango.[8]

Considered by many to be more the natural state of the temporal price structure for a storable commodity, contango proved to be inconvenient for the massive USO fund and other oil funds, and detrimental to the development of oil as an investable asset class. In a nutshell, prevailing contango structure means the fund is always buying more expensive contracts for future delivery, and sells them cheaper, when they mature. Every time the fund 'rolls' the contract (sells the maturing contract and buys a new one for later delivery), losses are incurred. Such losses act as a large fee for holding the oil contract and undermine the profitability (if any) of the fund.

A great example of contango working against those 'rolling' long paper-oil positions was the case of a German industrial conglomerate Metallgesellschaft (MG), which at the time of a trading disaster employed some 63,000 people.[9] The company pursued an aggressive strategy of selling long-term, fixed price oil contracts—reportedly up to 160 million barrels—to consumers and distributors while hedging its exposure by purchasing near-term futures and forward contracts on the NYMEX and through swap dealers. As long as the market remained in backwardation, MG's strategy worked: they could roll their positions forward and collect a premium. However, when the market structure flipped to contango—partly driven by traders anticipating and front-running MG's rolls—the strategy unravelled. The company ultimately reported a staggering $1.3 billion loss in 1993. In response, Deutsche Bank enlisted Nancy Kropp, an ex-Morgan Stanley trading manager, to unwind MG's positions, much as they had done seven years earlier in the Kloeckner fiasco,[10] while simultaneously working to rescue MG from bankruptcy.

The MG debacle has been extensively analysed, including by Nobel Prize-winning economist Merton Miller.[11] Both its risk management approach and the subsequent liquidation of its positions remain subjects of debate, serving as a cautionary tale of the complexities of commodity hedging and market dynamics.

The third category of investable products was the Structured Product. Comprising layers of credit, swaps, options, and unique payouts tied to the price of oil, these instruments were often constructed by Quants and Strategists and sold to investors by the firm's sales forces.

The Quants differed significantly from the brash and charismatic traders and salespeople involved in investor products. Their ideal situation was to be in front of a computer screen enjoying midnight pizza and lounging with gym-shoed feet on their desks, engrossed in esoteric articles about Gaussian functions in Energy Risk magazine.

While few individuals in the Investor Product business became household names—most prominent hedge fund figures were already well established—the characteristics of some participating companies offered a touch of humour. It wasn't the asset management firms like Tiger, Ospraie, Harvard, Calpers, or Ontario Teachers that provided this amusement, but rather the banks involved in the sector. In a tongue-in-cheek article titled 'If Banks Were Musicians' published in Bloomberg Magazine, the so-called 'Masters of the Universe' found themselves the subject of playful mockery.[12]

U.K. bank Barclays had a history of fluctuating involvement in oil and commodities over the years. The authors humorously designated them as 'Oasis', after a famous British rock band: '*Chaotic in the 1990s, gained some focus in the early 2000s, but now appearing a bit bloated and self-indulgent*'.

Morgan Stanley was likened to Coldplay—'D*eadly earne*st', while Goldman Sachs was compared to the Rolling Stones—'U*niversally regarded as arrogant*'. Deutsche Bank was described as Fleetwood Mac 'Y*ears of infighting*'; Merrill Lynch as Madonna—'U*mpteen attempts at reinvention*', and HSBC as any boy band—'*The true performers earn peanuts*'. How perceptively accurate!

Increased oil price transparency and the availability of a large number of derivative instruments both OTC and on the exchanges made it easy and cheap for a wide range of non-oil, financial market participants to gain access to a range of oil-related products, which they could use to improve returns through diversification and macro-indicator hedging. The latter is particularly important as it involves using oil-related derivatives to allow portfolio managers to take opposite positions on specific assets they expect to be heavily impacted by macroeconomic events. As a result, portfolio managers and traders tended to 'herd', collusively or otherwise, and that was to put one-way pressure on prices and volatility.

Oil markets, though fast developing, were tiny relative to financial markets in, say, currencies and so when the weight of the money usually associated with these traditional markets came to bear on oil, there was bound to be an effect. Commodities as assets under management of commodity-based funds grew from $40 billion in the early 2000s to $300 billion in 2012.[13] And this was to manifest itself most especially in the price and volatility over the course of 2008, a period about which more analytical ink has been spilt than any other in the history of oil markets, perhaps only absent OPEC's heyday.

The Great Recession

In 2008, oil prices surged dramatically, reaching approximately $140 per barrel in July before plummeting to $40 per barrel by the year's end, propelled by the financial crisis (see Fig. 16.1). The bubble had burst. As with any bubble in the past, this price trajectory sparked intense debate over whether it was driven by fundamental factors related to the actual supply and demand for physical oil or by speculators treating oil as a financial product.[14]

Prominent economists, both within and outside the oil industry, have argued their positions in numerous research papers, books, and during face-to-face encounters with investigative committees of regulatory agencies and government bodies.[15] As is usually the case, this led to calls from some for a regulatory framework, particularly aimed at limiting the capacity of 'swap providers' to offer unrestricted liquidity in oil futures markets.[16]

As discussions evolved, this became the second focal point of the dialogue, following the initial questions of causation.[17] This is a complex issue, as futures officials emphasise the need to regulate OTC markets, while members of the oil community rally supportive economists to highlight the potentially dangerous unintended consequences of intervening in competitive markets.

Some argued that short-term volatility and extreme price movements do not really matter. In the longer term, spikes and troughs will average themselves out and markets will return to some form of dynamic disequilibrium.[18]

Short-term volatility is nonetheless a big problem for industry participants (even if less damaging to the general public). The most obvious transmission mechanism for distress is through the process of margin financing. Assume that oil prices are plummeting and an airline that has forward-purchased futures and over-the-counter contracts to hedge against rising jet fuel prices is facing a dilemma. As prices fall, the airline's hedge positions result in a paper loss. Both the futures and forward contracts will require the airline to post collateral to cover these potential losses. Consequently, the airline must raise so-called 'margin' finance to meet these requirements.

Given the volumes and price fluctuations involved, the funding requirements can reach billions,[19] as was the case for Emirates Airlines in late 2008.[20] Emirates had faced a three-dimensional problem—volatility, outright price collapse, and a significant shift in the shape of the forward curve. Not six months earlier, Emirates President, Gary Chapman had outlined the more than $1 billion benefit of hedging since inception in 2000.[21] These market moves undermined confidence not only in the Emirates but also in Dubai, and international banks began to withdraw liquidity from the Sovereign. Although the airline managed to secure funding locally and, with patience and some restructuring, repaired the position, a bankruptcy and global financial crisis could have easily followed. Not everyone has been as fortunate, and margin distress is a significant reason why some view hedging as a perilous endeavour in volatile oil markets.

As it is often the case, it is likely that both fundamental and speculative factors contributed to the events of 2008. Leading up to the peak price, there was an increasing belief—fuelled by insights from banks' research notes—that future oil markets were becoming imbalanced. Many speculated that oil production might be peaking, while China's insatiable appetite for middle distillates seemed to know no bounds as its economy continued to expand.

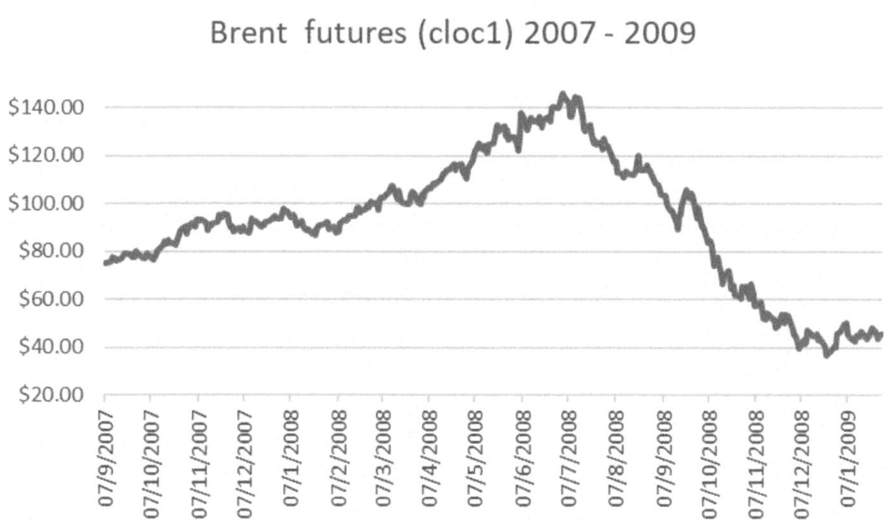

Fig. 16.1 Brent prices. Authors, using ICE data

Recall from Chapter 5 how supply shortfalls in middle distillates can quickly impact WTI prices due to the transparent and regular publication of stock levels in middle America (PADD 2). Additionally, there were concerns about supply at the time: Mexican production was declining, strikes and explosions were affecting the oil sector in Nigeria,[22] and output from the middle distillate-rich Forties field in the U.K. North Sea was curtailed due to widespread corrosion in the pipeline.[23]

However, it is likely that financial players were herding, aggressively bidding into a vacuum as offers receded and prices kept rising. With no restrictions on their ability to place substantial volumes in futures or forward markets, swap dealers were encouraging their clients to join the trend. After all, fostering one's own sales credits while ensuring the success of their clients created a 'win–win' scenario. As a result of both fundamental and speculative enthusiasm, the market surged higher.

The collapse came in July and the 'blame' for the market's turnaround is often pinned on George Soros deciding to sell out his long position. Yet, one bank, which believed information gained from its physical business complemented its financial trading activities in oil, sensed that middle distillate demand had peaked. They contended that the reason for the turnaround was fundamentally driven, even if the magnitude and speed of the price collapse were influenced by speculative behaviour, much like the preceding upcycle.[24]

Another point, perhaps previously overlooked, is that financial bubbles may have a positive role to play—something economists have often neglected in the past. Prices, after all, serve as signals, conveying critical information about scarcity to market participants. Reacting by 'shooting the messenger' does not address the underlying issues. Similarly, attempting to curb price increases through legislation often proves counterproductive, as it fails to tackle the root causes of the bubble.

'Now, though, a growing body of research suggests that bubbles may have advantages, even when many of the investors involved lose money'.[25] According to newer academic insights, markets tend to 'work' over the long run. As the adage goes, 'The best cure for high prices is high prices'. Elevated prices attract more investment and simultaneously suppress demand. Extreme price spikes amplify this effect, leading to the familiar cycle of 'boom and bust'.

Fundamental or speculative? A reasonable observer might recognise causation in their intertwined roles. A paper by the World Bank points seems to confirm pointing to a combination of: ... *both long- and short-term factors... upward surprises in oil supply, downward surprises in demand, unwinding of geopolitical risks that had threatened production, change in OPEC policy objectives, and an appreciation of the U.S. dollar'*. In their view: '*Changes in supply conditions appear to have played a dominant role, with the OPEC strategy aimed at supporting its market share significantly deepening the drop in prices that was already underway*'.[26]

But, whatever the causes of the turmoil, it led to a seismic shift in the oil markets: a demise of the banks from the largest commodity market in the world.

Of Banks, Trading and Horses

The sound of dogs barking down the corridor was far from typical for a five-star hotel. Yet, unmistakably, there were dogs barking. Perhaps they were the same ones that had taken the elevator from the lobby up to the suite level at the elegant Normandy Barriere in Deauville, France. Here, a dog or two as part of the clientele was hardly unusual. These particular dogs likely belonged to former oil trader and broker John Corbani. An avid racehorse owner and esteemed horse breeder,[27] John had a tradition of booking an extra suite at the Normandy during the horse sales—just for his two loyal dogs.

John Corbani was a significant figure in the oil markets throughout the 1980s and '90 s, holding influential roles at J. Aron and other firms. However, he chose to retire early to support his wife's career, which would reach the highest echelons of Goldman Sachs. Known in the horse racing world as Madame Isabelle Corbani, she is more familiar within the oil trading industry as Isabelle Ealet

An Economics graduate of the Ecole Supérieure in Marseille, Isabelle advanced to Goldman Sachs after postgraduate studies at Sciences Po and early successes as a middle distillate trader at the French oil giant Total. Her expertise and leadership eventually earned her the title 'Queen of Commodities' as she led Goldman's Commodities business. Beyond oil, Isabelle expanded Goldman's reach into metals and coal acquisitions and developed its power and gas trading capabilities, leaving a lasting mark on the commodities world.[28]

Known for her integrity and fair dealings, though famously intolerant of incompetence, Isabelle retired in May 2018 after reaching the position of Co-Head of Goldman Sachs' Securities division. Stepping away from her remarkable career, she shifted her focus to pursue excellence in the world of thoroughbred racing and breeding, among other interests. It's a world that has long captivated the trading community, where both oil trading and betting on horses are seen not as gambling, but as calculated risks grounded in skill and insight.[29]

The allure lies in the challenge of predicting which horse might win a given race, considering factors like race distance, ground conditions, recent form, competition strength, assigned handicaps, jockey skill, and more. For oil traders, this world of probabilities and risk/reward dynamics feels right at home. Breeding presents a similar intellectual puzzle: pairing the right sires and dams in pursuit of a future champion. It's an industry steeped in statistics, though often with sample sizes too limited for drawing statistically sound conclusions—an aspect that only deepens its complexity and appeal.

From the well-respected Nova trading company's renowned products trader Mike Watson to Hamilton Bros' Duncan McGregor, former BP 'super trader' and manager Paul Adams, and Peter Fagin of Castleton Commodities, who owns Deerpark Stud in Ireland, countless figures from the trading world—including this author—have invested their hard-earned City profits into the racing and horse breeding industry, whether by acquiring prized horseflesh or frequenting smoky turf accountant offices. Gary Ross, the esteemed oil market researcher from PIRA and confidant to OPEC ministers, earned his doctorate through studies on New York's off-track betting industry. Likewise, other former Wall Street heavyweights like John Mack and the late Peter Karches, CEO and President of Morgan Stanley, often found themselves slipping away from the trading floor for a few lunchtime hours at Belmont Park, drawn by the thrill of the races.

Departure

Isabelle's departure coincided with a decline in the fortunes of the Wall Street refiners. From their beginnings in 1984, these firms had steadily climbed to dominate oil trading, pioneering unique trading methods, creating innovative products, and advancing asset-based trading strategies. Now, nearly 35 years later, their reign was finally coming to an end.

In reality, this decline had been set in motion nearly a decade before. The 2008 Financial Crisis devastated Wall Street, leaving millions worldwide financially diminished. Major names in finance, including Lehman Brothers, AIG, Merrill Lynch, and Bear Stearns, collapsed into bankruptcy or merged with others, reshaping the financial landscape and permanently altering the role of banks in global oil trading.[30]

While many of these names maintained some involvement in oil trading, none were as integral to the industry as Morgan Stanley and Goldman Sachs.

On the weekend of 11–12 October 2008, Morgan Stanley was on the brink of collapse. Had Morgan Stanley not been saved by an eleventh-hour investment from Japan's Mitsubishi UFJ Financial Group that saved it, Goldman Sachs would likely have been the next in line, facing the crisis's unforgiving fallout.

Neither oil nor commodities trading had triggered the crisis, yet these sectors would arguably suffer the most severe repercussions. The U.S. government's decision to convert Morgan Stanley and Goldman Sachs into bank holding companies, combined with what many later described as a stifling wave of over-regulation on their commodities trading arms, effectively sidelined the very activities that had bolstered these institutions in their darkest hour. In 2008, the 'refining' divisions of Wall Street's powerhouses generated crucial revenue, arguably staving off their collapse. Ironically, it was these 'saviours' that were ultimately marginalised, while those more directly responsible for the crisis regrouped and continued with business as usual.[31]

Not only the Wall Street Refiners were impacted. In 1999, a partial repeal of the 1933 Act known as Glass Steagall, which had separated the activities of Commercial and Investment banks, led to a challenge to MS and GS as the likes of JP Morgan (JP), the United Kingdom's Barclays, and Citicorp got stuck into the physical oil and commodities world.[32] Their rise was also about to be cut short.[33]

JP Morgan had spent the 1990s and early 2000s focussed on the oil derivatives business, and it was not until 2008 under the aegis of a rising star in the bank, Blythe Masters, that they started acquiring oil and other commodities businesses and upping the ante.

Masters, another trader with horses in her blood (although the more dignified equestrianism as opposed to the bustle of the racetrack),[34] had transitioned from credit trading, followed by a stint as CFO of the Investment Banking division, and was intent on leaving her mark. More imperious in style than her Goldman counterpart, Isabelle Ealet, Masters possessed a keen understanding of the Wall Street game—cultivating a commanding presence through employing a piercing intellect, strategic power dressing, and carefully cultivated networks. Not shy of invective, she famously informed her staff on a business-wide conference call in 2010 that JP Morgan's rivals were 'scared shitless of us'.[35] Her connection to the equestrian world extended to her husband at the time, Daniel Masters, a former Phibro oil trader and a key player in JP Morgan's energy business in the late 1990s. Interestingly, Danny's father was a professional bookmaker.

J.P. Morgan's ascent into the upper echelons of the trading world began in 2008 when the financial crisis provided an opportunity to acquire Bear

Stearns. Bear Stearns came with a sizable energy business, offering a solid foundation for growth. In addition to various non-oil commodities, J.P. Morgan expanded its reach by acquiring UBS's Canadian energy arm in 2009 and RBS Sempra's oil business in mid-2010. By 2011, J.P. Morgan proudly reported revenues that rivalled those of Goldman Sachs and Morgan Stanley during their peak years of 2008 and 2009.[36]

Not only had JP acquired businesses, but they had also, more importantly, captured talent. None more so than when the acquisition of Bear Stearns bequeathed them intellectual, physicist and trader, Etienne Amic. He would stay for more than ten years before going on to found Vortexa[37] and take on the CEO role at VAKT,[38] both very successful technology-heavy entities supporting decision-making and operations in oil markets and embryonic of the 'new age' ways in oil trading.[39]

During this period, Barclays was also thriving under the leadership of the polished French engineer Benoit de Vitry. A taciturn figure, de Vitry spoke in a quiet manner, and his heavily accented English could be challenging to understand at times. Nonetheless, he was one of the pioneers of oil derivatives in the 1990s, having served at Paribas, Merrill Lynch, and the Canadian Imperial Bank of Commerce (CIBC) before joining Barclays in 2000. His exceptional intellect quickly caught the attention of Barclays Capital CEO Bob Diamond and his close associate Jerry del Missier, leading to his appointment as the company Treasurer.

De Vitry's tenure at Barclays was marked by significant advancements in oil and commodities trading, largely achieved through strategic hiring rather than acquisitions. However, he ultimately decided to resign in 2013, around the same time that increasing regulatory burdens began to weigh heavily on the sector.[40]

During that period, Barclays' overall commodities revenues peaked at around $800 million in 2010, based on recollections from that time. Notably, when De Vitry left the bank, he passed the reins to Roger Jones, who would later join the significant independent trader Mercuria in 2012. This is interesting because, while independent traders have leveraged the substantial returns they've seen in the 2020s to invest in their operations, Mercuria appears to have focussed more on investing in talent rather than acquiring businesses, especially in comparison to Vitol and Trafigura.

Citigroup recognised the importance of talent and brought in former coal trader Stuart Staley to help propel the bank forward as the 2008 shakeout began. If you picture the quintessential clean-cut, highly intelligent, and engaging American MBA type, Staley fits that description perfectly. With a confidence likely shaped by his years at Enron, Staley, similar to Ealet at

Goldman, Bryce at Morgan, Masters at JP, and De Vitry at Barclays, eventually took on larger roles within these firms. However, he was to be proven wrong when commenting in 2014 that' I don't lose sleep about the competition from trading houses and oil majors eager to eat into banks' market share'.[41]

The key components of the regulatory response to the Financial Crisis that impacted oil trading at banks included the Bank Holding Company Act (BHC),[42] the Volcker Rule,[43] Dodd-Frank Act,[44] and, on a global scale, the Basel III regulatory framework for banks.[45] Interestingly, despite the common challenges faced, there was minimal communication among the major banks at the head-of-business level. Instead, it was left to Manhattan law firms like Davis Polk to represent the banks, particularly on matters concerning the Bank Holding Company Act and the Volcker Rule.

Regulators, especially the Federal Reserve Bank of New York, began to question the safety and soundness of bank holding companies involved in owning mines, storing metals, transporting oil by ship, and generating power. This scrutiny inevitably drew the attention of senior executives at these banks. While Goldman's Chairman and CEO, Lloyd Blankfein and Gary Cohn, were well-versed in commodities risk, this wasn't necessarily true for executives at other institutions. With profits surging in the early 2000s, there was probably little incentive to investigate deep down into the commodities operations, even though the financial and credit risks were understood.

Rules and Regulations

What if a vessel carrying oil experienced a catastrophic spill or a power plant exploded? For risk-averse CEOs like Morgan Stanley's James Gorman, there was no need for a second warning; the firm's commodities and highly regarded oil trading operations were already on borrowed time.

Even if some decision-makers at Morgan Stanley and other firms were prepared to resist, they faced strong opposition from Federal Reserve Board Governor Daniel K. Tarullo. With a presence that seemed to blend comedian Steve Martin with the archetypal tall American Bald Eagle, Tarullo was determined to remove banks from physical businesses. His stance was clear and 'non-negotiable.' While Goldman hesitated on compliance, Citigroup and JPMorgan began to divest their physical interests, and Gorman at Morgan Stanley was decidedly proactive.[46]

Having exhausted their last-ditch efforts to justify their continued involvement—by attempting to be grandfathered under previous legislation or seeking exemptions from stringent BHC regulations through merchant banking allowances—the Fed made its stance clear in late 2013. This marked the beginning of a significant shift, as the much less regulated and opaque independent trader community eagerly anticipated the opportunities that lay ahead.

Dodd-Frank was enacted relatively quickly and aimed to establish centralised clearing for over-the-counter derivatives. It also introduced legislation that tightened regulations on U.S. swap dealers, raising their costs through stricter capital requirements.[47] On its own, Dodd-Frank might not have had a significant impact, but combined with the globally applied Basel III proposals—implemented after more than a decade of delays—that targeted leverage ratios, liquidity requirements, and counterparty risk concentration, the banks' operations faced even greater challenges.[48]

The Volcker Rule, intended to limit the proprietary trading activities of U.S. banks, was included in the 2010 Dodd-Frank Act but faced delays and wasn't implemented until 2015.[49] There was significant concern that the definition of proprietary trading—as short-term trading aimed at profiting from the difference between purchase and sale prices—was overly simplistic. Regulators did not fully grasp the complementarity between this activity and the essential provision of discretionary liquidity to oil markets through market-making and client servicing. The advantages of stabilising revenues through hedging in liquid markets and how this could reduce costs for clients were also overlooked.

Regulators seemed more focussed on public backlash regarding bank failures, excessive bonuses, and instances of misconduct, such as the Iraq Oil-for-Food scandal, which we heard of in the previous chapter. For sure, the distinction between market-making and proprietary trading was not clearly understood by many of those pushing for regulatory changes.

Criticism was widespread. Coca-Cola expressed concerns that Goldman Sachs, through its ownership of Metro, was inappropriately influencing aluminium prices. Additionally, there were numerous soundbites from Congress, many of which were more political than intellectually rigorous or grounded in reality. One notable example came from anti-bank Congress representative Elizabeth Warren, who stated during a Senate hearing on October 8, 2013, that 'banks had adopted a business model favoured by Enron'. It was unclear whether she was implying that banks were engaging in criminal activities similar to those of Enron.

Many believed that, despite being targets of public criticism, banks provided services in a way that their potential competitors would not. The independent traders, poised like wolverines to capitalise on the opportunity to scale up and compete with BP, Shell, and Total, were unlikely to prioritise liquidity provision for 'clients' in the future. As a result, oil trading was set to increasingly bifurcate into two distinct areas: asset-backed trading benefiting the firm itself, and proprietary trading driven by quantitative modelling, algorithms, and data science. Although the latter did generate some liquidity, it did not typically focus on market-making.

The potential revenue at stake was substantial. Morgan Stanley led in oil revenues from 2006 to 2009, peaking at $1.25 billion in 2008. With profits before tax (PBT), and after expenses, reaching up to 60% of total revenues, the returns from oil trading were significant for the banks. The period from 2003 to 2009 was marked by strong growth, and according to consultant Oliver Wyman, the bank commodities businesses share of oil trading revenues peaked at $5.1 billion in both 2008 and 2009. However, by 2013, this figure had plummeted to just $1.8 billion.[50]

Even accounting for an overall decline of about 50% in commodities revenues at banks during this period, the 65% drop in oil revenues signifies a dramatic shift. This decline led to a significant reallocation of revenues towards oil majors and independent traders.

For Sale

For both Morgan Stanley and JP Morgan, the process of divesting their physical businesses began. Already facing regulatory issues with the Federal Energy Regulatory Commission (FERC) due to alleged manipulation of power markets in California and Michigan, JP Morgan announced in early 2014 that it was in exclusive negotiations with the rising trading house Mercuria.[51] The sale, widely reported at around $800 million, would serve as a springboard for Mercuria in its efforts to compete with industry giants like Vitol, Trafigura, and Glencore.

The sale process for Morgan Stanley proved to be far more complicated. Valuing a trading business largely comprised of people, short-term contracts, client relationships, and a few owned assets is quite challenging. Why acquire such a business as a going concern when you could simply hire the talent? Buying the entire operation risks losing key personnel in the process. Consequently, Morgan Stanley needed to seek out a less conventional buyer to facilitate a sale.

Their senior commodities team in London had established a strong relationship with the Qatar Investment Authority for oil hedging. Based in Doha, with a somewhat incongruous London office accessed through an unmarked door next to the bikini section in the Qatari-owned Harrods, both parties were well acquainted. Behind that door lay a world of luxury.

In late 2012, they reached an agreement to form a new company that would incorporate much of Morgan Stanley's physical commodities business, alongside assets and contributions from the Qataris. A deal price of around $1 billion was established, but last-minute negotiations fell apart when the Qatari Prime Minister took offense at Morgan Stanley CEO James Gorman's inability to travel to Doha on short notice for a final discussion.

With that setback, the firm returned to the drawing board and soon struck a deal with Rosneft, the Russian oil company led by Igor Sechin. However, U.S. regulatory hurdles ultimately prevented the transaction from going through, despite the agreement.

Further talks occurred with Sinopec, who were unhappy with being turned down by Morgan Stanley, and ENI, under the expansionist vision of Marco Alvera, a protégé of former CEO Paulo Scaroni. Neither negotiation resulted in a deal, nor did attempts at a management buyout backed by private equity succeed. Ultimately, Morgan Stanley sold its physical oil business—minus head trader Michael Brennan, who opted to leave for a consultancy career—to Castleton Commodities, a U.S. trader.[52]

Deutsche Bank also complied and announced in December 2013 that it would exit physical commodities activities.[53] Goldman Sachs ultimately sold a coal mine in Colombia and a controversial metals business, Metro, which Ealet had acquired in 2010, but otherwise continued its operations largely unchanged, defying regulators. There was no doubt, however, that the banks had been significantly weakened.

What followed was nothing short of remarkable: a golden age of revenue prosperity in oil and other commodities that flooded the independent trader community with riches, as we discovered in previous chapters, along with the leading oil majors that had weathered the storm—BP, Shell, and Total.

Alongside these veterans emerged a new breed of quick-thinking operators, empowered by data mining and the use of quantitative techniques in trading strategies. These 'paper boys', however, were far from uniform—they ranged from large global financial traders to scrappy startups, with some serving clients and others simply serving themselves'.

Notes

1. https://dfpi.ca.gov/consumers/investing/investing-101/learn-more-about-investment-products/.

2. A string of seaside communities known as a summer destination for affluent New York City residents in the East end of Long Island's South Fork.
3. A private gated community located on the western tip of New Providence island in The Bahamas.
4. Hedge funds are investment vehicles which use a wide-range of financial instruments in order to secure returns regardless whether the market is rising or falling.
5. For a detailed discussion on the subject, see: 'Theory of Storage and Market Structure' in Chapter 3 of Imsirovic, A. (2024).
6. Because the position was 'rolled' from one month into the next.
7. Authors conversation on 10/04/2024 with a commercial bank dealer active at the time.
8. In general, 'Contango' is caused by the excess of supply over demand for prompt oil relative to future deliveries.
9. https://papers.ssrn.com/sol3/papers.cfm?abstract_id=2394915#:~:text=In%201993%20Metallgesellschaft%20nearly%20collapsed,allowed%20Metallgesellschaft%20to%20continue%20operation.
10. See Chapter 9.
11. https://ideas.repec.org/a/bla/jacrfn/v7y1995i4p62-76.html.
12. Gilbert, Mark Bloomberg News 11/05/2006.
13. See Baffes and Haniotis (2010).
14. Indeed, both might well have mattered.
15. For a good summary of the debate, see Baffes et al. (2015).
16. We discuss in this chapter.
17. For an interesting review of the literature on the subject, see this academic blog: https://blogs.darden.virginia.edu/brunerblog/2018/12/the-financial-crisis-of-2008-a-review-of-notable-books/.
18. Dynamic disequilibrium is a useful shorthand phrase to apply to a market where neither the short run nor the long run marginal cost of production tends to provide other than widely different price benchmarks for the observer.
19. One Singapore trader who worked in several banks (but wished to stay anonymous) commented on the leveraged trades: 'Citi used to write 5 to 1 collars for Asian airlines. Standard Chartered wrote 3 and 4 to 1. Also, we used to sell deep in the money collars to Asian airlines!'.
20. Kelly (2014), pp. 79–81.
21. Jain, Shweta: Emirates Saves $1 Billion By Hedging Fuel Costs EB247 24/01/2008.

22. https://www.wilsoncenter.org/sites/default/files/media/documents/publication/Omeje12.pdf.
23. See: https://www.ogj.com/pipelines-transportation/pipelines/article/17221898/corrosion-control1-unmitigated-mic-prompts-integrity-management-changes.
24. Kevin O'Reilly cites the fact that the oil desk was handed back two cargoes of diesel by Chilean entities was a sign of something not seen for many months.
25. https://www.economist.com/finance-and-economics/2025/01/02/would-an-artificial-intelligence-bubble-be-so-bad.
26. Baffes et al. (2015), page 41.
27. John and his wife raced and bred the stallion City Light now standing successfully in France.
28. Blas J and Farchy J: Goldman Loses Its 'Queen of Commodities' Marking End of An Era Bloomberg 14/05/2018.
29. Grounded in science, neither are seen as games of chance. It has been said that people who lack the ability to assert control over the probabilities associated with their choices are gambling and not investing or trading.
30. Merrill Lynch particularly had been in and out of commodities trading in the 1990's while AIG had focussed their business on the provision of complex derivatives to the corporate and investor worlds.
31. See: https://www.rba.gov.au/education/resources/explainers/the-global-financial-crisis.html.
32. The 1999 Gramm-Leach-Bliley Act also known as The Financial Services Modernisation Act was that which partially repealed the original Glass Steagall Act of 1933.
33. Between 2003 and 2008, around a dozen banks received permission from the Fed to trade physical commodities. https://www.reuters.com/article/business/fed-rethinking-move-allowing-banks-to-trade-physical-commodities-idUSBRE96I17B/.
34. '… well-spoken, horse-mad British woman called Blythe Masters' in 'The Dream Machine', FT Magazine, March 25–26, 2006. Page 24.
35. JP Morgan's Masters Says Don't Panic as Commodities Unit Slips Dawn Kopecki Bloomberg 03/08/2010.
36. Of the order of $2.5bn according to sources such as Oliver Wyman, Coalition and Bernstein Research at the time. Source: annual private presentations to MS from OW, C and BR across the whole 2008–14 period. Also, see the Bernstein Research article 'The Long View:

Divvying Up the Industry-Implications of Investment Bank Withdrawal from Commodities' by Bead Hintz et.al. May 7, 2014.

37. https://www.vortexa.com/.
38. https://www.vakt.com/.
39. Vortexa developed a business providing intelligence on waterborne freight movements while VAKT is a multi-party owned operations and finance support firm applying blockchain technology to oil contracts processing and settlement.
40. Barclays were effective at tying their commercial bank lending capabilities into the newly constructed oil trading business and this was to lead to deals such as one to supply Stanlow Refinery in the UK with crude oil as part of a financing package.
41. Pengelly, M: Energy Risk 06/06/2014.
42. https://www.govinfo.gov/content/pkg/COMPS-252/pdf/COMPS-252.pdf.
43. https://www.federalreserve.gov/supervisionreg/volcker-rule.htm.
44. https://www.cfr.org/backgrounder/what-dodd-frank-act.
45. https://www.bis.org/bcbs/basel3.htm.
46. Discussion with Colm Kelleher 01/07/2024.
47. Dodd Frank refers to the Wall Street Reform and Consumer Protection Act of 2010.
48. There was a special disagreement between regulators and the regulated over the capital envisaged as needed to counter Credit Valuation Adjustment (CVA) risk, a cost which greatly worried the banks.
49. Volcker prohibited proprietary trading except in connection with market making, in connection with business done for customers and in connection with certain risk reducing activities.
50. Authors discussion with OW executives in 2014.
51. https://www.reuters.com/article/business/jp-morgan-sells-commodity-arm-to-mercuria-for-800-million-sources-idUSKCN0HS1J9/.
52. A sale took place reportedly at book value. https://www.reuters.com/article/business/castleton-joins-oil-trade-titans-with-morgan-stanley-deal-idUSKBN0NW24O/.
53. Deutsche Bank also complied and announced in December 2013 that it would exit physical commodities activities.

Bibliography

Baffes, J. and T. Haniotis. 2010. "Placing the Recent Commodity Boom into Perspective." In Aksoy, A. and B. Hoekman (eds). "Food Prices and Rural Poverty". World Bank.

John Baffes, M. Ayhan Kose, Franziska Ohnsorge, and Marc Stocker: 'The Great Plunge in Oil Prices: Causes, Consequences, and Policy Responses,' World Bank Policy Research Paper, March 2015 (PRN/15/01).

Bouchouev, Ilia: 'Virtual Barrels Quantitative-Trading in the Oil Market', Springer 2023.

Dicker, Dan: 'Oil's Endless Bid', Wiley 2011.

Fattouh, Bassam: 'The Financialization of Oil Markets', Oxford Institute of Energy Studies. 2012.

Gkanoutas-Leventis, Angelos: 'Spikes and Shocks-The Financialization of the Oil Market from 1980 to the Present Day', Palgrave Pivot, 2017.

Imsirovic, A (2023): 'Brent Crude Oil Genesis and Development of the World's Most Important Benchmark', Palgrave McMillan.

Imsirovic, A (2024): 'International Oil Markets in the Age of Climate Change', Palgrave, 2024.

McLean, B and Elkind, P (2003): The Smartest Guys in the Room- The Amazing Rise and Scandalous Fall of Enron Penguin.

Kelly, Kate: 'The Secret Club That Runs the World', Penguin 2014.

O'Sullivan, Daniel: (2009) 'Petro Mania, Black Gold, Paper Barrels and Oil Price Bubbles', Harriman House.

17

Paper Boys

'Paper Boys'

Very few global organisations would historically have had their headquarters in the Cromwell Road area of London. Sure, the HQ of the Boy Scouts sits just around the corner on Queensgate and there is a museum or two close by. Mostly though, Cromwell Road is really just a traffic jam on the way to Heathrow Airport.

There are certainly no oil companies there—at least not of the old school. But step forward Onyx Capital Group. Located in an Arcade just off the Cromwell Road, this is not like Piccadilly's Burlington Arcade filled with purveyors of expensive gentlemen's toiletries and smoking jackets; the Gloucester Arcade is more sandwich shop and key cutters.

Don't underestimate Onyx though, as they are a serious player in today's oil markets, and they possess an innate ability to demonstrate those and other attributes via a slick marketing agenda. That agenda includes regular podcasts by staff and the firm's leadership, the employment of highly regarded industry veterans as advisors and Board members, and the publication of a readable and interesting book on oil derivatives by co-founder, Greg Newman.[1]

Along with his colleague of the time, Omar Kayaam, Greg left Mandara and founded Onyx in 2016. Founded in 2009 by Muwaffaq 'Alf' Salti, a former trader at Goldman Sachs, Morgan Stanley, and JP Morgan Chase. Mandara rapidly gained prominence as a key player in the once-niche over-the-counter (OTC) swaps markets. Along with another company—Geneva Energy Markets—also founded by an ex-Wall Streeter, Mark Vonderheide,

A. Imsirovic and C. Bryce, *The Rivers of Money*,
https://doi.org/10.1007/978-3-031-91806-3_17

operated as market-makers serving clients in areas that had traditionally been dominated by investment banks.

Similar to Mandara, DV Trading, Dare, XTX, and others, Onyx was stepping in to fill the gap left by the heavy regulation imposed on firms like Morgan Stanley, Goldman Sachs, and JP Morgan in the aftermath of the Great Recession.

While Vitol, Trafigura, Mercuria, BP, and Shell, along with smaller entities such as EDF Trading, Koch, and Cargill had stepped in to fill the void in physical trading, none of these companies really wanted to bother with serving clients by providing a market-making service for paper barrels.[2]

Newman and Kayaam's speciality was not new then, just rebranded and much the same as Morgan Stanley and Goldman Sachs started doing in the mid-1980s, providing liquidity to investors and those with an oil price exposure to manage.

By the mid-2010s, two offshoots formed by former Mandara 'graduates'—Onyx and DV Trading—had entered the space. Collectively, these firms earned the nickname 'curve scrapers', generating small margins on high volumes through trading on-screen, directly with counterparties, or via OTC voice brokers. They bring oil derivatives liquidity to the market in return for collecting a bid-offer margin.

For companies like these, gaining market share is a key objective, as it allows them to access the earliest bids and offers and execute trades internally, thereby minimising risk. When hedging opportunities are unavailable in one market, positions are managed in alternative markets using meticulously researched and calibrated models. For instance, a fuel oil trade might be hedged using Brent crude oil, while a contract-for-difference swap in the Dated Brent market could be offset with a Brent futures spread—until conditions permit closing the position in the original market.

In the same way as Morgan Stanley and Goldman Sachs did with the creation of ICE, Onyx, and others promulgate transparency and fairness in their dealings as an incentive for clients to return for repeat business.

And they love STEM.[3] Prominent in their marketing is the clear marker that the co-founders are Engineering graduates, and electronic delivery is at the heart of their offering. Yet, the benefits of emotional intelligence are not ruled out in a market where human contact still plays a part and so the firm's literature focusses on the required skills of humility, resolution, and accountability.

This harks back to lessons learned while the founders trained with their mentor Alf Salti's firm, Mandara. Salti, a renowned fuel oil trader in the banking world before setting up his own firm, believed in assessing new recruits for their medical and emotional suitability for trading by running tests with heart monitors and other idiosyncratic methods assisted by an ex-SAS commando, James King.

Having attracted $3.5 million seed capital, the Onyx pair got going and '*where there was steady money to be made, expand*'.[4] Now, like the way in which we saw earlier that Marc Crandall acted in the early days of Trafigura, Newman and Kayaam would '*do the trade, if scratch after costs*'.[5]

Onyx has grown reputationally in the ten years of its existence providing liquidity to clients most especially in the lighter products derived from the oil barrel such as naphtha and gasoline, although in recent days they have been pivoting from being a trading business to being a service business, providing brokerage and research to clients.

Of course, there are competitors, and some, for example, Jane Street, are significantly bigger fish. They are involved in much more than oil but do much the same thing. Jane Street is also 'humble' according to its PR and, like Onyx, STEM, and data orientated, and its provision is electronic.

Dare International, DV Trading, and XTX are other competitors, and the new world of paper trading is not inhabited by the 'lunch-a-lot' types of the 70s and 80s but by the rather cooler types in their open-necked shirts and ¾ zip gilet uniforms, sipping their latest vegan coffee creation.[6]

At an altogether different scale are the 'New Titans of Wall Street'.[7] These are the high-frequency traders who programme computers with complex algorithms which supposedly take human emotions out of the trading equation and which can quickly analyse reams of data and place the most optimal trades in the fastest time and at the lowest cost.

Citadel, Susquehanna, Millenium, DRW,[8] and others fall into this bracket but, unlike Onyx and friends, they are not servicing the needs of the investor and hedging communities in oil. Rather, they have stepped into proprietary trading- an area where the banks have been excluded since the passage of the Volcker rule post the 2008 financial crisis.

Heavy on technology and data mining to support their decision-making processes, they have come to dominate paper market liquidity on public markets taking maximum risk. They are '*momentum creators*'.[9]

Citadel and Millenium, the two most active, operate at opposite ends of the risk scale. Citadel is a maximum-risk organisation, which is confident in its deep data-led views. They are willing to sit with losing positions until they hopefully come right and they trade large-sized positions. Their willingness to hold onto positions harks back to the methods employed by Phibro in the Andy Hall days and is a methodology experiencing a revival in firms such as Vitol as deep data spawns confidence that markets will eventually do what the data says they will do. One only needs deep enough pockets and, in a 'size matters' world, the likes of Citadel and Vitol have this advantage.

Millenium on the other hand is tightly risk controlled. Set up in a structure of individual risk 'pods', their traders are kept on a much shorter leash. Consequently, they have not experienced the large losses and profits of a Citadel.

Generally, though, hedge funds and CTA's (Commodity Trading Advisors) are market followers. Often referred to as 'momentum' traders,[10] they follow signals and trends, going with and exaggerating the flow with their rules-based form of trading. And they do it as a pack. Their growth has been explosive.[11] Strategies of these funds differ greatly,[12] but all of them often move in the same direction and exacerbate directional price moves and volatility in the short run.[13]

As cited by Ilia Bouchouev, 'financial volumes have more than doubled since 2008–2009' as 'oil trading has dramatically changed over the last decade'.[14] The new, highly quantitative side of the oil trading business and the types of firms involved are well described by Bouchouev in his excellent book, 'Virtual Barrels'.[15]

Even veteran analysts like economist Phil Verleger have commented that 'Artificial Intelligence (AI) is driving the oil market'.[16] Certainly, this is now a business with less 'colour', one that is possibly less interesting as a cultural study, more rote, less spontaneous, and less alcoholic.

Support systems have grown up around the thirst for data and the desire to reduce transaction costs and enhance the efficient operation of the oil trading business. Vortexa are an example of a firm that provides detailed ship tracking intelligence to the trading community—important for understanding the physical flows taking place particularly when, unlike BP, Shell and other traders, newbies don't do physical oil themselves.

A further example is VAKT, set up by a number of physical oil market participants in 2017 and got going by former CEO and ex-JP Morgan trader, Etienne Amic. VAKT employ blockchain technology to take 40% of the cost out of the process of a physical oil trade between inception and final settlement. And then there is 'commodity tokenisation' most publicly promulgated by ex-Shell executive Maryam Ayati's Watr Protocol organisation.

It was in the same year, 2017, that the author recalls a discussion with Jeff Sprecher at the retirement function for outgoing ICE Europe Chairman, Sir Bob Reid. All Sprecher wanted to talk about and to focus on in discussion that evening was '*data*'- *it's value, it's future*'.

Whether technology can take over the role of the trader in totality is a most moot point. Traders are '*artisans, restless, humans with heightened sensory perception. They can pick up the signals from the things not said*'.[17] On the other hand, there are those who believe that the human touch of the trader creating value is of lesser consequence. Paul Chapman, the managing partner of search firm HC comments that' *difference due to human perspicacity and brilliance has gone away*'.[18]

Algos in Fast-Changing Markets

And whether the speed of execution enabled by technology and so prized by the algorithmic traders really offers any economic or social value beyond that accruing to the computer operator and his firm, is also moot. In any case, the growing volatility of energy markets in the 2020s has been a fertile ground for the return of automated trading, 'black boxes' and Artificial Intelligence (AI)—a fancy name for an old technology based on neural networks, only wrapped up in a new package, turbo-charged by the increased processing power of graphics chips.

Neural networks are computer systems inspired by the human brain and go back to the 1940s.[19] They consist of many small processing 'nodes', which are densely connected together in layers. Data is moved through these layers, starting at the input layer and ending at the output layer, always moving in one direction only. Each connection between nodes has a number called a 'weight'. When a node receives data, it multiplies the data by these weights and adds them up to get a single number. If this number is below a certain 'threshold', the node does nothing. If it's above the threshold, the node sends the result to the next layer. To train the network, the weights and thresholds start with random values. Example data is sent through the network, and the system adjusts the weights and thresholds over time so it can produce the correct answers consistently for similar data.

The breakthrough came with computer games and modern Graphic Processing Units (GPUs) with an architecture very similar to that of neural networks. Their structure enabled the building of networks of tens of layers (as opposed to one or two before), giving rise to the term 'deep learning'. The breakthrough came at the turn of the century when NVIDIA released the first GPU on a single chip, making the 'deep learning' models easier and cheaper to build.[20]

These models or modern 'algorithms' have proved to be ideal in fast-changing markets, flooded with large and complex information such as historical prices, volumes, and external economic indicators, which are often non-linear and hard to model using traditional mathematical tools. Algorithms used in trading are sets of rules or instructions designed to automate the process of buying and selling fast-changing financial assets associated with liquid markets and fast-changing prices. Energy transition and electrification proved to be fertile ground for this new form of automated trading.

Due to human-induced climate change, there has been an urgent need to transition our economy to cleaner fuels.[21] Such energy transition has involved electrification of the economy and the introduction of clean, renewable sources of power.[22] However, most renewable sources of energy are intermittent and their supply is unpredictable and weather-dependent. The increased use of intermittent renewables has put high demands on stabilising the system using energy storage, demand response, and backup sources such as gas turbines. This was exacerbated by geopolitical events such as the Russian invasion of Ukraine in 2022 and the French nuclear power crisis in the very same year.[23]

The balancing of the electricity grid has become a short-term affair requiring automation. '*The closer we get to delivery, the better we can predict what type of power source can supply electricity and when, and we can trade the power right up to a few minutes before it is to be consumed. Since the time horizon is so short, we need support from our mathematical algorithms to make the right decisions*', claims Europe's largest renewable energy producer, Statcraft.[24]

A report by The Netherlands Authority for Consumers and Markets (ACM) in collaboration with the Dutch Authority for the Financial Markets (AFM) states: '*The energy transition moves market participants to use algorithms, as the need for constantly balancing positions increases especially during last-minute trading*'.[25] As a result, the volatile 2022 electricity markets saw some 83% of all orders submitted on EPEX SPOT's[26] continuous market platform from application programming interface (API) apps, according to the power exchange data.[27]

Algorithm-based trading has been a somewhat familiar feature in the oil markets for some time. However, the declining cost of computation and its widespread adoption in other markets such as electricity have significantly accelerated its prevalence in the oil markets.[28]

With increased geopolitical risks and increased government intervention in the oil markets,[29] some form of Algo-trading in the oil industry is likely to stay with us.

Back in the old smokestack world of physical oil, Brent as a benchmark was under pressure from within the industry and a change was badly needed.

Is WTI Midland in the Brent Contract a Trojan Horse?

Concern for the volume of oil underpinning the Brent benchmark goes a very long way back. Alleged squeezes in the early 2000s led to the introduction of a number of grades in the basket.

An important role in introducing the alternative delivery was played by Jorge Montepeque, an S&P Global Platts (Platts) employee who arrived in London in 2001 in the middle of an alleged Brent squeeze. To prevent it from happening again, Platts, (with the muscular efforts of Montepeque in the lead), introduced the alternative delivery barrels into the Brent contract, Oseberg and Forties making the contract 'BFO'. Ship-to-ship transfers were also included in the assessment process and the nomination 'window' was widened to thirty days to allow for more cargoes included. Eventually, this led to the 'BFOET basket' of deliverable grades: Brent, Forties, Ekofisk, Oseberg, and Troll.[30]

Such efforts brought increasing complexity to the benchmark. The inclusion of new grades required sulphur, quality, and freight adjustments. Rules governing the eligibility of bids, offers, and trades have been tightened over time, and electronic trading platforms introduced to facilitate the assessment process.[31] What remained of Brent was just a brand name for the benchmark of incredible complexity.

However, after each adjustment, production would inevitably decline, raising concerns about the adequacy of the oil volumes supporting the benchmark. By 2022, Brent's production had dropped to around 700,000 barrels, making it clear that urgent action was required to preserve the benchmark's relevance.

Scrapping Brent in favour of an entirely new benchmark was not an option. Countless forward contracts, futures, and other derivatives—representing millions of barrels—were pegged to the Brent price and extended far into the future. The industry had a pressing need for Brent to remain operational and reliable, ensuring its continued use without disrupting the valuations of these existing contracts.[32]

The lifting of the U.S. export ban at the end of 2015 caused a major shift in crude oil flows. And it is the change in flows that usually lead to changes in pricing and benchmarks. Traditionally an importer of light, sweet oil from Europe and West Africa, the United States suddenly became an exporter of crude of a comparable quality. Fast-growing economies in Asia were happy to absorb these volumes, enabling them to widen their sources of supply and improve energy security. European refineries were also happy customers. The shorter sailing distance, very liquid and transparent markets, as well as lower credit risk, made them an obvious target for U.S. oil exporters.

The idea to introduce WTI into the Brent assessment was probably first publicly proposed at a Platts forum in London in 2017.[33] The idea came following a breakfast meeting with David Povey who was, at the time, a senior trader at Occidental Petroleum in Houston. David suggested that: '*When WTI hit the water, it was essentially Brent*', meaning that it was trading on a Brent-related price. It was well known that most of the WTI Midland cargoes were pricing based on Brent, but the notion that the U.S. crude could be a part of the Brent benchmark was so radical that most people just laughed at it.

But your author took the idea seriously enough to write a couple of papers on the subject, published in 2019.[34] PRAs took it seriously too. Much earlier, in March 2016, Platts launched a brand-new assessment for Dated Brent based on a delivered, CIF (Cost, Insurance and Freight) Rotterdam price. However, the published assessment had not gained much traction with the trading community. But the existing assessment had its use and on 25 February 2019, Platts announced the inclusion of delivered, or CIF Rotterdam offers of North Sea oil cargoes into FOB Dated Brent.[35] A competing PRA, Argus Media was already publishing its '*New North Sea Dated*' assessment which included delivered assessments of non-North Sea grades.[36] In a way, the ground was well prepared for the possibility of including U.S.-produced oil delivered to Europe in the Brent assessment.

In December 2020, S&P Global initiated an industry consultation to explore such solutions. Subsequently, in February 2021, it announced plans to incorporate WTI Midland into new CIF Dated and cash Brent assessments, effective July that year.[37]

The proposal immediately caused a large shift in the dated-to-frontline (DFL) Brent derivative market.[38] The unwritten rule of the oil trading industry had always been that PRAs assessed prices and reported on the market, and did not influence it. Clearly, the rule was broken.

The problem was that for Platts, the key PRA in assessing the Brent market, the flagship benchmark was the Dated Brent assessment. Dated Brent quotations sold the publication and brought the bulk of the money for the oil side of the business. On the other hand, the Intercontinental Exchange (ICE) appeared to believe that the expiry of the forward Brent contract did not matter so much as long as the Brent Index turned out to be some reasonable number for the few participants left long or short the contract to settle. This is probably because most of the financial players and market-makers, who trade most of the futures contracts (and bring most of the revenue), exit their futures positions well before the contract expires.

The fact was that both Dated Brent and Forward Brent were critical components for the benchmark's functionality. As Kurt Chapman, a former head of oil at Mercuria, a Swiss oil trading company commented: '*Dated and Forward Brent are one and the same oil, only separated by time and loading period - normally referred to as convergence'. Value of one is closely interlinked with value of the other. Addressing issues with Dated Brent without ensuring the proper and equivalent functioning of the forward contract could jeopardise the functioning of the Brent futures market*'.[39]

This is simply because Dated Brent is the Forward Brent, which has come to be delivered and for which loading dates have been nominated.[40] This key point was also emphasised by Kurt Chapman and Adi Imsirovic in a series of papers published during the period of a heated discussion on the subject.[41]

Eventually, both Platts and ICE recognised a need to coordinate their actions. Even more consultations followed. These discussions were highly technical due to the complexity of the benchmark: Brent had its forward and futures contracts, partials, CFDs, EFPs and DFLs, EFS, TAS, and many other indices and markers. Its price was assessed with the help of derivatives markets as well as with the help of FAF, sulphur, quality adjustments, and many other methods that are often unfathomable to a newcomer to this benchmark.[42]

Divided Market

There was some opposition to the inclusion of WTI Midland into the contract. A few traders and one PRA favoured the inclusion of the prolific Norwegian Johan Sverdrup (JS) crude oil instead of the 'foreign' (WTI Midland) barrels. However, JS was a lot heavier and higher in sulphur content than most of the other 'sweet' grades in the 'Brent basket'. The key issue was that the inclusion of JS would have given Equinor, the Norwegian oil company, large control of the benchmark.[43]

WTI Midland was a more natural choice since, as soon as the oil '*hit the water*', WTI Midland was bid and offered on a Brent-related basis. In Europe, WTI Midland (with a density of 42 API and sulphur content of 0.2%) became the 'base-slate'[44] of many refineries and directly competed with the similar Norwegian Ekofisk (with a density of 38.5 API and 0.19% sulphur) which was already deliverable in the Brent contract.

Following the publication of a joint white paper with ICE, on February 2022, S&P Global Platts announced a new proposal for an FOB (rather than CIF) Brent contract. The idea behind this second proposal was to include cargoes of WTI Midland crude oil in both its Dated Brent crude oil benchmark and forward contracts (starting with June 2023 deliveries), but to maintain the assessment on an FOB basis.

By sticking with the FOB assessment, all the futures and other derivative contracts would remain relatively unchanged, without jeopardising their existing open interest. However, the details involved in this change were immense. They included increasing the cargo size of the North Sea grades eligible for the assessment to 700,000 barrels,[45] a comprehensive rewriting of the Shell general terms and conditions (GT&Cs), changing WTI Midland FOB nominations, vetting of the U.S. loading terminals, narrowing down of the quality specifications and so on.[46]

In another surprising turn of events, shortly after the Platts announcement, Shell—a key participant in the Brent market—revealed to have another problem. They noted complications surrounding the transfer of title within U.S. territorial waters, under U.S. jurisdiction.[47] In response to this concern, they wrote a new set of STASCO 2022 Cash BFOETM GT&Cs.[48]

However, forward Brent was to remain an FOB contract by using a freight adjustment mechanism, assessing the delivered WTI Midland 'as if it was loaded in the North Sea'. While the usual FOB contract specifies title transfer at the loading port, the new contract would have the title change hands in the international waters, outside U.S. jurisdiction.[49]

All of this made the contract far more complex than anyone intended it to be. Highly regarded ex-trader and founder of the energy consulting firm Consilience, Liz Bossley, asks the question in a recent report 'When Does Complex Become Too Complicated'.[50] However, given all the constraints, options were limited. Performing the additional calculations was something all participants in the Brent market were already doing throughout the day. The prize of the inclusion of WTI Midland in Brent was a massive and immediate boost to the liquidity of the benchmark by a good 1.5 mbd of additional oil. At the same time, all of the associated Brent derivative contracts, including Brent futures, would remain unchanged. '*The inclusion of WTI Midland in the Brent contract has been a success, as witnessed by the boost in trading liquidity in the Platt's window*', according to Chapman.[51]

But there is no free lunch. Aside from the odd teething pains associated with nominations and delayed deliveries,[52] WTI Midland started to dominate Brent,[53] with Midland setting the price of the benchmark the majority of the time. In theory, there is nothing wrong with one grade being dominant. Forties dominated the 'Brent basket' for many years. But this gave the critics of the 'new' Brent ammunition to claim that the 'new' benchmark was superfluous, since it was the FOB value of WTI Midland that was at the heart of the price determination, regardless whether it was sailing for Europe or Asia.[54] In theory, the argument had some merit.[55] The volumes of various WTI FOB USGC contracts were growing steadily, creating a competitive market among the PRAs and exchanges.[56]

All these new price assessments were very useful. However, they were all still linked to the price discovery mechanism of the WTI Cushing futures contract. As long as the financial players, who take most of the outright positions in WTI Cushing, were happy with it, the WTI price for Cushing delivery was to remain a dominant price discovery mechanism and a benchmark. The old rule that 'liquidity always trumped basis risk' worked. Traders preferred a liquid contract approximately reflecting the market fundamentals rather than an illiquid one, which perfectly reflected them.[57]

Debates and consultations regarding the changes in the Brent benchmark of the early 2020s have left the oil trading industry rather tired and bruised. Traders, brokers, PRAs, and others spent years working out appropriate changes in both WTI Midland and Brent, and nobody was in the mood for another major change any time soon.[58]

However, in the long run, these changes could have laid groundwork for the development of a new benchmark around WTI Midland loading in the USGC. With falling oil demand in Europe, refinery closures there, and continuing exports from the United States, one-day WTI may well have to carry the mantle of a global oil benchmark alone.[59]

In the meantime, as long as the two conjoined benchmarks continue to perform reasonably well, with no more negative prices (as in the case of WTI in April 2020) or defaults and delays in delivery (always a possibility in any delivered contract such as WTI Midland inside Brent), the two benchmarks could happily coexist side-by-side for many years to come.

Old School Lives On

Not all present-day market operators have abandoned the past. Certainly not the large independent traders like Vitol and Trafigura, BP and Shell. This is just as well as if they had done so and had abandoned their asset-backed optionality-mining physical trading business, they would have missed out on three of the most remunerative years ever experienced in oil markets—in the 2021–23 period. Partly due to the effects of COVID-19, partly due to the disruption of the normal flows of commerce consequent on Russia's invasion of Ukraine, and partly due to the growth of U.S. shale oil as an internationally traded stream, these companies were able to adapt and profit.

Historically low interest rates over the past decade significantly fuelled investments by independent trading companies in assets and long-term contracts, leaving them well-positioned to capitalise on market imbalances and exogenous crises as they arose. During this period, Vitol reported annual net revenues hovering around $15 billion, while Trafigura achieved approximately half that figure. Even Mercuria, the smallest among the top five independent traders, recorded net revenues of $2.7 billion in 2023, nearly matching their record-high of $2.92 billion from the previous year.[60]

Of course, these were not all oil revenues and, indeed, the oil portion has been declining as gas, power, and renewables markets have come into prominence. But oil is the alma mater of these groups and remains the baseload revenue stream and the identity of all of them. And shale has been one of the big stories of the last fifteen years or so.

Shale is a type of sedimentary rock composed of flaked layers of minerals that may contain organic matter, resulting in deposits of gas and oil. The technique of extracting hydrocarbons from this rock is hydraulic fracturing or 'fracking'. Oil produced from shale is often referred to as 'tight' oil. Fracking is a collection of technologies, developed over time and adopted to particular rock formations, involving horizontal drilling. It was a set of technologies that would change the structure and workings of the global oil industry itself.

The advent of shale was a game-changer for U.S. oil production, geopolitics, and oil trading. For a start, a large oil production (about 20 million barrels of oil liquids) is coming from a relatively safe country, which is outside the oil cartel. Almost three-quarters of the country's production is from shale resources.[61] U.S. oil exports are freely traded in open markets with no destination restrictions. Since 2023, WTI Midland has been a major component of the key international oil price benchmark, Brent.[62] This has improved price discovery and liquidity in the international oil markets. It has also reduced volatility as safer oil exports from the United States have been replacing the barrels from the more volatile Middle East.[63]

Major oil companies have flocked to U.S. shale assets. Fracking technologies are far more acceptable in the United States than in most other places, especially in Europe. This is partly due to legal reasons since the European Napoleonic law assigns all the subsoil property rights to the state and not the owner of the land above. As a result, the discovery and production of tight oil in Europe brings the owners of the land and local population only noise and other forms of pollution. The owners of land rich with shale in the United States get fat checks every month, which goes a long way to soothe the pain and inconvenience of fracking. The density of the population is obviously a factor too.

There are other advantages of shale 'plays'. Shale investments are 'short-cycle', for production of not more than a couple of years forward. Reserves are well known and accessible. The investment has predictable returns and the price risk is easy to hedge. Unlike investments in conventional oil production, which are made for a decade or more into the future, involving billions of dollars, shale investments are spread among many different wells, each of which requires far smaller investments, making them less risky. The short cycle characteristic of shale also avoids the risk of stranded assets.

This strategy is reflected in their actions. Oil mergers and acquisitions in the United States in 2023 amounted to $186 billion. In October 2023, ExxonMobil announced the purchase of a large shale producer in the United States, Pioneer, for $60bn.[64] Soon, this was followed by Chevron's $53bn deal to buy another major U.S. producer, Hess.[65] Having acquired Pioneer, ExxonMobil has obtained some of the best acreage in the Permian, boosting its reserves in the region, with possible production of about 2m barrels of oil equivalent (the region produces oil, gas, and condensates) by 2027.[66]

The advent of shale oil production is important for a number of reasons. The shale basins are enormous and widely spread across the globe.[67] While it takes a significant effort to produce shale hydrocarbons, there is far less uncertainty in shale exploration and production. The investments can be distributed over a number of small plays and require short-cycle financing, making the price risk easy to hedge.

Shale oil production is highly sensitive to price fluctuations. When market prices rise above production costs, shale output typically rebounds quickly. Combined with ongoing cost reductions and productivity improvements,[68] this makes shale oil production exceptionally resilient. This resilience poses a significant challenge to short-term, revenue-focussed cartels like OPEC, as shale oil becomes a formidable competitor.

Finally, shale production technologies are likely to be exported and adopted worldwide, enhancing global oil reserves and better depletion of existing reservoirs. This will reduce costs, increase supply, and all things equal (they never are), put downward pressure on oil prices. As these technologies become more common and widespread, unconventional production methods are expected to transition into mainstream practices and become 'conventional' production.

Despite shale being a 'Texas/Oklahoma business', there has been little evident increase in the number of trading companies locating in Houston. Paul Chapman, Managing Partner of search firm Human Capital (HC), comments that: '*Shale made no difference to Houston as a trading centre*'. Only when this U.S. oil became WTI Midland at the Gulf Coast—and thence became Brent, did it make a difference to international oil trading through its effect on Brent pricing and it's destination reach as an acceptable stream of light sweet crude oil.

COVID-19, 'Essex Boys' and Negative Oil Price[69]

The COVID-19 pandemic in 2020 posed one of the greatest challenges to the oil markets, particularly for producers, as demand dried up. The measures implemented to curb the pandemic triggered an unprecedented demand shock that disrupted oil prices and benchmarks.[70]

Among these, the WTI contract faced the most severe impact. On April 20, 2020, the WTI May delivery contract settled at an astonishing −$37.63 per barrel.[71] On that day, the May WTI contract price plummeted from $17.73 into negative territory, closing at −$37.63 per barrel (see Fig. 17.1).

Any storable commodity can reach a point where its price turns negative when storage costs exceed the commodity's value. For instance, natural gas prices at the Waha hub in the Permian Basin had frequently traded below zero.[72] This situation arises when an abundance of cheap supply drives up demand for storage, causing storage costs to rise exponentially. If no storage is available at the contractual delivery point, the cost of finding alternative locations dictates the price. Gas producers can afford to sell at negative prices

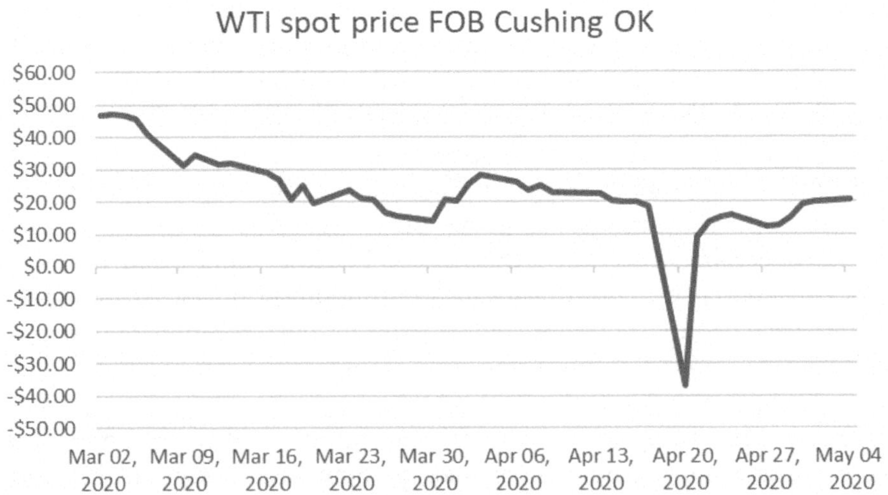

Fig. 17.1 Price of West Texas Intermediate crude oil futures in 2020 (data from CME)

at Waha as they make money on oil production, and associated gas cannot be vented or flared.

CME Group's WTI crude oil futures contract requires physical delivery in Cushing, Oklahoma. Traders with long positions expiring on the contract must secure storage for delivery there. In the midst of the demand shock caused by COVID-19 (estimated globally at 8.7 million barrels per day), stocks at Cushing surged towards the 65 million barrel marker.[73] As storage levels approached capacity, the likelihood of negative prices became apparent. Historical precedents of high inventory levels were observed between 2016 and 2018, driven by the shale oil boom and insufficient pipeline capacity linking new production areas and Cushing to export terminals on the Gulf Coast. Anticipating this, the CME enabled the system facility allowing for negative prices well before the event.[74]

While a landlocked contract like WTI, with limited alternative delivery and storage options, could feasibly go negative, the magnitude of the price drop was extraordinary. On the same day, the June WTI contract settled \$58.06 a barrel higher than the May contract.[75] This price spread implied that alternative storage or delivery options, such as Houston, should have been viable at costs well below \$58.06.[76] In other words, traders buying oil at −\$37.63, transporting it all the way to Houston, keeping it there for a month and delivering it back into Cushing the following month would have made a fortune. But they did not.

The details of what transpired remain unclear, as comprehensive data on market participants and their positions is not publicly available. Such data could be reviewed by the Commodity Futures Trading Commission (CFTC),[77] responsible for overseeing U.S. commodity markets. The CFTC issued a preliminary report on November 23, 2020, after seven months of investigation. While the report cited contributing factors like an oversupplied global market, demand collapse due to COVID-19, and concerns over global storage availability, it failed to explain the extreme price fall.

Anecdotal evidence suggests that Exchange-Traded Funds (ETFs) may have played a role in the crash, potentially as both contributors and victims.[78] ETFs, marketed to retail investors for oil exposure, often hold large, publicly known positions.[79] Professional traders (price-makers) can exploit this transparency, particularly during predictable 'roll' periods when ETFs transition from one contract month to another.[80]

It is very likely that, on 20 April 2020, one or more ETFs were victims of a 'long squeeze'. Professional traders[81] might have anticipated large ETF liquidations in the May contract, purchasing substantial volume of the Trade at Settlement (TAS) futures contracts.[82] Indeed, the CFTC report points out that, at 31.1%, TAS futures were the largest constituent of 'All Traded Sides of May 2020 NYMEX WTI Contract.'[83]

As settlement approached, these traders likely sold additional May futures at a loss, driving prices sharply lower. They lost on a small volume of trades but made money on a very large TAS position.[84] Locked into selling their positions, ETFs were forced to accept the negative prices set by professional traders. A class action was filed against a group of former IPE traders, so-called 'Essex Boys' who remained active in oil trading through a company called Vega Capital London, after parent-company ICE closed the London IPE floor down in 2005.[85]

While the CFTC report highlighted retail investors' lack of understanding of complex contracts as a contributing factor, it likely doesn't tell the whole story. It appears that professional traders profited significantly from the event, raising concerns about the risks posed by derivative contracts.

Russia and Ukraine

Completing the trilogy of events (Shale, COVID-19, and the Ukraine War) that have conspired to shower riches on the oil trading world is the last of these, the impact on global hydrocarbon flows of the Russian invasion of Ukraine in 2022.

After Russia invaded Ukraine, European buyers aimed to cut energy ties with Russia. The U.S. Treasury Department and the EU approached this issue from the 'having their cake and eating it' perspective. Their aim was to keep oil markets supplied (hence keeping the ever politically sensitive gasoline prices low), while reducing Russia's revenues per barrel of oil exported. They introduced price caps on Russian crude and petroleum products, enforcing these through restrictions on G7 and EU support services for transactions above certain price levels. The idea was that Russia's reliance on G7 and EU services would force compliance, leading to caps of $60 per barrel for crude, $45 for lower value products, and $100 for higher value ones.[86]

However, Russia had time to prepare, purchasing tankers and securing alternative insurance. New entities emerged in places like the UAE and Hong Kong, facilitating Russian oil exports. The compliance process was ineffective,[87] as oil is traded weeks in advance, making it impossible to verify if the price cap is met. Sellers inflated costs to keep prices under the cap, aided by Russia's growing independent shipping capacity.

While Russia discounted its oil due to embargoes, the main buyers—India and China—had more bargaining power and pushed prices lower.

Longer shipping distances allowed Russia to obscure real prices and further circumvent the cap.

Rising oil prices exposed the flaws in the price cap. As Brent oil surged above $90 per barrel, the cap became irrelevant.[88] Russian ESPO crude, sold primarily to China, has traded above the cap for months.

The original EU sanctions would have impacted Russian oil exports more significantly if not for the price cap, which aimed to minimise that impact. However, it has failed to reduce Russia's oil revenue, with recent monthly revenues exceeding $7 billion.[89] Sanctions on Turkish and UAE shipping companies are unlikely to be effective, given Russia's expanded independent capacity.

In reality, since price caps increased demand and reduced supply, but with OPEC keeping oil prices high and Russia needing revenue, the system was gamed. To truly reduce Putin's oil revenue, the G7 should have removed the cap, focussed on embargoes, and enforced secondary sanctions on violators.

And so....

On the debit side in oil trading is the continuing inability of some participants to stay clear of scandal and allegations of illegality. And there is a long and unhappy history of 'mischief' in oil trading. Paper markets have suffered from front-running, spoofing, and abuse of dual capacity. At times they have invited abuse and their trading arrangements have been unfit for purpose. TAS is a good example of a trading arrangement that makes trading at the settlement of the exchange an invitation to have a disproportionate (leveraged) effect on price and is, arguably, a trading arrangement that should have been abolished many moons ago.

Despite the episodes of bad behaviour, whether in futures, forwards, or physical markets, it is well worth remembering that the great majority of market participants are acting in good faith. It is those who have made money trading oil but have resisted the temptation to engage in market manipulation or bribery who can take great credit for trading profitably, transparently, and honestly. They are the ones who have added true value in the process of directing oil and oil products from source to the most efficient and effective place of disposal and who have, by application of trading instruments available in futures and forward markets, made things cheaper for people. They lower the cost of capital, reduce the chance of unexpected risks, and facilitate profitable investment for their wide range of clients. Their service is socially useful.

Notes

1. Newman, Greg: World of Oil Derivatives Amazon 2023. Ex Vitol leaders, Peter Smith and David Fransen sit on the Board while Jorge Montepeque is an Advisor.
2. They can all be categorized as users rather than providers of liquidity.
3. Science, Maths Engineering and Technology.
4. Discussion with Greg Newman 02/04/2024.
5. Ibid.
6. See City A.M. newspaper 01/10/2023.
7. FT 30/09/2024.
8. https://www.drw.com/.
9. Discussion with Peter Smith 07/12/2024.
10. https://www.rjoasis.com/what-is-a-cta/.
11. https://www.eurekahedge.com/Research/News/1388/Introduction-to-CTAs-and-their-Role-in-Portfolio-Allocations.
12. https://www.cmegroup.com/education/courses/managed-futures/comparing-cta-strategies.html.
13. https://www.bloomberg.com/news/articles/2024-06-04/oil-algorithmic-traders-amplify-crude-price-rout-after-opec-s-surprise.
14. Bouchouev, Ilia: Energy Qauntamentals-Who is Who in Financial Barrels January 2024, p. 4.
15. Bouchouev, Ilia: Virtual Barrels Quantatative Trading in the Oil Market Springer 2023.
16. Verleger, P- The Oil Casino-AI Stacks the Odds Energy Intelligence 16/03/2022.
17. Interview with ex-trader and playwright Brendan Connellan who wrote 'Kill the Bid', a play centred on a trading floor and performed Off-Broadway.
18. Discussion with Paul Chapman 27/02/2024.
19. This is based on the following article: https://news.mit.edu/2017/explained-neural-networks-deep-learning-0414#:~:text=Neural%20networks%20were%20first%20proposed,the%20first%20cognitive%20science%20department.
20. See: https://aws.amazon.com/what-is/gpu/#:~:text=Evolution%20of%20GPU%20technology,learning%20(AI/ML).
21. https://www.ipcc.ch/report/sixth-assessment-report-cycle/.
22. https://www.iea.org/reports/net-zero-by-2050.

23. https://maintenanceworld.com/2023/05/03/france-struggling-with-nuclear-reactor-maintenance-crisis/#:~:text=Posted%2005/03/2023,defects%20and%20found%20stress%20corrosion.&text=After%20this%20discovery%20EDF%20began,to%20maintenance%20work%20and%20repairs.
24. https://www.statkraft.com/newsroom/explained/physical-algorithmic-trading-quick-decisions/.
25. See: https://www.acm.nl/system/files/documents/rapport-marktstudie-algoritmische-handel-energiemarkt-public_0.pdf page 3.
26. https://www.epexspot.com/en.
27. See: https://www.spglobal.com/commodity-insights/en/news-research/latest-news/electric-power/083123-power-markets-boost-algorithmic-trading-amid-changing-sector-dynamics.
28. https://www.bloomberg.com/news/articles/2024-06-04/oil-algorithmic-traders-amplify-crude-price-rout-after-opec-s-surprise.
29. https://www.csis.org/analysis/oil-market-interventions-and-consequences#:~:text=The%20trend%20of%20government%20intervention,avoid%20disrupting%20global%20energy%20flows.
30. See Imsirovic (2021, Chapter 11).
31. For more details, see Kurt Chapman's chapter in Imsirovic (2023, chapter 5).
32. Needless to say, Platts and ICE had a lot to lose if I Brent was scrapped.
33. Your author suggested this idea in the conference during his presentation about oil benchmarks.
34. 'Changes to the 'Dated Brent' Benchmark: More to Come', https://www.oxfordenergy.org/publications/changes-dated-brent-benchmark-come/ and 'Benchmarks Face 2020s Evolution' in https://pemedianetwork.com/petroleum-economist/articles/trading-markets/2019/benchmarks-face-2020s-evolution/.
35. The CIF assessment was to be 'netted-back' to FOB price using the assessment of the prevailing freight or shipping rates.
36. https://view.argusmedia.com/New-North-Sea-Dated.html.
37. See A. Imsirovic (March 2021).
38. Ibid.
39. Interview with Kurt Chapman on 24/1/2025.
40. Forward and futures contracts are closely tied to the forward contract via the EFP (exchange of futures for physical) mechanism.
41. The papers were:

'The Future of the Brent Oil Benchmark—A Radical Makeover', A. Imsirovic and K. Chapman in Oxford Energy Comment, March 2022. https://www.oxfordenergy.org/wpcms/wp-content/uploads/2022/04/The-Future-of-the-Brent-Oil-Benchmark-A-Radical-Makeover.pdf.

The Brent Benchmark—Where Do We Stand?', A. Imsirovic and K. Chapman in OIES Energy Comment, July 2022. https://www.oxfordenergy.org/wpcms/wp-content/uploads/2022/07/The-Brent-Benchmark-%E2%80%93-Where-Do-We-Stand.pdf.

'The New Forward Brent Benchmark', With Kurt Chapman, Oxford Energy Comment, March 2023. https://www.oxfordenergy.org/wpcms/wp-content/uploads/2023/03/The-New-Forward-Brent-Benchmark.pdf.

42. Brent partials usually trade as 100,000-barrel part-cargoes in the physical, forward market. Contracts for Difference or CFDs are swaps between Dated Brent and forward Brent prices (usually traded on weekly basis). Dated-to-FrontLine or DFLs are swaps between Dated Brent and the futures front month Brent settlements (usually on monthly basis). Exchange of Futures for Swaps are derivatives linking swaps, usually Dubai, usually on monthly basis with futures markets (usually Brent). Brent index is the price at which the futures market contract expires at the end of the month. Brent can be Traded At Settlement (TAS). The assessment for Dated Brent is made using the forward dated Brent curve, constructed using the observed CFD trades. Freight Adjustment Factor or FAF is used to adjust all the freight costs to a common denominator. Sulphur and quality adjustments are made to reduce the discounts or premiums of grades in the Brent 'basket' (Brent, Forties, Oseberg, Ekofisk and Troll—BFOET or often BFOE for short) for an easier comparison—a handicap system of sorts.
43. Equinor already had a dominating role in production of Ekofisk, Oseberg and Troll.
44. Dominant, preferred grade of oil in the refinery against which all other grades are measured in value.
45. Deliveries of WTI Midland to Europe were based on the 'new' AFRA vessels with approximately same capacity.
46. For details, see Imsirovic and Chapman (July 2022).
47. Your author remembers meeting Dave Ernsberger, Co-President, S&P Global Commodity Insights at an OIES conference. Dave's face dropped when he conveyed then fresh news.

48. General Terms and Conditions (GT&Cs): https://www.shell.com/business-customers/trading-and-supply/trading/general-trading-terms-and-conditions/_jcr_content/root/main/section/simple/call_to_action_456169931/links/item0.stream/1692805078655/9bff1771c5c2e79f19230207a5d3487b4551e6b1/stasco-bfoetm-2022-v1-two-revised.pdf.
49. More precisely: '..., the risk and title in the Crude Oil will pass to the Buyer immediately after the Vessel carrying the Crude Oil leaves the waters comprising the exclusive economic zone of the United States of America (USA) or the territories of the USA.' Ibid., clause 44.
50. LizOutLoud The Price of Oil: When Does Complex Become Too Complicated January 16th 2025.
51. Interview with Kurt Chapman on 24/1/2025.
52. In the original WTI Midland contracts, it was the buyer who would nominate the loading dates, not the seller!
53. This statement, in statistical terms, depends on the methodology used as well as the period in question. Platts use the term 'define' the benchmark rather than 'set' the benchmark because WTI Midland may be the cheapest grade in one week, while Forties or Oseberg (including quality premiums) can be the cheapest in another week—given that Dated Brent is assessed over a period of 30 days. For example, using Platts methodology, Forties was by far most dominant grade in January 2024.
54. https://www.argusmedia.com/en/news-and-insights/market-opinion-and-analysis-blog/the-crude-report-wti-swallows-brent.
55. One of the earlies such observations was in Imsirovic: 'Oil Benchmarks Under Stress', Oxford Energy Comment, April 2020, p. 4. https://www.oxfordenergy.org/publications/oil-benchmarks-under-stress/.
56. For details, see A. Imsirovic (2024, page 177).
57. In other words, traders generally found liquidity risk to be more important than basis risk.
58. Authors' impression following discussions with the industry participants.
59. See Imsirovic and Chapman (March 2023, p. 9).
60. See Farchy, J.: 'Vitol Hands Traders Record $6.5 Billion after Profit Boom,' LinkedIn post.
61. https://www.eia.gov/tools/faqs/faq.php?id=847&t=6#:~:text=The%20U.S.%20Energy%20Information%20Administration,crude%20oil%20production%20in%202023.&text=Last%20updated:%20March%2028%2C%202024.

62. See A. Imsirovic (2023, chapter 9).
63. In order to support prices, OPEC members have generally been producing well below their allocated quotas.
64. Other 'High-profile oil-focused combinations to be announced in the last four months alone include ExxonMobil's planned purchase of Pioneer Natural Resources in a deal worth $59.5b, Chevron's $53b acquisition of Hess, Occidental Petroleum's $12b purchase of CrownRock and APA's $4.5b acquisition of Callon Petroleum.' Also, there were about $6 bn of gas-related acquisitions. https://pemedianetwork.com/petroleum-economist/articles/corporate-finance/2024/shale-gas-industry-consolidates-in-the-shadows/.
65. https://www.woodmac.com/news/opinion/what-does-the-chevron-hess-deal-mean-for-oil-and-gas/.
66. https://corporate.exxonmobil.com/news/news-releases/2024/0503_exxonmobil-completes-acquisition-of-pioneer-natural-resources.
67. See: https://www.eia.gov/todayinenergy/detail.php?id=14431.
68. https://www.reuters.com/markets/commodities/new-technology-helps-us-shale-oil-industry-start-rebuild-well-productivity-2024-04-24/.
69. 'Essex Boys' name was coined by Bloomberg to denominate a group of senior traders of Vega Capital London: https://www.bloomberg.com/news/articles/2022-05-04/-essex-boys-legal-woes-spill-into-u-k-after-negative-oil-trades.

    WhatsApp of the traders who allegedly manipulated WTI when it turned negative was 'Legends XXX'; on 20 April 2020. See: https://www.ft.com/content/432e279f-04e4-44c0-9e72-3d614f1e667d.
70. For details, see: https://www.oxfordenergy.org/wpcms/wp-content/uploads/2020/04/Oil-Benchmarks-Under-Stress.pdf.
71. https://www.nytimes.com/2020/04/20/business/oil-prices.html.
72. Associated gas was produced with crude oil which was more profitable. Given limitations for flaring, it still made sense to produce and sell crude and sell gas at negative prices (i.e. pay for it to be taken away. See: https://www.reuters.com/article/us-usa-natgas-texas/texaswaha-natgas-prices-drop-to-negative-now-but-soar-post-coronavirus-idUSKCN2231TD.
73. See A. Imsirovic (2001, page 196, Figure 13.4).
74. Your author recalls 20 April 2020 well. When prices went into single figures, he called a senior CME officer and suggested prices may go negative. The reply was that CME anticipated that possibility and switched the facility allowing for trading negative prices a week before!

75. Commodity Futures Trading Commission (2020, p. 9).
76. Pipeline cost is normally no more than $2 a barrel each way.
77. https://www.cftc.gov/.
78. For example, the OTC contract, known as Yuányóu Bˇao, sold by the Bank of China. See: https://www.reuters.com/article/china-bank-of-china-oil/update-1-bank-of-china-deeply-disturbed-about-investors-loss-on-oil-productsidUKL3N2CC3JV/?edition-redirect=uk and https://www.reuters.com/article/china-bank-of-china-oil-regulator/regulator-fines-bank-of-china-over-loss-making-product-linked-to-crude-oil-dINKBN28F0EA.
79. Rolling long ETF positions is usually done on pre-announced dates, before the expiry of the contract.
80. Recall the chapter 16 where banks made the fund roll into a '*business*.'
81. '… traders associated with Vega Capital London made out like bandits when crude oil futures dropped $56 a barrel into negative territory ahead of expiry on April 20, 2020. Bloomberg's regular coverage has dubbed them the Essex Boys.' https://www.ft.com/content/432e279f-04e4-44c0-9e72-3d614f1e667d.
82. This is simply an agreement to buy or sell a volume of commodity at whatever price the exchange settles.
83. Commodity Futures Trading Commission (2020, p. 15. Table 1). 31.1% includes TAS spreads.
84. This 'leveraged' type of trade is illegal in most jurisdictions.
85. The proposed class action was led by coin collector Mish International Monetary Inc., alleges violations of antitrust laws and the Commodities Exchange Act. https://www.qcintel.com/article/london-traders-lose-first-round-of-negative-wti-antitrust-case-5365.html.
86. https://ec.europa.eu/commission/presscorner/detail/it/ip_22_7468.
87. See: https://pemedianetwork.com/petroleum-economist/articles/trading-markets/2023/the-russian-price-cap-myth/.
88. https://www.brookings.edu/wp-content/uploads/2024/05/20240528_ES_Sanctions_JohnsonWolfram_Final.pdf.
89. https://www.reuters.com/business/energy/russian-oil-gas-budget-revenues-up-15-september-mm-official-data-2023-10-04/.

Bibliography

Brusstar and Karas (2020): Why Cushing Matters: A Look at the WTI Benchmark, OIES, May 13, 2020.

Bouchouev, Ilia (2023): 'Virtual Barrels Quantitative Trading in the Oil Market,' Springer 2023.

Bouchouev, Ilia (January 2024): 'Energy Qauntamentals-Who is Who in Financial Barrels,' OIES, January 2024.

Commodity Futures Trading Commission (2020): 'Trading in NYMEXWTI Crude Oil Futures Contract Leading up to, on, and around April 20, 2020' Interim Staff Report, November 23, 2020, https://cftc.gov/PressRoom/PressReleases/8315-20.

Imsirovic, A. (March 2021): 'CIF Brent Benchmark?', OIES Energy Comment. https://www.oxfordenergy.org/publications/cif-brent-benchmark/.

Imsirovic, A. (2021): 'Trading and Price Discovery for Crude Oils,' Palgrave.

Imsirovic, A. ed. (2023): 'Brent Crude Oil - Genesis and Development of the World's Most Important Oil Benchmark,' Palgrave.

Imsirovic, A. (2024): 'International Oil Markets in the Age of Climate Change', Palgrave, 2024.

Imsirovic A. and Chapman K. (March 2022): 'The Future of the Brent Oil Benchmark—A Radical Makeover', A. Imsirovic and K. Chapman in Oxford Energy Comment https://www.oxfordenergy.org/publications/the-future-of-the-brent-oil-benchmark-a-radical-makeover/.

Imsirovic A. and Chapman K. (July 2022): The Brent Benchmark—Where Do We Stand?', A. Imsirovic and K. Chapman in OIES Energy Comment, https://www.oxfordenergy.org/wpcms/wp-content/uploads/2022/07/The-Brent-Benchmark-%E2%80%93-Where-Do-We-Stand.pdf.

Imsirovic A. and Chapman K. (March 2023): The New Forward Brent Benchmark', With Kurt Chapman, Oxford Energy Comment, https://www.oxfordenergy.org/wpcms/wp-content/uploads/2023/03/The-New-Forward-Brent-Benchmark.pdf.

Newman, Greg (2023): World of Oil Derivatives, self-published.

18

Epilogue

Market as a Social Construct

The emergence of the modern oil market in the early 1980s was no accident. It stemmed from the collapse of market control by the oil Majors and the liberalisation policies taking hold in the West at the same time. Not even the powerful OPEC cartel could resist this trend. The river of money gathered strength and by the late 1980s, all major crude oil prices were trading at market-related levels.

Oil trading evolved as new products were developed and participants from other markets entered, bringing financialisation to the industry. Independent traders gained prominence while regulators pushed banks to the periphery. Throughout this process, a series of geopolitical disruptions emerged that could have undermined the market but ultimately created new opportunities.

However, this book has not been about geopolitics or abstract economic shifts. 'The market' is socially constructed being made up of real people—individuals with human stories, sometimes ordinary, sometimes extraordinary. It was 'they' who were the forceful currents that moved this mighty river of money along the path of lowest cost and maximum profit. A few oil traders became exceptionally wealthy, but most transitioned to less stressful and more stable careers. While not everyone loved oil trading, they all agree on one thing: it is a unique profession. Moving tens of millions of dollars' worth of oil across the globe, buying and selling it for profit, offers one of the ultimate ego trips. In the right organisation, it can be highly rewarding, with profit-sharing opportunities adding to the allure.

A. Imsirovic and C. Bryce, *The Rivers of Money*,
https://doi.org/10.1007/978-3-031-91806-3_18

Yet, not all oil traders make money or keep their heads above the swirling waters of the rivers of money—a reality few of them are eager to discuss. Traders live with their position, weekends and holidays are often filled with phone calls to colleagues, managers, and operators, along with a constant watch on geopolitical events. The adrenaline, the stress of daily volatility, and the shared experience within a team naturally fosters camaraderie. The never-ending thirst for information makes oil trading an exceptionally social profession (subject to one's preference), where networking and conversations often lead to valuable market insight. However, it is bad for the blood pressure.

This social aspect of trading worked as much for Robin Burley in the early 1970s as it did for the members of the 'Singles Club' in the 1990s and the 'paper traders' such as Alf Salty and Greg Newman in 2020s. That social aspect might have taken shape in the premises of Madame Claude, the infamous Parisian 'Madame', where a Philipp Brothers trader befriended the Shah of Iran, a PVM ski trip in Chamonix where the elite of the Brent trading fraternity liked to meet or just a quick pint after work in a local pub or bar, something the London, New York and Singapore trading fraternity regularly indulged in. That is how business has been done for decades.

As the international trading industry grew, initially it found its natural home in London. With English as the spoken language, a trusted legal system and a strong capitalist attitude towards contractual obligations and free markets in general, London was the place to be. Then, just like now, the world of oil would gather every February under the auspices of the Institute of Petroleum (IP) week, now called the International Energy (IE) week. Then and now: '*Park Lane became a playground for oil executives, who staggered from grand dinners to after-hours diversions in salons…*'. Places were always important in oil trading and London has always had everything one may desire—fine dining, gentlemen's clubs, and lots of great, simple pubs.

Changing Times

As W.S. Gilbert aptly put it, 'the hours creep on apace',[1] and oil trading has hardly stood still. Much has changed over the past 50 years. Where once the business thrived in the high-society venues—top restaurants and nightclubs—the arenas of trade have evolved. The oil exchange trading floors took centre stage, and when those colourful, chaotic environments with their vibrant jackets, exaggerated gestures, and high-energy frenzy came to a close, the market moved 'upstairs'. Initially, these new spaces mirrored the old frenzied atmosphere, marked by phone slamming, misogynistic antics, and perhaps a bit of substance abuse. But over time, they transformed into calm sanctuaries as technology advanced, and traders shifted from streetwise instincts to STEM[2] expertise. The pirate spirit was replaced by the academic and emotionally intelligent polymath.

Different competencies were becoming necessary for the rounded trading firm—salespeople, marketers, structurers, originators, quants, and analysts were all finding a role and the Smithian division of labour promulgated a more efficient business. Trading very much became a team game.

Technology supercharged latency. In the early days, a deal would take several days to conclude until the forwards and futures markets came along and lunch had to be taken at the desk as deals were being done all day long. Posh bankers like Goldmans would have Saville Row tailors brought to the office to fit suits. Then, following the example of other financial market, the algorithmic traders and the data scientists brought transaction speed to the party and took over, at least on the 'paper' side of the oil market. This, in spite of the fact that liquidity borne of speed (empty liquidity) is no more than a passing gossamer, confusing the signals from the real market and adding little to the process of price discovery.

It is surprising that speed has been unaffected by permissibility as the creep of legislation and regulation has affected the business in other ways. This has been no more so than in the regulations that led to the demise of the banks as critical liquidity providers. The subsequent rise of the independent traders to prominence has not filled the void left by the client-serving banks.[3] Independent traders and the 'Paper Boys' add liquidity, but it is liquidity for their own proprietary ends and not liquidity directed at price risk management and the service of clients.

The benefits brought by the independent trading community are different. They are the distributors, the logistical experts and it is they who direct resources from the points of production to the most efficient point of consumption and who can 'turn on a sixpence' when global economics, politics, or extraneous events dictate. The outbreak of war between Russia and Ukraine is a prime example where traders were able to redirect flows to those deprived of Russian diesel and to replace the loss of volumes of Urals and other Russian crude oil streams. They made sure that the flow of oil never stopped.

NYMEX and ICE brought transparency to the table even if trading houses continue to like hunting amongst the mangroves in the swamp. Unlike captains of industry and other celebrity businesspeople, traders are not well known publicly and have not suffered the same public persecution that others attract. That oil trading, the biggest least known business on the planet—a business, which penetrates every aspect of everyday life—is able to quietly operate unseen in its small corner after 50 years, is quite staggering. The traders like it that way—they like fishing in the darkness and under the radar.

There is another dark side though—the 'underbelly' of the trading industry—and its modern era began with the 'legislative arbitrage'. Nixon's Emergency Petroleum Allocation Act of 1973 almost immediately created a frenzy of 'trading' activity in the United States. Marc Rich and Pincus Green might have been late to join in, but they learned valuable lessons, which they perfected for the rest of their careers—linking foreign and domestic deals and moving their whole operation to offshore tax heavens—a practice most oil trading companies use to this day.

The duo also planted the seeds of 'market fundamentalism' into the industry—a belief that the only right actions are the profitable ones, with a lesser concern about the moral, ethical, and sometimes legal consequences. There is probably corruption in all commercial activities. Arms deals,[4] construction,[5] and many other businesses are probably far more associated with it. But oil trading touches something that all our lives are totally dependent on—transportation fuels, industry, and pretty much anything we use. This should make the business more subject to public scrutiny.

From the late 70s through the 80s, the dark side of oil trading was associated with another 'legislative arbitrage'—sanctions-busting. Rhodesia, South Africa and Israel were either legally or morally sanctioned during this period. Fast forward some five decades and replace Rhodesia and South Africa with Russia, Iran and Venezuela, and not that much has changed—except the players.

Bribery was probably rampant in the industry throughout this period and was usually associated with obtaining access to oil from countries where poorly paid individuals hold the power to direct resources and are able to personally benefit. Oil sourced in this way often ended up in the refineries and forecourts of the household name companies. How much did they know about where the oil came from and did they turn a blind eye?

Corruption not only disrupts social values and norms, but it leads to the misallocation of resources and reduces growth in countries with corrupt governments.[6] 'The invisible hand never picks up the tab'.[7] Yet, we should also caution that we, as Western-world authors, operate with a certain conditioned 'gaze' and that others from a different era, with different backgrounds and from different places may view things differently.

But the growth of the international oil markets over time has created far more price transparency, and such deals are today very obvious to spot. As a result, the oil trading has becoming cleaner over time, even if part of a trading managers job is to 'corral the amoral'.

In the paper markets, front-running, price manipulation and spoofing[8] are just some of the illegal behaviours that, for some, were considered to be fair game tactics—at least until law enforcement came calling, which it has more recently begun to do.

Despite its 'dark underbelly', the other side of the ledger reveals the immense social and economic benefits that trade brings. In the authors' view, these benefits far outweigh the disruptions caused by its darker aspects. Oil trading, to a significant extent, serves a vital social and economic function—an importance that cannot be overstated.

Trust

For the authors, this has been an intellectual and an emotional adventure reliving our own past. A big part of the reason for writing this book was to memorialise these individuals and events before they are 'covered by the sands of time'. But a far more important reason are the lessons for all those interested in trading.

Across the fifty years, volatility, complexity and contango have been the traders' friends, making they and their companies much money. So far, the rivers of money these 'friends' have enabled show no signs of drying up. Despite strong opposition from the most extreme advocates of the energy transition, oil traders and the vital role they play will remain a fixture for the foreseeable future—even as the overall significance of oil is likely to decline.

Time, geopolitics and technology may have changed the way trading has been done. Long meetings and lunches are now substituted by a click of a mouse—less socially but more technologically constructed. But serious, long-term trading business still very much relies on trust—not only trust in the deal but equally trust in 'those who bring the deal' much like we heard was the Marc Rich way in the early days.

Probably the most important lesson is that traders, like the river of money, naturally follow the least cost, greatest profit contours to reach their goals. Least cost exchange is beneficial and society should make every effort to facilitate it. Prices are just signals—messages about the state of the market. Shooting messengers has never been a good policy. If our society wants to tame the river of money, it should focus on the underlying causes for the river to flow outside the banks set by our values, aspirations and goals.

Whether they are price freezes of the Nixon administration in the 1970s or Russian oil 'price caps' of 2020s, these seemingly easy policies always have unintended consequences. The former led to fuel shortages and the latter to the creation of a trading 'underworld', which not only evades the global financial system, but may lead to a potentially devastating ecological catastrophe. In fiddling with well-functioning global markets, our political leaders must focus on legislating our values and norms and not prices. Selling oil to a higher bidder outside the country is fine—but bribing someone to do is not.

Most energy prices today are globalised and their prices are set by the international market. Banning exports, subsidising imports and capping prices will not change the underlying value of a commodity. If you dam a river at some point, its level will only rise somewhere else. We cannot freeze a river at our whim. But we can help it carve beautiful landscape, irrigate fields, and sustain distant communities, from farms in the upstream, to the sprawling cities in the downstream. We can let its flow carry energy and opportunity, enriching the land and the lives of those it touches.

Notes

1. From the operetta, HMS Pinafore.
2. Science, Technology, Engineering, Mathematics.
3. To some extent, liquidity providers (see Chapter 17, 'Paper Boys') slipped into that space but in a much smaller way than the behemoth banks who were promulgating all sorts of liquidity provisions—from hedging simple risk all the way through to helping countries such as Egypt get lower costs of funding or Mexico with their price protection and in size) (large volume).
4. https://www.sipri.org/yearbook/2011/01.
5. https://www.sipri.org/yearbook/2011/01.
6. https://www.imf.org/EXTERNAL/PUBS/FT/ISSUES6/INDEX.HTM.
7. https://www.patheos.com/blogs/gloriouslife/2020/10/the-invisible-hand-never-picks-up-the-check/.
8. https://www.thefederalcriminalattorneys.com/stock-market-manipulation

Index

A. Imsirovic and C. Bryce, *The Rivers of Money*,
https://doi.org/10.1007/978-3-031-91806-3

The manufacturer's authorised representative in the EU is Springer Nature Customer Service Centre GmbH, Europaplatz 3, 69115 Heidelberg, Germany. If you have any concerns regarding our products, please contact ProductSafety@springernature.com

Printed and bound by CPI Group (UK) Ltd, Croydon, CR0 4YY
28/08/2026
02205642-0004